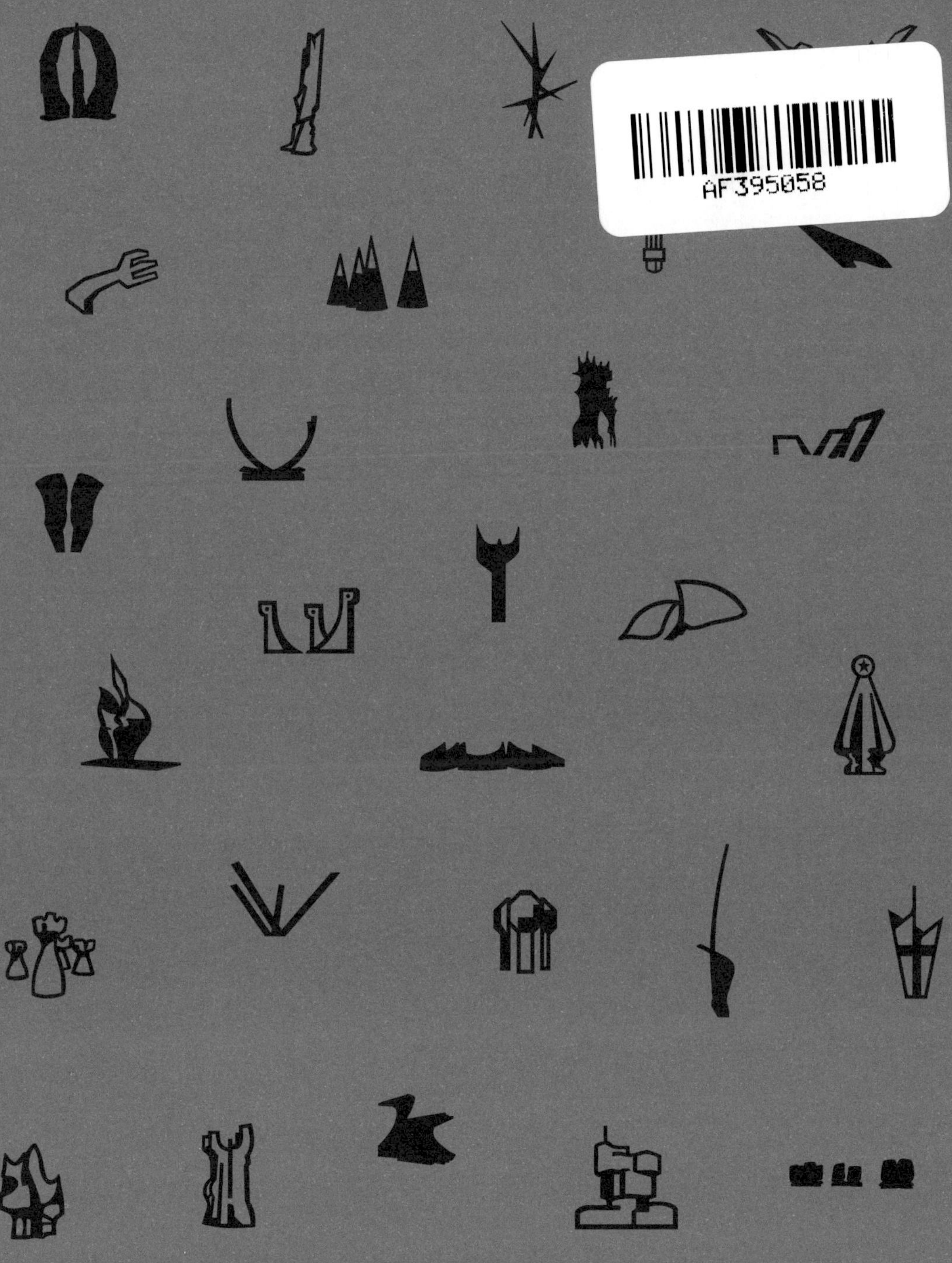
AF395058

SPOMENIK MONUMENT DATABASE

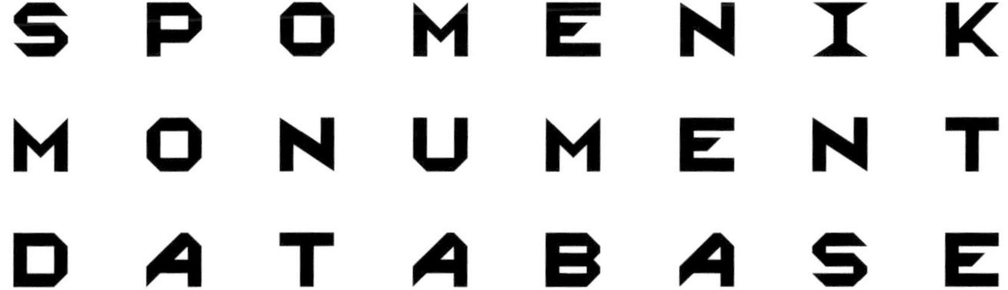

DONALD NIEBYL

FUEL

INTRODUCTION

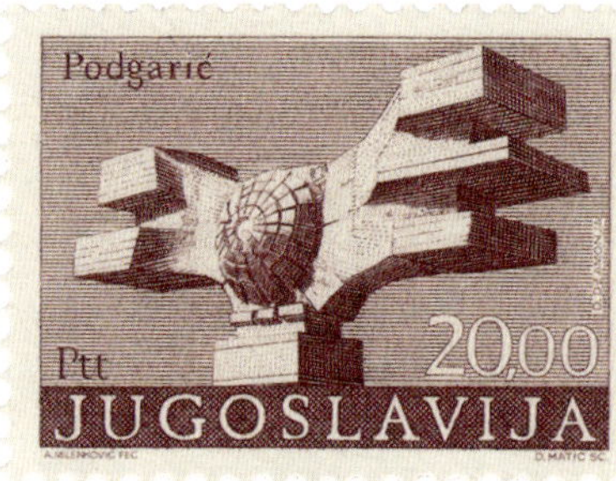

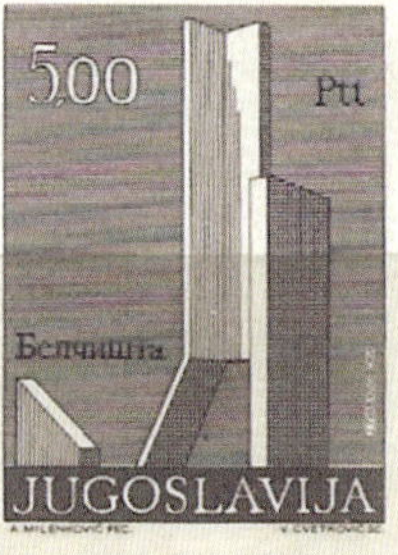

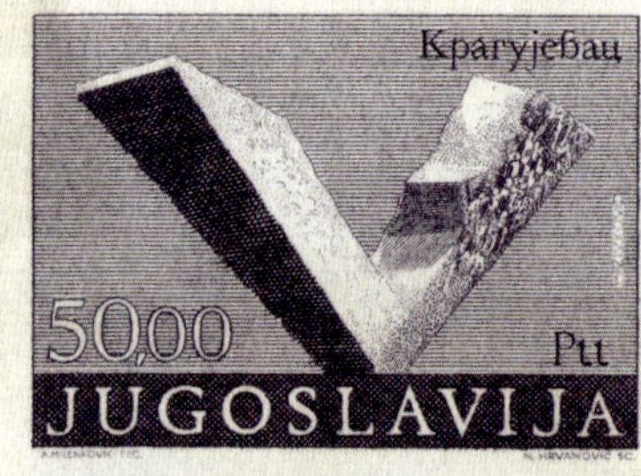

Yugoslav postage stamps featuring spomeniks, 1974

When Austrian writer Robert Musil famously stated that 'there is nothing in the world as invisible as a monument'[1], he added some exceptions: 'those memorial towers that block off an entire landscape, or ... that form a series, like the Bismarck monuments scattered all over Germany.' The species of monument discussed in this book are rendered visible not just by their prominence and ubiquity, but also by the ideology of effortful unification that produced them: they aspire to the status of powerfully imposing symbols of a set of shared philosophies. But while the initial symbolic meaning of a monument is determined by the context in which it was created, its interpretation thereafter is never fixed.[2,3] Any significant cultural or political shift can result in its transformation from a unifying object to a divisive one. Yet however ambivalent a society may be towards its monuments and the history they memorialise, they nevertheless reveal much about its values, attitudes and beliefs.

This book explores the enduring, unique and controversial monument heritage of the former Socialist Federal Republic of Yugoslavia (see map on inside of dust jacket), including the story of their origins, and of more recent events that have left Yugoslavia and much of its legacy of ambitious memorials in ruins.

These evocative monuments, these spomeniks – the word 'spomenik' is Serbo-Croatian for 'memorial', derived from the root 'spomen-' meaning 'memory' – have been routinely omitted from surveys of 'European' or 'World' architecture and sculpture.[2] And while it is true that images of them have recently proliferated across the internet, the accompanying information about their origins has typically been sparse, or confused, or misleading.

The genesis of the spomeniks dates from World War II (known in Yugoslavia as the National Liberation War), with the invasion of the Kingdom of Yugoslavia by the combined Axis forces of

Germany, Italy, Bulgaria and Hungary. Over the course of that war, a home-grown, anti-fascist, communist, partisan resistance army formed, led by the charismatic Josip Broz Tito. This army instigated a series of popular uprisings in an attempt to topple the occupying Axis forces and their domestic collaborators. Although they received some assistance from the Allies, the improbable size of the task and the bravery of those involved cannot be underestimated, especially given that they ultimately succeeded in liberating the region.

In the aftermath of World War II, Tito's victorious movement founded the multi-ethnic Socialist Federal Republic of Yugoslavia.

The nascent Yugoslavia spanned the regions of present-day Bosnia and Herzegovina, Croatia, Kosovo, Macedonia, Montenegro, Serbia and Slovenia. It comprised a wide range of ethnicities and religions as well as divergent political and social groups. Many of these factions had fought each other during the war, some even committing atrocities against others. To bind these often competing groups together, it was crucial that the country's political elite developed an appropriate national narrative that could become the 'vocabulary of the revolution'.[3] This would serve not only to forge productive relationships between individuals and society as a whole, but would also lay the groundwork for that most important of Yugoslav ideals, 'Brotherhood and Unity.'[5] While a variety of methods would be used to define and propagate this official collective memory, one of the most pervasive and enduring tools employed by Yugoslavia's Communist Party was the creation of a vast network of monuments and memorial spaces across the entire country.

While these new 'altars of the secular religion of socialism,'[2] varied in their scope and design, the primary sculptural style which ultimately came to define this prescribed-memory policy from 1960 onwards was that of an often highly abstract socialist modernism, which is perhaps the most intriguing aspect of these structures.

The route to this redefinition of the traditional concept of a war memorial began with a political falling out. In the latter stages of World War II, the Red Army had helped Tito's partisans, and

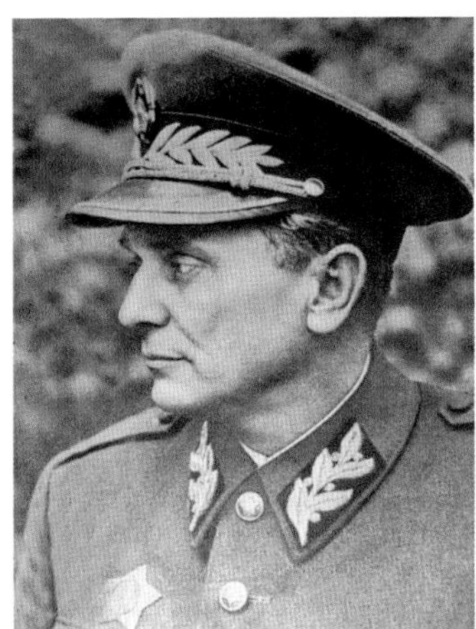
Josip Tito, c.1943

the two communist countries shared close ties. Throughout the 1940s and 1950s, Yugoslav monuments mirrored the prevailing Soviet socialist realism of the time. This highly structured and dogmatic style was characterised by heavy-handed imagery of working-class hero soldiers, often wielding weapons, alongside communist hammer-and-sickle motifs.

In 1948, a rift between President Josip Tito and the General Secretary of the Communist Party of the Soviet Union, Joseph Stalin, led to the expulsion of Yugoslavia from the Cominform (the forum of the international communist movement). The Soviets claimed the conflict was a result of the disloyalty of Yugoslavia, while in the West and in Yugoslavia, Tito was presented as unwilling to allow his country to become a Soviet satellite state. Today, historians emphasise the importance of Stalin's refusal to allow Tito's plan to absorb Albania and Greece, in co-operation with Bulgaria, in order to create a powerful Eastern European bloc outside Moscow's control.

With emancipation from the structure of 'paternalistic Soviet influence',[3] a new style of artistic expression began to emerge in Yugoslavia. This self-determined trajectory, or 'Third Path',[2] experimented with more abstract forms of art and architecture, influenced by Western artistic culture, so allowing Yugoslavia to become culturally distinct from both the USSR and the US, the two dominant powers of the era. The leaders of the Yugoslav Communist Party realised that through the abandonment of socialist realism and the adoption of a less rigid system of artistic expression for its remembrance projects – an 'aesthetically sophisticated,'[7] socialist modernism, using the idiom of abstract universalism[7,8,9] – it could present itself to its population as a revolutionary saviour, while simultaneously providing a utopian vision of a united, modern and progressive Yugoslavia.

During the Yugoslav era, several thousand monuments honouring the partisan struggle and the socialist revolution were built across the country's landscape, almost exclusively by Yugoslav artists, designers and architects.[8] The government framed this massive project as a legitimate achievement of a united, collectively minded people.[5]

It is not the case, however, that abstract forms were directly decreed by the Yugoslav government.[2,6] Initially, during the late 1940s and through the early 1950s, there was little direct intervention from the Yugoslav state about what form a monument should take.[2] In the mid-1950s, the government veterans' association, SUBNOR, assumed responsibility for the commissioning of remembrance sites in Yugoslavia.[2,5] Using design competitions, SUBNOR carefully reviewed potential artists and proposals, invariably selecting schemes that would best fit the desired narrative.[6] Yet this was not entirely a top-down method of regulating or controlling artistic expression.

The creation of these works was a collaborative effort negotiated between SUBNOR, its sub-committees, the individual republics, local communities and the artists.[7] This system, aimed at engendering universal reconciliation,[8] enabled the development of an ideologically consistent, yet regionally representative, visual language for the nation's monuments, that would also avoid the difficulties that would arise with specific, literal and visceral depictions of the atrocities inflicted and endured by the various Yugoslav ethnic and religious groups. The mythical history of a shared revolutionary struggle over fascism, steeped in the multi-ethnic, secular harmony of 'Brotherhood and Unity', became the official narrative of the socialist state.[2,3,6,10] Accordingly, the monuments are ideological[11,12] attempts to 'master the past in order to control the future'.[9]

It is no surprise then that so many of these monuments assert themselves through great size and mass. Their immovable presence within the landscape is intended to give an impression of indisputable permanence in contrast to the tenuous nature of the state itself.[3]

A further striking aspect of many spomeniks is their dramatic placement in the natural environment. Traditionally, monuments are situated in town squares and on main streets. The majority of spomeniks, however, are situated at former battlefields and the locations of revolutionary uprisings.[6,13,14]

The Yugoslav government believed that this strategic placement of these politically ascribed sites of memory in remote locations could act as a conduit between the growing urban population and the country's history. It was hoped that such a connection could help Yugoslav youth relate to a socialist war narrative they had not personally experienced.[6] With this in mind, these monument complexes were conceived of as more than simply sites for grand commemorative sculpture – they were hybrid complexes, often containing hotels, sports and leisure centres, parks and museums.[13] One of the most crucial components was the amphitheatre, which served as an open-air classroom, from which the political doctrines of 'Brotherhood and Unity' and 'Socialist Revolution' could be preached.[14] There are many examples of such structures and purposes being directly integrated into the monuments themselves.[8,13,14]

Constructing memorials with varied ways of engaging visitors encouraged people to come and spend a greater amount of time there. Such active participation would cultivate a deeper relationship with the official narrative,[8] in which the monuments stood as enduring and optimistic testaments to the socialist regime.

The period of the 1960s to the 1970s was one of relative stability and consensus for Yugoslavia. During this time, remembrance sites within this vast network, which was central to the spirit of the nation, were visited by hundreds of thousands of people every year. Families across the country

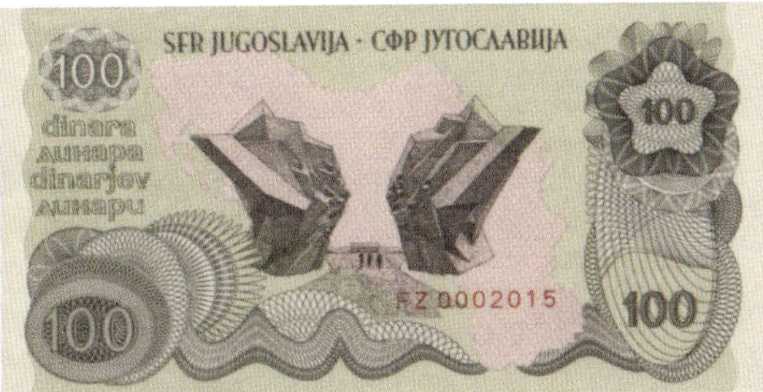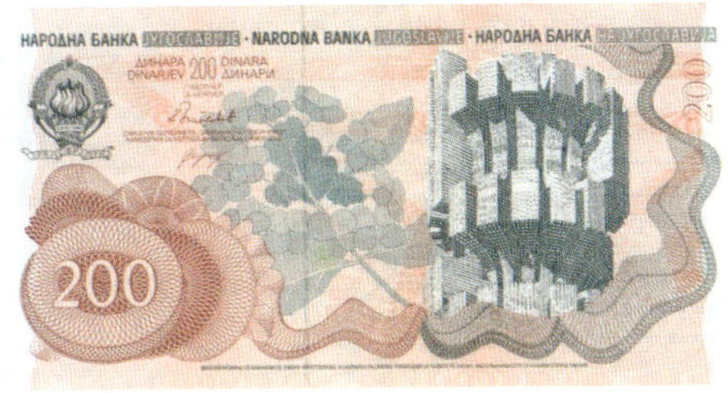

Spomeniks depicted on Yugoslav 100 and 200 dinara banknotes, c.1989

would set out on pilgrimages to them, particularly during associated national holidays.

While overt displays of actual, transcendent religion were of course intensely discouraged by Yugoslavia's Communist Party,[17] these designated sites for the socialist religion became 'symbols of Yugoslav cultural identity',[16] to be actively exalted and venerated. At the altar of these monuments people celebrated their revolution; listened to rousing political speeches; learned about the struggles of Tito and the partisans; mourned their fallen comrades; communed with the history of the site; and interacted with their communities and families.[14,16] Rather than the passive, invisible memorials of yesteryear, these monuments aimed, through the active participation of communities, to achieve 'transfer of memory'.

Children were encouraged to visit the monuments from an early age. The Union of Pioneers of Yugoslavia was a political youth movement for young people aged seven to seventeen, existing as the first stage in the state-sanctioned 'political socialisation' of Yugoslav youth. A crucial component of this process involved children being taken on mass tours of the country's memorial infrastructure. The tours were a method of communicating the state's official historical account,[14] so forming a vital part of the pioneers' patriotic education.

Gathering in large numbers, the children, dressed in their uniform of a red neckerchief and blue Titovka hat, would march ceremoniously to the monuments. Once there, they would receive political lessons, collectively recite political oaths and sing songs of the Yugoslav revolution.

Speaking of her time in the Yugoslav pioneer movement, writer Marijana Belaj remembers that they 'recited in unison the initiation oath which bound us to pursue moral values such as "diligence" and "good comradeship", as well as to respect everyone who "strives for liberty and peace". But the same oath also bound us – though we were unable to fully comprehend it – "to love the self-managing homeland and to develop Brotherhood and Unity and the ideas Tito [had] fought for".'

In 1975, the Yugoslav government was rocked by the Zaliv Scandal – the publication of an interview with political activist Edvard Kocbek, in which the 1945 summary killing of 12,000 Slovene Home Guard prisoners of war by the Yugoslav communist regime was openly discussed for the first time.

Over the following decades, other previously suppressed accounts of atrocities were gradually brought to light. These were not only crimes committed by communist partisans, but also those of domestic collaborators with the Germans, such as the Ustaše and Chetniks. These acts had long been kept secret by the Yugoslav government, through fear that such revelations could inflame inter-ethnic animosity and compromise its efforts to construct 'Brotherhood and Unity'. These scandals reignited traditional ethnic and religious positions, undermining the official dogma of Yugoslav identity, as it gradually 'ceased to address the people'.[3]

Following the death of Josip Tito in 1980, the Yugoslav government was unable to control the increasing economic and political challenges that eventually brought about the dismantling of the

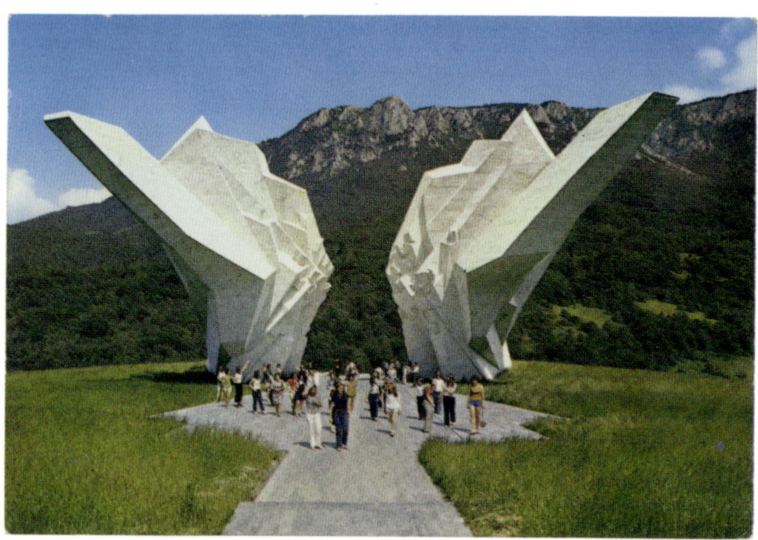

A postcard of the Battle of Sutjeska Memorial Monument Complex in the Valley of Heroes, Tjentište, built in 1971

nation in the early 1990s. Subsequently, through the 1990s and 2000s, a series of independence movements (some of which led to long-drawn-out wars) resulted in the creation of seven distinct nations, largely dominated by ideologies of ethnic and religious nationalism.[6]

It is not uncommon during periods of war for the cultural heritage of a region to be 'symbolically unmade and remade in order to influence collective memory'.[3] Predictably, some of the first symbols to be attacked in many of these newly independent nations were the monumental vestiges of the former Yugoslav state.[2,3,7]

Most of this destruction occurred in regions where the Yugoslav ideology of the monuments diametrically opposed that of the nationalist government (as in Bosnia and Croatia).[2,6,8,9] In Croatia alone, the country's Association of Anti-fascist Veterans estimates the number of destroyed or damaged partisan monuments to be around 3,000.[7] While the majority of the Croatian casualties were smaller, traditional plaques, markers or busts, among them were also many large abstract spomeniks, such as those at Kamenska, Petrova Gora and Bijeli Potoci. Generally, this destruction was committed anonymously by clandestine groups of anti-communist or anti-Yugoslav vandals. It was often also prescribed or 'supported by official politics',[2] as such monuments acted as obstacles to the attainment of long-buried, supposedly authentic, national identities.[3,9,13] In many cases, new monuments were erected on the ruins of the old, to celebrate these revised mono-ethnic histories and national narratives, reinforcing the idea that 'societies construct their past rather than record it'.[6]

In other areas of the former Yugoslavia, such as Serbia, Slovenia or Macedonia, the destruction of spomeniks was not as actively pursued. Here, the partisan history and the heritage of socialist revolution could sometimes be recontextualised and absorbed into the new nationalistic ideologies.[2] Where this could not be achieved, however, the monuments were simply left to decay in obscurity.[2,6]

Across the current landscape of the former Yugoslav states, an appreciable number of the spomeniks have been successfully integrated into these new countries and continue to be celebrated in their local communities (such as those at Kragujevac, Kozara, Kruševo and Maribor).

In some locations, attempts are even being made to restore dilapidated monuments for a new generation. At the same time, the decaying ruins of those monuments deemed incompatible with present-day political and religious situations linger on the peripheries of the landscape, just below the surface of collective memory.[5]

In this limbo, they quietly 'haunt, if not undermine, the new national regimes',[3] since their abstract, universalist symbols of progress still resonate with many former Yugoslav citizens,[3,6,8] almost as if the monuments represent some unrealised utopia.[8] Such nostalgia is especially pertinent to the current economic and social issues faced by some of these countries. Yet in spite of this latent enthusiasm, many monuments continue to suffer vandalism and destruction.

Large, architecturally complex and sophisticated socialist monuments were built in many communist countries in the post-World War II era (such as Bulgaria, the DDR, Hungary, Lithuania, etc.). However, it is the immense scale of the Yugoslavian project, coupled with its intricate planning and ideological engineering, that makes it unique. Exactly how this legacy should be addressed within the context of these new nations is the subject of open debate across the former Yugoslav states today.[3,8]

Saddled with this memorial legacy, it falls to the incumbent political class to determine whether the sites become 'tools for reconciliation' or 'fault lines that perpetuate unresolved conflicts'.[7] Further complicating such discussions is the recent worldwide interest in these visually arresting icons. The largely untapped potential of this heritage to promote the former Yugoslav republics also has to be considered when deciding their fate.

Whether these monuments are simply useless politicised relics of the communist past, or important historical artefacts worthy of preservation, will be debated far into the future. Nevertheless, their creative ambition should be recognised and admired.

1. Musil, Robert. *Posthumous Papers of a Living Author*, Eridanos Press, 1987.

2. Đurić, Iskra. *Memorials Without Memory: Bogdan Bogdanović and Yugoslav memorial architecture in the changed social and political context*, presented at *AR(t)CHITECTURE – An International Conference at The Technion*, Israel Institute of Technology, 2015.

3. Begić, Sandina and Mraović, Boriša. 'Forsaken Monuments and Social Change: The Function of Socialist Monuments in the Post-Yugoslav Space', Chapter 2, *Symbols that Bind, Symbols that Divide*, Springer, 2014.

4. Kempanaers, Jan and Neutelings, Willem Jan. *Spomenik*, Roma Publications, 2015.

5. Jauković, Marija. 'To Share or to Keep: The Afterlife of Yugoslavia's Heritage and the Contemporary Heritage Management Practices', *Croatian Political Science Review*, Vol. 51, No. 5, 2014.

6. Videkanic, Bojana. *Non-Aligned Modernism: Yugoslavian Art and Culture from 1945-1990*, PhD paper for York University in Toronto, Canada, November 2013.

7. Pavlaković, Vjeran and Perak, Benedikt. 'How Does This Monument Make You Feel?: Measuring Emotional Responses to War Memorials in Croatia', Chapter 12, *The Twentieth Century in European Memory*, Lund University, 2017.

8. Burghardt, Robert and Kirn, Gal. 'Yugoslavian Partisan Memorials: Between Memorial Genre, Revolutionary Aesthetics and Ideological Recuperation', *Manifesta Journal*, Vol. 16, 2012.

9. Musabegović, Senadin. 'Symbolic significance of monuments in Bosnia and Herzegovina', *Monumenti: the Changing Face of Remembrance*, Centar za kulturnu dekontaminaciju, Belgrade, 2012.

10. Dragojević, Mila and Pavlaković, Vjeran. 'Local Memories of Wartime Violence: Commemorating World War Two in Gospić', *Suvremene teme*, Vol. 8, No. 1, 2016.

11. Dimitrovski, Valentino. 'Back to the Past: Monuments and Remembrance in Macedonia, Monumenti: the Changing Face of Remembrance', Centar za kulturnu dekontaminaciju, Belgrade, 2012.

12. Maković, Zvonko. 'Denkmalplastik auf dem Gebiet Jugoslawiens. (1945-1991): Paradigma einer Zeit, Die Ikonographie des Antifaschismus', *Beton International*, 2015.

13. Burghardt, Robert and Kirn, Gal. 'Hybrid Memorial Architecture and Objects of Revolutionary Aesthetics', *Signal: A Journal of International Political Graphics & Culture*, Vol. 3, 2014.

14. Kirn, Gal. 'Counter-archive: Poetry, Sculpture and Film on/of the People's Liberation Struggle', *Slavica TerGestina*, Vol. 17, 2016.

15. Šešić, Milena. *Cultural policies, cultural identities and monument building – new memory policies of Balkan countries*, proceedings of Faculty of Drama Arts Belgrade: University of Cultural Policy Belgrade, 2010.

16. Putnik, Vladana. 'Second World War monuments in Yugoslavia as witnesses of the past and the future', *Journal of Tourism and Cultural Change*, Vol. 14, Issue 3, 2016.

17. Ordev, Igor. 'Erasing the Past: Destruction and Preservation of Cultural Heritage in Former Yugoslavia: Part 1', *Occasional Papers on Religion in Eastern Europe*, Vol. 28, Issue 4, George Fox University, 2009.

ANDRIJEVICA (ahn-DREE-yeh-vee-tsa)

NAME: Monument Park Knjaževac
LOCATION: Andrijevica, Montenegro
YEAR COMPLETED: 1967
DESIGNER: Vojislav Vujisić
COORDINATES: N42°44'15.1", E19°47'13.9"
DIMENSIONS: 22 metres high
MATERIALS: White marble

HISTORY

In 1941 Montenegro was invaded and occupied by Italian forces. Close family ties between the two countries (Italian Queen Elena was the daughter of Montenegrin monarch Nicholas I) meant the Italians anticipated few problems; however, the population quickly became angered by their presence. There was dissatisfaction with their administration of food resources, the mass influx of refugees and heavy-handed oppression.

In the town of Andrijevica organised resistance was growing. On 17 July 1941, a group of 235 partisan rebels overthrew the local Italian garrison, killing more than 200 Italian troops and effectively (if briefly) liberating Andrijevica. The Italians recovered control of the town, but the partisans continued to fight. During the course of the war Andrijevica changed hands more than fifteen times. The Andrijevica partisans fought successful conflicts all over Montenegro, including victories in Bistrica, Lokva, Zekova and Glava. In June 1944, the 21st Waffen Mountain Division (1st Albanian unit) of the Waffen-SS were deployed in the region. In Andrijevica they murdered over 400 innocent Orthodox Christians. The town was finally liberated by partisan troops on 17 November 1944.

DESIGN AND CONSTRUCTION

This monument was built to commemorate the 600 partisan fighters and 900 civilian victims from the area, who died during the National Liberation War. Located in Andrijevica's Knjaževac Monument Park on a terrace overlooking the Lim river, it was opened in July 1967. The 22-metre-tall, white marble sculpture, designed by sculptor Vojislav Vujisić, is made up of six connected pillars that support a central raised eternal flame. The six pillars are intended to represent the six republics of the former Yugoslavia. The park contains several smaller monuments commemorating various events of World War I, the Balkan Wars and World War II.

STATUS AND CONDITION

While there is some damage to the façade and base of the main spomenik, it is in a reasonable condition. The Vujisić spomenik is used to advertise the town, there is directional signage to the monument and informational plaques on site. The park is well visited and remembrance events are held here every 13 July, to mark Montenegro's Statehood Day.

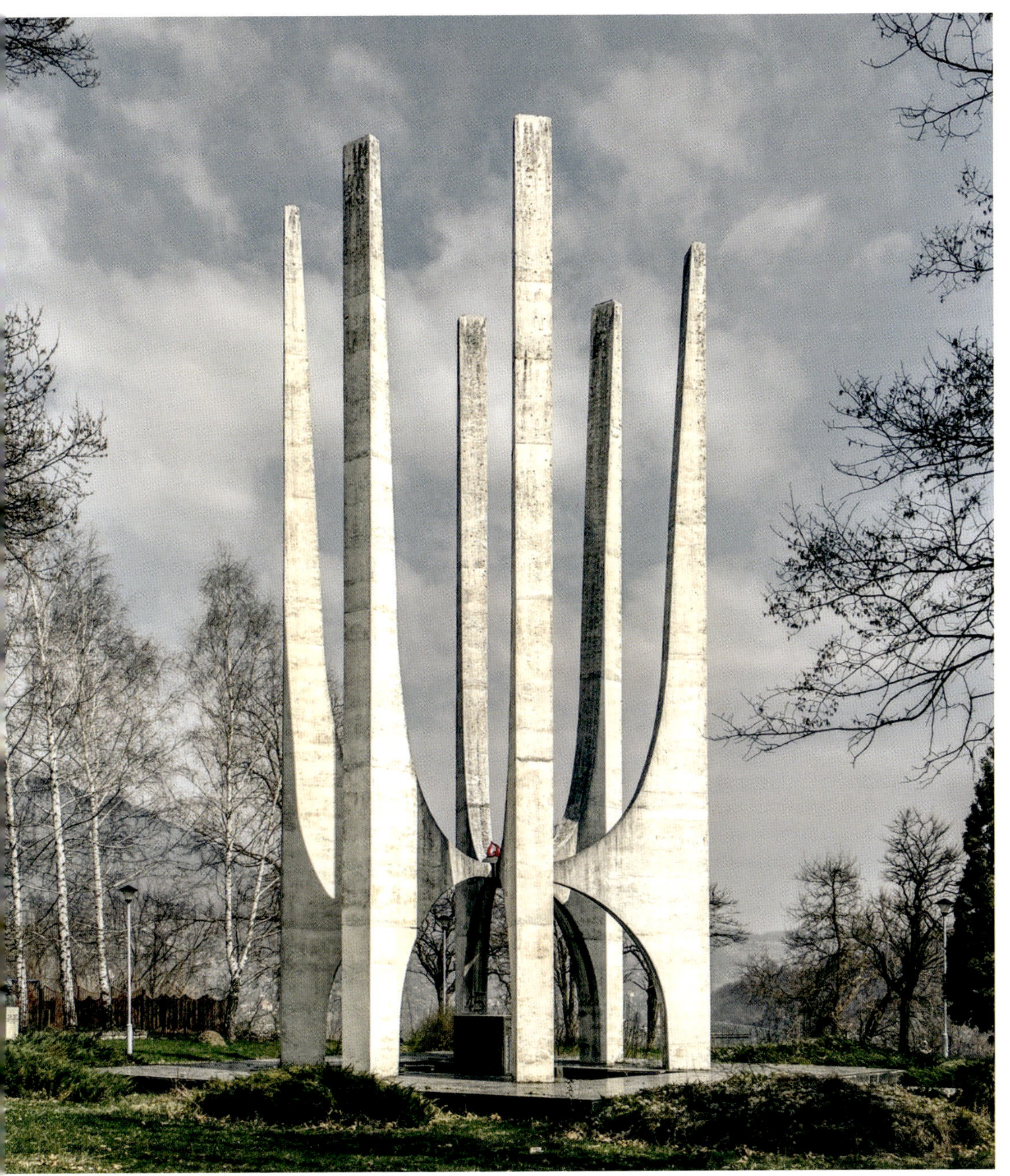

AVALA (AH-vah-lah)

NAME: Soviet War Veterans Monument
LOCATION: Near Pinosava village on Mount Avala, Belgrade, Serbia
YEAR COMPLETED: 1965
DESIGNER: Jovan Kratohvil
COORDINATES: N44°41'19.7", E20°30'50.6"
DIMENSIONS: 5 metres high
MATERIALS: Bronze

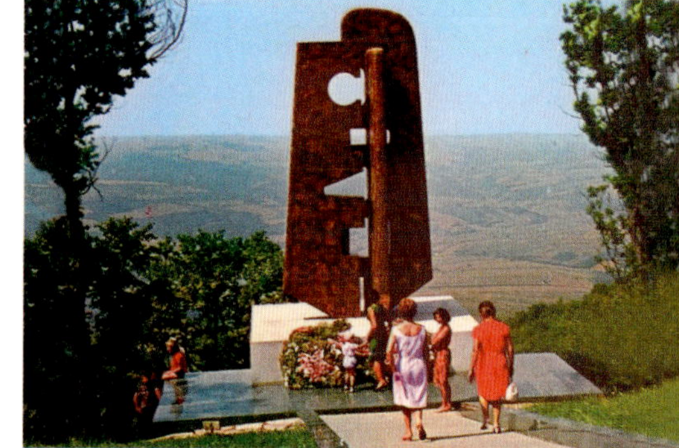
A postcard of the monument shortly after its construction in 1965

HISTORY

On the morning of 19 October 1964, a group of 22 Soviet dignitaries and veterans were flying from Moscow to Belgrade to take part in a ceremony marking the 20th anniversary of the Liberation of Belgrade. The plane was expected to land at 11.30am at the Belgrade Batajnica Military Air Base. At 11.34am, just as it was approaching the airfield, it veered off course and crashed into the nearby Mount Avala. All 33 passengers and crew were killed. Various explanations were put forward as to the cause of the crash. While no conclusive reason was found, the possibility of sabotage was ruled out. Following the tragedy, two days of nationwide mourning were held across Yugoslavia.

DESIGN AND CONSTRUCTION

In 1965, a memorial, designed by the Belgrade Olympic athlete and sculptor Jovan Kratohvil, was built near the crash site. His 5-metre-tall bronze monolith, accessed via a pair of grand stone staircases, stands on a marble pedestal overlooking the Serbian countryside. This spomenik, along with the Avala Tower (completed the same year) complement Mount Avala's main attraction, the Monument to the Unknown Hero.

STATUS AND CONDITION

Through the 1960s up to the 1990s, this was an extremely popular tourist area. However, in the late 1990s the mountain was shelled by NATO during the Kosovo War. In 1999, the Avala Tower was completely destroyed and the Monument to the Unknown Hero suffered bomb damage. However, the Soviet War Veterans spomenik was largely unharmed.

Today, Avala again attracts thousands of visitors each year. The spomenik is well maintained, with many commemorative and ceremonial events still being held on 23 February (Red Army Day) and 20 October (Belgrade Liberation Day) to honour the Red Army veterans who died here.

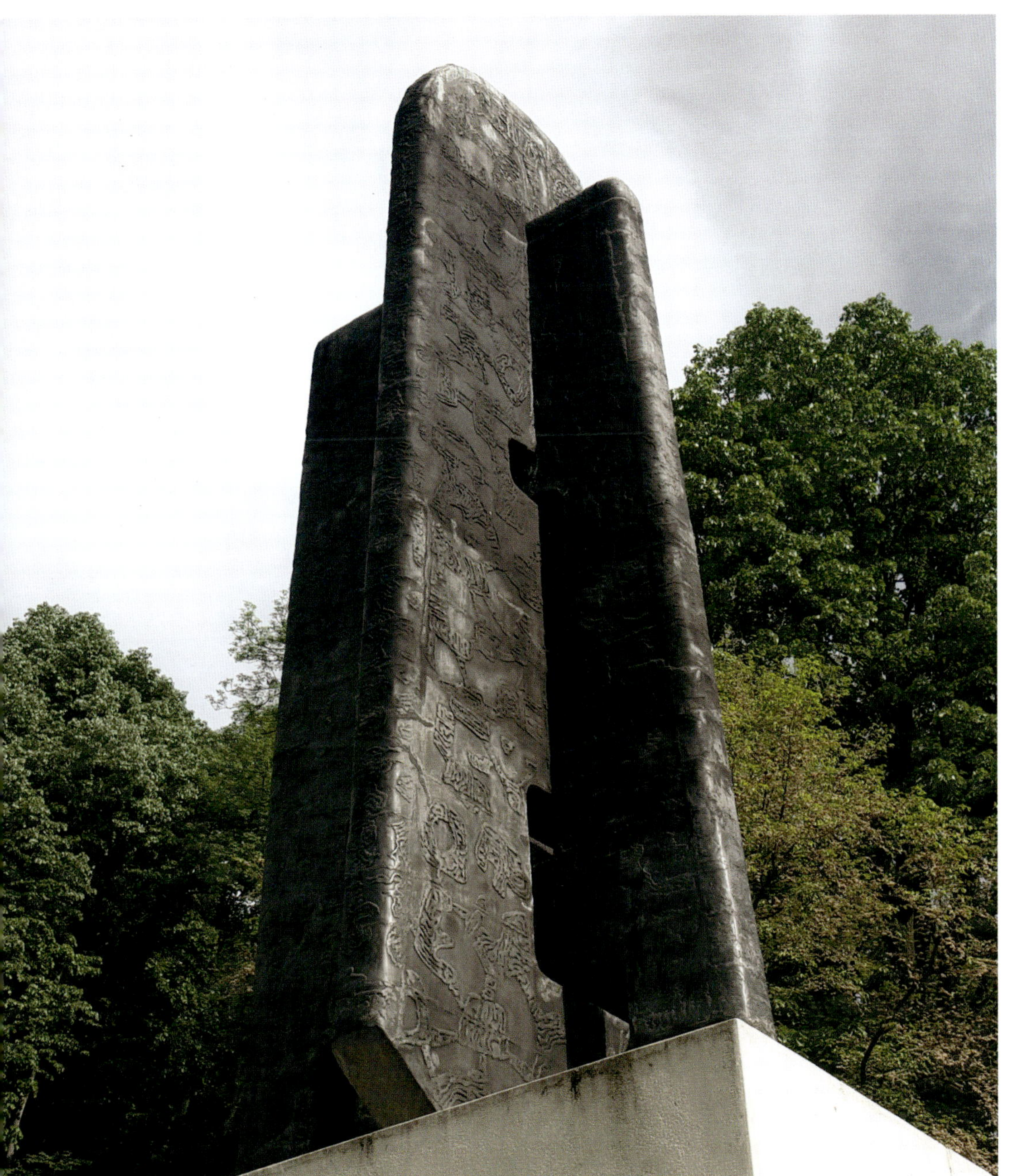

BARUTANA (bah-ruh-TAH-nah)

NAME: Monument to the Fallen Soldiers
LOCATION: Barutana, Montenegro
YEAR COMPLETED: 1980 (5 years to build)
DESIGNER: Svetlana Kana Radević
COORDINATES: N42°23'38.3", E19°08'30.3"
DIMENSIONS: Eight 12 metre high pillars
MATERIALS: Poured concrete and rebar

HISTORY

The First Balkan War: Montenegro, ambitious to expand its territory into Ottoman-controlled Sandžak (a region between Montenegro and Serbia), made an alliance with Serbia, Greece and Bulgaria, forming the 'Balkan League'. Montenegro declared war on 8 October 1912. Victory was eventually sealed with the signing of the Treaty of London in May 1913, ending 500 years of Ottoman presence in Europe. Montenegro was granted half of the Sandžak region. Around 150 people from the Barutana region died during the war.

World War I: Austria-Hungary, alongside Germany, the Ottoman Empire and Bulgaria (the Central Powers) held Serbia responsible for the assassination of Archduke Franz Ferdinand of Austria in Sarajevo on 28 June 1914. As a result of Serbian defiance, Austria-Hungary declared war. Montenegro, Serbia's ally, soon followed. Hundreds of fighters from the Barutana region fell during the war. Following the surrender of the Central Powers in 1918, Montenegro's territory was integrated into the new Kingdom of Yugoslavia, becoming part of Zeta Banovina province.

World War II (also known as the National Liberation War): the Kingdom of Yugoslavia was invaded by Axis powers in April 1941. On 16 April, Italian forces occupied the Zeta Banovina region, intending to re-establish the Kingdom of Montenegro under Italian control. A popular uprising began on 14 July 1941. Within weeks the Montenegrins had almost retaken the entire country. Mussolini dispatched an overwhelming force to crush the rebels, resulting in the deaths of thousands of fighters and civilians. After the Italian surrender in September 1943, resistance forces again progressed with the liberation of the region. Although German troops quickly replaced the Italians as occupiers, their numbers were insufficient. By December 1944, all Axis forces had withdrawn from Montenegro. Over the course of the war, several hundred citizens of the Barutana region were killed. In 1945, Montenegro became one of six republics within the new Socialist Federal Republic of Yugoslavia.

DESIGN AND CONSTRUCTION

Following a nationwide competition, native Montenegrin architect Svetlana Kana Radević's design was selected. The monument, commemorating those who died in these conflicts, was officially opened to the public in July of 1980, 26 years after the partisan liberation of the Barutana region. The central element consists of eight free-standing concrete pillars, 12 metres tall. Towards the top, they break from the vertical into sharply angled 'C' shapes, giving the impression of a bud on a stem or supplicating hands. A large amphitheatre was built adjacent to this element for educational and political presentations. The complex had its own lighting, to facilitate its use in night-time events. On the stone-paved pathway that leads to the spomenik are three circular areas with smaller memorial elements, dedicated respectively to the victims of the First Balkan War, World War I and World War II.

STATUS AND CONDITION

Although the central monument is in reasonable repair, other elements of the site are deteriorating. During the Yugoslav era, the complex was maintained by children from the local school, but the population slump in the village since the breakup of the country is reflected in the condition of the site today. It is possible the site is still used to hold commemorative events, but there is no obvious evidence of this, and there is no directional signage to the spomenik, nor information at the site itself.

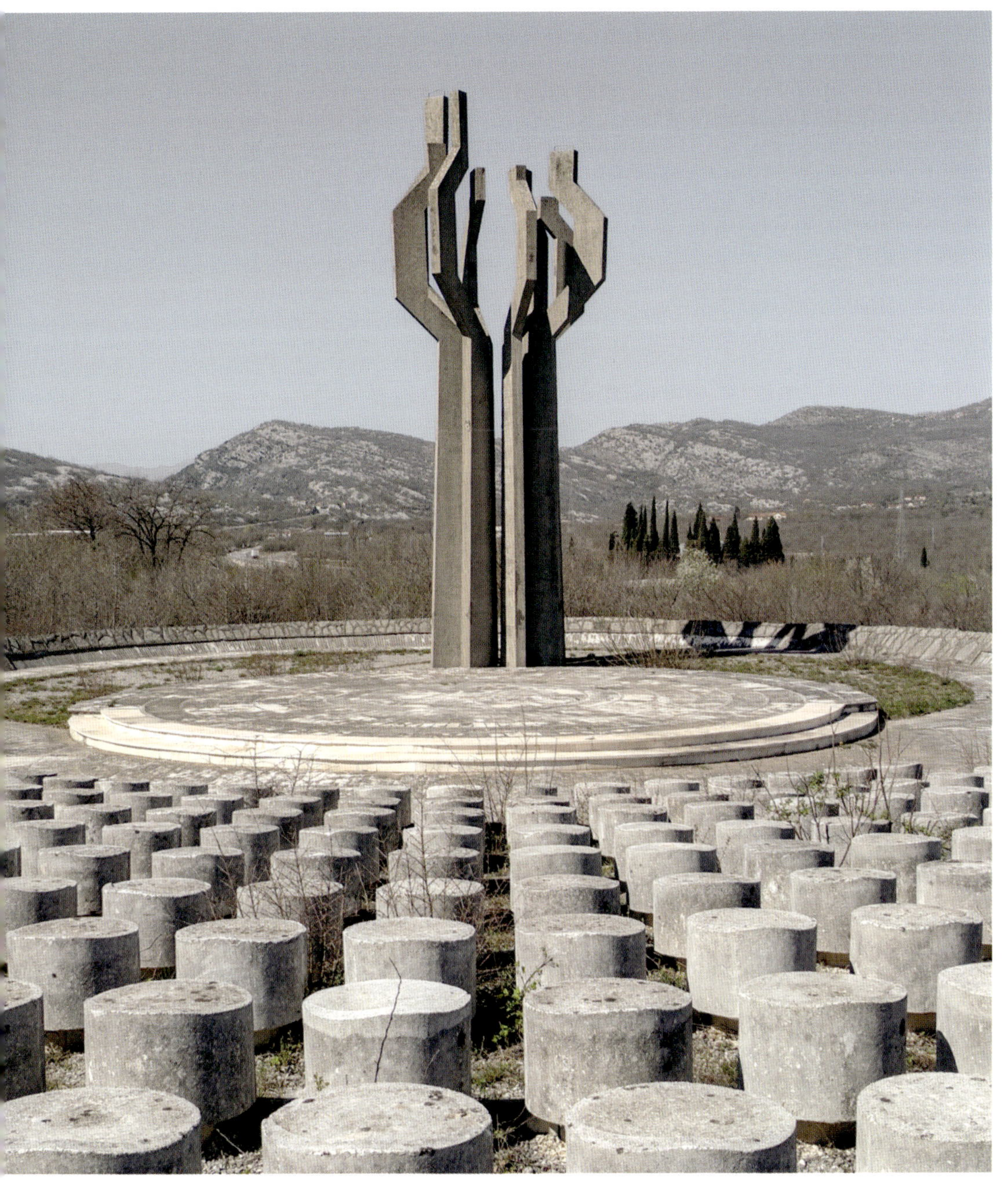

BIHAĆ (BEE-hach)

NAME: Garavice Memorial Park of the Victims
of Fascist Terror
LOCATION: Bihać, FBiH, Bosnia and Herzegovina
YEAR COMPLETED: 1981
DESIGNER: Bogdan Bogdanović
COORDINATES: N44°49'20.0", E15°50'24.3"
DIMENSIONS: fifteen monoliths, 4–6 metres high
MATERIALS: Bihacite stone blocks

HISTORY

Following their occupation of Croatia and Bosnia, the Axis Italian and German forces created the Independent State of Croatia (NDH), using the ultra-nationalist Ustaše forces to impose order. In June 1941, the mayor of Bihać, NDH-aligned Ljubomir Kvaternik, passed new laws expelling ethnic-Serbs and Jews from the city and its surrounding areas. However, many remained and consequently Kvaternik ordered all ethnic-Serbs and Jews, regardless of gender or age, to be arrested. From July into August, these civilians were murdered in their thousands at sites across Bihać, the majority of executions taking place at Garavice Hill, west of the city.

The first liberation of Bihać occurred on 4 November 1942, when 6,000 partisan fighters stormed the city, overpowering 4,000 Ustaše and Homeland occupying forces. The city was declared an independent territory and named the Bihać Republic. However, the partisan victory was short lived, as German troops from the SS 7th Division managed to retake the city on 29 January 1943. It was not until April 1945 that Bihać was fully liberated from Axis control, when partisan troops from the 4th Yugoslav Army descended on the city and defeated the German 15th Mountain Corps as part of Operation Lika-Primorje. It is estimated that, during the course of the war, between 12,000 and 15,000 people were killed in Bihać.

DESIGN AND CONSTRUCTION

In 1949, a modest memorial was constructed at the foot of Garavice Hill to commemorate the site of the killings. Twenty years later, the municipality of Bihać commissioned architect Bogdan Bogdanović to create a more ambitious scheme. His memorial complex would be located at the top of the hill, with the surrounding area acting as a mass grave for the thousands who were killed there. However, many years passed before plans were finalised and construction could actually start. It was not until 1981 that the completed memorial was finally unveiled to the public.

The memorial consists of fifteen stone columns, between 4 and 6 metres tall, spread across a wide area where the killings occurred. Thirteen columns stand on the Garavice hillside, a paved stone path twisting through them, while two additional columns stand at a mass grave, a kilometre north of Garavice Hill, on the other side of the Kolkot river.

STATUS AND CONDITION

Today the spomenik complex is neglected and damaged. After the breakup of Yugoslavia, the site fell into disrepair. Besides being a target for vandals, it was also scarred by fighting and shelling throughout the Siege of Bihać (1992-95), during which nearly 5,000 people were killed. Today, beneath the graffiti, most of the columns

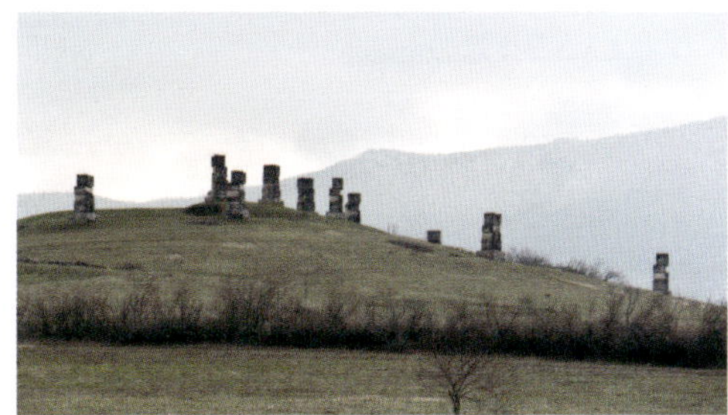

are in a reasonable state and could easily be restored to their original condition.

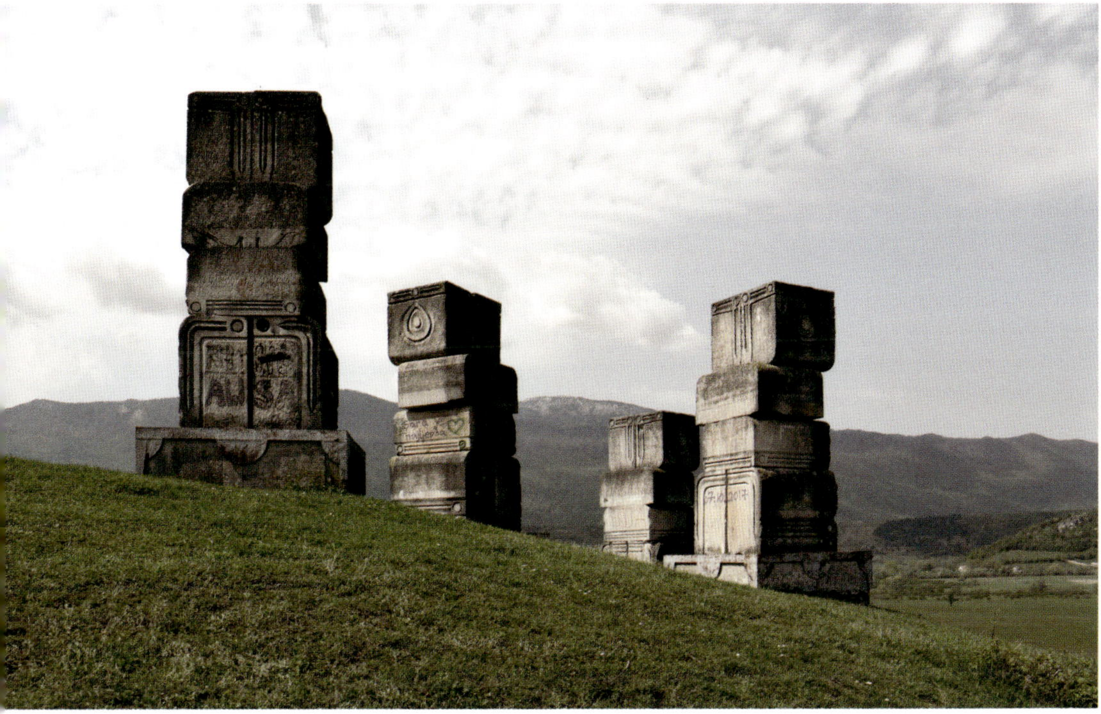

In September 2011, Garavice was assigned protected status, coming under the Bosnia and Herzegovina Commission for the Preservation of National Monuments. Recognising the need for restoration at the site, the Bosnian government called on 'competent State authorities to work within all legal means and with real and detailed actions to both preserve and improve this anti-fascist heritage'.

In recent years, annual ceremonies have once again been held at the memorial, often attended by local and regional government officials, and there are fresh plans to renovate the site.

BOTUN (BOH-toon)

NAME: Monument to the Uprising at Debarca
LOCATION: Botun, Macedonia
YEAR COMPLETED: unknown
DESIGNER: unknown
COORDINATES: N41°16'43.7", E20°47'01.3"
DIMENSIONS: Two 4–5 metre high monoliths
MATERIALS: Poured concrete and rebar

HISTORY

In April 1941, following the Axis occupation of the Kingdom of Yugoslavia, present-day western Macedonia was incorporated into an Italian puppet state called the 'Kingdom of Albania'.

The region of Debarca was deeply affected by these changes. Its occupation and oppression by Italian and Albanian Axis-aligned forces pushed its citizens to breaking point. As a consequence, a significant anti-fascist movement evolved. This resistance was so strong that Debarca became an important centre for the co-ordination of uprisings (mainly organised by the communist-led partisan resistance group) across much of present-day western Macedonia. This success was largely thanks to enraged and committed citizens, along with the region's tough mountain terrain, which favoured the partisans' guerrilla-style warfare.

In spring 1943, partisan fighters overwhelmed and disarmed all the Italian garrisons in Debarca, completely liberating the district from Axis control and creating the first free territory in Macedonia.

On 18 August, a group of around 100 fighters met on Mount Slavej, north of Botun. They used the weapons confiscated from the Italians to establish the first formal partisan military unit, called the 'Mirče Acev Battalion' (in honour of the freedom activist who had been killed in custody in January 1943). One of the region's most accomplished partisan units, they operated across the Kingdom of Albania and Bulgarian-occupied Vardar Macedonia.

Practically every man in the free-territory of Debarca was mobilised into a militia, while the women took supporting roles and organised resistance activities. Schools in the free-territory were able to teach the Macedonian language, which had been forbidden during the occupation. However, when the Italians surrendered to the Allies in September 1943, they were quickly replaced by German forces, instigating a two-month-long stand-off with partisan fighters. Eventually Debarca fell under German control. It was not until November 1944 that the Botun region was liberated by partisans for the last time.

DESIGN AND CONSTRUCTION

Situated to the south of Botun, this monument was constructed during the Yugoslav era to honour the resistance fighters of Debarca who gave their lives in the struggle for freedom from Axis forces (as explained on the plaque linking the two sections of the sculpture). It has not been possible to discover any background information about when the monument was created or who designed it. It is possible that the two sections of the spomenik represent the two main ethnicities in the region: Macedonian and Albanian.

STATUS AND CONDITION

This spomenik, formed of two deteriorating concrete monoliths resting on a fractured and overgrown paved platform, is completely abandoned. There is no sign of ceremonial activity (although the formation of the 'Mirče Acev Battalion' is still widely celebrated in Macedonia on 18 August, under the name 'Army Day').

The exact reason for the neglect of this spomenik is unknown, but it is likely thanks to the perception of the partisan struggle as a Yugoslavian cause that holds little relevance for Macedonians interested in cultivating their own distinct identity. This may explain why it is abandoned but not vandalised – Macedonians may not necessarily feel anger towards it (as has been the case with many spomeniks in post-Yugoslav Croatia and Bosnia), but ambivalence or indifference.

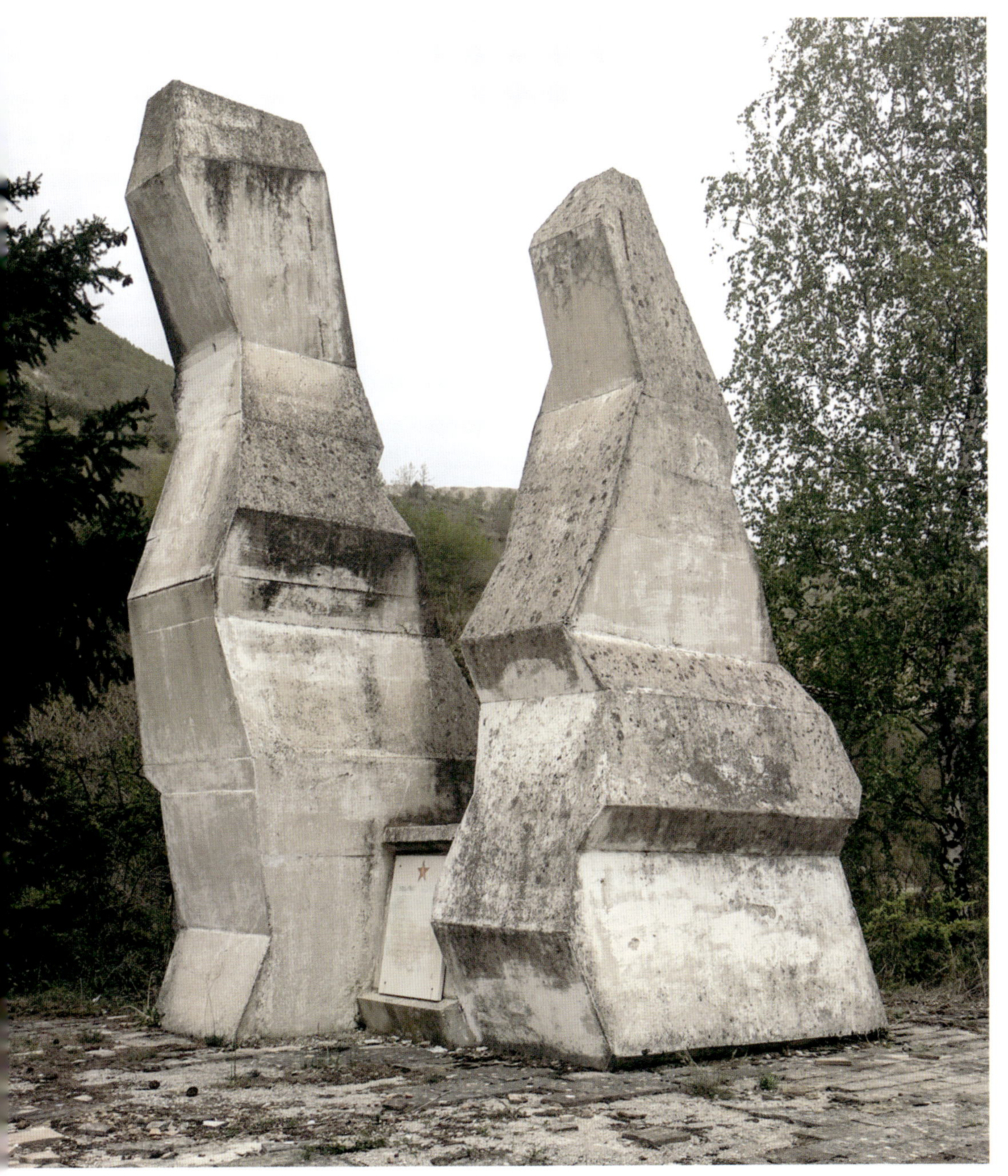

BRATUNAC (BRAH-tuh-nats)

NAME: Bratunac Memorial Park
LOCATION: Bratunac, Republic of Srpska, Bosnia and Herzegovina
YEAR COMPLETED: 1978
DESIGNER: Petar Krstić
COORDINATES: N44°11'02.8", E19°19'43.5"
DIMENSIONS: 17 metre obelisk
MATERIALS: Steel pipes

HISTORY

The Independent State of Croatia (NDH) was established following the invasion of the Kingdom of Yugoslavia in April 1941 by Axis Italian and German forces. This puppet state contained much of present-day Bosnia, including the Podrinje region where Bratunac is located. The nationalist Ustaše militia, acting for the NDH, brutally enforced racial laws oppressing ethnic-Serb, Roma and Jewish populations. Ethnic-Croats and Muslims were not subjected to such oppression, unless they were suspected of collaboration with political dissidents or anti-Axis resistance groups.

Resistance to Axis occupation began in eastern Bosnia on 8 August 1941, when ethnic-Serb rebels in Kravica (a small village just west of Bratunac) rang the bells of the local Orthodox church in a defiantly symbolic act of freedom.

Hundreds of local citizens joined the two main resistance groups: the communist-led partisan rebels and the nationalist Chetniks. Throughout 1941, these two groups worked together, fighting against Ustaše and Axis forces, and liberating many towns in southeast Bosnia. In late 1941, during Operation Uzice, a rift between the partisan and Chetnik groups of west Bosnia turned them against each other, the Chetniks siding with German forces. However, they continued to fight together in eastern Bosnia until January 1942, when the Germans launched Operation Southeast Croatia, an offensive aimed at eliminating all partisan resistance. The Chetnik-led insurgents offered no resistance to the Germans, many withdrawing east over the Drina river into Serbian territory. The loss of the Chetniks considerably weakened the strength of the partisans, who were pushed back towards Foča, leaving 2,000 of their number either dead or captured. The partisans broke off all co-operation with the Chetniks, viewing their action as an unforgivable betrayal. Bratunac again fell under Ustaše control until April 1942, when Serb Chetniks used guerrilla tactics to retake the area, making it part of a large Chetnik liberated zone, often referred to as Mihailović's Island of Freedom, after the supreme Chetnik commander Draža Mihailović.

However, in the same month the territory was retaken (as part of Operation Trio, a German-Italian counter-insurgency offensive) by the Ustaše's notorious Black Legion unit, commanded by Jure Francetić. He ordered all Serb villages in the area to be burnt to the ground, leading to the massacre of many ethnic-Serb civilians. In the nearby town of Vlasenica, the Black Legion was reported to have raped and killed nearly 900 Jewish and ethnic-Serb residents. Francetić died in December 1942 when his plane was shot down near the NDH town of Slunj.

Bratunac continued to change hands during the course of the war, but was finally liberated from Axis and Chetnik control by partisan forces in March 1945.

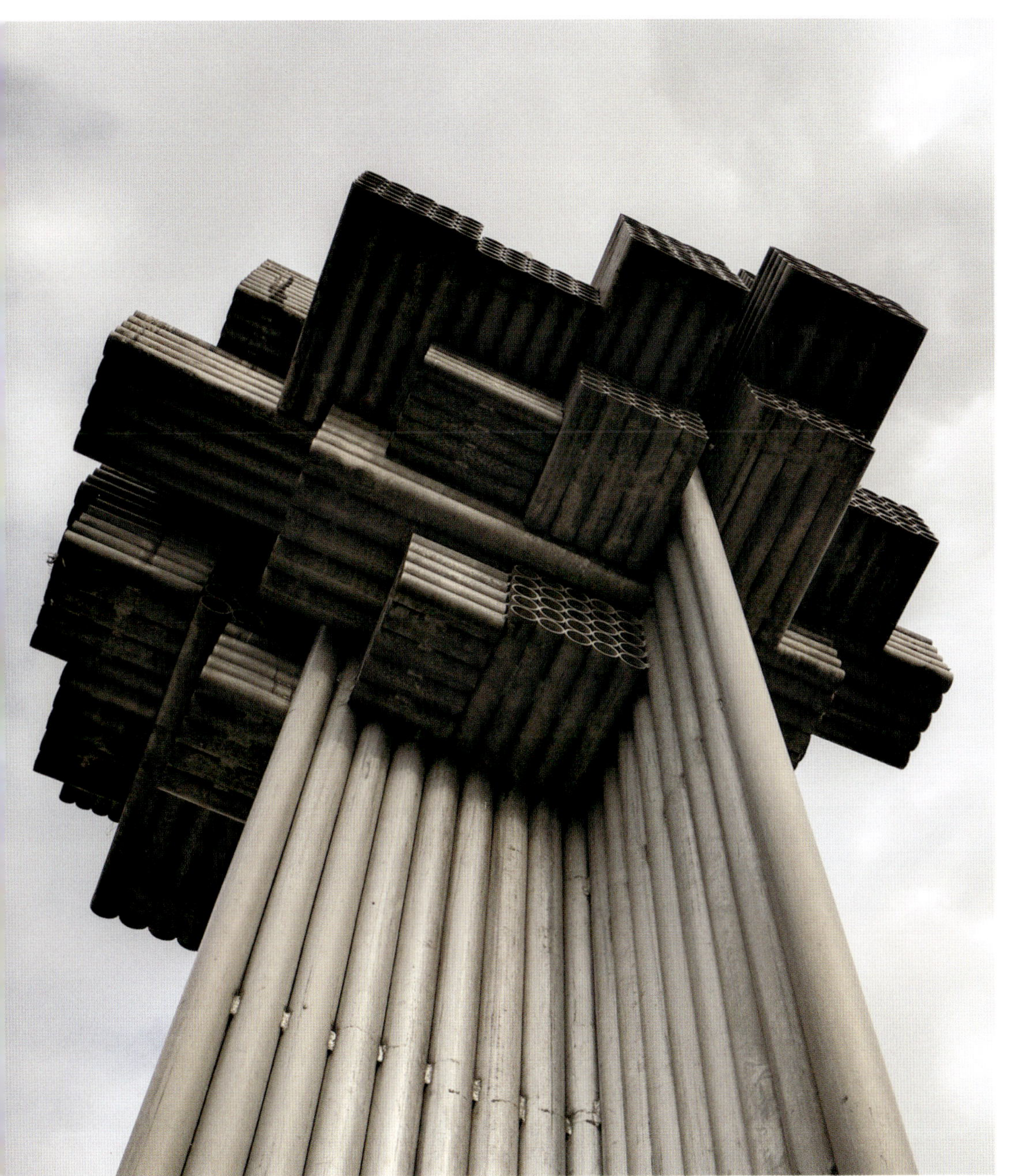

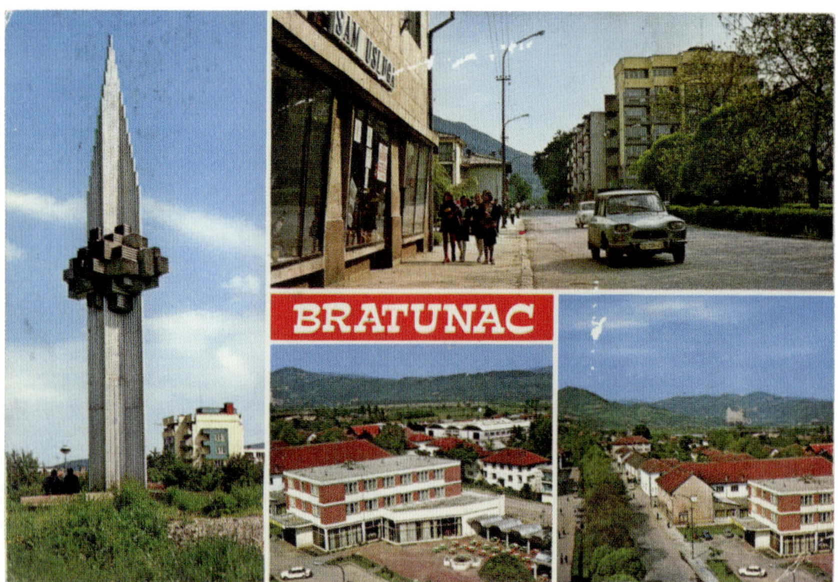

A postcard from the 1980s showing the Bratunac spomenik

DESIGN AND CONSTRUCTION

This spomenik, created by sculptor Petar Krstić and completed in 1978, commemorates the partisan fighters and civilians from this region who were killed during World War II. The central element consists of a 17-metre-tall tower constructed from metal tubes, tapering towards the top and standing on a curvilinear concrete mound. Towards the middle of the structure, shorter lengths of tubing are arranged at right angles to the main body of the spomenik in what might be seen as a kind of knotty interruption to the otherwise serene upward flow of the tower.

STATUS AND CONDITION

On 29 February 1992, the Socialist Republic of Bosnia passed a referendum for independence, leading to the further dismantling of the Republic of Yugoslavia. Tension built as Bosnian Serbs refused to recognise Bosnia's declared indepen-dence. This conflict led to the Bosnian War between Bosnian Serbs and Muslim Bosniaks (who supported Bosnian independence). The spomenik complex at Bratunac was in the middle of a Bosnian Serb-held region called the Republic of Srpska (RS). As fighting intensified, the spomenik fell into disrepair. The army of the Republic of Srpska (VRS), commanded by Ratko Mladić, attempted to ethnically cleanse the RS region. They committed many atrocities in the process, including the infamous massacre at the nearby town of Srebrenica, where more than 8,000 Muslim Bosniaks (mainly men and boys) were killed in July 1995. The war ended on 14 December 1995.

Today, the Bratunac spomenik remains in poor condition, with most of the complex's surrounding elements being damaged, defaced or destroyed. While the central monument appears structurally sound, its concrete base is in a bad state of repair. There is no indication that memorial events are held here. There are no directional signposts to the monument and there is no information about its significance at the site itself.

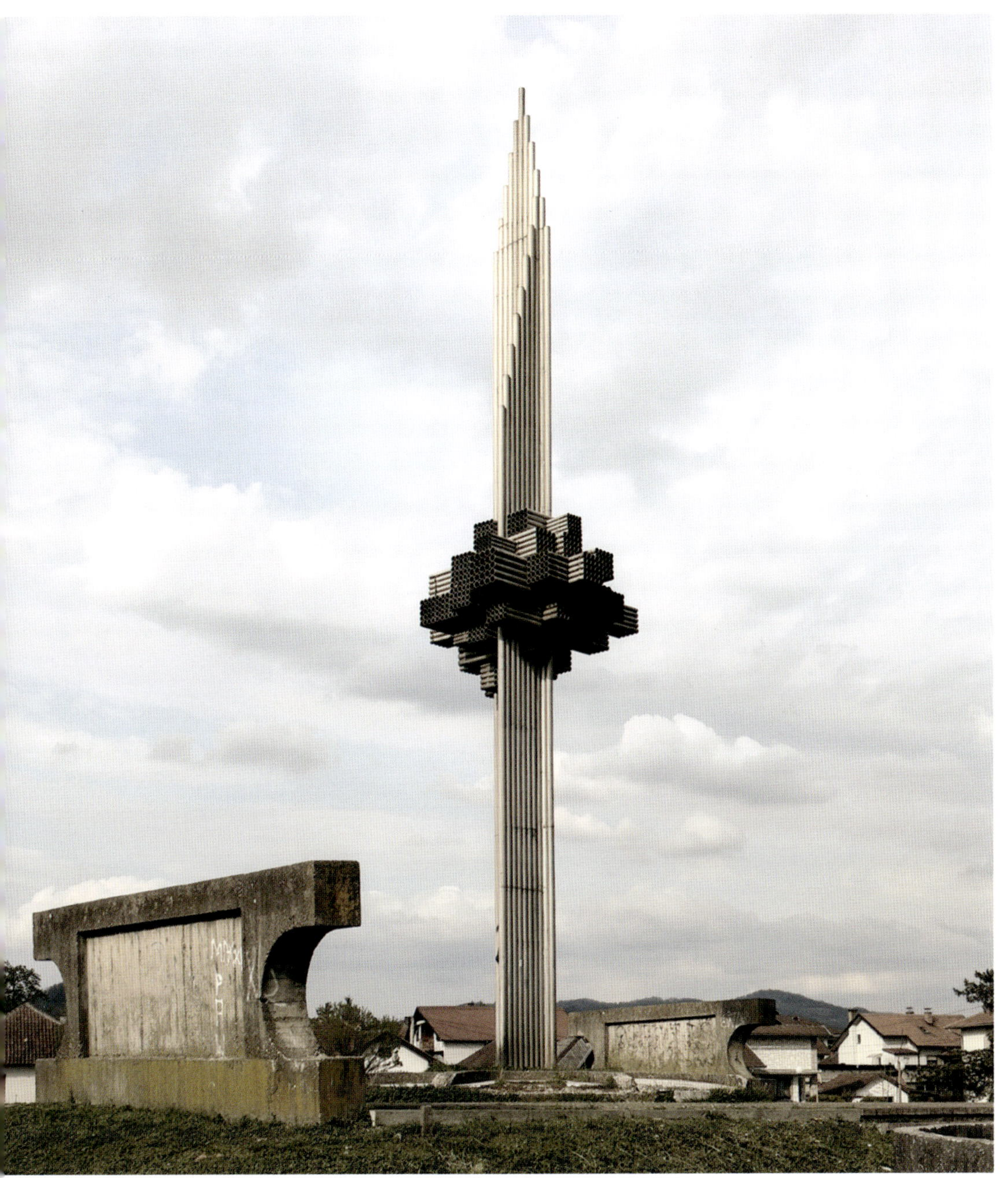

BRAVSKO (BRAHV-skoh)

NAME: Monument to the Fallen Fighters of the
National Liberation War
LOCATION: Bravsko, FBiH, Bosnia and Herzegovina
YEAR COMPLETED: 1972
DESIGNER: Mirko Radulović
COORDINATES: N44°32'56.4", E16°34'54.5"
DIMENSIONS: 7 metres high
MATERIALS: Poured concrete and rebar

HISTORY

In April 1941, with the Kingdom of Yugoslavia occupied by Axis forces, modern-day Croatia and Bosnia (including the Bosanska Krajina region where Bravsko is located) were absorbed into a new puppet regime called the Independent State of Croatia (NDH). Its nationalist Ustaše militia brutally enforced new racial laws, persecuting ethnic-Serb, Roma and Jewish populations. Inspired by the Yugoslav communist partisans, ordinary citizens across the Bravsko region began to make plans to fight back, gathering weapons and holding secret meetings. When 60 peasants and railway workers were killed by Ustaše soldiers in the nearby village of Klenovac, the resistance fighters of the Bravsko region joined together to form the Bravsko Company, under the command of Gliša Raca. By the end of 1941, they numbered more than 100 men and had already carried out a number of offensives and sabotage missions against Ustaše and Axis units. Their constant attacks were a problem for the Ustaše and so, on 6 January 1942, the Ustaše launched a surprise offensive against the Bravsko Company camp. However, the resistance fighters had been alerted in advance and defeated their attackers in an ambush. On 28 February 1942, similar tactics were used against an Italian offensive near the village of Majkić.

The Bravsko Company continued to fight against the Ustaše and to liberate areas of western Bosnia (such as Ključ, Krasulje, Vrhpolje and Sanica). On 22 August 1942, at the village of

Kamenica near Drvar, they were incorporated into the newly formed 3rd Krajina Partisan Brigade, consisting of 1,000 fighters, in four battalions.

In November 1942, members of the 3rd Krajina Brigade took part in the liberation of Bihać, which led to the creation of the Bihać Republic, a territory made up of partisan-liberated areas, including the town of Bravsko. However, the Bihać Republic was retaken by German troops on 29 January 1943 during Case White, the Axis offensive intended to eliminate Tito and his partisans from western Bosnia.

Throughout the war, the 3rd Krajina Brigade fought across occupied Yugoslavia, including battles at Neretva, Sutjeska and the Sremski Front (one of the last, and bloodiest, battles of the war). The Bravsko region was finally liberated by partisans in May 1945. During the course of the war, over 500 local residents perished, both civilians and those fighting in resistance units across Yugoslavia.

DESIGN AND CONSTRUCTION

This spomenik honouring the Bravsko Company fighters killed in the war was designed by Yugoslav architect Mirko Radulović. It also commemorates partisans Trivo Latinović and Mile Latinović, who were made Yugoslav National Heroes. Trivo died in 1943 in nearby Ključ, while leading an assault against a German bunker. Mile died commanding the 5th Battalion of the 3rd Krajina Brigade at the Sremski Front in 1944. Opened in 1972, the centrepiece of the complex is a 7-metre-tall concrete sculpture consisting of a square central pillar, with five corrugated rectangular sections radiating horizontally from its apex. Gliša Raca, the Bravsko Company commander, also has a tomb at the site.

STATUS AND CONDITION

The basic structure of the memorial is in good condition; however, this remote site is overgrown and appears neglected. There is no directional signage to the memorial, or information at the site. In addition there is no evidence of any remembrance ceremonies being held here.

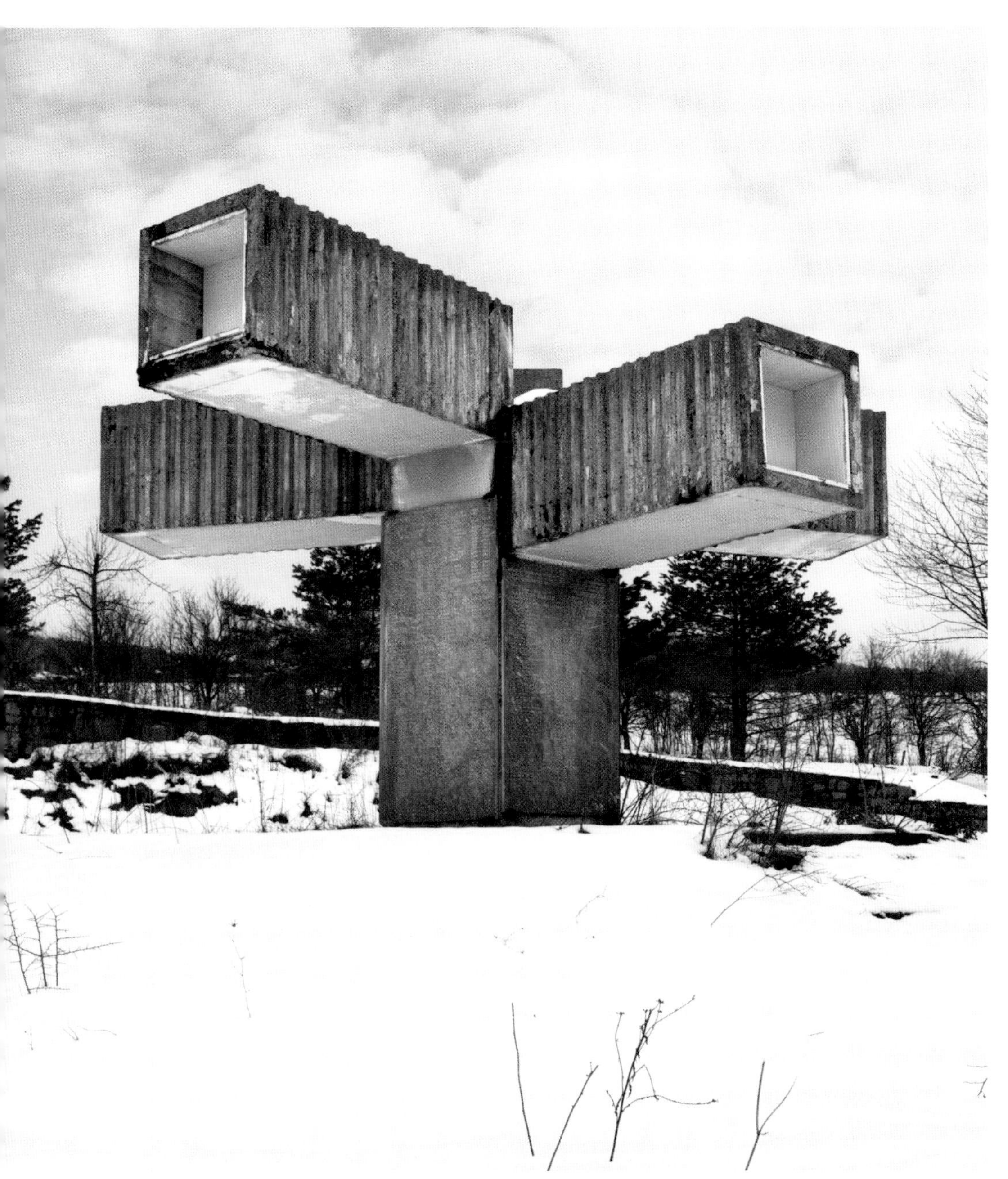

BREZOVICA (BREH-zoh-vee-tsa)

NAME: Monument to the Šar Mountains Partisan Unit
LOCATION: Brezovica, Kosovo
YEAR COMPLETED: 1964
DESIGNER: Svetomir Basara
COORDINATES: N42°13'12.3", E20°59'50.0"
DIMENSIONS: 9 metres high
MATERIALS: Poured concrete, rebar and steel

HISTORY

Following the invasion of Axis forces in April 1941, the Šar Mountains region was annexed into the Italian puppet state called the Kingdom of Albania. While some Albanians were appeased by promises made to them by the Italian forces, others joined Serbs across the region to fight Axis occupation. On 3 November 1942, rebel fighters from the regions of Ferizaj and Brezovica formed the Šar Mountains Partisan Unit. However, they were immediately pursued by well-armed Bulgarian Axis troops and forced to disband. Twenty of the original unit reformed in March 1943 and began to mine chromium (for aeroplane parts) near the Albanian border. However, local anti-communists had tipped off the Italian forces, who attacked the partisans and killed or captured most of the unit.

In May 1943, the Šar Mountains Partisan Unit absorbed two other partisan detachments and a few months later a further two battalions, bringing their number to more than 220 fighters. They fought most notably in the Kičevo and Debarca regions of Macedonia. In October, 50 members of the unit helped Albanian partisans to defend the Albanian town of Peshkopi against (anti-communist, Axis-collaborating) Balli Kombëtar forces, who had surrounded the town with artillery.

After a two-day battle, the partisans successfully drove all Balli Kombëtar out of the town.

In September 1944, the unit's members were merged with other Kosovo Metohija liberation brigades, and the Šar Mountains Partisan Unit was disbanded. After the war, twelve former members of the unit were awarded the Order of the People's Hero, while five others were made Yugoslav People's Army (JNA) generals. The unit's chief, Branko Šotra, went on to become the head of all JNA forces in Serbia during the 1960s and 1970s.

DESIGN AND CONSTRUCTION

Opened in 1964, the Monument to the Šar Mountains Partisan Unit was designed by sculptor Svetomir Basara, who originally came from the nearby village of Ševc. The main monument stands at the far northern end of the park, which consists of two high, curved concrete walls (9 and 7 metres tall respectively), intended by the artist to suggest a pair of lungs, breathing life into the resistance. These are set around a 7-metre-tall, black, steel, abstract construction. At the centre of the park is a circular, stone-lined fountain from which stone-paved pathways lead to the park entrance to the south and the monument to the north. Symmetrically located on the east and west sides of the park are circular courtyards, surrounded by decorative concrete benches.

STATUS AND CONDITION

While the majority of the park's elements are relatively intact, many have been damaged and vandalised. The primary monument is in reasonable condition, but has been defaced with graffiti. There is no evidence that remembrance events are held here. A children's playground has recently been built within the site.

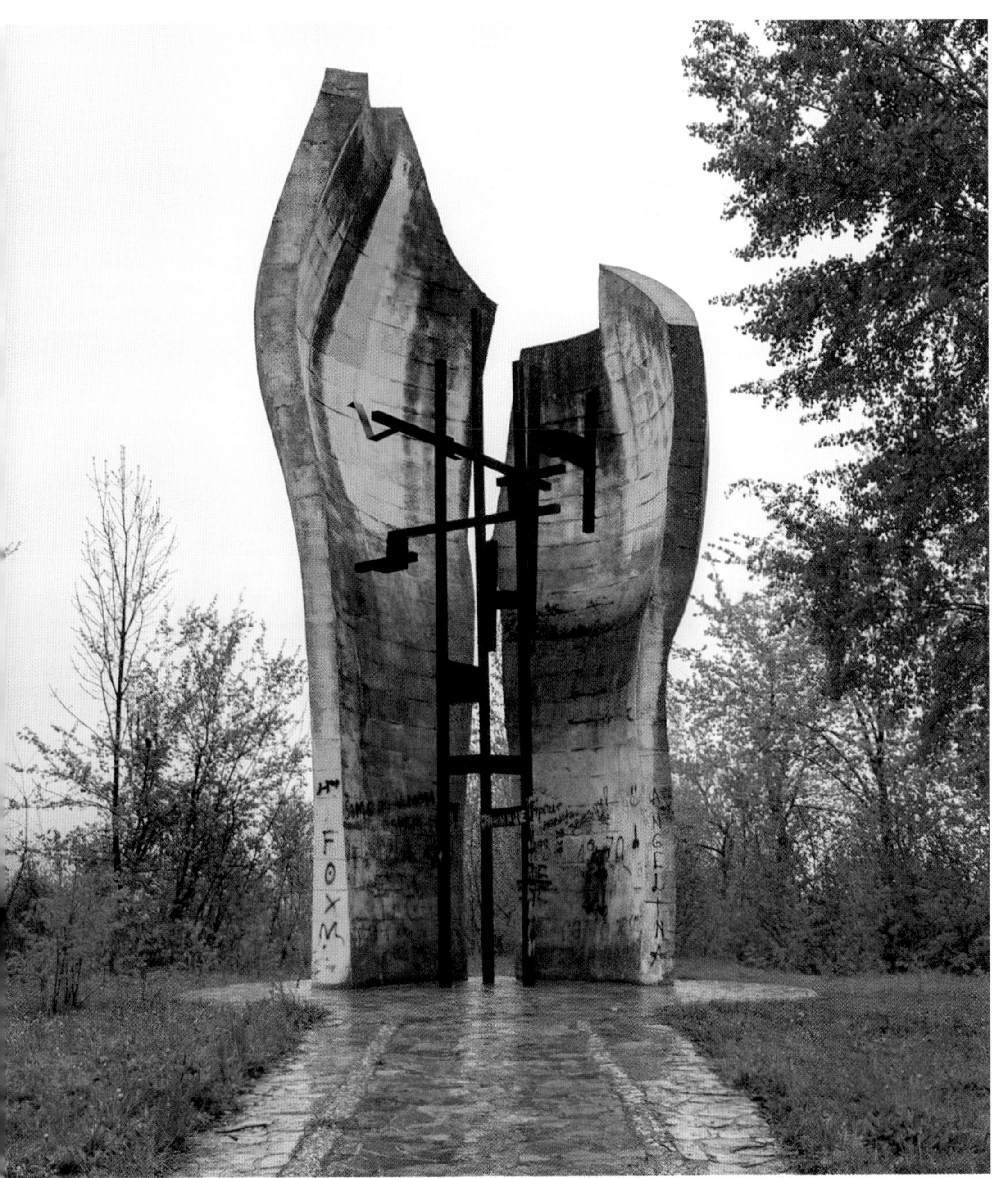

BRZEĆE (ber-ZEH-cheh)

NAME: Mramor Monument
LOCATION: Brzeće, Serbia
YEAR COMPLETED: 1969
DESIGNER: unknown
COORDINATES: N43°16'38.8", E20°52'31.1"
DIMENSIONS: 15 metres high
MATERIALS: Marble

HISTORY

In May 1944, partisan commanders were planning their final push for the liberation of Serbia from occupying Axis forces and their Chetnik collaborators. The 1st Krajina Proletariat Strike Brigade had successfully defeated the Germans and Chetniks in Novi Pazar, the Sandžak region and the Ibar river region. Now they continued to pursue Axis units into the Kopaonik Mountains, along the rugged border of present-day Serbia and Kosovo.

In early August 1944, partisan intelligence reported the massing of the Chetnik 4th Assault Corps near the small village of Brzeće. The 1st Brigade dispatched their 2nd Proletariat Shock Division, under the command of Petar 'Peko' Dapčević, to intercept and attack them. From 6 to 8 August 1944, the partisans engaged and comprehensively defeated the Chetniks in the foothills south of the village. This victory was pivotal for the partisan resistance and the continued advance towards Belgrade, as the 4th Assault Corps were reported to be one of the strongest and best-armed Chetnik fighting forces in Serbia. Furthermore, their defeat allowed the 1st Krajina Proletariat Strike Brigade to link up with previously isolated partisan detachments in Jablanica and Toplica.

Through the increase in joint operations between partisan groups, along with the help of the Red Army during the Belgrade Offensive, Serbia was completely freed from German control by the end of 1944. After the war, Peko Dapčević was made a Yugoslav National Hero and promoted to the rank of Lieutenant General in the JNA.

DESIGN AND CONSTRUCTION

Completed in 1969, the Mramor Monument commemorates the Battle of Kopaonik, one of the final partisan victories against Axis forces in the Kopaonik Mountains. It is a 15-metre-tall, forked, marble structure, reminiscent of a bridge strut, with an ornate circular design at its centre and a broad altar-like plaque at its base. It is located in the southern foothills area of Brzeće, close to the site of the pivotal battle. Its architect is not known.

STATUS AND CONDITION

The structure of the main memorial is sound, although it is severely weather-stained and the altar-like base is showing signs of cracking. It is listed locally as a point of interest and cultural attraction. Although there are no signposts, its position on one of the main highways through the Kopaonik Mountains means the memorial receives a small trickle of visitors. Well-attended commemorative events are held here, usually on the Day of Uprising against Fascism (7 July).

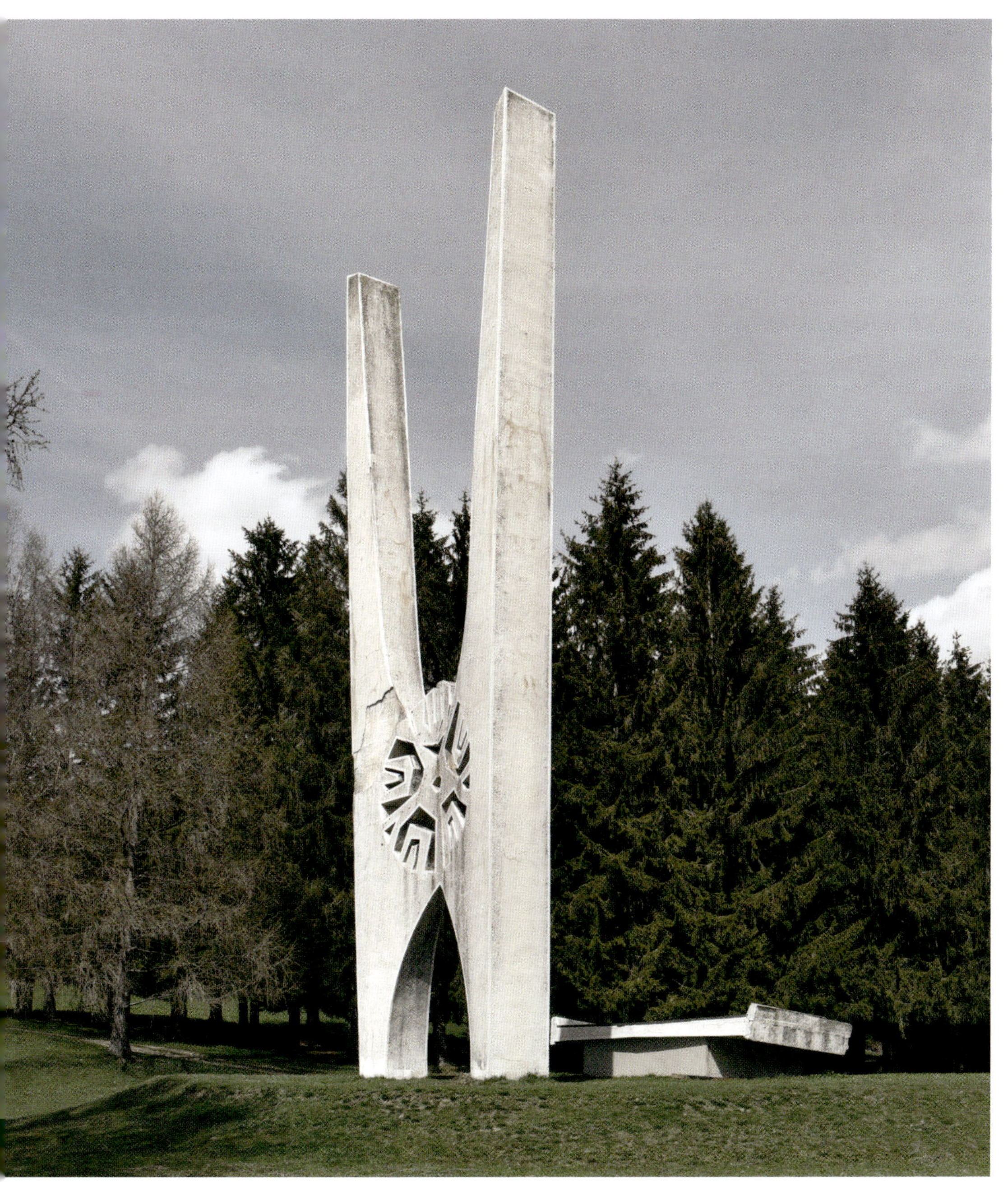

ČAČAK (CHA-chuk)

NAME: Mausoleum of Struggle and Victory
LOCATION: Jelica Mountain, Čačak, Serbia
YEAR COMPLETED: 1980 (4 years to build)
DESIGNER: Bogdan Bogdanović
COORDINATES: N43°52'34.8", E20°20'05.0"
DIMENSIONS: 12 metre high megaron in a 36 hectare memorial park
MATERIALS: Gabbro stone blocks and wood

HISTORY

In July 1941, responding to occupation by German forces, the city of Čačak formed a fully armed and mobilised partisan detachment. Quickly growing to number over 500 fighters, these partisans, along with their Chetnik allies, fought Axis forces in western Serbia to create the short-lived Republic of Užice (see also Kadinjača page 64 and Popina page 154), the first liberated region in Europe during World War II.

However, a rift developed between the Čačak partisans and the Chetniks over strategy. The situation became so divisive that on 6 November 1941, Chetnik commander Draža Mihailović ordered his troops to attack the partisans. They then sided with the Germans, fighting with them to retake the Republic of Užice from partisan control. The Chetniks captured the Čačak partisan celebrated political commissar, Ratko Mitrović. He was hanged in the town centre on 11 December 1941. Despite this loss, the Čačak partisans continued to fight. The arrival of the Partisan Strike Force to western Serbia in spring 1944 brought renewed energy to local partisan detachments and on 4 December the city of Čačak was finally liberated. This victory came great loss of life for both Čačak civilians and soldiers, with more than 4,600 dead by the end of the war.

DESIGN AND CONSTRUCTION

In October 1976, acclaimed architect Bogdan Bogdanović was commissioned to design a memorial to those who had died during the liberation of Čačak. Completed in December 1980, its primary element is a 12-metre-tall stone and wood triple megaron, covered with 620 carved heads of mythological beasts. Downhill from this centrepiece is a smaller dolmen-like structure, standing in front of a 5-metre-tall mass burial mound containing bodies of those killed in Čačak during the war.

When Bogdanović was interviewed about the design, he stated: 'I have always held to the great Adolf Loos' idea, that every good architectural design can be described in words… [for the Čačak memorial] these words can be exhausted in the following semantic chain: a gate, a small gate in a large gate, three long gates in a long axial plane, three gates in a single megaron.'

STATUS AND CONDITION

After the fall of Yugoslavia, the memorial complex fell into disrepair. Today, while the park itself is used for recreation, the spomenik elements remain neglected. However, in December 2016, the Serbian Ministry of Labour, Employment and Social Policy granted 160,000 Euros for the restoration and conservation of the complex. The site is still used for commemorative events, which are held here annually every 7 July, the Day of Uprising against Fascism, despite this holiday having been officially abolished by the Serbian government in 2001.

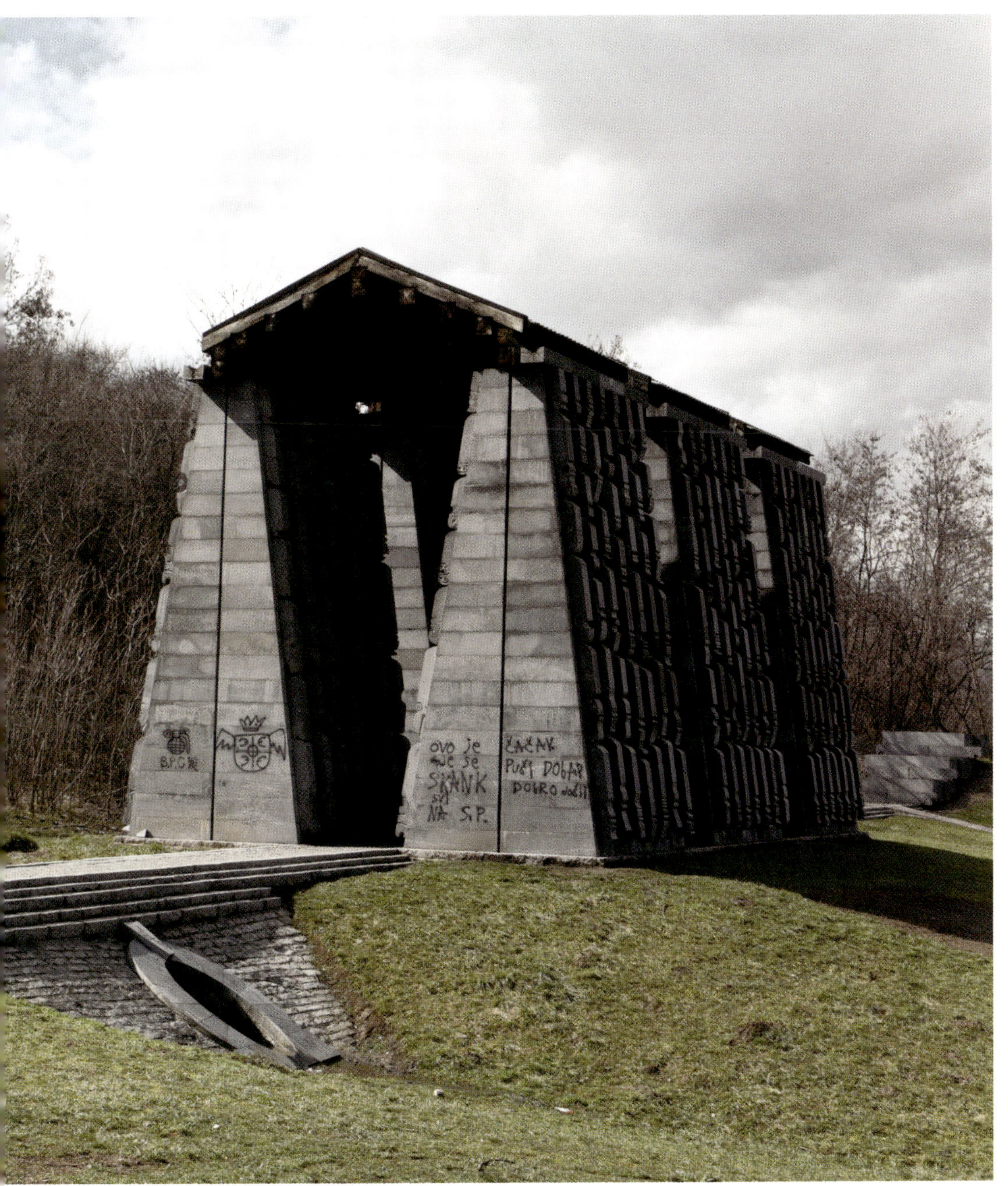

ČENEJ (CHEH-ney)

NAME: Monument to the Novi Sad Partisan Detachment
LOCATION: Čenej, Vojvodina, Serbia
YEAR COMPLETED: 1971
DESIGNER: Pavle Radovanović
COORDINATES: N45°19'23.3", E19°49'44.9"
DIMENSIONS: Three monoliths up to 6 metres high
MATERIALS: Brick and mortar

HISTORY

After its invasion by the Axis powers in April 1941, the former Kingdom of Yugoslavia was partitioned into separate territories administered by different countries. Miklós Horthy's Hungarian Axis forces annexed Novi Sad and its greater region. The Hungarian Honvédség troops, who occupied the city, did so with considerable ferocity.

Brutal crimes were committed against the city's Serbian and Jewish populations. The most notorious is known as the Novi Sad Raid, in which, during January 1942, Honvédség troops killed between 3,000 and 4,000 civilians across the region. Though this was ostensibly a means of suppressing the partisan resistance, historical records show that the Hungarian government was attempting to improve its standing with Germany. In addition, the persecution of non-Hungarians (the removal of Serbs, Jews, Roma and other dissidents) allowed Hungarian families to occupy newly vacant homes. In the city of Novi Sad, more than 1,000 citizens were marched across the frozen Danube river and were then shelled from the shore. Victims were blown up or fell through the ice sheet, while others were pushed into the now exposed freezing water or were simply shot.

But the atrocities carried out by the occupiers were not enough to prevent the Vojvodina partisan resistance from recruiting more than 2,000 fighters from a diverse range of ethnicities (Serbian, Slovak, Hungarian, etc.) In September 1944, as part of the Belgrade Offensive, the Red Army entered Vojvodina, weakening German and Hungarian forces in the area. On 23 October, the Novi Sad Partisan Detachment freed the city from Hungarian Axis control. Even though it was liberated in 1944, the Bačka region remained under communist military rule until 1945. During this period, thousands of ethnic-German and Hungarian civilians (along with Serbian–Axis collaborators) were killed in reprisal actions.

In 1945, the region was assimilated into the Autonomous Region of Vojvodina within Serbia, with Novi Sad as its capital.

DESIGN AND CONSTRUCTION

The construction of a spomenik to commemorate the Novi Sad Partisan Detachment was organised by regional government and veterans' groups. Local Novi Sad sculptor Pavle Radovanović was commissioned to create the monument, which consists of three yellow-brick forms, the tallest of which is 6 metres high. It was officially unveiled, on 7 July 1971, to mark the 30th anniversary of the uprising against Axis occupation. Situated 10 kilometres north of the city, near the small village of Čenej, it stands in the middle of a grassy field surrounded by farmland.

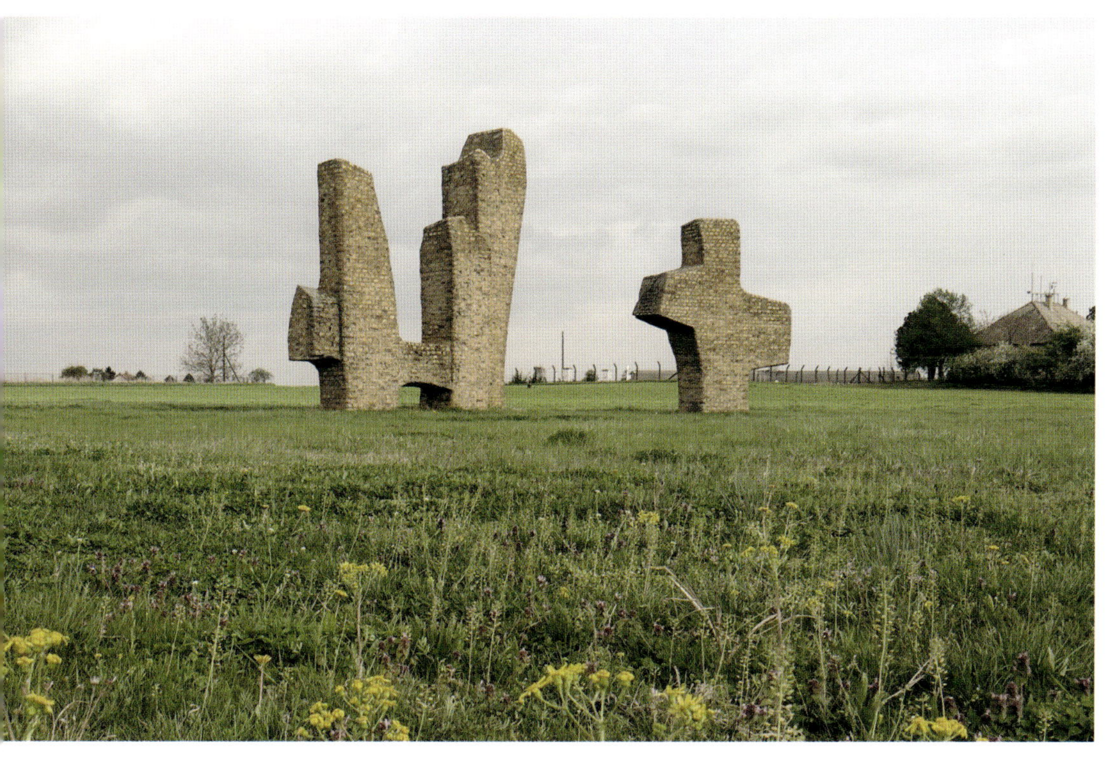

After the fall of Yugoslavia, the Čenej spomenik fell into a state of disrepair. Most of the surrounding paths are overgrown and many of the sculpture's bricks are in poor condition. There are remnants of other destroyed or stolen elements around the site. The original engraved memorial stone at the entrance to the complex was replaced in 2001 after being damaged beyond repair in the 1990s.

Although the site is seldom visited, Novi Sad government officials still hold commemorative events here on 7 July, the Day of Uprising against Fascism and 23 October (Novi Sad Liberation).

ČRNI KAL (CHER-nee KAL)

NAME: Monument to the National Liberation War
and to Victims of Fascist Violence or Monument
to the Overseas Brigade
LOCATION: Črni Kal, Slovenia
YEAR COMPLETED: 1966
DESIGNER: Edo Mihevc
COORDINATES: N45°33'12.0", E13°52'21.3"
DIMENSIONS: Three monoliths, 5 metres high
MATERIALS: Marble blocks

HISTORY

In April 1941, following the invasion of the
Kingdom of Yugoslavia by Axis forces, the Istrian
peninsula (where Črni Kal is located) was occupied
by Italian troops. Many Slovenes in the Črni Kal
region fled this brutal occupation: those who
remained were subject to violence and cultural
oppression. Italian was made the official language
and Slavic was outlawed. All Slavic newspapers,
schooling and cultural traditions were also
prohibited. Thousands of Italians were moved
into Istria, displacing the locals. Armed rebel
movements were established across Istria, as the
people of the region organised against the
occupation. Through 1942, these groups, mostly
communist partisan resistance units, were little
match for the weight of the Italian Army.

Istrian partisans were encouraged when the
Italians surrendered to the Allies in September
1943. However, the German Army quickly
reoccupied the area, designating it the
Operational Zone of the Adriatic Littoral (OZAK).
Under the command of feared SS and Police
Leader Odilo Globocnik, a number of genocides
were committed. He established an Istrian
concentration camp, imprisoning more than
25,000 Italian, Slovene, Croatian and Jewish
civilians, about 5,000 of whom were killed there.
The village of Črni Kal was burned by German
troops on several occasions, resulting in the
deaths of dozens of villagers. Despite these
actions, partisan activity continued and in May
1945, Črni Kal was finally liberated.

Thousands of Italians who had settled in the
Istria region during the occupation were forced
to leave by the partisans. Some were even killed
in the Foibe massacres (see also Plovanija page
144). After the war, the proximity of Črni Kal to
the Free Territory of Trieste (a kilometre away)
meant that the village was involved in the political
issue of the Trieste Question (the argument
between Italy and Yugoslavia over territorial claims
to the Free Territory of Trieste). This situation was
only fully resolved in 1975 with the signing of the
Treaty of Osimo, which ceded to Slovenia the
former area of the Free Territory of Trieste.

DESIGN AND CONSTRUCTION

In the early 1960s, Slovenian architect Edo Mihevc
was commissioned to construct a spomenik
complex just outside Črni Kal, commemorating
the citizens from eighteen surrounding villages
who died during World War II. In addition, the
monument honours the dead of the Prekomorske
(Overseas) Brigades, many of whom were from
this region. Unveiled in 1966, the memorial
consists of three semi-abstract curved sculptures,
constructed from marble blocks, symbolising
historic Istrian barges of antiquity.

STATUS AND CONDITION

Since the collapse of Yugoslavia in the 1990s,
interest in this once popular attraction has faded.
While the memorial is still visited and hosts local
commemorative events, general maintenance of
the site has declined considerably. There are no
directional signs to the spomenik and the only
information at the site itself is a small plaque
engraved in Slovenian. However, in 2004, the
construction of the A1 motorway Črni Kal viaduct
was completed, making access to the site much
easier. Veterans groups in Istria have been
discussing whether to designate this site the
'centre of Partisan resistance' during World War II.
If this proposal is upheld, it would result in a
brighter future for the complex.

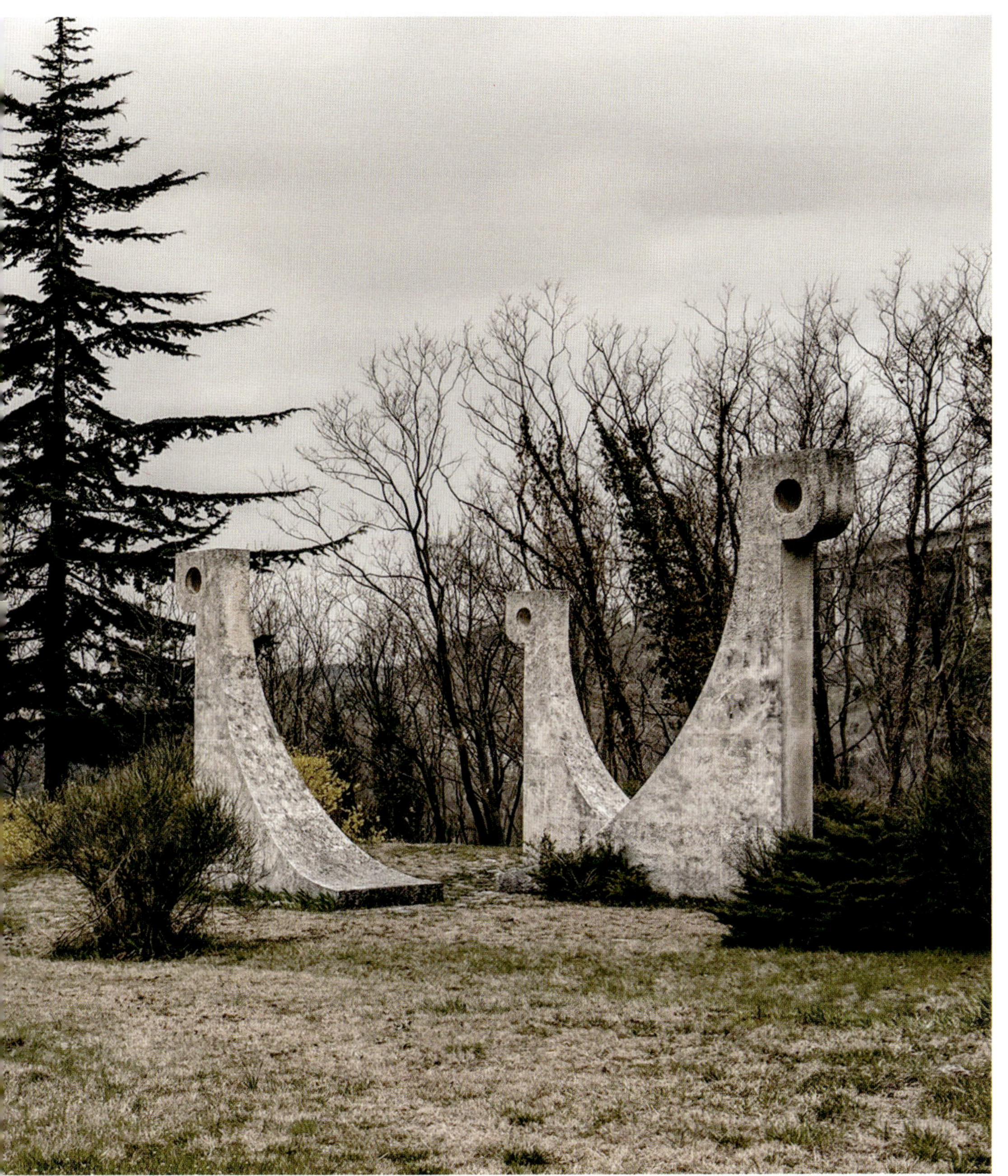

DOTRŠČINA (doh-trsh-CHEE-nah)

NAME: Dotrščina Memorial Park
LOCATION: Zagreb, Croatia
YEAR COMPLETED: 1968 (5 years to build); elements added until 1993
DESIGNERS: Vojin Bakić and Josip Seissel
COORDINATES: N45°50'34.3", E16°01'40.1"
DIMENSIONS: 2 metres high and 4 metres wide in a 365-hectare monument park
MATERIALS: Stainless steel

HISTORY

In April 1941, following the Axis invasion of the Kingdom of Yugoslavia, the puppet Independent State of Croatia (NDH) was formed, with Zagreb as its capital. Ustaše forces, charged with maintaining NDH rule, pursued a ferocious campaign against anyone they considered to be politically or racially undesirable. Most at risk were the city's ethnic-Serb, Jewish and Roma populations and any ethnic-Croat civilians the Ustaše viewed as dissidents or rebels. In May 1941, the NDH passed racial laws requiring 'undesirables' (such as Serbs, Jews and Roma) to either leave Zagreb or be killed. Executions occurred in several locations around the city, including in the concentration camps just beyond its borders, and, perhaps most significantly, in the Dotrščina forest. Shootings and burials by the Ustaše took place at Dotrščina with varying regularity until the end of the war. While the remains of only a few hundred people have been found and positively identified, some estimate that more than 7,000 civilians might have been executed here. Not all victims were buried in the mass graves as citizens were often allowed to claim the bodies of family members.

On 5 May 1945, a battle began against the Axis occupation of Zagreb. After three days, the Axis forces were defeated and the 45th and 28th Divisions of the 2nd Yugoslav Army marched into the city. Around 18,000 Zagreb residents were killed during the war, the majority at Dotrščina.

DESIGN AND CONSTRUCTION

After the war, locals marked the area of Dotrščina forest, where the killings had occurred, with a series of scattered, makeshift tombstones. In 1960, sculptor Vojin Bakić, architect Dr Josip Seissel and writer Juri Kaštelan were commissioned to create a more co-ordinated memorial and expansive sculpture park, which opened in 1968. The central monument is a 4-metre-wide, polished, faceted, stainless-steel form, mounted on a black marble plinth. Bakić said of this monument: 'I came to the realisation that the crystal, made of this gleaming material, reflects what the victims who have fallen there represent for us: purity, permanence, eternal light... The bright mass of the steel reflects light in such a way as to arouse singing from among the tombstones, as well as the motivation to rediscover the physical and ideological radiance of the free-hearted people who are interred there.'

In 1975, the Yugoslav government bestowed the honour of Hero City on Zagreb under the Order of the People's Heroes of Yugoslavia. In celebration, the construction of a number of additional monuments, along with an expansive museum complex, was planned at the site. Four of these additional monuments were completed during the 1980s and 1990s. However, with the political upheaval of the 1990s and the subsequent dismantling of Yugoslavia, all further work was halted, leaving other monuments and the museum complex itself unrealised.

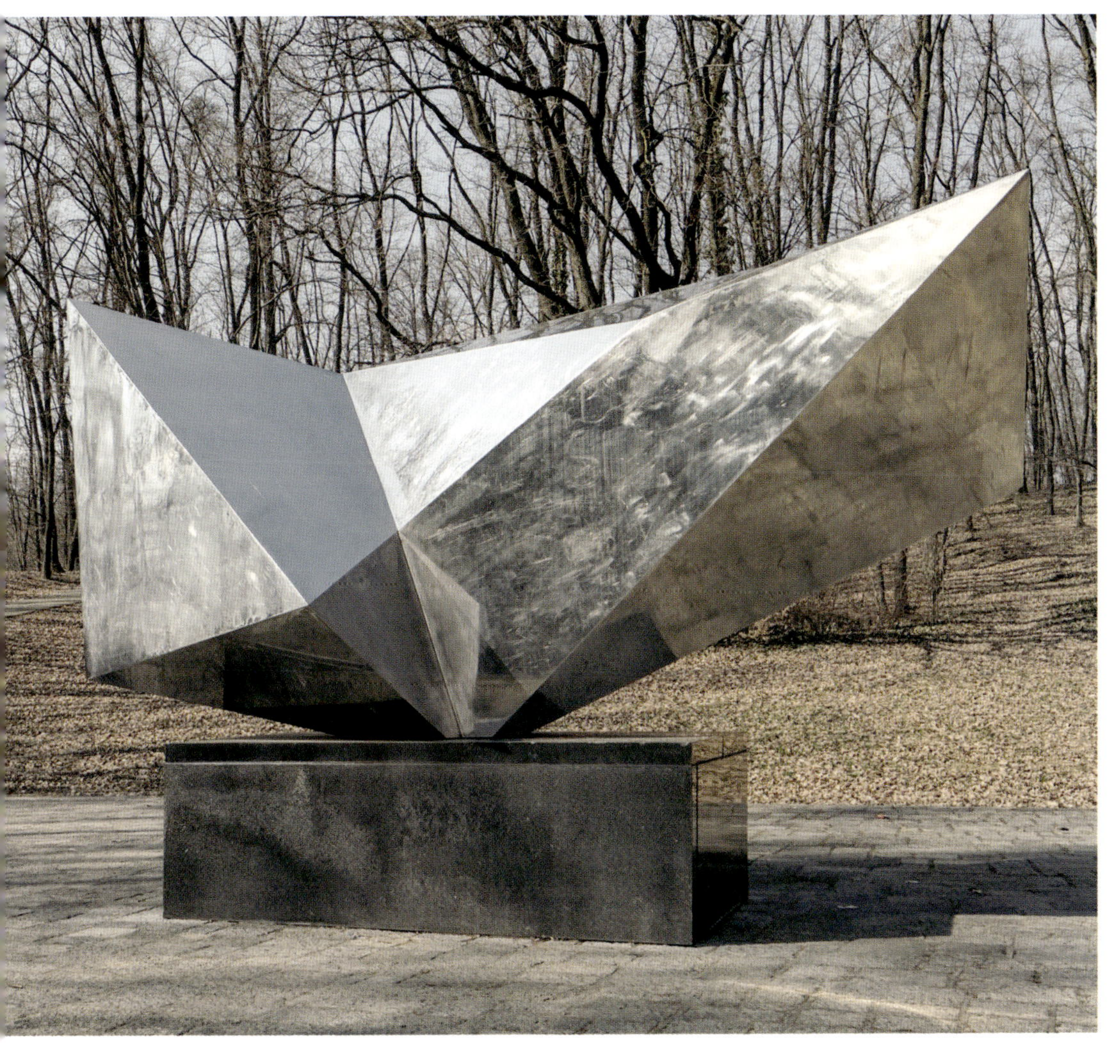

Today, the memorial park is well looked after. As in most large cities, there is a continuous problem with graffiti, but this is usually dealt with quickly by park officials. Plans for more significant restoration by the Dotrščina Virtual Museum (an online resource dedicated to increasing awareness of the spomenik complex) have been frustrated because of lack of financial support from local and national government bodies. Despite these setbacks, the number of remembrance ceremonies, cultural events and community activities held at the memorial park is growing.

DRAŽGOŠE (DRAZH-goh-sheh)

NAME: Monument Cankarjev Battalion in Dražgoše
LOCATION: Dražgoše, Slovenia
YEAR COMPLETED: 1976
DESIGNERS: Boris Kobe, Stojan Batič and Ive Šubic
COORDINATES: N46°15'08.5", E14°09'59.8"
DIMENSIONS: 12 metres high and 13 metres wide
MATERIALS: Poured concrete and rebar

HISTORY

On 9 January 1942, a group of 240 partisans from the Cankar Battalion organised a defence of the Slovenian village of Dražgoše against 2,000 advancing German soldiers intent on deporting the local population to concentration camps.

In deep snow and freezing temperatures, the outmanned and out-equipped partisans suffered only eight casualties, inflicting 26, in what became known as the Battle of Dražgoše. After three days, the partisans were forced to retreat to the mountains, pursued by German forces.

In reprisal, the Germans killed 35 villagers and deported the rest to the Šentvid internment camp. The village was then looted and razed to the ground. This was the first major confrontation between Slovene partisans and German forces in World War II; it was also one of the largest and fiercest resistance offensives the Germans had faced in Europe so far.

At the time, the actions of the partisans were considered heroic. However, these events have since been reappraised, and recent studies assert that the Catholic populace believed the partisans were using their villages to stage such battles, in the knowledge that Catholics would be targeted for reprisals, and that the partisans refused to leave when asked to by the villagers. It is further claimed that the partisans intended, through such displays of defiance and the inevitable subsequent reprisals, to turn the population against the Germans.

DESIGN AND CONSTRUCTION

Despite a number of earlier plans, it was not until 1975 that construction began on a complex to commemorate the actions of the Cankarjev Battalion at the Battle of Dražgoše. The spomenik was unveiled on 3 May 1977 at a ceremony attended by Tito and his wife Jovanka. Conceived by a Slovenian team consisting of architect Boris Kobe, sculptor Stojan Batič and painter Ive Šubic, the spomenik serves both as a memorial and as a platform from which the battleground can be viewed. Its shape evokes that of a fortified Slovene hayrack, a symbol of indigenous culture and identity. The design incorporates two sets of bronze partisan figures (by Batič) set in opposing 'V' formations, pointing hands and guns towards the surrounding mountains.

Set into a niche in the hillside opposite the spomenik is a 7-metre-wide mosaic (by Šubic, who actually took part in the Battle of Dražgoše). He has included a Slovene hayrack within his depiction of events, further assimilating these actions into a broader Slovene identity.

STATUS AND CONDITION

The spomenik complex is in very good condition, well maintained and visited. Commemorative ceremonies are held here annually every 9 January, to mark the anniversary of the battle. These are regularly attended by crowds of more than 10,000 people.

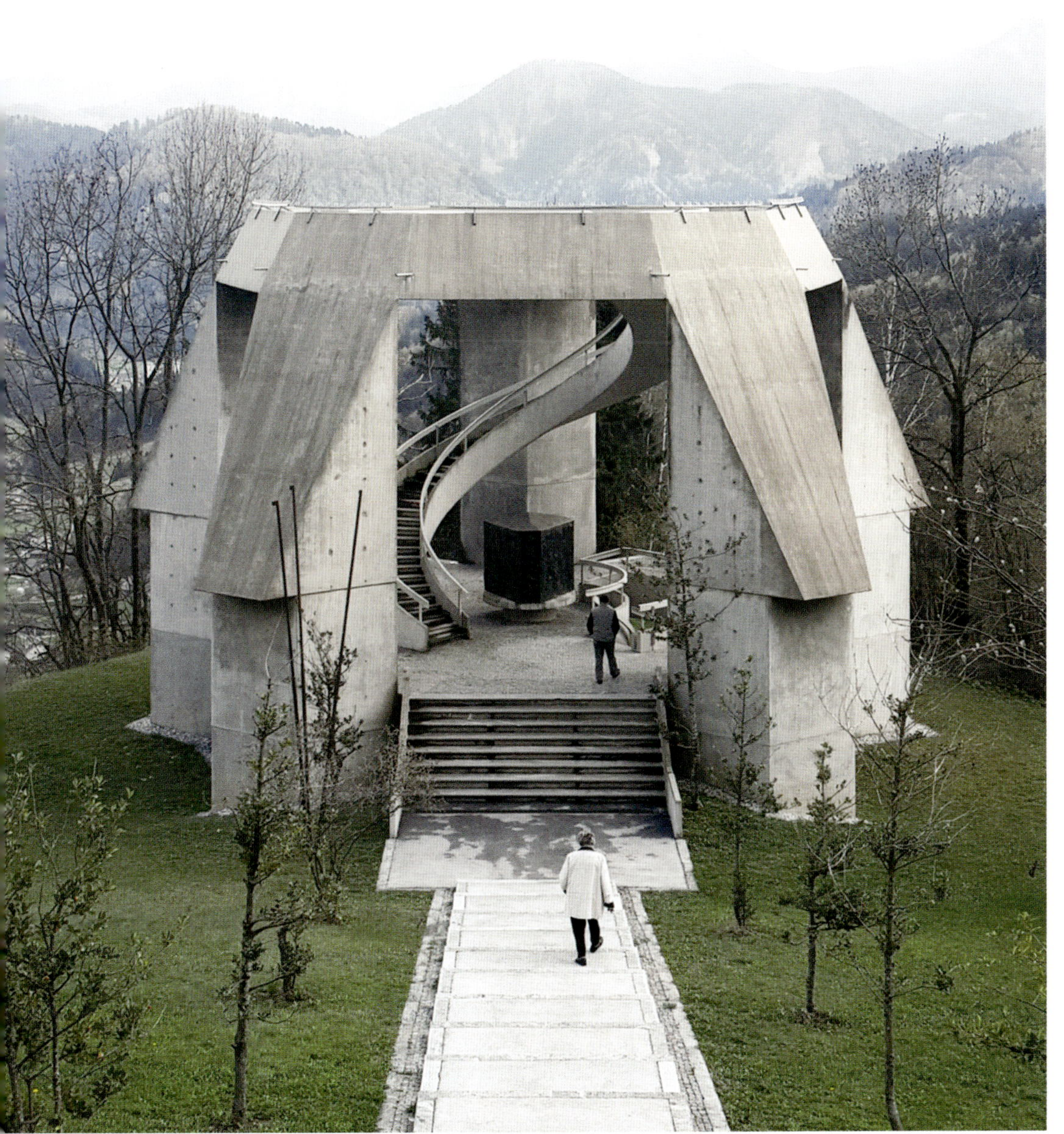

DRVAR (DER-var)

NAME: Monument to the Fallen Fighters of the
National Liberation War from Drvar
LOCATION: Šobić Hill, Drvar, FBiH, Bosnia and
Herzegovina
YEAR COMPLETED: 1967
DESIGNERS: Lujo Šverer and Marijan Kocković
COORDINATES: N44°22'27.3", E16°22'58.9"
DIMENSIONS: Four pointed pillars, 20 metres high
MATERIALS: Poured concrete and rebar

HISTORY

The invasion of the Kingdom of Yugoslavia in
April 1941 by Italian and German forces led to
the formation of a new Axis-controlled country,
the Independent State of Croatia (NDH). The NDH
used the Ustaše, a nationalist militia, to brutally
subjugate its citizens. People from across the
Drvar region joined the partisan resistance led
by Josip Tito to fight the occupying forces. First
liberated by partisans in mid-1942, Drvar was
subsequently lost and regained several times. In
September 1943, following the Italian surrender,
Tito seized more territory in western Bosnia,
making his headquarters in a cave nestled in the
steep mountains overlooking the town.

On 25 May 1944, with partisan resistance
escalating, the Germans launched Operation
Rösselsprung (Knight's Leap), intended to destroy
the partisan headquarters at Drvar and kill Josip
Tito. The 500th SS Parachute Battalion would
drop by air, while the XV Mountain Corps would
combine with the Croatian (NDH) 1st Regimental
Group 373rd to descend on Drvar, eliminating
Tito as the Luftwaffe bombed the town. Despite
a vast amount of planning by German intelligence
and tactical commanders, and though Tito was
actually in the town as the air assault began, the
partisan leader escaped to the island of Vis in
the Adriatic. Although more than 4,000 partisans
were killed in the battle, Tito's dramatic escape
proved to be a significant propaganda victory.

The Drvar region was finally liberated by
partisans in May 1945. At the end of the war,
more than 800 civilians (mostly ethnic-Serbs) had
been killed and 90 per cent of the town destroyed.

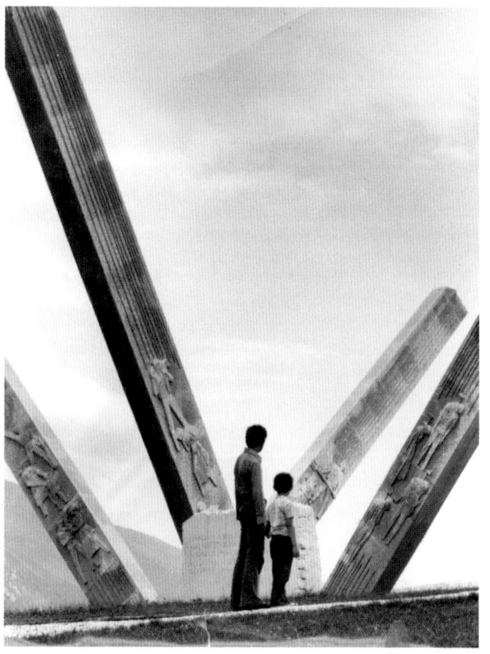

DESIGN AND CONSTRUCTION

This monument, situated on Šobić Hill in the
centre of Drvar, honours the soldiers who died
here during World War II. Designed by Dubrovnik
sculptor Marijan Kocković and architect Lujo
Šverer it was unveiled on 25 May 1967. The main
feature consisted of four 20-metre-tall concrete
pillars, radiating upwards and outwards from a
central point. Each pillar was adorned with low-
reliefs depicting scenes from the war. In 1981, as
a tribute to the town's partisan history, Drvar
changed its name to Titov Drvar.

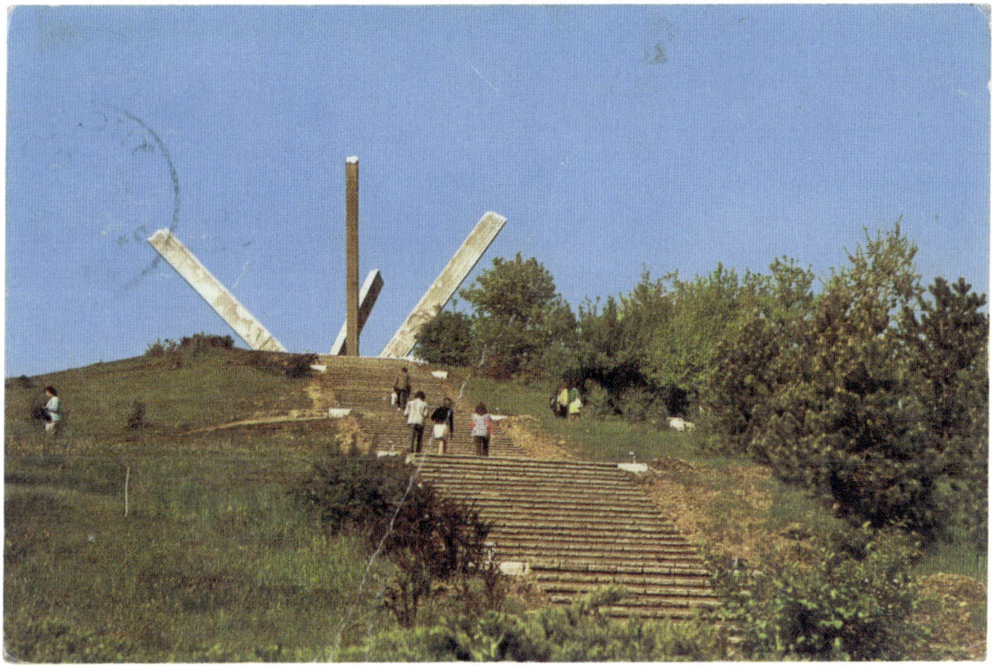

left: A photograph from the late 1960s showing relief details (image from the Marijan Art Gallery, Dubrovnik); *above*: A postcard from the 1970s
below: The remains of the monument today

STATUS AND CONDITION

During the Yugoslav era, the monument was very popular, as locations related to the battle became busy tourist sites attracting thousands of visitors every year. In 1991, as Yugoslavia fell apart, the town changed its name back to Drvar. In 1992, at the start of the Bosnian War, Drvar was taken over by the Republic of Srpska. In 1995, the Croatian Army captured the town and much of the ethnic-Serb population fled, leaving the town almost deserted. When the Dayton Peace Accord was signed at the end of 1995, the Drvar region was handed to the ethnic-Croat/Bosniak Federation of Bosnia and Herzegovina, at which point around 10,000 ethnic-Croats moved into the displaced ethnic-Serb homes. In 1996, the spomenik on Šobić Hill was destroyed and other historic sites vandalised.

Commemorative ceremonies are intermittently held at the site, but these are not officially sanctioned. Rival ceremonies honouring Croatians killed in retaliatory partisan actions are often held at the same time. Despite the slow return of the ethnic-Serb population, the monument is still in ruins. Currently, a monument to local victims of the 1990s Bosnian War is being planned, on or near the location of the smashed memorial.

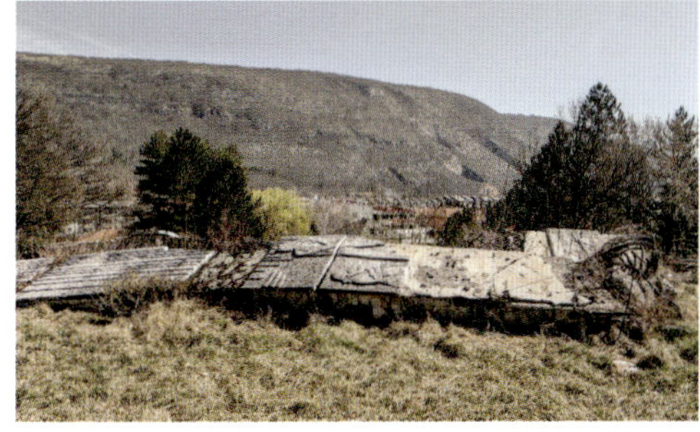

GEVGELIJA (gev-GELL-ee-ah)

NAME: Monument to Freedom or 'The Flower of Freedom'
LOCATION: Mrzenski Hill, Gevgelija, Macedonia
YEAR COMPLETED: 1969
DESIGNER: Jordan Grabul
COORDINATES: N41°09'29.6", E22°30'02.1"
DIMENSIONS: 12 metres high and 8 metres wide
MATERIALS: Steel frame, aluminium plates

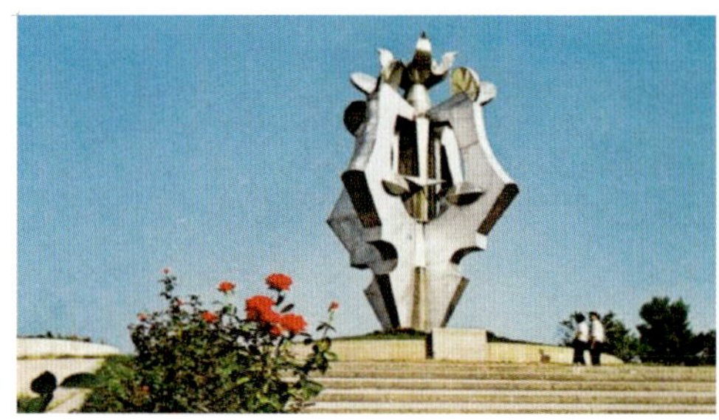
The Gevgelija spomenik in the 1970s

HISTORY

When Axis forces invaded the Kingdom of Yugoslavia in 1941, they renamed the eastern two-thirds of modern-day Macedonia 'Vardar Macedonia' (after the river running through it) and allocated control of the region to Bulgarian troops. The population suffered greatly under their oppressive rule.

In May 1943, 50 rebels convened on the foothills of Kožuf Mountain to the west of Gevgelija. Here they formed the Gevgelija Partisan Detachment, the first resistance unit in this part of southern Macedonia. The detachment was nicknamed 'Sava Mihajlov' after the former Duke of Gevgelija, a Macedonian revolutionary who participated in the 1903 Ilinden Uprising against the Ottoman Empire.

Quickly growing in size to 95 members, the unit fought Bulgarian soldiers, disrupted Axis troop movements and sabotaged supply lines. Following these successes, in September 1943, the unit was integrated into the much larger People's Liberation Battalion, named 'Strašo Pindžur' after the Yugoslavian partisan hero who was tortured by the Bulgarians and died in captivity. The unit continued to fight in this battalion until the end of the war.

The city of Gevgelija was finally liberated from Bulgarian forces on 7 November 1944.

DESIGN AND CONSTRUCTION

In the mid-1960s, the city authorities of Gevgelija commissioned renowned Macedonian sculptor Jordan Grabul to build a spomenik complex in honour of the Gevgelija Partisan Detachment. The primary element of his design is a 12-metre-tall structure covered in polished aluminium plates, which could be interpreted as four abstract figures all holding a central flower or flaming torch. The finished complex, situated on Vardar Hill, was opened in 1969.

STATUS AND CONDITION

This once popular site fell into disrepair during the Yugoslav Wars in the 1990s. The situation worsened when it was decided to excavate the Bronze Age/Roman ruins discovered during the monument's construction. In addition, plans were made to construct the major E-75/A1 motorway just metres from the complex. As a result, in 2005, the spomenik was relocated from Vardar Hill to Mrzenski Hill, around 2 kilometres northwest of the original site. Local veteran groups were promised that it would be developed into a suitable memorial complex – however, this did not materialise. Since the move, most of the monument's polished aluminium plates have been stripped from the framework.

Although visible from the nearby motorway, the site is not promoted or protected by the local municipality, and there is no evidence that it is used for commemorative events. As a final indignity, in 2017 a communications tower was built within a few metres of the memorial.

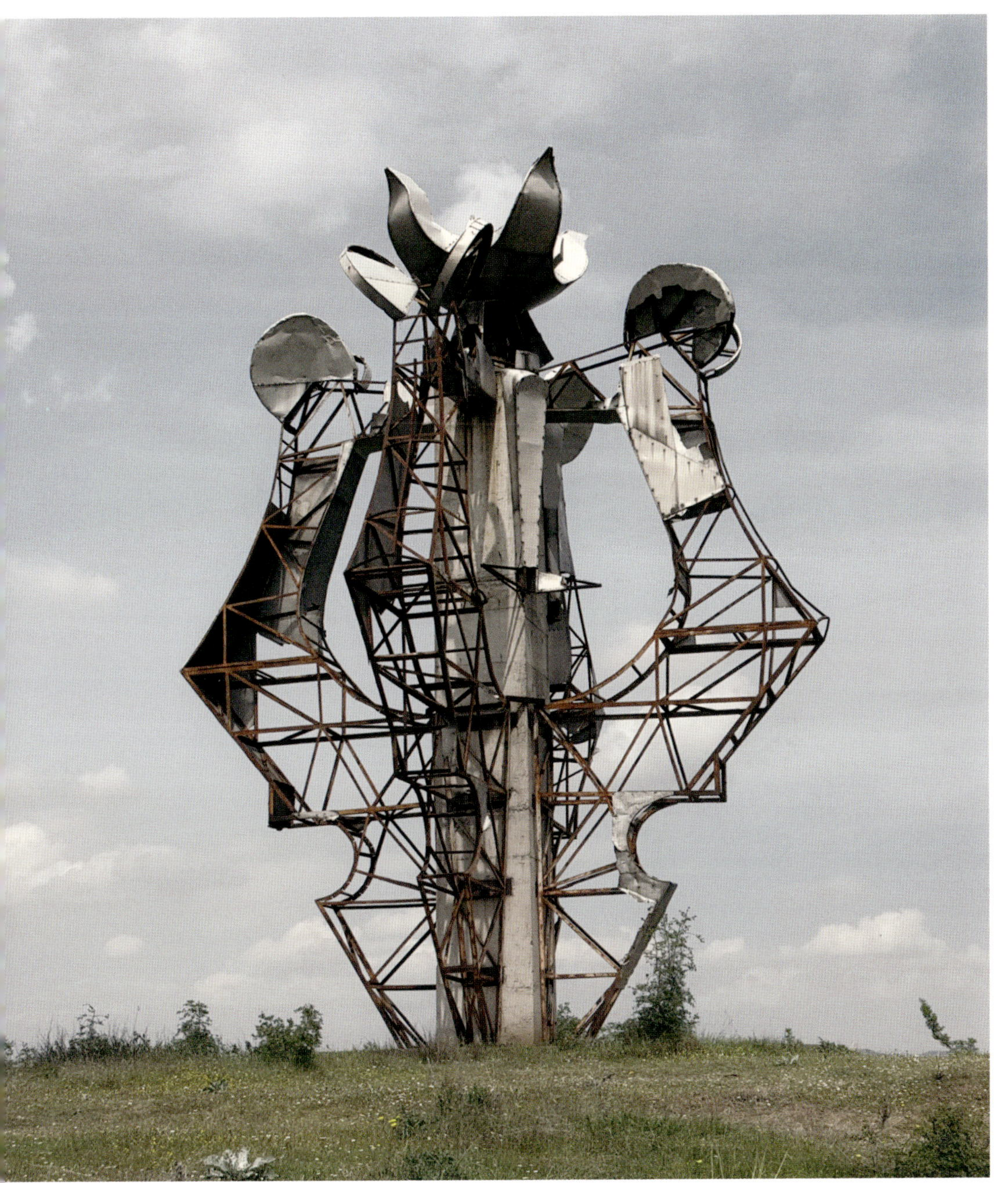

GLAMOČ (GLAAH-moch)

NAME: Monument to Ivo Lola Ribar
LOCATION: Glamoč, FBiH, Bosnia and Herzegovina
YEAR COMPLETED: 1978
DESIGNER: Mirko Ostoja
COORDINATES: N44°04'20.3", E16°49'14.1"
DIMENSIONS: 5 metres high
MATERIALS: Steel

HISTORY

Born in Zagreb on 23 April 1916, Ivo Lola Ribar spent his childhood in Belgrade. He studied law at the University of Belgrade, where he joined the (then illegal) Young Communist League of Yugoslavia (SKOJ). He attended communist conferences in Brussels (1935), Geneva (1936) and Paris (1937). His actions came to the attention of Josip Tito, then Secretary-General of Yugoslavia's Communist Party, who appointed him as Secretary to the party's Central Committee in 1937. While in this post, Ribar, who was dynamic and energetic, organised communist newspapers, rallies, speeches and student movements. He graduated from the University of Belgrade in 1939.

In January 1940, Ribar was arrested for communist activities and sent to a newly established prison for political dissidents in Bileća, Bosnia. By May, however, Ribar and the rest of the inmates had been released, after public protests over the prison's existence.

A few months later, in April 1941, Axis forces invaded and occupied the Kingdom of Yugoslavia. Ribar worked within the Communist Party leadership to organise local rebel groups and co-ordinate resistance. He established and ran several anti-fascist youth magazines and in 1942 was a founding member of the Unified League of Anti-Fascist Youth of Yugoslavia.

A member of the Partisans' Supreme Command, in October 1943 he was named chief of the first partisan military mission to the Middle East Command (part of the British forces in Egypt). However, on 27 November 1943, as he and his team were about to fly from an airfield near Glamoč to Cairo, their plane was bombed by a German aircraft, killing all those on board. Ribar was 27 years old.

During the Yugoslav era, Ribar was hailed as an icon of the National Liberation movement. The majority of his family had also been killed in the war, along with his fiancée, who died in a Banja Luka death camp. Consequently, he was regarded as a leader who had given everything for the freedom of the people of Yugoslavia.

DESIGN AND CONSTRUCTION

This spomenik, built as a tribute to Ribar, is situated in the centre of a newly planted pine forest located near the airfield where he was killed. Designed by sculptor Mirko Ostoja, it was officially unveiled on 27 November 1978, to mark the 35th anniversary of Ribar's death. Lengths of metal recovered directly from the wreckage of the plane in which Ribar died have been worked into tapering blade-like and serrated shapes, arranged to form an abstract configuration evocative of a tangle of thorns. On the stone pathway to the sculpture stands a memorial wall, engraved with quotes from both Ribar and Tito. Other smaller memorial elements are scattered around the site. A small museum containing exhibits detailing Ribar's life once stood to the east of the monument.

STATUS AND CONDITION

Ribar's legacy, promoted by the Communist Party, made this a popular tourist destination during the Yugoslav era. As Yugoslavia fell apart, the monument was neglected and other elements were damaged (particularly the small museum). Today the sculpture is in reasonable condition, but the surrounding area is overgrown and completely unmaintained. Veterans' groups have expressed interest in restoring the site, but to date no action has been taken. The site is now part of a military installation and should not be visited without official authorisation.

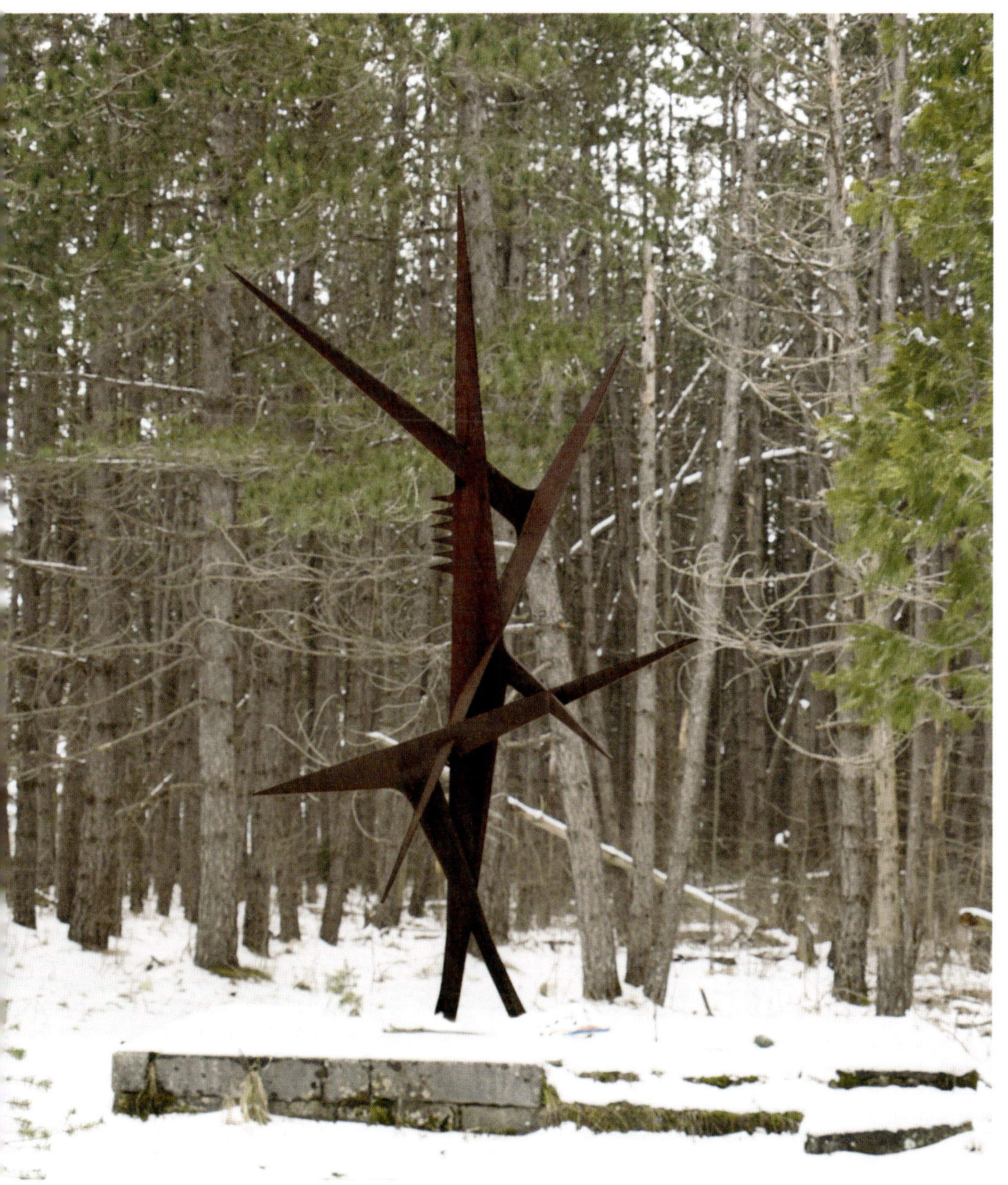

GLIGINO BRDO (glih-GEE-no BER-doh)

NAME: Freedom Hill Monument
LOCATION: Gligino Hill, Dobrljin, Republic of Srpska, Bosnia and Herzegovina
YEAR COMPLETED: unknown
DESIGNER: Ahmed Bešić
COORDINATES: N45°08'32.3", E16°29'47.5"
DIMENSIONS: 10 metres high
MATERIALS: Poured concrete and rebar

HISTORY

In April 1941, with the Axis invasion of the Kingdom of Yugoslavia, the leaders of the Croatian nationalist Ustaše movement formed the puppet Independent State of Croatia (NDH), comprising most of modern-day Croatia and Bosnia. The Ustaše aimed to create an ethnically pure Croat state, and proceeded to persecute ethnic-Serbs, Jews, Roma and dissidents.

The population quickly banded together to form resistance movements against this oppression. In the Bosnian region of Bosanska Krajina, some of the first organised rebel activity occurred around the small town of Dobrljin. This resistance was thanks in large part to a Bosnian Serb, Mirko Zec. Raised in a modest farming family, in 1938 Zec had left to serve in the Yugoslav Royal Army. On his return, he worked in the local coal mines. Respected by the community, he was a natural leader who had a reputation as an advocate for workers' rights. On 27 July 1941, he gathered a small group of fighters at Gligino Brdo, where they planned the region's first resistance efforts against the Ustaše militia.

On 31 July, a small detachment of Ustaše soldiers arrived in Dobrljin, where they were immediately ambushed and killed by Zec and his comrades. This action instigated a widespread uprising against occupying Axis and Ustaše forces across the region. Zec, along with thousands of other Bosnian rebels and dissidents, joined the communist-led partisan resistance movement. In 1942, he was promoted to commander of the 3rd Battalion, 1st Krajina Brigade, and he was promoted again in 1944 to commander of the 6th Brigade, 25th Serbian Division. He was killed in the town of Kozluk in April 1945.

It is estimated that more than 200 Bosnian Serbs were executed by Ustaše forces in Dobrljin. The town was liberated by partisans in June 1944.

DESIGN AND CONSTRUCTION

The spomenik on Gligino Hill marks the location of the region's initial uprising in July 1941. Designed by sculptor Ahmed Bešić, the exact date of its construction is unknown, though its design suggests it was built in the 1970s.

The 10-metre-tall, ridged, concrete sculpture resembles a heavy rosette or flower head mounted on a hollow cylindrical pillar. A small amphitheatre was originally located a few metres south of the monument.

STATUS AND CONDITION

The site has been neglected and its remote location means it is seldom visited. While the primary sculpture is in good structural condition (although covered in graffiti), other memorial elements are missing or have been completely destroyed. The monument is not promoted locally, though there is a plaque at the site giving basic information. There is no sign that commemorative events are held here.

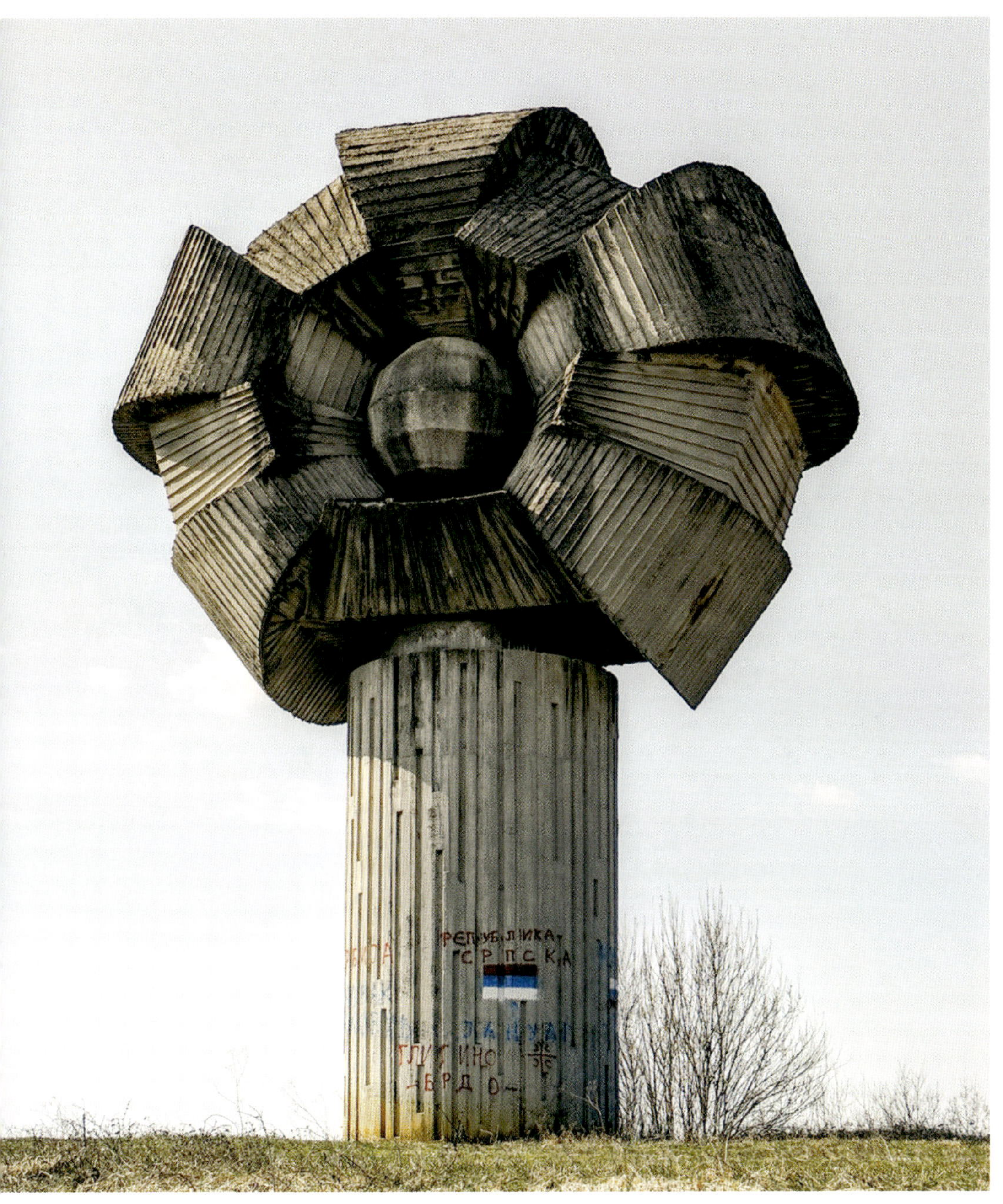
РЕПУБЛИКА
СРПСКА
ГЛИГИНО
БРДО

GOLUBOVCI (goh-luh-BOHV-tsee)

NAME: Monument to the Fallen Fighters
of Golubovci
LOCATION: Golubovci, Montenegro
YEAR COMPLETED: 1974
DESIGNERS: Slobodan Boba Slovinić and Vukota
Tupa Vukotić
COORDINATES: N42°19'35.6", E19°13'11.8"
DIMENSIONS: 7 metres high
MATERIALS: Poured concrete and rebar

HISTORY

Before World War II the region of Montenegro had been part of a province of the Kingdom of Yugoslavia called Zeta Banovina. Following invasion by Axis forces in April 1941 it became an Italian auxiliary state and was renamed the Kingdom of Montenegro.

Montenegrins across the country organised themselves into an armed resistance, launching an uprising on 14 July 1941. Within three weeks, they had liberated almost the entire region from Axis control. Mussolini retaliated by sending a force of nearly 90,000 troops to brutally crush the uprising. The resistance was destroyed. Nearly 10,000 rebels were killed across Montenegro and over 20,000 interned in camps (many from the town of Golubovci and the regoin around the city of Podgorica).

The Italians exercised total control over Podgorica for nearly two years, until their surrender to the Allies in September 1943. Subsequently, the region was re-occupied by the German Army. Recognising the strategic value of Podgorica as a supply route for its campaigns in Albania and Greece, the German command increased the movement of German troops and armaments through the city. Josip Tito, leader of the partisan resistance, notified the Allies about this activity, recommending the city be targeted with a bombing campaign. The first strike took place on 25 October 1943, directed at the German Luftwaffe based at the city's Golubovci Airport. Podgorica

and its airport were repeatedly bombed through the remainder of the war, with the most intense raid on 5 May 1944. Golubovci was finally liberated by Tito's partisan forces on 19 December 1944. Around 90 per cent of Podgorica had been leveled and nearly 5,000 fighters and civilians killed.

On 13 July 1946, Podgorica officially changed its name to Titograd in tribute to Josip Tito.

DESIGN AND CONSTRUCTION

In 1972, the local government commissioned well-known Montenegrin architect Vukota Tupa Vukotić to construct a monument in Golubovci to commemorate local soldiers and civilians who died during World War II. The memorial was officially unveiled in December 1974.

The primary element is a 7-metre-tall, C-shaped, asymmetrical, slatted, concrete form suggestive of a cupped or gripping hand. It is situated on top of a large burial mound containing the remains of fallen partisan fighters. Two large bronze relief panels depicting battle scenes by the artist Slobodan Boba Slovinić are built into the architecture of the main monument. The entire complex was originally surrounded by an elaborate fountain system.

STATUS AND CONDITION

During the conflicts of the early 1990s, Titograd reverted to its original name of Podgorica. Despite these conflicts having a dramatic effect on the area (the airport was targeted during NATO bombings in 1999), the spomenik complex is in good condition. The municipality has spent more than 30,000 Euros to maintain the memorial over the past few years. However, it still suffers from graffiti and the site's extensive fountain system no longer functions.

The site is not promoted and there is no information at the memorial. Small annual commemorative events are held here on 13 July (Montenegrin Statehood Day). In 2017, it was announced that a children's playground would be built within the site, along with improvements to lighting and fences, To date, however, this work has not begun.

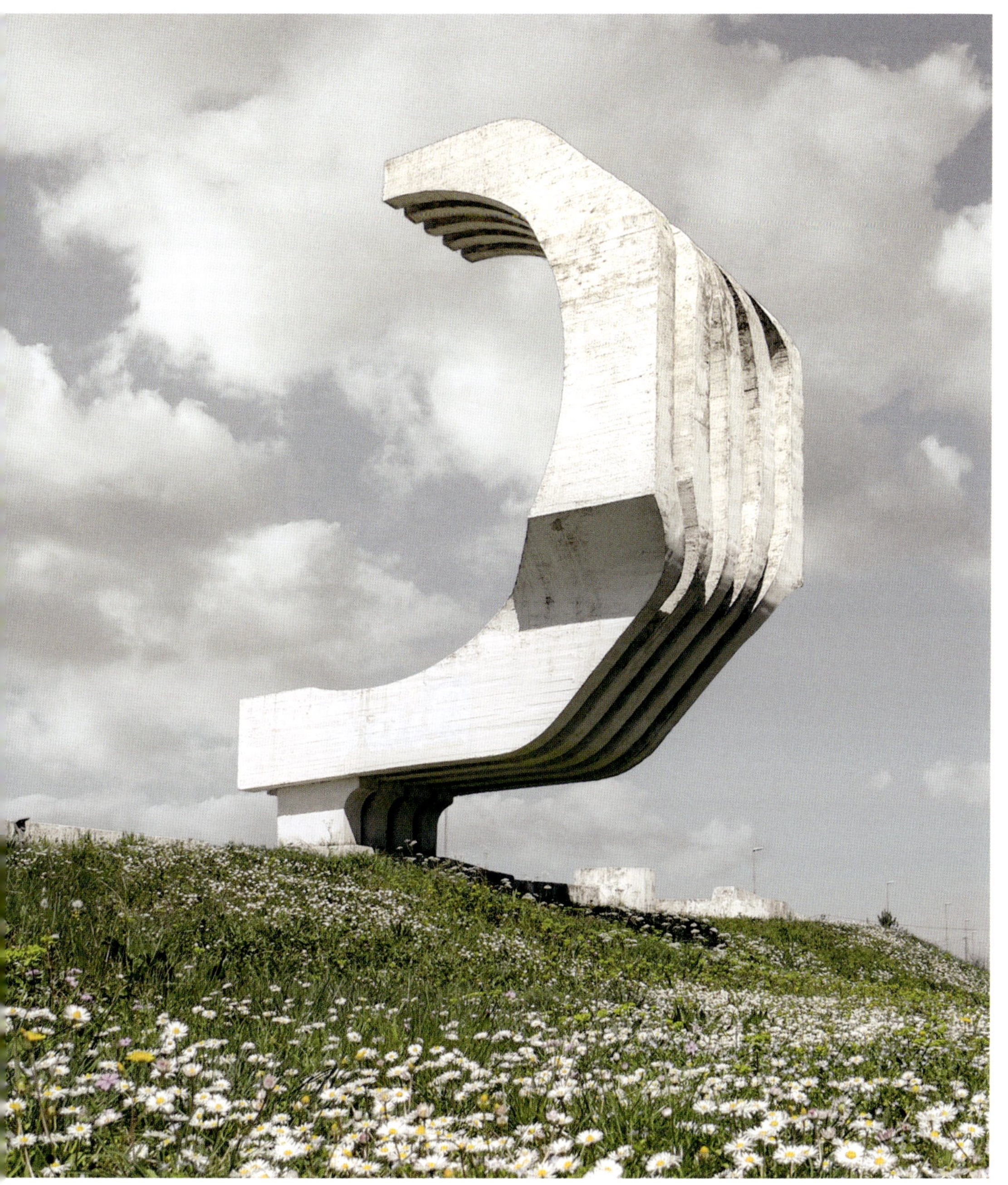

GRMEČ (GER-mech)

NAME: Monument to the Revolution or Monument to the Bosanska Krajina Partisan Hospital or Monument to Korčanica
LOCATION: Grmeč Mountain, FBiH, Bosnia and Herzegovina
YEAR COMPLETED: 1979
DESIGNER: Ljubomir Denković
COORDINATES: N44°41'14.1", E16°26'15.5"
DIMENSIONS: 15 metres high
MATERIALS: Marble blocks and concrete

HISTORY

During 1941, as the partisan resistance liberated more territory from Axis powers in northwest Bosnia, their support forces constructed a large hospital complex hidden in the Grmeč Mountain forest. Consisting of nineteen buildings arranged around a central hospital, 36 by 8 metres in area, the sprawling facility contained workshops, a bakery and even a power station, while on-site printing presses produced communist propaganda. Initially built to treat soldiers from the three units of the 1st Krajina Detachment stationed in the Grmeč Mountain, as the war continued, the hospital cared for wounded partisans from across the region. In November 1942, the liberated area of Grmeč Mountain was able to merge with other freed territories in western Bosnia, becoming the Bihać Republic.

However, in January 1943, the Germans began Operation Case White (see page 26) with the objectives of retaking the liberated Bihać Republic, eliminating all partisans from western Bosnia and capturing their leader, Josip Tito. On 20 January the area around Grmeč Mountain was overrun by German forces, who pushed the partisans south into a trap they had prepared at the Neretva River. Despite the speed of the German advance on Grmeč, the hospital personnel and wounded soldiers were all safely evacuated. Over the course of its existence (from January 1942 to February 1943), the hospital successfully treated thousands of partisan soldiers.

DESIGN AND CONSTRUCTION

Serbian sculptor Ljubomir Denković was commissioned to create a spomenik complex to commemorate the hospital on the site of its compound. Completed in 1979, it consists of two large, curved concrete forms – reminiscent of a natural item such as a split nut, seed or flower bud – roughly 15 metres high, with a raised, ramped pathway running centrally between them. On the internal, concave sides of these forms, two staircases lead down from the ramped path to a lower section that originally held a large-scale model of the mountain and the hospital, illuminated by a skylight set into the path above. A shallow, 18-metre circular reflection pool is situated in front of the monument at ground level. To the west, a network of forest trails leads to various smaller concrete memorial elements.

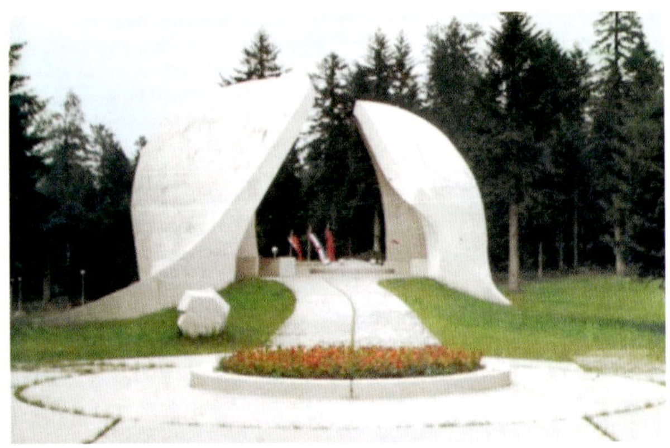

The Grmeč spomenik in the 1980s (image from the Ljubomir Denković Archive)

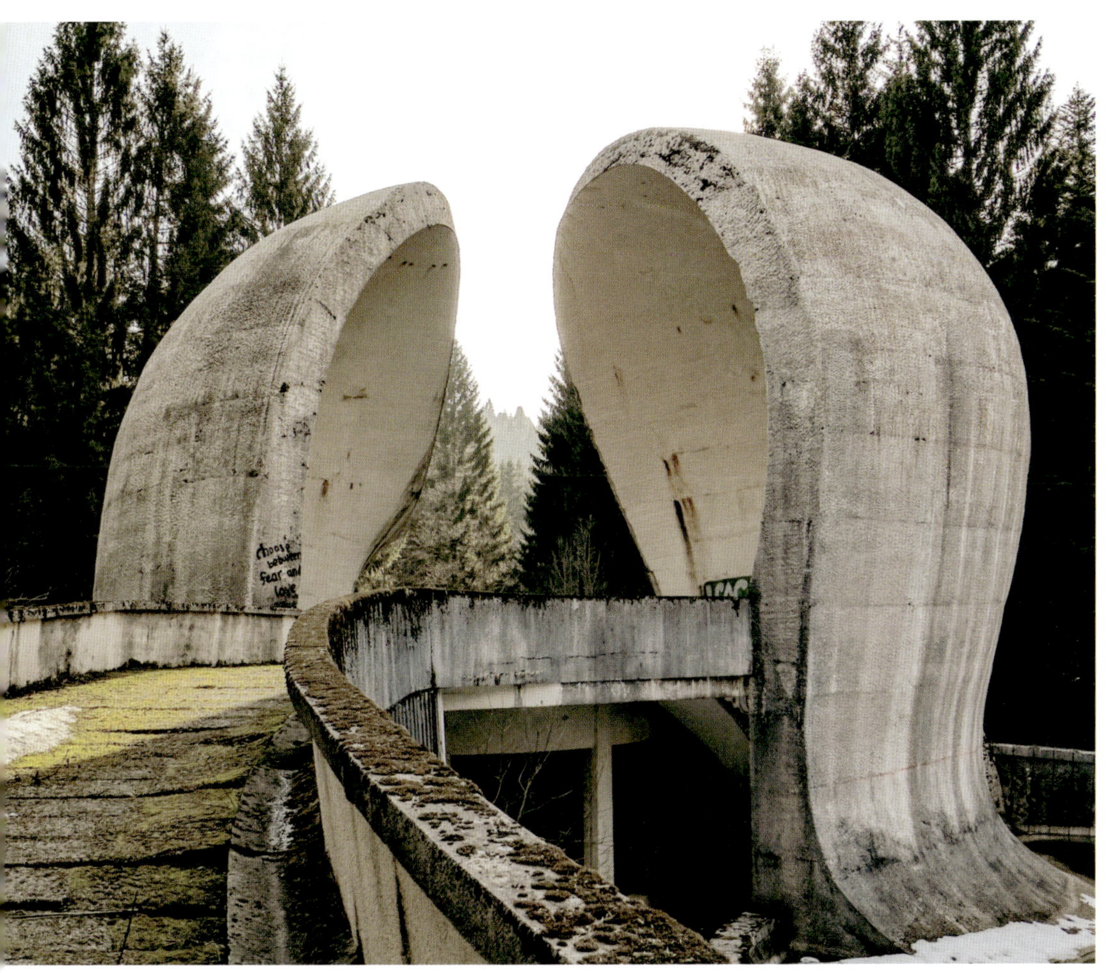

STATUS AND CONDITION

The spomenik began to fall into disrepair in the early 1990s, at the time of the Yugoslav and Bosnian Wars. During this period, many elements were vandalised or destroyed. While the durable concrete structure is still relatively intact, the rest of the monument is completely derelict. It receives very few visitors, and there is no indication that commemorative ceremonies are held here. The spomenik does not appear on the Bosnian government's list of protected monuments. While there is evidence of four or five additional memorials, it is difficult to determine the exact number, as the trails that lead to them are completely overgrown. Near the beginning of the path to the spomenik stands the abandoned Grmeč Hotel. Originally built for holidaying Yugoslavs in the 1970s, this structure is also completely derelict and tenanted by vagrants.

ILIRSKA BISTRICA (i-LEER-ska BIS-tree-tsa)

NAME: Monument on Freedom Hill
LOCATION: Ilirska Bistrica, Slovenia
YEAR COMPLETED: 1965
DESIGNERS: Janez Lenassi and Živa Baraga-Moškon
COORDINATES: N45°34'07.7", E14°14'24.7"
DIMENSIONS: 8 metre cube
MATERIALS: Poured concrete and rebar

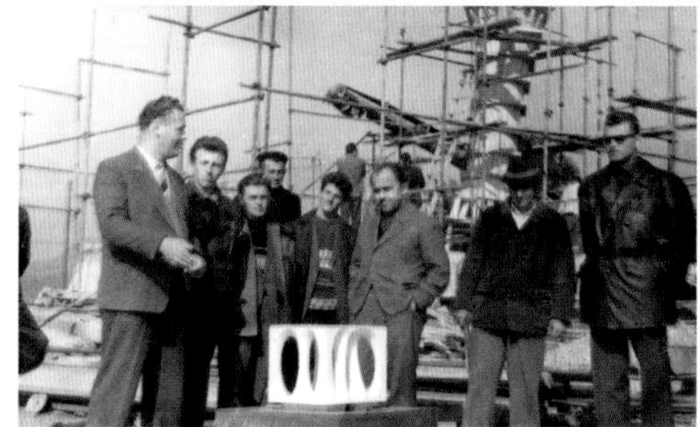
Examining a scale model at the construction site, 1963
(photograph by Vojko Čeligoj)

HISTORY

Following invasion by Axis forces in April 1941, Slovenia was assigned to Italian control and the everyday activities of its citizens were subject to suppression. Resistance against Italian occupation flourished. As an important location for the movement of troops to the Adriatic, Ilirska Bistrica saw particularly fierce combat. After the Italians surrendered in 1943, they were replaced by German forces, resulting in continued brutality against rebels and civilians alike.

On 7 May 1945, the city was finally liberated, as the 4th Yugoslavian Army Brigade (helped by local militiamen) fought through the region on their way to Trieste. This spomenik honours the 284 fighters of the brigade killed during this offensive. Their bodies are entombed beneath the monument. Also commemorated are the fighters from the Istria and Slovene Littoral (Primorska) regions, who were members of the Yugoslav Prekomorske (Overseas) Brigades (units of the National Liberation Army who fought outside Yugoslavia, mostly in Italy).

DESIGN AND CONSTRUCTION

Slovenian sculptor Janez Lenassi and female architect Živa Baraga-Moškon were commissioned to create this spomenik complex and ossuary dedicated to the fighters of the 4th Yugoslavian Army Brigade. The complex was unveiled in May 1965 at a ceremony attended by thousands of local citizens and politicians from across Slovenia.

The primary element of the monument is an 8m-tall-hollow concrete cube, held upright by nine internal tapering columns. The crypt lies directly underneath. The spomenik's form and shape evoke the famous cave systems across the region, most notably at Postojna and Škocjan. The series of tightly packed and fluted columns are intended to mirror the geological formations common in the karst topography of this part of Slovenia, while also representing the bones of the fallen partisan fighters. The monument was considered a sensation of modern design and Lenassi was honoured with the coveted Slovenian Prešeren Award for artistic achievement.

STATUS AND CONDITION

The monument is in excellent condition and is well maintained. As with many others in Slovenia, it has been spared the damage typically suffered by others across the former Yugoslav states during and after the Yugoslav Wars.

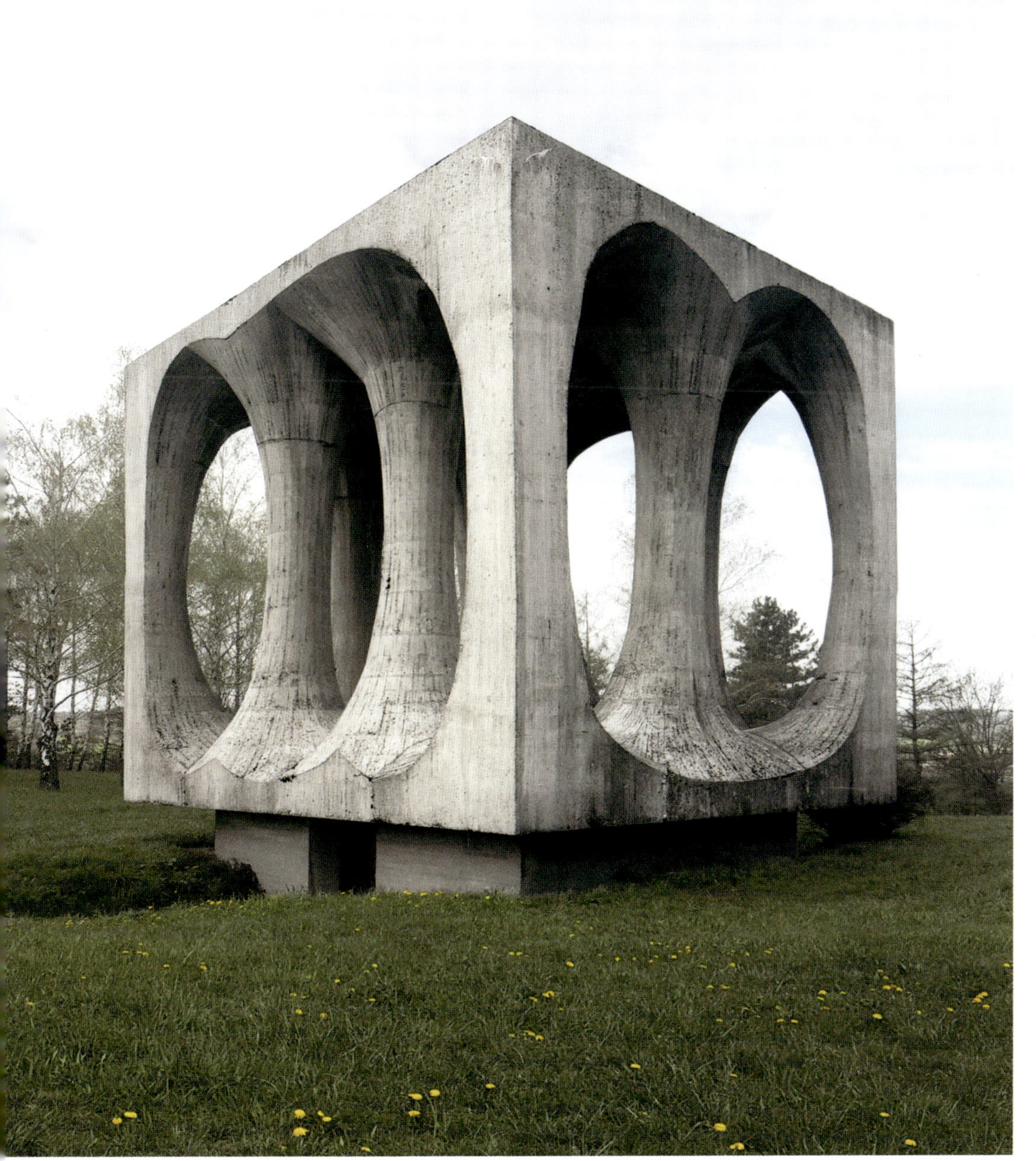

JABUKA (YAH-boo-kah)

NAME: Stratište Memorial Complex
LOCATION: Jabuka, Serbia
YEAR COMPLETED: 1981
DESIGNER: Nebojša Delja
COORDINATES: N44°55'43.6", E20°38'01.8"
DIMENSIONS: Monument complex of 2 hectares
MATERIALS: Poured concrete, rebar and bronze

HISTORY

Following the invasion of the Kingdom of Yugoslavia by Axis forces in April 1941, the Germans installed the puppet Government of National Salvation in Serbia, with Yugoslav Army General Milan Nedić as its prime minister.

Axis forces took control of the region, targeting anti-fascist dissidents, Serbs, Jews and Roma. As their oppression intensified, so did the resistance movement against them. In July 1941, uprisings resulted in the deaths of hundreds of Axis troops. This enraged German commander Franz Böhme, who implemented Hitler's order authorising the killing of 100 civilians in retaliation for every German soldier killed, and 50 civilians for every German soldier wounded (see page 88). In addition, Jews, communists and suspected rebels were to be held hostage and executed if any further German soldiers were killed or attacked.

Accordingly, thousands of male civilians were arrested and whenever Germans were killed around Serbia, these captives were executed. The killings were carried out on the Pančevo–Jabuka road, behind a high embankment of the River Tamiš. Recovered German records indicate that from 1941 to 1944 more than 10,000 Jews, Serbs, communists and Roma were executed here, in what is often referred to as the Pančevo Holocaust. In April 1944, realising the war might be lost, the Germans attempted to destroy the evidence of their crimes, spending months exhuming the mass graves and burning the bodies.

The Pančevo and Jabuka area was liberated in October 1944 during the Belgrade Offensive, a joint operation undertaken by the partisans, the Red Army and the Bulgarian People's Army.

DESIGN AND CONSTRUCTION

Immediately after the war, a modest pyramid monument was constructed at the site in memory of those killed. This was replaced in 1981 by a more substantial spomenik complex, designed by Belgrade artist Nebojša Delja. The primary monument is intended to symbolise the farming tradition of the region. Called 'Brazde' (Furrow), it consists of a pair of abstract concrete forms that mirror each other to represent ploughed soil. These are topped with four bronze elements that Delja intended would rust over time, to more closely resemble the colour of earth. A concrete altar with a bronze plaque stands in front of the monument. Behind it is a large amphitheatre overlooking the River Tamiš marshland. A small museum was also built at the site, exhibiting artefacts related to the Pančevo Holocaust.

STATUS AND CONDITION

After the conflicts of the 1990s, the popularity of this once well-visited monument dwindled. In the 2000s, the complex was wrecked by thieves and vandals and in 2016, two of the four large bronze elements were stolen. The lighting system has also disappeared, and even the wiring of the now derelict museum has been stripped out.

Despite the poor condition of the complex, annual commemorative events are still held here, and the spomenik is occasionally visited by educational and research groups. There has been renewed interest in restoring the site, and in 2016, a contract was agreed between the Institute for the Protection of Cultural Monuments in Pančevo and the Serbian Ministry of Labour, Employment, Veterans' Affairs and Social Affairs committing 116,000 Euros to its reconstruction.

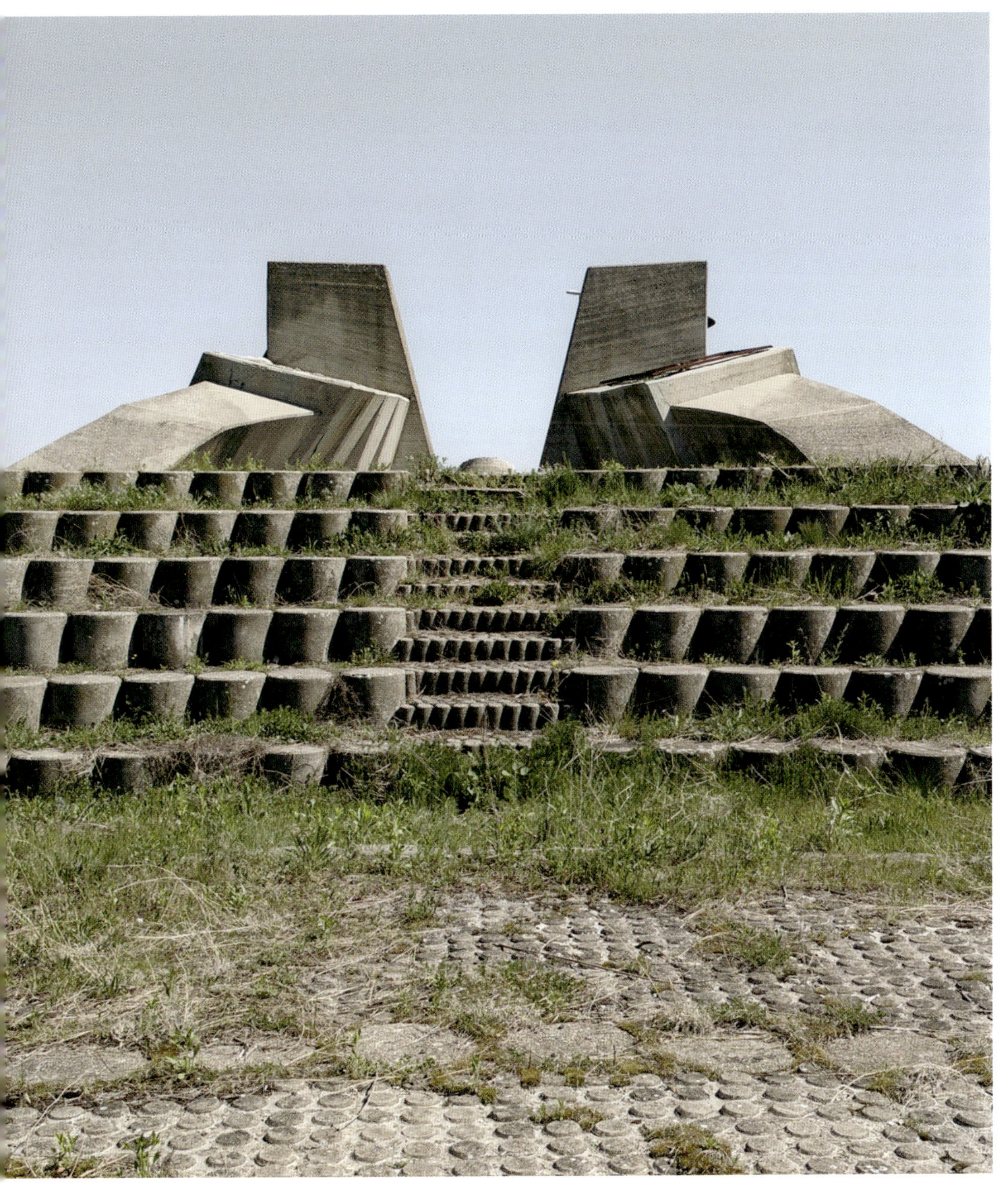

JASENICA (yah-SEH-neets-ah)

NAME: Podgrmeč Museum and Memorial Fountain
LOCATION: Jasenica, FBiH, Bosnia and Herzegovina
YEAR COMPLETED: 1979
DESIGNER: Marijan Kocković
COORDINATES: N44°48'11.3", E16°15'30.1"
DIMENSIONS: Two half spheres, 3 metres high
MATERIALS: Brač limestone

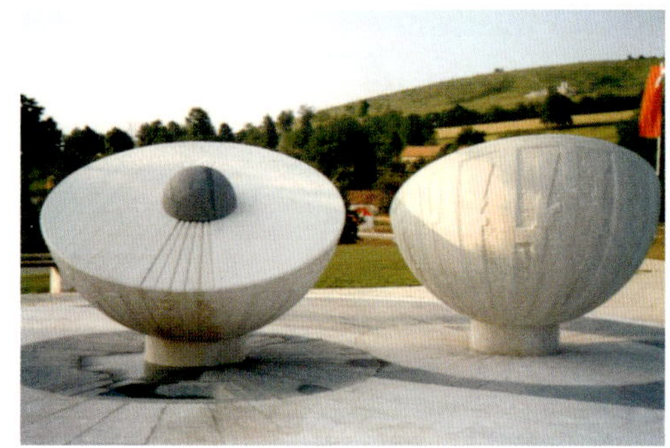

The spomenik in its original condition, c.1980
(image from Marijan Art Gallery, Dubrovnik)

HISTORY

In April 1941, with the invasion of the Kingdom of Yugoslavia, the village of Jasenica in the Podgrmeč region was absorbed into the Axis puppet regime newly named the Independent State of Croatia (NDH). Resistance against this occupation began almost immediately, mainly organised by communist-led partisan forces.

During 1942, many local residents joined the 1st and 5th Krajina Partisan Detachments under the command of Zdravko Čelara, fighting to free territory across northwest Bosnia, and by the end of that year, Axis forces had been driven from the area. Jasenica and other surrounding liberated territories were merged into the partisan-run Bihać Republic, and the village sheltered child refugees from the Jastrebarsko youth concentration camp who had been rescued by Kordun partisans.

On 7 January 1943, Supreme Commander Josip Tito passed through the village on his way to Bihać, and delivered a rousing speech to troops of the 4th Krajina Division in front of the snow-covered schoolhouse.

However, just a few weeks later, the partisans were forced to flee Jasenica as Axis forces advanced in the Case White offensive (see page 26) aimed at retaking the whole of the Bihać Republic, expelling partisans from the region, and capturing Tito (whom they considered the most dangerous man in occupied Yugoslavia). The German operation was successful in all of these objectives, although Tito managed to escape captivity.

Jasenica was finally freed in April 1945, when troops of the 4th Yugoslav Army liberated the entire Podgrmeč region.

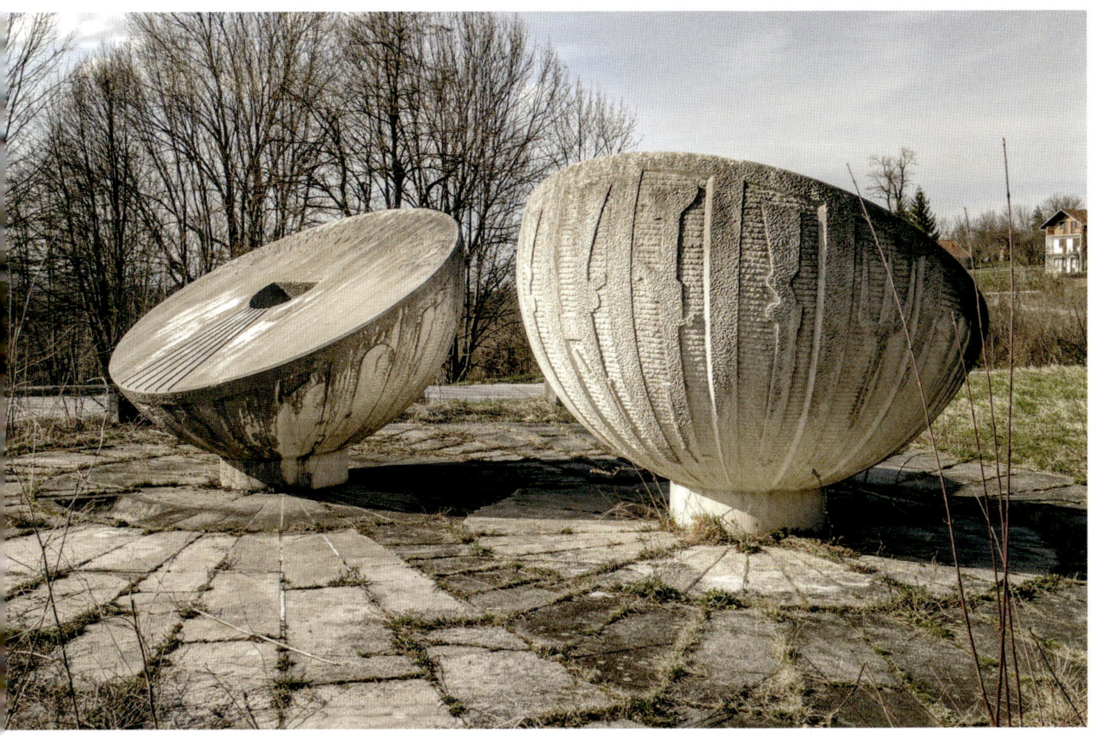

After the war, the Jasenica's schoolhouse was turned into the Podgrmeč Museum and Memorial, displaying wartime artefacts, a fresco honouring the 4th Krajina Division, and busts of local Yugoslav National War Heroes.

In the 1970s, Dubrovnik sculptor Marijan Kocković was commissioned to create a fountain in front of the museum commemorating Tito's inspirational speech. Kocković's monument was opened on 27 July 1979. It consists of a pair of large hemispherical fountains, made of limestone quarried from the Croatian island of Brač, set on pedestals in the middle of a paved circular courtyard. Quotes by and about Tito are engraved into their sloping, flat faces, around the central water spouts, and partisan weaponry - pitchforks and scythes, as well as firearms - are depicted in relief on their curved outer surfaces.

A thriving tourist destination during the Yugoslav era, the region was overrun with conflict during the Bosnian War in the early 1990s. Many of the town's residents were driven from their homes, as infrastructure and buildings were destroyed, including the Podgrmeč Museum and Memorial. In 1995. At the end of the war, only around 50 of the former 1,000 residents returned, and much of the village is still abandoned to this day.

The future of the monument is also uncertain. There is no directional signage to the location or information about the monument at the site itself. The fountain sculptures are damaged and the museum is derelict. There is no evidence that the monument receives any visitors or that commemorative events are ever held here. In addition, it does not appear on the official list of protected monuments.

JASENOVAC (YAH-sen-oh-vats)

HISTORY

In April 1941, following the invasion of the Kingdom of Yugoslavia by Axis forces, the puppet Independent State of Croatia (NDH) was formed. This brought much of what is present-day Croatia and Bosnia under Axis control. Undesirables such as partisans, communists, anti-fascists, POWs and certain ethnic groups (Serbs, Jews, Roma, etc.) were detained in purpose-built camps across the region administered by the fascist Ustaše forces. Established around July or August 1941, the Jasenovac camp complex initially used forced labour to produce timber, bricks and leather goods. But in November 1941, work ceased and Jasenovac began operating exclusively as a death camp. The complex was made up of five sub-camps. Camp III (the Brickworks) and Camp V (Stara Gradiška – specially constructed for women and children) were where the majority of killings were recorded. (Before 1942, thousands of Jews were also killed at these sub-camps; after that date, most were deported to Auschwitz.)

Nearly all the prisoners were ethnic-Serb civilians, transported from the Kozara region for collaborating with partisan rebels. Most were killed on arrival. The total number of Jasenovac victims remains unknown; though estimates range from as few as 20,000 to over a million. These figures – low and high – are the subject of heated debates and politicised controversies, with the result that none is universally accepted by historians. Ongoing research at the Jasenovac Memorial Site Museum currently assesses the number at somewhere between 80,000 and 100,000, which accords with the findings of most modern sources. This makes Jasenovac one of the largest single extermination camps in Europe during World War II.

Although the Nazis had no direct involvement in the camp, they supported the NDH, which borrowed from their ideology in striving to create an ethnically 'pure' Croatia. Witness accounts reveal that the inhumanity at the camp was at least equal to that of the German extermination camps. On 24 April 1945, as partisan units closed in, and following a revolt in which dozens of prisoners escaped, Jasenovac was abandoned by Ustaše forces. Before leaving, they attempted to erase evidence of their crimes by liquidating the remaining prisoners and burning the camp to the ground. When partisan forces arrived on 2 May, all they found were ashes, charred buildings and the still-smouldering skeletons of hundreds of recently murdered victims.

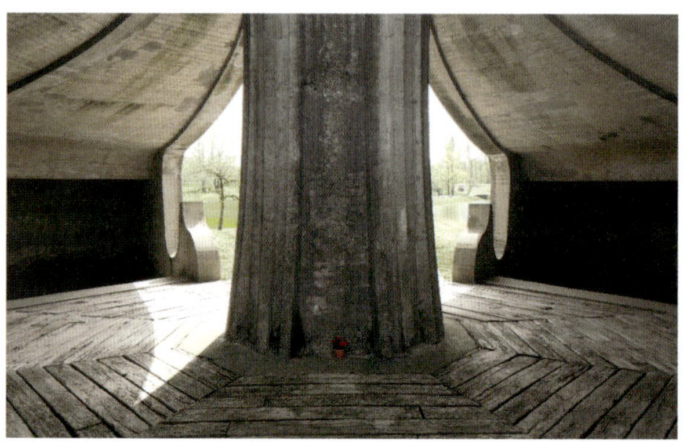

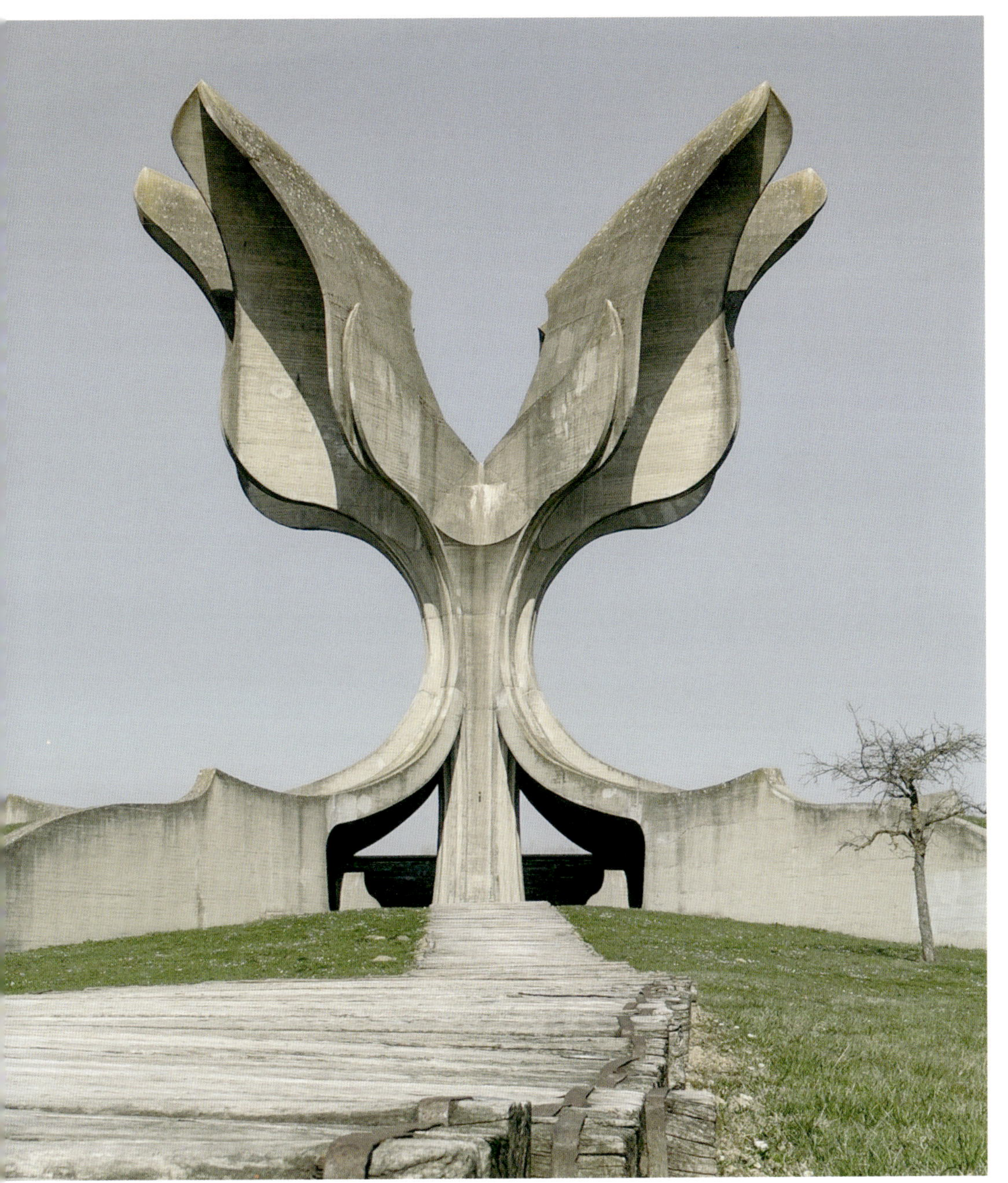

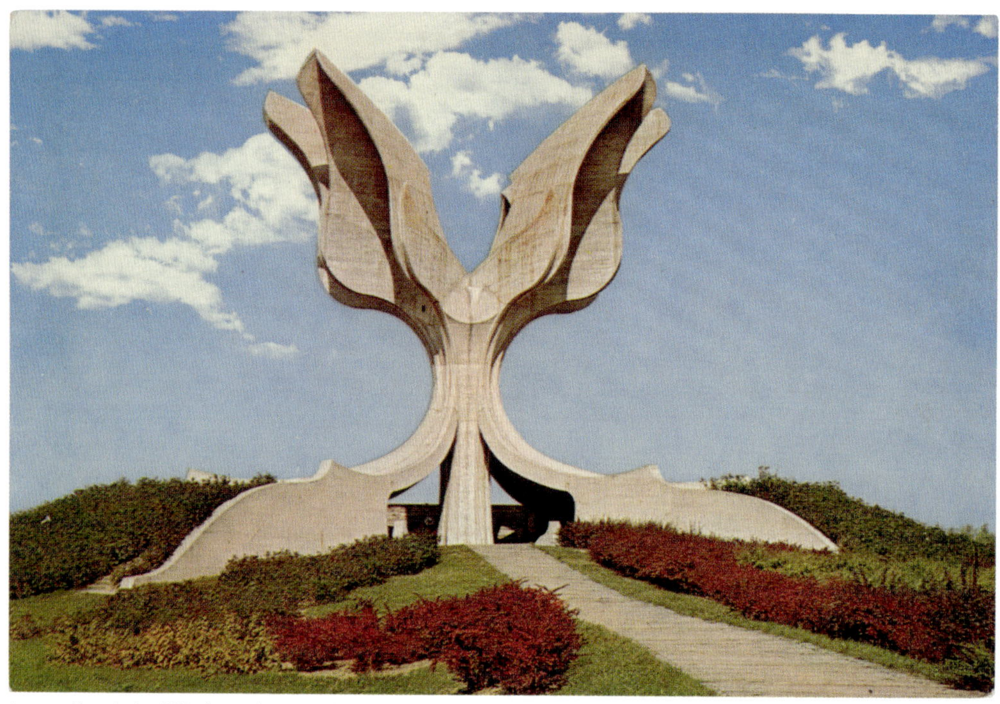

A postcard from the late 1960s showing the spomenik soon after construction

DESIGN AND CONSTRUCTION

For the next two decades, only a few small make-shift wooden memorials, erected by locals and survivors, marked the site. In the late 1950s, following pressure from families and victims, the Yugoslav government began to plan an official memorial to the victims of the Jasenovac forced labour and extermination camp.

In 1960, the proposal of architect Bogdan Bogdanović was chosen by President Josip Tito himself. The designer decided not to directly portray the atrocities that occurred at the site, considering them too horrific, as well as potentially contributing to ethnic tensions. Instead, he imagined a lyrical memorial, symbolising not only life and rebirth, but also reconciliation, the overcoming of suffering, and a 'termination of the inheritance of hatred that passes from generation to generation'.

His design called for the ruins of the camp to be cleared, allowing him to use the grounds as a blank canvas for his massive project. However, following a budget review, the huge scope of the original concept was drastically pared down. After years of compromise, redesign and construction, the monument was publicly unveiled at a large remembrance ceremony on 4 July 1966. Tito was conspicuous by his absence.

In his memoir *The Doomed Architect* (1997) Bogdanović recalls that during the inaugural address of the ceremony (held a kilometre away from the sculpture), a crowd of thousands burst through the ring of guards. Running across open ground, they reached the monument, swarming around it, screaming and wailing. Bogdanović described the scene as an 'unearthly sight' and expressed concern that the structure might be compromised by the tremendous weight of people standing directly on it. Fortunately, it held.

The primary element of the memorial complex is a 24-metre-tall, six-petal, flower-shaped concrete sculpture. Inside this structure is a crypt, the floor of which is lined with railway sleepers taken from the track that once brought prisoners to the camp. These sleepers are also used to form a pathway leading visitors to the monument, recreating the final journey of the victims.

In the landscape surrounding the monument, large earth mounds mark the locations of the former camp buildings. Torture areas and graves are represented by shallow, undulating mounds and hollows. Several man-made lakes help to create a serene atmosphere of reflection. The 'Flower Monument' complex is regarded by many as one of the most celebrated and striking genocide memorials in existence.

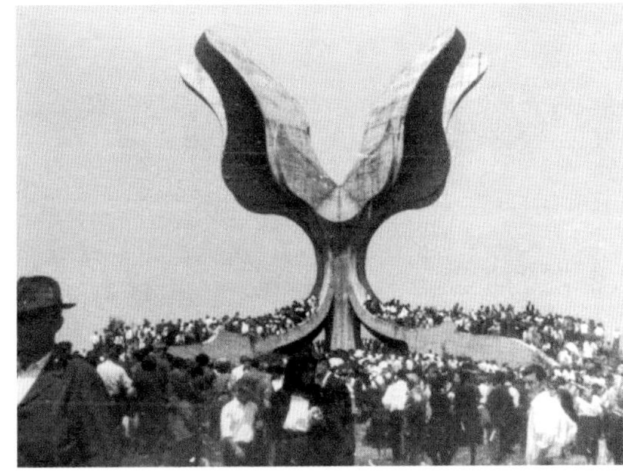

STATUS AND CONDITION

In the years after the fall of Yugoslavia and the ensuing wars, the Jasenovac spomenik was subject to intense bouts of vandalism and destruction. In 1991, Croatian soldiers smashed and looted many exhibits from the memorial site. Following the wars and a long period of restoration, the memorial was re-opened in 2006. Today the complex is in good condition and is well maintained. It is popular with both tourists and those paying their respects.

Commemorative ceremonies are held at the monument annually on 22 April (the date prisoners revolted and broke out of the camp in 1945). These are usually attended by some 2,000 visitors. However, some politicians in the Croatian government have been accused of attempting to diminish the importance of the Jasenovac atrocities in relation to Croatian history and of adopting 'pro-fascist stances'. These controversies have led to boycotts of official Croatian ceremonies at Jasenovac by some Serb, Jewish and anti-fascist groups, and to the staging of rival ceremonies at nearby locations.

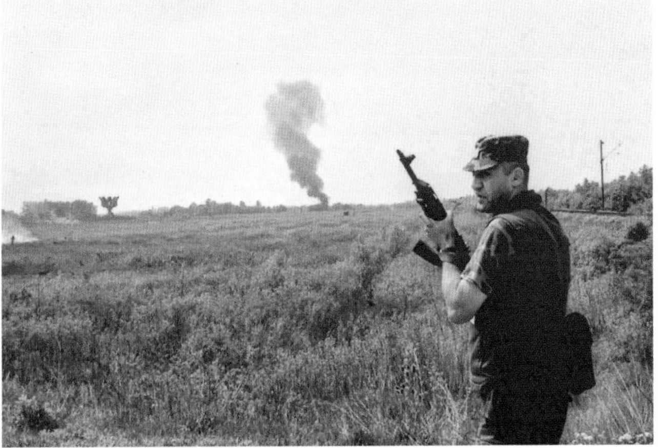

top: At the opening ceremony in 1966, crowds gathered around and stood on top of the monument in a spontaneous display of grief
below: The Jasenovac spomenik did not escape the destructive Yugoslav Wars of the 1990s, (images from the Jasenovac Memorial Site)

KADINJAČA (kah-DEE-nyah-chah)

NAME: Kadinjača Memorial Complex
LOCATION: 14km NW of Užice, Serbia
YEAR COMPLETED: 1979 (2 years to build)
DESIGNERS: Stevan Živanović, Miodrag Živković and
Aleksandar Đokić
COORDINATES: N43°54'43.7", E19°44'33.7"
DIMENSIONS: Large complex covering 15 hectares
MATERIALS: Poured concrete, rebar and granite
blocks

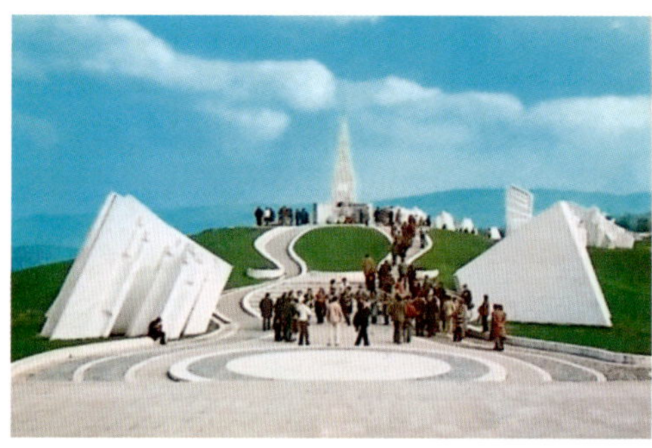

A commemoration at the site in the 1980s

HISTORY

In autumn 1941 the partisans liberated an area of Serbia around the city of Užice that had been under German control. Named the 'Republic of Užice' by the partisans, it was the first liberated territory within Axis-occupied Europe. In retaliation, the Germans initiated Operation Užice, the first German-led anti-partisan campaign of World War II. As part of a series of planned offensives, the operation aimed not only to recapture the partisan-held territory, but to eliminate the resistance movement altogether.

On 28 November 1941, Marshal Josip Tito ordered the Užice Workers' Battalion, along with two partisan units from Posavina and Orasje, to intercept the Wehrmacht 342nd Infantry Division advancing towards Kadinjača Mountain, 14 kilometres from Užice. Under the command of Andrija Đurović, 400 partisan fighters engaged more than 3,000 German soldiers at 8am on 29 November. Despite killing only two German soldiers, the Workers' Battalion managed to hold their ground against the enemy for more than six hours. Although German forces killed the great majority of the Workers' Battalion in combat, and recaptured Užice by the end of the day, their overall mission was a failure, as the citizens and partisan leaders of Užice were able to withdraw to the sanctuary of the Sandžak region.

After the end of World War II and the establishment of Yugoslavia, the town of Užice changed its name to Titovo Užice in honour of Tito and the establishment of the breakaway territory. The events of the battle and the fall of Užice were depicted in the Yugoslav film *Republic of Užice* (1974), directed by Serbian filmmaker Žika Mitrović.

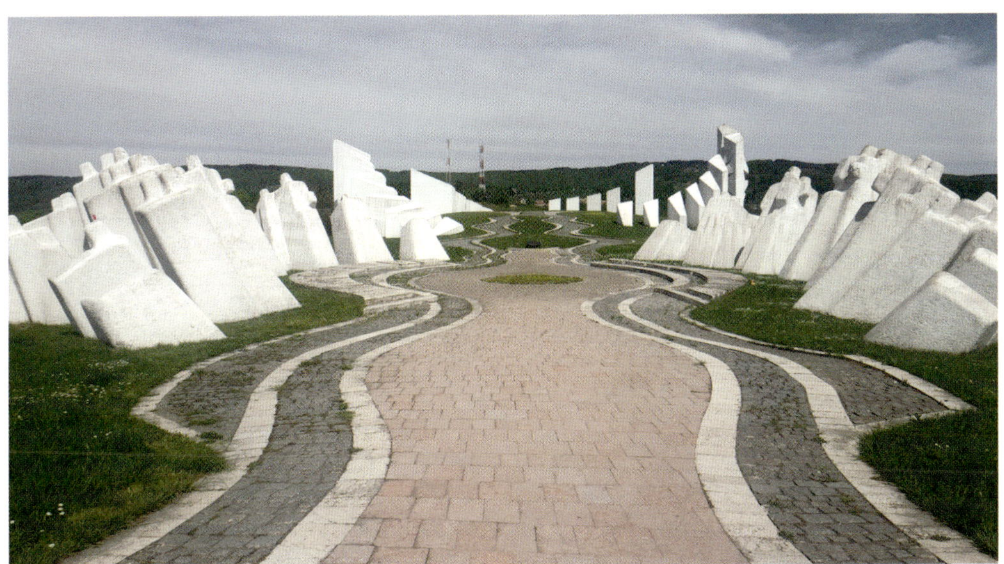

In 1952, an 11-metre-tall stone obelisk was built near the mountain peak to commemorate the Battle of Kadinjača. Created by Stevan Živanović, the design incorporated a crypt where the remains of the soldiers of the Workers' Battalion were interred. In 1962, veterans' groups and the municipalities of Užice and Bajina Basta devised a much more substantial memorial complex to complement the obelisk. In 1977, after an extended planning process, sculptor Miodrag Živković and architect Aleksandar Đokić were commissioned to expand the site. It was formally opened on 23 September 1979, at a ceremony attended by Yugoslav President Josip Tito, that attracted more than 100,000 people.

In addition to a new museum complex (designed by Aleksandar Đokić) at the south of the site, the large Amphitheatre of the Užice Republic was constructed to host educational presentations. To the north, the Plateau of Freedom is a circular formation of variously faceted concrete blocks, the largest two of which form a split pair with a central shape that resembles an artillery shell hole or the cracked iris of an eye. These points are connected by the Alley of the Workers' Battalion, a path flanked by a cluster of butress-like blocks with a hint of anthropomorphism. They all lean away from a central point, suggesting the location of a powerful impact. Živković's expansions of the memorial complex are arranged in such a way as to maintain the original 1952 obelisk as the main focus. An additional memorial called 'Partisan Woods' was added in 1984 when, on the hillside southwest of the museum, 88 trees were planted, one for each year of Tito's life.

STATUS AND CONDITION

The spomenik complex is in very good condition and is well maintained. It is easy to find, with directional and promotional signs in Užice and surrounding towns. This makes it a popular tourist attraction, with many thousands of visitors every year. Annual commemorative events are still held here, the main one being on 29 September in honour of the fighters of the Workers' Battalion.

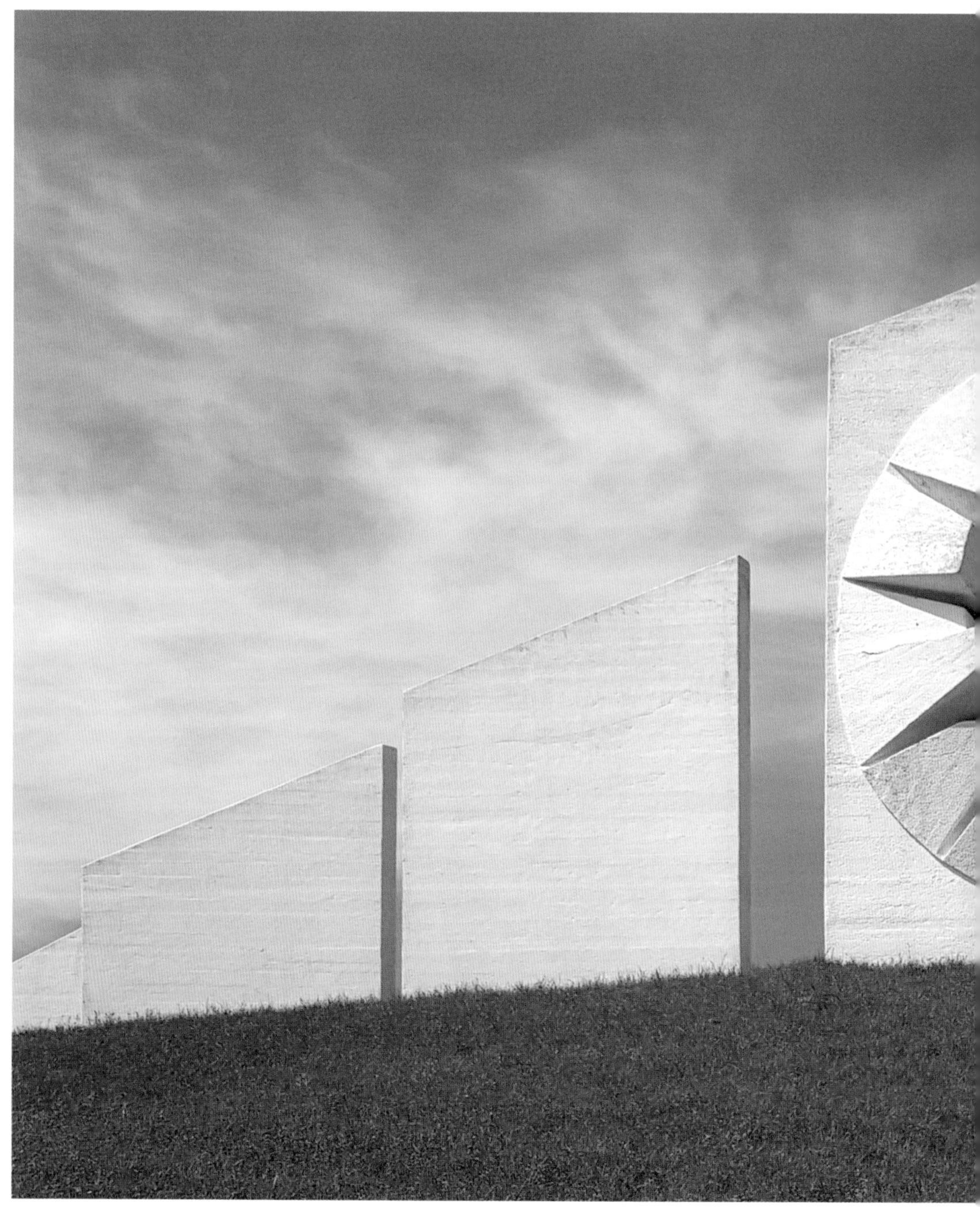

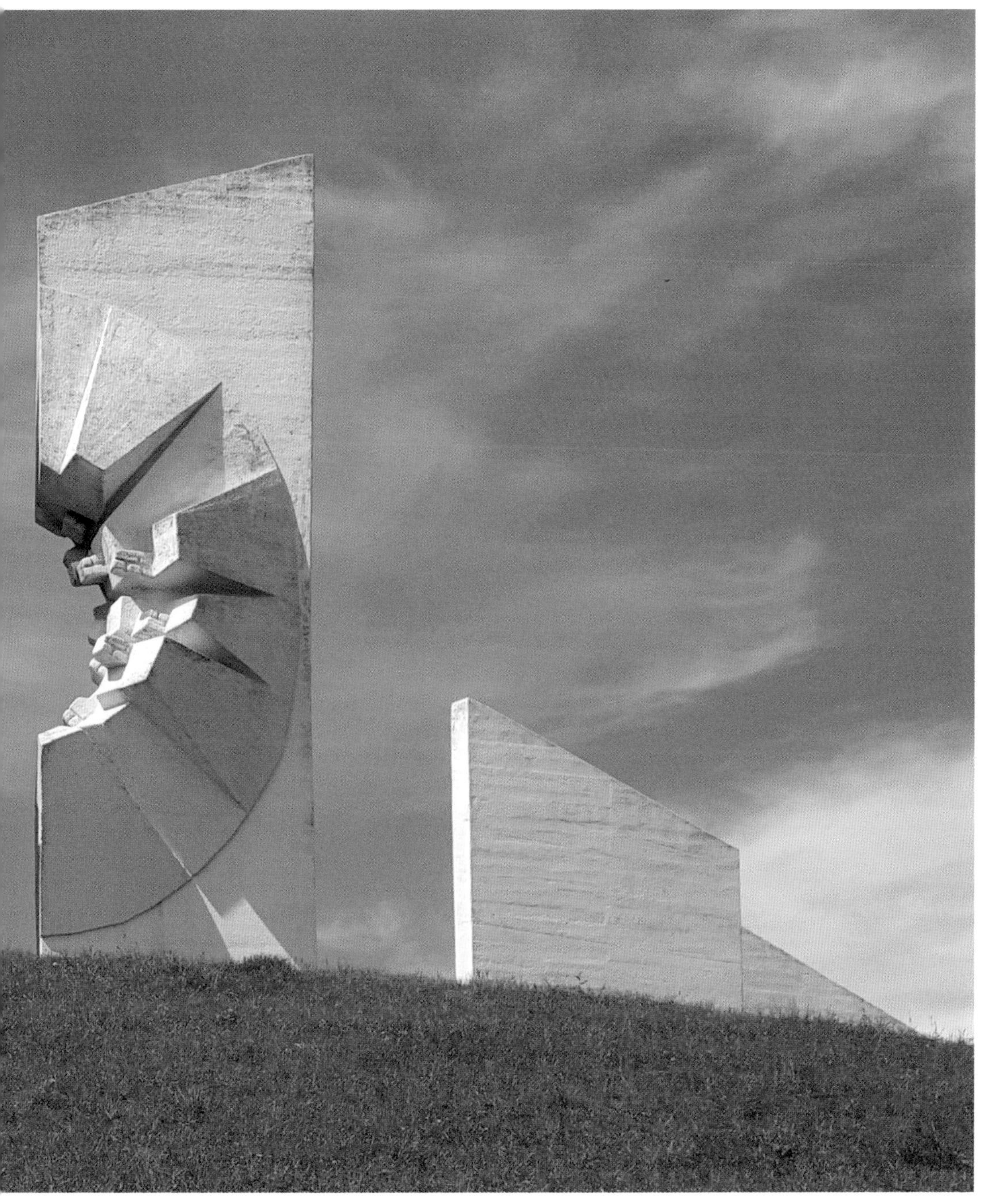

KAMENSKA (kah-MEN-skah)

NAME: Monument to the Revolutionary Victory of the People of Slavonia
LOCATION: Blažuj Hill, Kamenska, Croatia
YEAR COMPLETED: 1968 (2 years to build)
DESIGNER: Vojin Bakić
COORDINATES: N45°26'46.4", E17°28'36.4"
DIMENSIONS: 30 metres high
MATERIALS: Poured concrete, rebar and stainless steel

HISTORY

In 1941, with the Kingdom of Yugoslavia defeated by Axis forces, the region of Slavonia was integrated into the Axis-controlled Independent State of Croatia (NDH). Nationalist Ustaše militia enforced a brutal oppression, targeting ethnic-Serbs, Jews and Roma. Milivoj Ašner, Nazi collaborator and chief of the Ustaše in nearby Požega, orchestrated this persecution. He was allegedly responsible for many crimes against humanity, including ordering the execution of more than 400 Serbian civilians. Ethnic-Serbs and Croats joined resistance movements to fight the occupation and by 1943 they had retaken most of the Požega Valley. They battled to regain further territory, but it was not until April 1945 that the region was liberated. By then, more than 2,000 Slavonian partisan fighters had been killed.

After the war, Ašner fled to Austria. Changing his name to Georg Aschner, he lived in obscurity until he was exposed in 2004. Despite being indicted by Croatia in 2005 for crimes against humanity, Austria refused extradition on grounds of ill health. He died in 2011 in an Austrian nursing home, aged 98, having never been brought to trial. Until his death, Ašner was on Interpol's list of most wanted Nazi collaborators still at large.

DESIGN AND CONSTRUCTION

In 1960, Croatian sculptor Vojin Bakić was selected to construct a spomenik on Mount Papuk, near the town of Kamenska. It was here that the successful 12th Slavonian Division had formed in 1943 and where the commander of the 12th Slavonian Partisan Division National Hero Nikola Demonje, was buried. The shape proposed by Bakić required years of structural research. The Military Technical Institute in Žarkovo used a scale model to determine its behaviour in extreme weather conditions. Funded through public donations from citizens and organisations across nineteen municipalities in Slavonia and Baranja, the project took more than 150 workers two years to complete. It was unveiled on 9 November 1968 at a ceremony attended by Yugoslav President Josip Tito.

The 30-metre-tall monument, was covered in 1,600 m² of polished stainless steel panels and set on a black marble platform. Bakić employed stainless steel in a number of his spomeniks, with the idea that 'the search for light' was the ultimate symbol for Yugoslavia. Shaped like flames or wind-buckled wings, the Kamenska monument represents not only the bravery of the fighters, but could also be perceived as a Serbian national symbol (which may be a reason for its destruction – see below). When it was built, it was one of the largest modernist sculptures in the world.

STATUS AND CONDITION

This spomenik was destroyed in the wave of nationalism that followed Croatian independence. In August 1990, the area was drawn into the Yugoslav Wars, and sporadic fighting between ethnic-Serb paramilitary and Croatian Army units followed. In December, the Croatian 123rd Požeška Brigade entered the Papuk Mountain region. It is alleged that on 21 February 1991, they dynamited the monument, toppling it on their third attempt, after initial detonations weakened the structure. All that remains today is the crumbling marble platform. In 2010, anti-fascist organisations restored the Nikola Demonje memorial grave, which now hosts annual commemorative events.

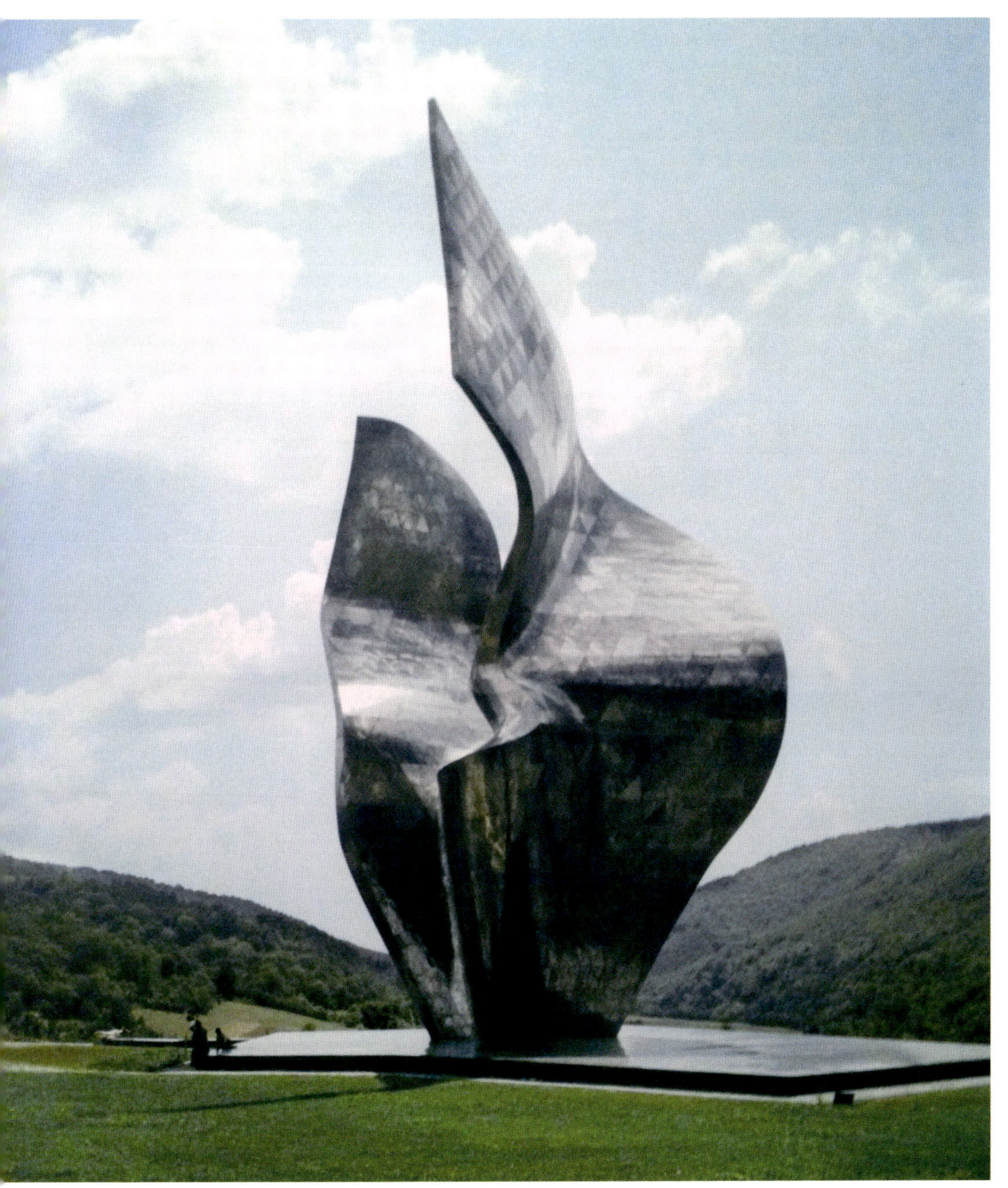

KAVADARCI (KAH-vah-dar-tsee)

NAME: Memorial Ossuary of Fallen Fighters
LOCATION: Kavadarci, Macedonia
YEAR COMPLETED: 1976
DESIGNER: Peter Muličkovski
COORDINATES: N41°25'57.8", E22°01'22.5"
DIMENSIONS: 13 metres high and 7 metres wide
MATERIALS: Poured concrete and rebar with iron gates

HISTORY

Following the invasion of the Kingdom of Yugoslavia in 1941, Macedonia fell under Axis control and was held in the grip of a brutal occupation. Armed resistance units grew in number across the country; fighting against particularly vicious and unrelenting Bulgarian forces, initially they enjoyed few successes. On 7 April 1944, a Bulgarian unit stumbled upon notorious 21-year-old partisan leader Kiro Krstev in a small house in Kavadarci. Determined to eliminate this threat, the Bulgarians called in 700 troops to surround the house. A seven-hour standoff ensued. Krstev attempted to break free under cover of darkness but was gunned down after only a few metres. He was posthumously made a Yugoslav National Hero in 1951.

In spring 1944, the 2nd Macedonian Partisan Assault Brigade commenced an all-out attack on Kavadarci in an attempt to liberate the city. However, their onslaught failed and the German troops continued to hold their positions. When Bulgaria sided with the Allies in September 1944, the partisans' rate of success against the remaining German forces dramatically increased, but it was only on 7 September 1945 that the 9th Macedonian Brigade was finally able to liberate the town.

DESIGN AND CONSTRUCTION

This memorial to fallen partisan fighters is situated on top of a 300-metre high hill in the middle of Gradski Park. Designed by Peter Muličkovski and constructed in 1976, it comprises a 'house' and a 'courtyard'. The house is a 13-metre tall, three-level concrete structure with a central spiral staircase. It is entered through wrought-iron gates modelled after the grapevines of the Kavadarci region. At ground level, granite plaques bear the names of those buried in the tomb beneath. The second and third levels provide viewing platforms. The shape of the memorial is reminiscent of a traditional Macedonian house of the Ohrid region, with inverted verandas, characteristic windows and the spiral staircase. Adjacent to the house, a

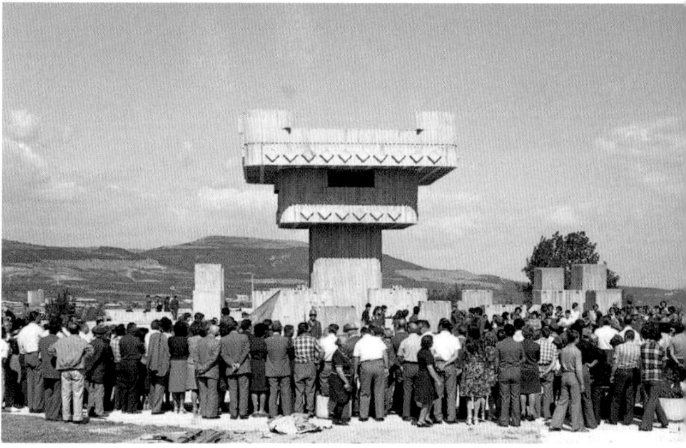

20-metre square concrete courtyard is bordered by grooved concrete blocks of varying sizes, with recessed amphitheatre-like tiers facing towards the centre.

A separate memorial composed of a 10-metre high obelisk and a small wall bearing a bronze relief is situated at the northwest corner of the park. It is dedicated to Kavadarci native and Yugoslav National Hero Kiro Krstev, and is set on the spot where he died.

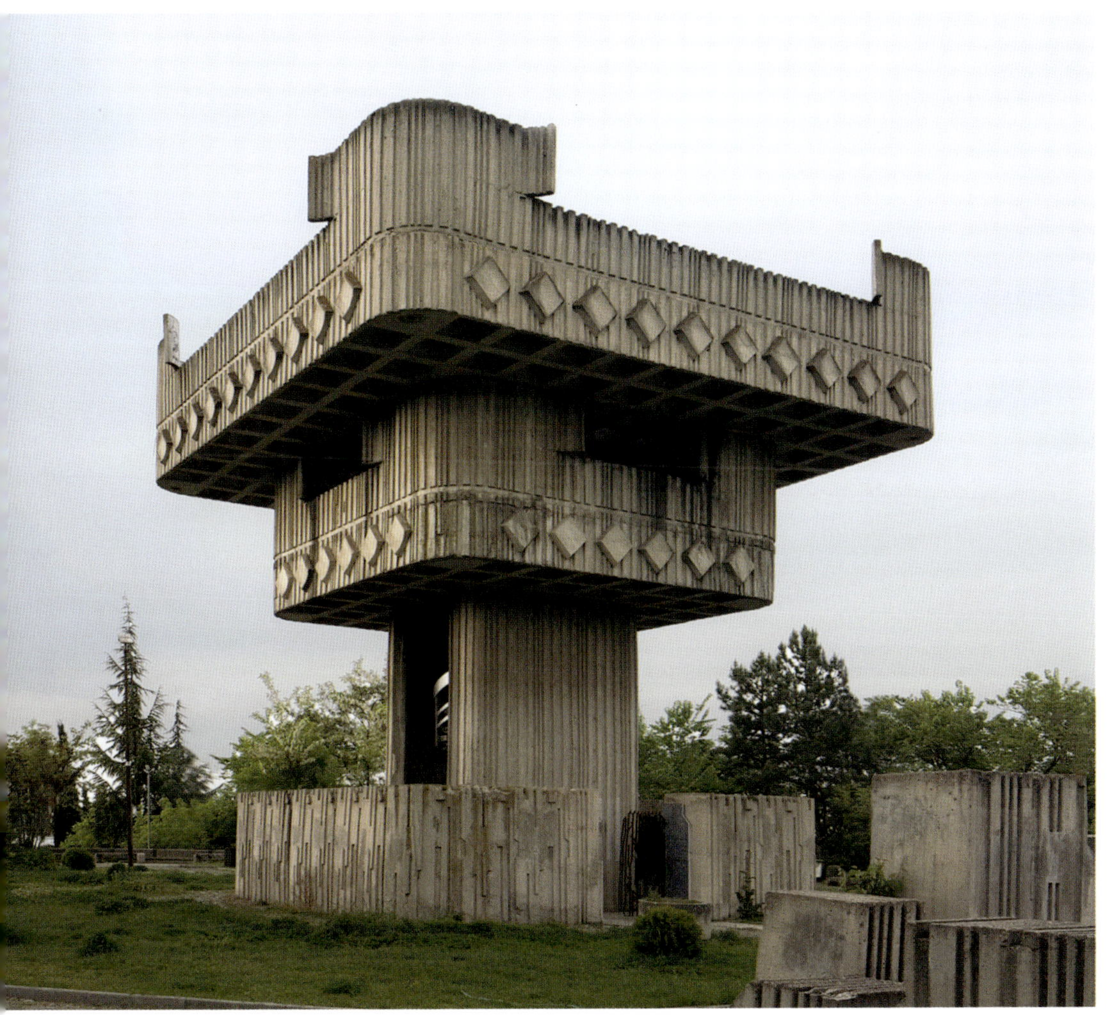

left: A commemoration takes place at the memorial, 1976, (image from the Kavadarci Museum Gallery)

STATUS AND CONDITION

The structure of the main monument appears solid, but overall the complex is in poor condition, with many parts overgrown. The granite plaques inside appear to be replacements for the originals. The monument has been vandalised so severely in recent years that the remains of the 328 partisans interred in the tomb were moved to the City Museum and Gallery for protection. Attempts have been made to erase graffiti from the façade and courtyard amphitheatre, but a considerable amount remains. There is no indication of any proposed renovations, or that ceremonies are held here to commemorate the city's 7 September Liberation Day.

KNIN (kuh-NEEN)

NAME: Monument to Croatian Victory or Monument to Salvation
LOCATION: Knin, Croatia
YEAR COMPLETED: 1969
DESIGNER: Đorđe Romić
COORDINATES: N44°02'19.6", E16°11'26.3"
DIMENSIONS: 25 metres high
MATERIALS: Poured concrete and rebar

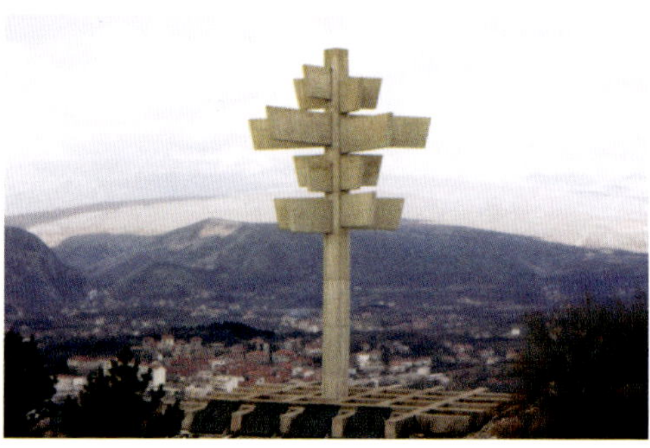
The spomenik with the city of Knin below, c.1978

HISTORY

At the end of 1944, the 8th Dalmatian Partisan Corps gained significant victories against Axis forces, weakening their grip on the Adriatic coast. On 3 November, the city of Šibenik – the last Axis stronghold on the Adriatic – was liberated. The retreating German troops, pursued by partisans, made their way to Knin (55 kilometres northeast of Šibenik). Their commander, General Gustav Fehn, was ordered to establish a fortified position at the southern end of the city and to defend it at all costs. German command intended Knin to be a stronghold on the new Axis front line. From 7 November to 9 December 1944, the 35,000 partisan fighters of the 8th Dalmatian Corps engaged 20,000 Axis troops in the Battle of Knin. A stalemate lasting around two weeks allowed Axis forces to begin to retreat north, providing an opportunity for the partisans to take the city. On 26 November, the partisans used tanks and artillery in an attempt to break the German lines, but without success. Finally, on 1 December, the partisans outflanked the Germans and encircled the city. On 3 December, the remaining German troops abandoned their posts, allowing the partisans to seize Knin. Around 700 partisans had been killed, while Axis losses numbered over 6,000. This victory heralded the total expulsion of Axis forces from the Dalmatian region.

At the end of the war, General Fehn was captured by British troops in Italy. He was later extradited to Ljubljana, where on 5 June 1945 he was executed without trial by partisans.

DESIGN AND CONSTRUCTION

In the late 1960s, young Knin architect Đorđe Romić was commissioned to design a memorial to commemorate the liberation of the city. Located on Spas Hill, the monument was unveiled in November 1969. The 25-metre tall concrete structure had fins projecting laterally from the top half, configured like a multi-directional signpost or rectilinear tree. This was set into a large concrete grid, with a number of heavy bronze plaques fixed to its west side.

STATUS AND CONDITION

The site of the monument made it a visible symbol of partisan victory to the citizens of Knin. For Croatian Axis collaborators, it would have been a bitter reminder of defeat. As the Yugoslav Wars began in 1991, the spomenik fell into disrepair. In July 1995, Croatian forces defeated the Bosnian Serb Army to occupy Knin. They then used explosives to topple the spomenik.

Today the ruins are overgrown and difficult to access. In 2007, the Croatian Ministry of Culture approved repairs, but no funding materialised. Some politicians want to erect a Christian cross on the site, but anti-fascist groups insist that the monument should be restored.

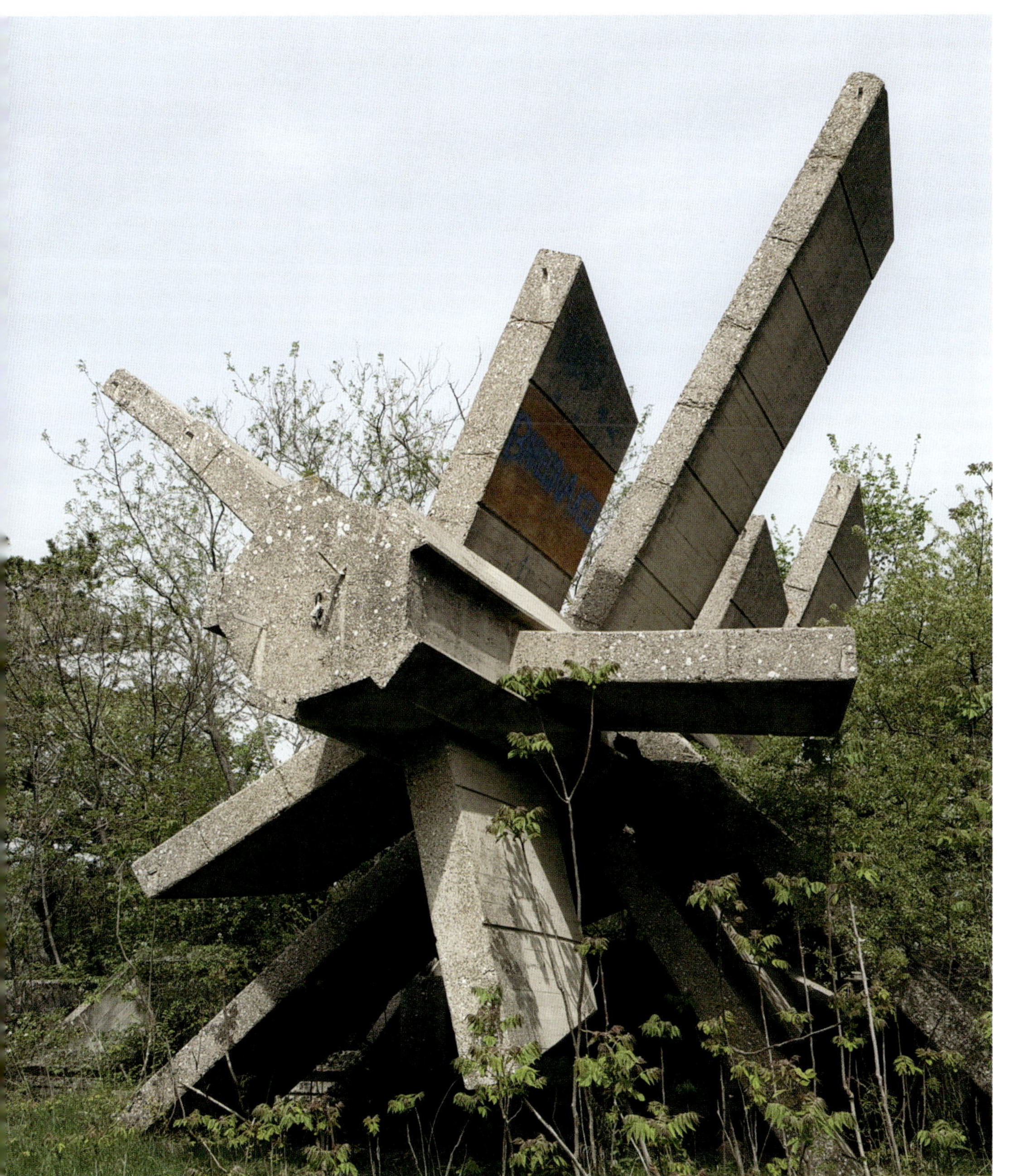

KOLAŠIN (koh-LAH-shin)

NAME: Spomen-dom or Kolašin Municipal
Assembly/Town Hall
LOCATION: Kolašin, Montenegro
YEAR COMPLETED: 1975 (4 years to build)
DESIGNER: Marko Mušič
COORDINATES: N42°49'27.2", E19°31'07.5"
DIMENSIONS: 3,220 square metres
MATERIALS: Poured concrete and rebar

HISTORY

On 17 April 1941, following the Axis invasion of the Kingdom of Yugoslavia, Kolašin was occupied by Italian forces and Montenegro subsequently suffered under the brutal command of General Pirzio Biroli. The resistance movement quickly established itself in two main groups: the communist partisans, primarily led by Kolašin native and Communist Party leader Milovan Đilas; and the Serbian nationalist Chetniks, led by former Royal Yugoslav Army officer Pavle Đurišić.

Fighting together, the two groups liberated a significant amount of Montenegro. But in August 1941, after a bloody Italian offensive resulted in crushing defeat, Đurišić and his Chetniks decided to stop fighting the Italians to avoid further loss of civilian life. The partisans wanted to continue however and a animosity developed between the factions. In January 1942, Đurišić met with Italian Army representatives to form an Italian-Chetnik alliance, working together to destroy the partisans.

As the Chetniks aligned themselves with the Italians, the partisans captured Kolašin from Italian troops. However, the partisans were not trusted by all residents (especially the Muslim population, as many had collaborated with the Italian occupiers). This mistrust was viewed by the partisans as 'opposition' and they killed up to 300 civilians who refused to co-operate with them.

These actions, which left many Montenegrins with deep resentment and anger towards the partisan forces, were condemned by the Communist Party leadership and later labelled as 'Leftist Errors'.

The Chetniks retook Kolašin on 23 February 1942, driving the partisans out of the region. Over the next eighteen months, fighting between the partisan and Italian-Chetnik forces was fierce, and Kolašin changed hands several times. With the surrender of the Italians in September 1943, the Axis front in Montenegro was weakened, allowing the partisans to take control of Kolašin once more. On 15 November, the Communist Party of Yugoslavia chose Kolašin to host an assembly to determine the future government of Montenegro. More than 500 delegates from across Montenegro attended the First Session of the Anti-Fascist Council of the People's Liberation of Montenegro and Boka, held in an old gymnasium in the town. Crucial decisions were made affecting the rebuilding of the country following the war. A further session was held on 14 June 1944.

A string of German-Chetnik offensives began in August 1944, in an attempt to retake Kolašin. However, each time the town was lost, the partisans were able to retake it. On 29 December 1944, Kolašin was liberated for the last time by the 5th Montenegrin Proletarian Brigade.

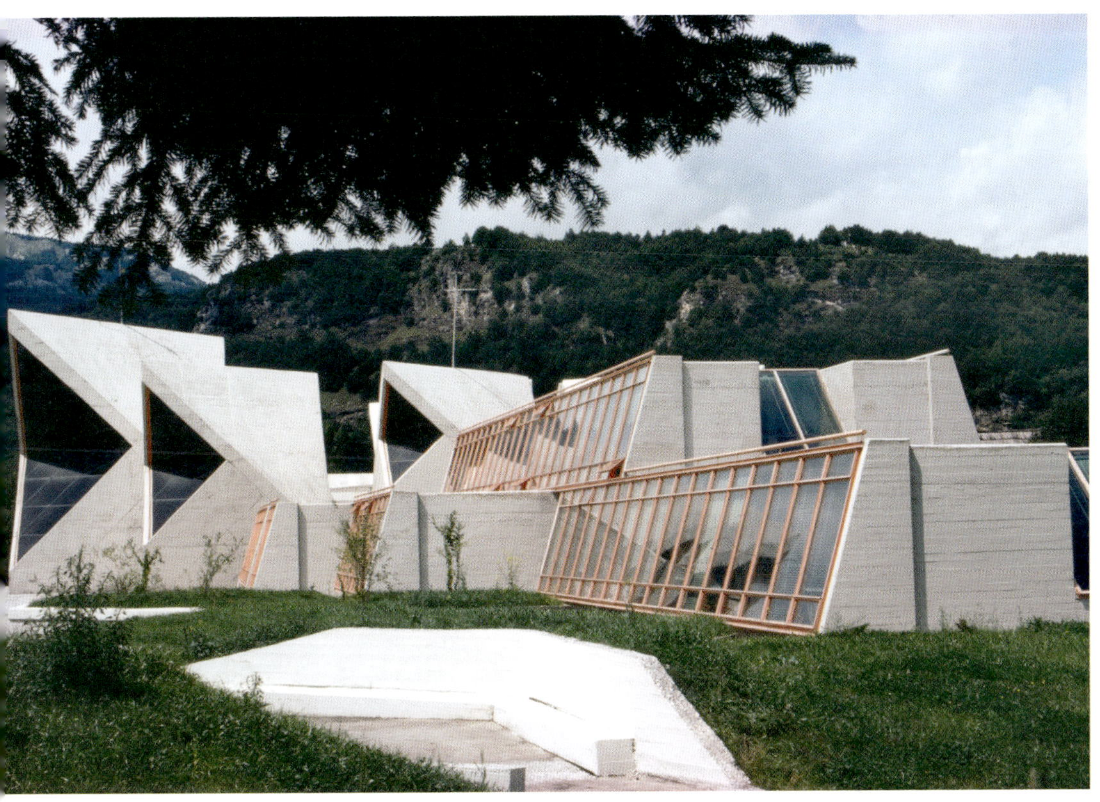

The Kolašin Spomen-Dom in the 1980s, (image from the Marko Mušić Archive)

In 1970, a Yugoslav-wide competition was held for the design of a spomenik complex and facility to commemorate the Kolašin Anti-Fascist Council gatherings of 1943 and 1944. A committee of artists, architects and politicians from across the country selected the design of Slovenian architect Marko Mušič. Work began in 1971 and the finished construction was opened on 15 November 1975. This spomenik complex, often referred to as the Spomen-Dom (Memorial House), is unique in that it acts as both a memorial structure and a fully functioning civic building. More than 3,000 square metres in size, it contains offices, exhibition spaces and a large Congress Hall, originally intended for civic events and government party functions. Considered by many to be a fine example of modern architecture, it won several awards, including the 1976 Slovenian Prešeren Award (the republic's highest art award) and the Yugoslavian 4 July Award.

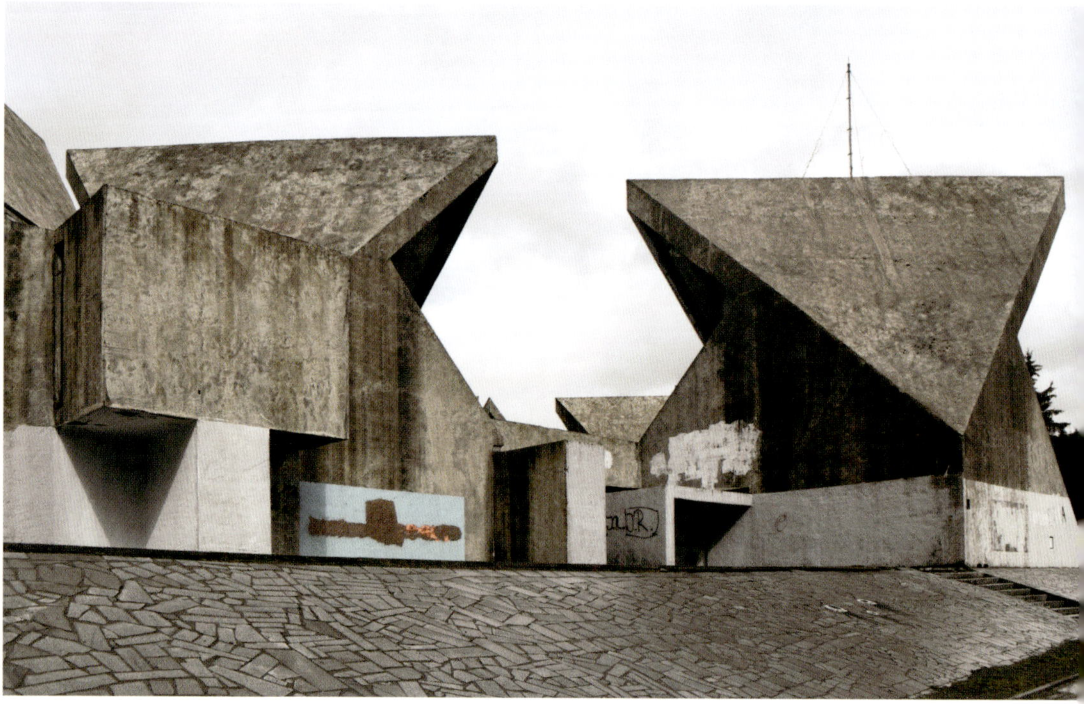

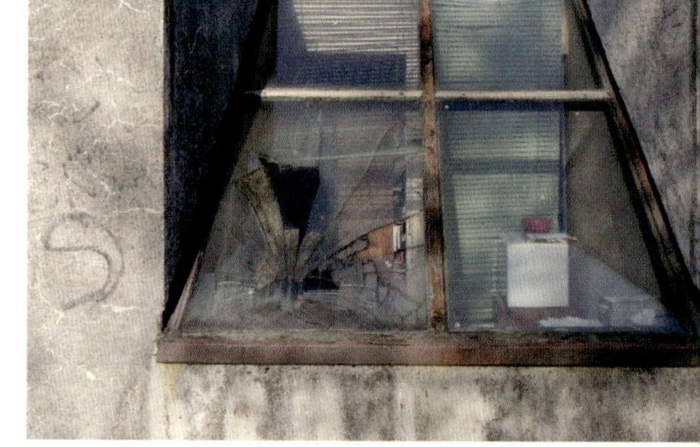

Since the dismantling of Yugoslavia in the 1990s and the ensuing conflicts across the region, this spomenik building has fallen into disrepair. Government funding was cut, which had a considerable effect on the maintenance of the structure, and because of its semi-derelict state, many locals viewed the building as an eyesore. In the late 2000s, plans were made for its demolition and the redevelopment of the site into a tourist facility, but thanks to a budget crisis these proposals were not realised. While the building is still in active use, it is suffering from cracks in the concrete, broken windows, stained walls, severe water damage and invading vegetation. Despite this neglect and its poor condition, the Spomen-Dom is still considered one of Montenegro's most significant examples of post-war architecture.

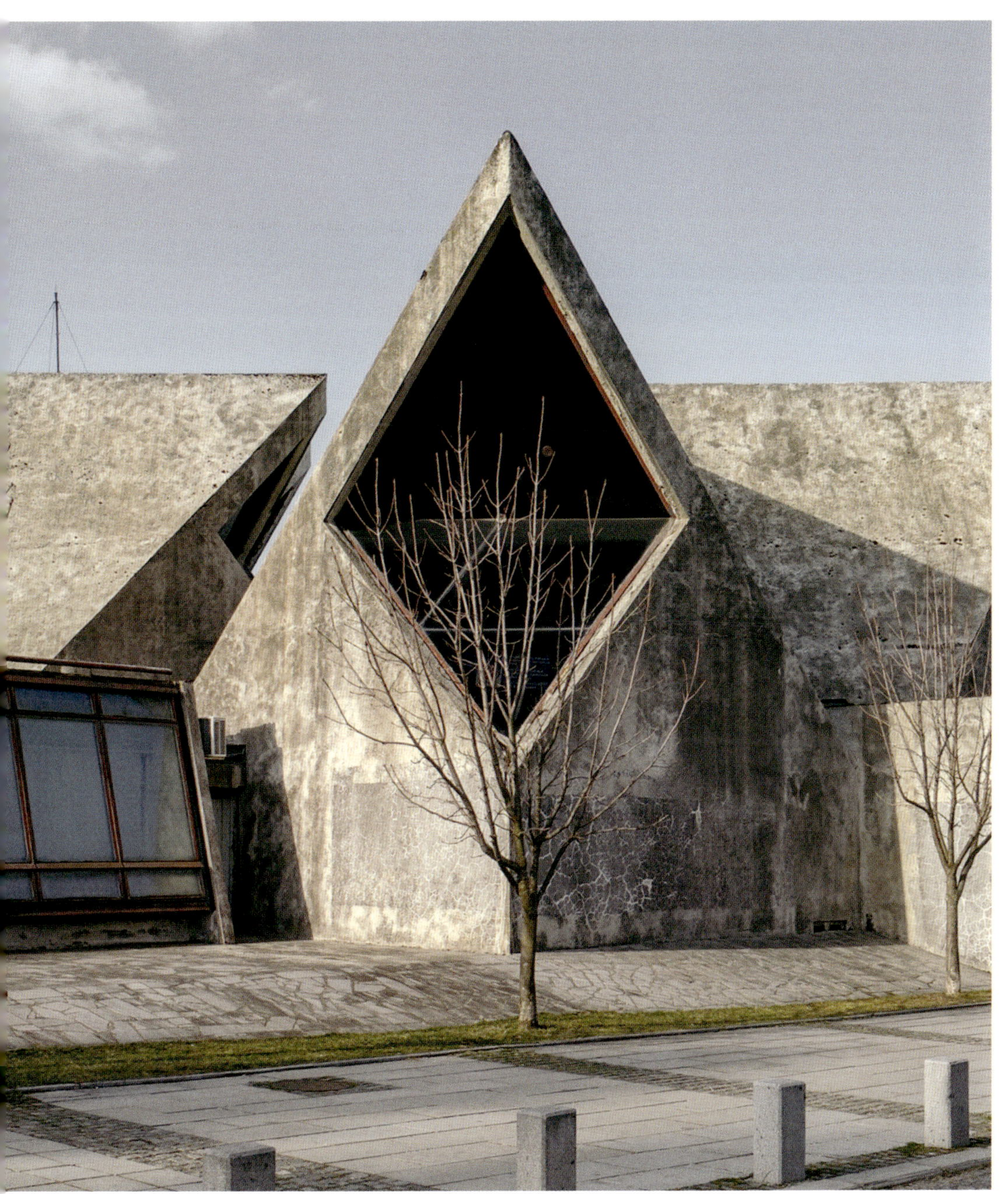

KORENICA (koh-REN-ee-tsa)

NAME: Central Monument of the White Streams,
Kamensko Memorial Area
LOCATION: 18km southeast of Korenica, Croatia
YEAR COMPLETED: 1981
DESIGNERS: Vladimir Ugrenović and Berislav Radimir
COORDINATES: N44°40'26.5", E15°50'54.8"
DIMENSIONS: 15 metres high
MATERIALS: Poured concrete, rebar and steel

HISTORY

Following the Axis occupation in April 1941, this region fell under the control of Axis-aligned Ustaše militia. While the majority of the population was Croatian, the Korenica area was inhabited by hundreds of ethnic-Serbs. They were severely oppressed, their Orthodox churches were destroyed, their rights were limited, and they were expelled from their homes and deported. Throughout the war, hundreds of Serbs from this region were liquidated in German and Ustaše death camps.

On 27 July 1941, in the village of Srb, ethnic-Serbs staged an uprising. Supported by partisans and Chetniks, the rebels successfully defeated the Ustaše. The Korenica region became part of a liberated territory spanning much of present-day Dalmatia and western Bosnia. The rebels mostly targeted Axis forces, but they also committed atrocities against Croat civilians, whom they viewed as collaborators.

In January 1943, the Germans initiated Operation Case White with the objective of ending the partisan problem in Yugoslavia. They began by pushing the partisans out of the mountains towards Mostar, where they had set a trap at the Neretva river. By the end of January, the partisans had been forced to retreat from their positions in the Korenica region, but not before inflicting several decisive strikes of their own. Case White was not a total success: it did not completely eliminate partisan operations in the region or capture resistance leader Josip Tito. However, it was a significant setback for the partisans, with more than 11,000 fighters killed and the western Bosnian and Dalmatian mountains no longer under their control. It was not until 1945 that Axis-aligned forces were finally expelled from the Korenica region.

DESIGN AND CONSTRUCTION

In the late 1970s, designers Vladimir Ugrenović and Berislav Radimir were commissioned to create a monument to commemorate the fallen fighters and civilian victims of the war from the surrounding region. The chosen location was a small and remote forested valley in White Steams Park, which had been a partisan stronghold during the Case White offensive. Unveiled in 1981, the finished monument consisted of four steel triangular shapes, resembling yacht sails, resting on a circular concrete platform.

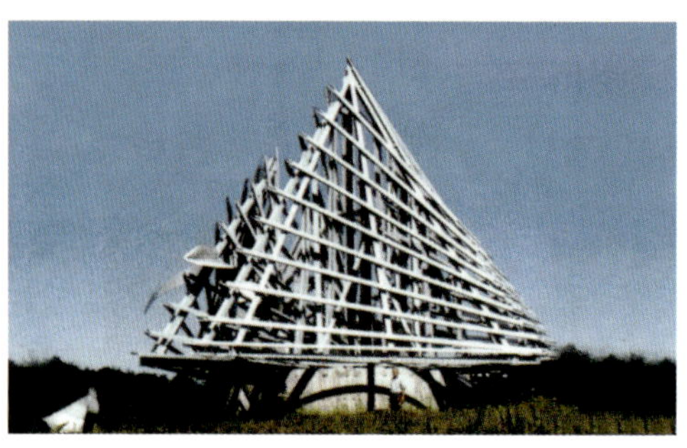

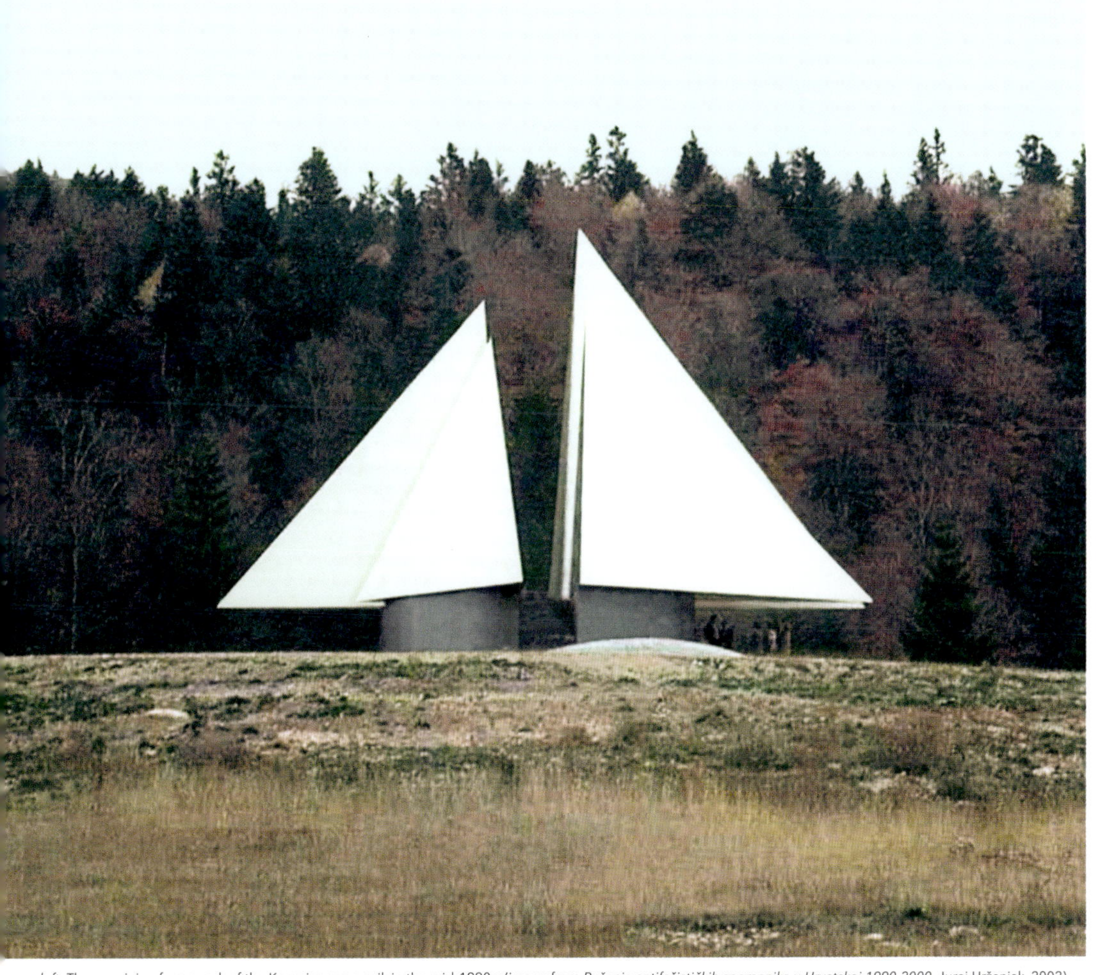

left: The remaining framework of the Korenica spomenik in the mid-1990s; (image from *Rušenje antifašističkih spomenika u Hrvatskoj 1990-2000*, Juraj Hrženjak, 2002)
above: The spomenik in the 1980s, (image from the Institute of Art History, Zagreb)

STATUS AND CONDITION

During the Yugoslav Wars of the 1990s, the site became part of a new ethnic-Serb breakaway territory called the Republic of Serbian Krajina. Almost immediately, the spomenik's metal panels were stolen and the monument fell into disrepair. In 1995, the breakaway territory was re-integrated into Croatia, but the spomenik was not repaired. Around 2008, the remaining steel structure was also stolen. Today, all that survives of the spomenik is its circular concrete base. The site is unmarked and no commemorative events are held here. There are no plans to rebuild this structure.

KOSMAJ (KOS-mahy)

NAME: Monument to the Fallen Soldiers of the Kosmaj Partisan Detachment
LOCATION: Kosmaj Mountain Park, Serbia
YEAR COMPLETED: 1970
DESIGNERS: Vojin Stojić and Gradimir Medaković
COORDINATES: N44°28'04.3", E20°34'18.3"
DIMENSIONS: 40 metres high
MATERIALS: Poured concrete and rebar

HISTORY

In the summer of 1941, citizens opposed to the brutal Axis occupation of Serbia began forming armed resistance groups, organised by Tito's communist partisan rebels, alongside the Chetnik Nationalists led by Draža Mihailović. On 2 July 1941, a secret meeting was held on top of the mountain of Kosmaj (55 kilometres south of Belgrade). Members of two separate partisan detachments, one from the Kosmaj area, the other from the Sava river region, were brought together to form one cohesive unit. Initially composed of around 95 fighters, by the end of 1941, their number had grown to nearly 300. That September, the detachment adopted the nickname 'Rade Jovanović' in honour of their deputy commander who had been killed during their first major battle near Sopot. In December - following the first German counter-insurgency, which led to the fall of the partisan Republic of Užice - they fled to the Sandžak region of western Serbia. On 22 February 1942, they attempted to disrupt German supply lines to Belgrade from the small village of Tulež, but were quickly discovered by German troops. In the ensuing battle, hundreds of partisans were killed; of the unit's 300 fighters, only thirteen were able to escape.

In May 1943, the Kosmaj Detachment was reformed in the Makovic forest at Kovačevac. From an initial group of 60 soldiers, the detachment grew quickly. By September 1944, it had expanded to more than 1000 fighters, renaming itself the Kosmajska Brigade. In November, the brigade took part in the liberation of Belgrade; it then moved on to the Syrmian Front, driving the Germans out of Mandjelos and the Matore forest. In March 1945, the brigade was disbanded, having lost hundreds of fighters during the four years of its existence.

DESIGN AND CONSTRUCTION

In the late 1960s, designers Vojin Stojić and Gradimir Medaković were commissioned by the Yugoslav government to create a monument on top of Kosmaj Mountain. Completed in 1970, it honours the Kosmaj Partisan Detachment and those who died during the National Liberation War (World War II). A wide concrete staircase leads from the road through the surrounding forest to the monument. The spomenik consists of five separate 40-metre-tall concrete double-pointed fins. On the ground at their centre is an engraved circular stone platform. Together the fins make a star-like shape echoing the red five-pointed star that the partisans added to the Yugoslav flag during the war.

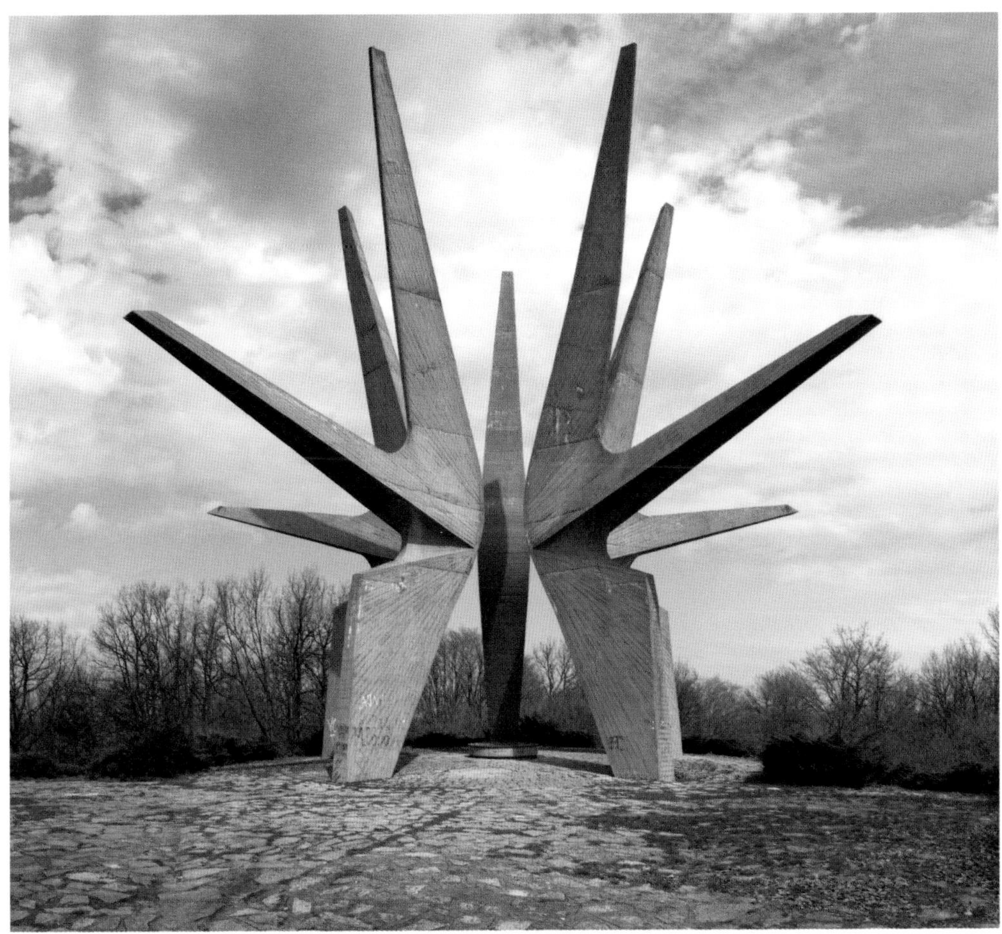

Structurally the monument is in a reasonable state, but there are signs of damage. The complex under the monument, the surrounding grounds and the staircases leading to it are all in poor condition, vandalised and crumbling. In 2014, the main plinth at the centre of the monument was smashed and its circular bronze relief stolen. Although repairs were made, they were to a lower standard than the original construction. Despite such obvious neglect, the monument is well promoted and popular with tourists. Flowers and other tributes are still left at the site and small commemorative events are held here.

Situated at the centre of the Kosmaj Mountain Park, designated a 'landscape of outstanding features', the monument enjoys protected status, although substantial work would be required to bring it back to pristine condition.

KOŠUTE (KOH-shoo-teh)

NAME: Monument to the 1st Split Partisan Detachment
LOCATION: Košute, Croatia
YEAR COMPLETED: 1961
DESIGNER: Vuko Bombardelli
COORDINATES: N43°37'40.1", E16°41'29.9"
DIMENSIONS: 17 metres high
MATERIALS: Poured concrete and rebar

HISTORY

In the months leading up to the Italian annexation of Dalmatia, occupying Ustaše forces escalated their oppression, persecuting dissidents and suspected anti-fascists. In April 1941, members of the League of Communist Youth of Yugoslavia raided Ustaše weapons depots to stockpile arms. In August, as the city of Split was officially annexed by Italy, partisan recruiters Pavle Pap Šilja and Mirko Kovačević arrived with orders to form three armed resistance detachments. Kovačević, a veteran of the Spanish Civil War, led the first detachment. Once assembled, all three were to relocate to Dinara, a mountain 80 kilometres north of Split. They left on the night of 11 August, using guides to lead them across the terrain. Halfway to Dinara, Kovačević's detachment of 45 partisans was separated from the others, losing contact with their guide and becoming disoriented. On 14 August, hungry and thirsty, a desperate Kovačević sent two of his group into the small village of Košute for supplies. Angry villagers immediately alerted Ustaše and Italian forces. Kovačević was the first to die in the ensuing battle, severely affecting the unit's morale. After a day, the partisans were defeated: thirteen had escaped, but four were dead and twenty-eight captured. Twenty-one of those captured were subsequently shot by firing squad (see page 162).

DESIGN AND CONSTRUCTION

In 1951, Mirko Kovačević was made a National Hero of Yugoslavia in recognition of his bravery. In the late 1950s, plans were made by local government and veterans' groups to create a spomenik at the location of the fighting near Košute, commemorating the 1st Split Partisan Detachment. On 14 August 1961, the 20th anniversary of the battle, Croatian architect Vuko Bombardelli's monument complex was unveiled.

Its primary element was a 17-metre-tall, six-pointed form, set on bare rock. Throughout the Yugoslav era, the memorial complex was a significant and popular landmark with veterans, locals and tourists.

STATUS AND CONDITION

In the early 1990s, with the breakup of Yugoslavia and the beginning of the Croatian War of Independence, the monument became a symbol of the old system for nationalist Croatians. As a consequence, in August 1992, it was rigged with explosives and destroyed. Today it remains in ruins. There is no evidence that the site is used for commemorative events, or that there are any plans to restore the monument.

right: The spomenik in the 1960s
(image from the Institute of Art History, Zagreb)
below: The spomenik today

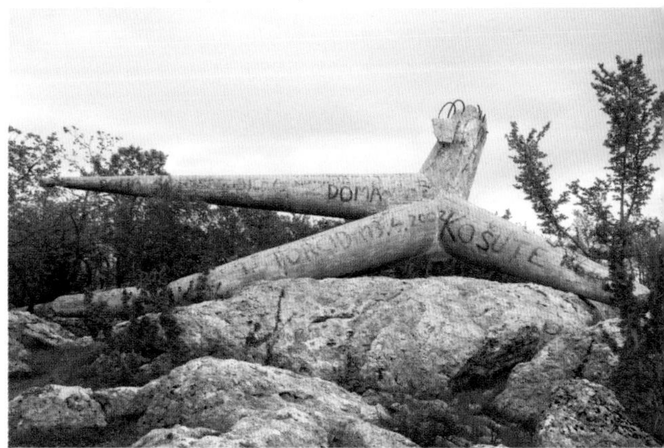

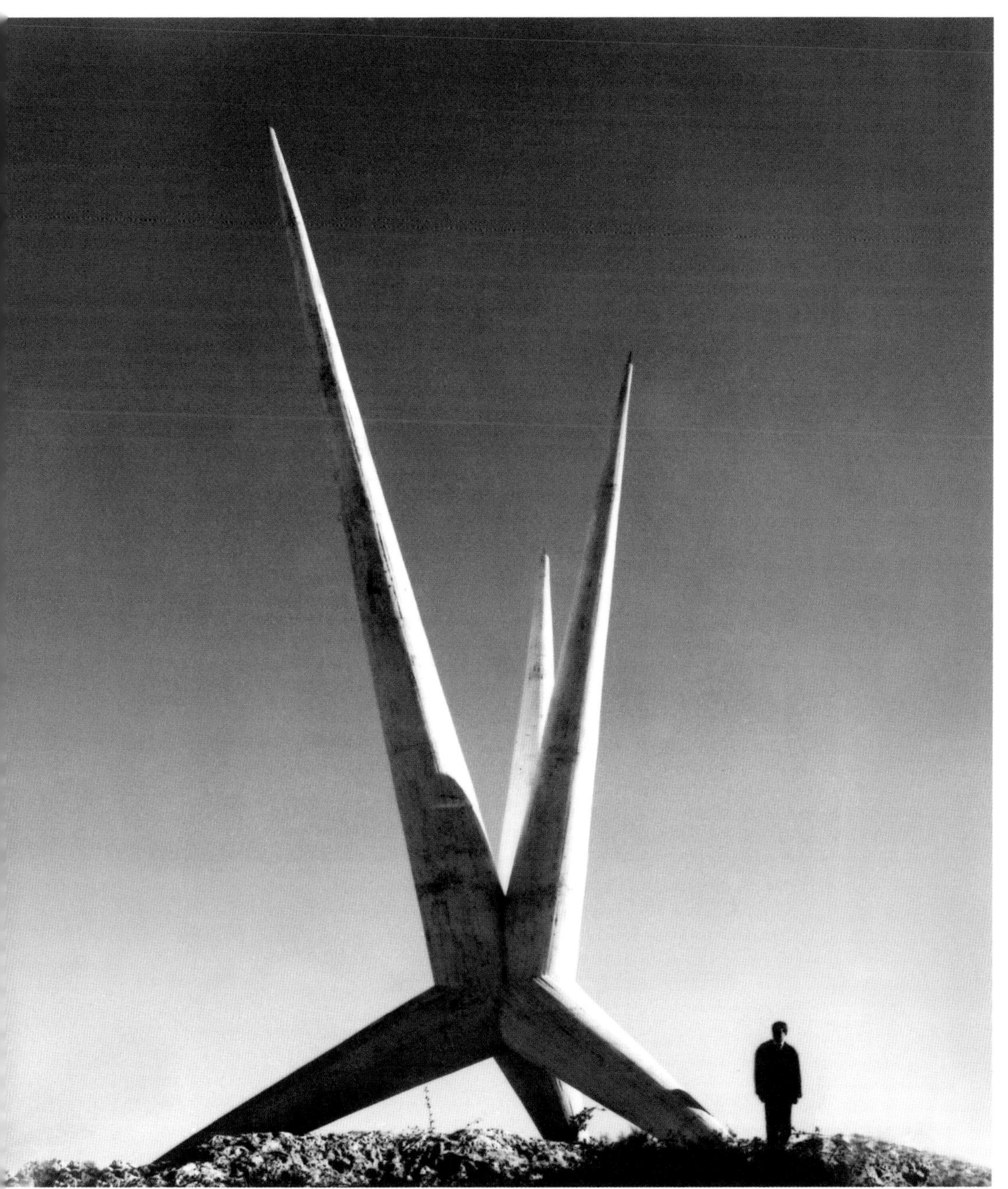

KOZARA (KOH-zah-rah)

NAME: Monument to the Revolution
LOCATION: Mrakovica area of Kozara National Park, Republic of Srpska, Bosnia and Herzegovina
YEAR COMPLETED: 1972
DESIGNER: Dušan Džamonja
COORDINATES: N45°00'49.7", E16°54'32.9"
DIMENSIONS: 33 metres high and 8 metres wide
MATERIALS: Poured concrete, rebar and steel plates

HISTORY

In 1942, after the partisans had liberated several towns in the central and west Bosnian regions, Axis command realised that its regional headquarters at Banja Luka could come under attack. In response to this threat, they launched the Kozara Offensive, mobilising 15,000 German, 22,000 Ustaše and 2,000 Chetnik troops, supported by five Hungarian gunships on the Sava river. Their objective was to eliminate the partisans and any support they might have in the villages of the Kozara region. Against them stood the regional partisan resistance forces, consisting of only 3,000 soldiers aided by 60,000 untrained civilian volunteers (mostly ethnic-Serbs) from the surrounding liberated territory.

On 10 June, Axis forces began their siege of the partisan headquarters in the Mrakovica area of the Kozara Mountain. The conflict, which lasted around two months, eventually saw the defeat of the partisans. During the course of the offensive, 2,100 partisan fighters perished, while 25,000 mostly ethnic-Serb civilians were killed and 40,000 transferred to Ustaše concentration camps.

The 900 partisan survivors went on to form the 5th Krajina Brigade. Their commander, Josip Tito, moved from east to west Bosnia to reorganise his remaining forces. While this was a significant defeat for the partisans, it became an important component of Yugoslav post-war mythology, which celebrated the bravery and selflessness of the partisan soldiers who gave their lives to fight fascism in the face of overwhelming odds.

DESIGN AND CONSTRUCTION

After the war, the Mrakovica site was not deemed to be important in terms of general Yugoslav war heritage; its legacy was only considered relevant to only local Bosnians. Initially, numbers at the annual commemorative gatherings were small. But over the years, the legend of the events that occurred here grew, as did the crowds.

In 1962 – five years after the site was officially designated a place of historical significance by the Socialist Republic of Bosnia and Herzegovina – an open competition was held for the design of a new memorial complex dedicated to the partisan fighters and civilians who died in the bloody Kozara Offensive in spring 1942. The concept proposed by Macedonian artist Dušan Džamonja was selected from 49 entries. Funding for the monument was secured exclusively from donations from 400,000 individuals and more than 1,000 organisations. Construction began in 1971, with the Bosnian President Hamdija Pozderac laying the corner-stone of the project. The spomenik was officially unveiled on 10 September 1972, at a commemorative ceremony inaugurated by the President of Yugoslavia, the former partisan commander Josip Tito.

The primary monument is situated at the centre of Kozara National Park on a plateau near the top of Mrakovica Mountain, one of the highest peaks in the Kozara range. It is a 33-metre-tall cylinder, made up of 20 vertical fins with intermittent, protruding, stainless-steel covered planes. The cylinder is divided along vertical lines into four sections to create a rhythmic profile. Džamonja states that his intention was to create 'a game of light and dark', with the 'positive' steel protrusions representing life and victory and the 'negative' hollows representing death and defeat. The construction required 1,000 tons of cement, 4,000 cubic metres of aggregate and 200 tons of structural steel. The concrete fins that radiate along the ground from the centre of the monument represent the oppressing forces of

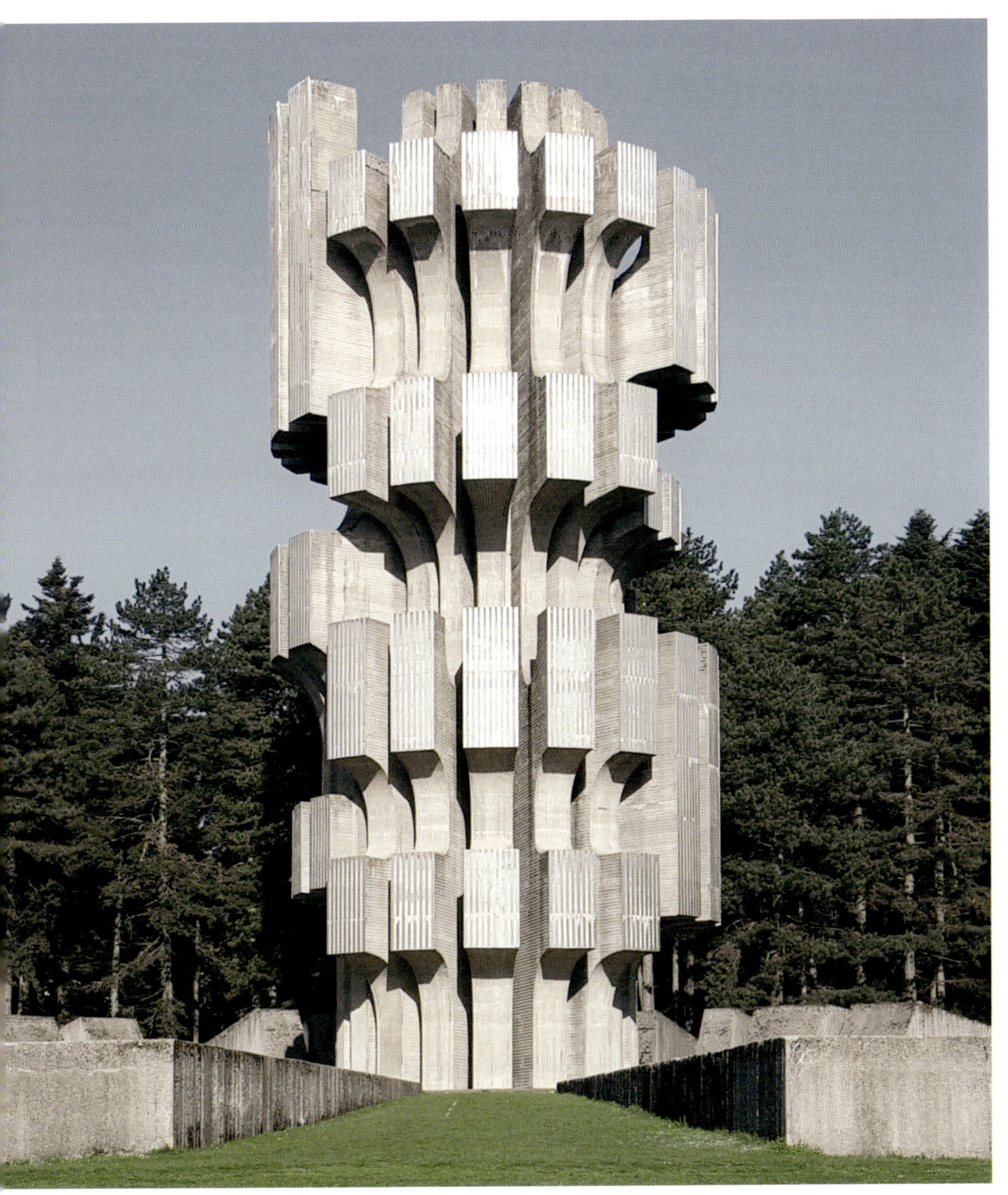

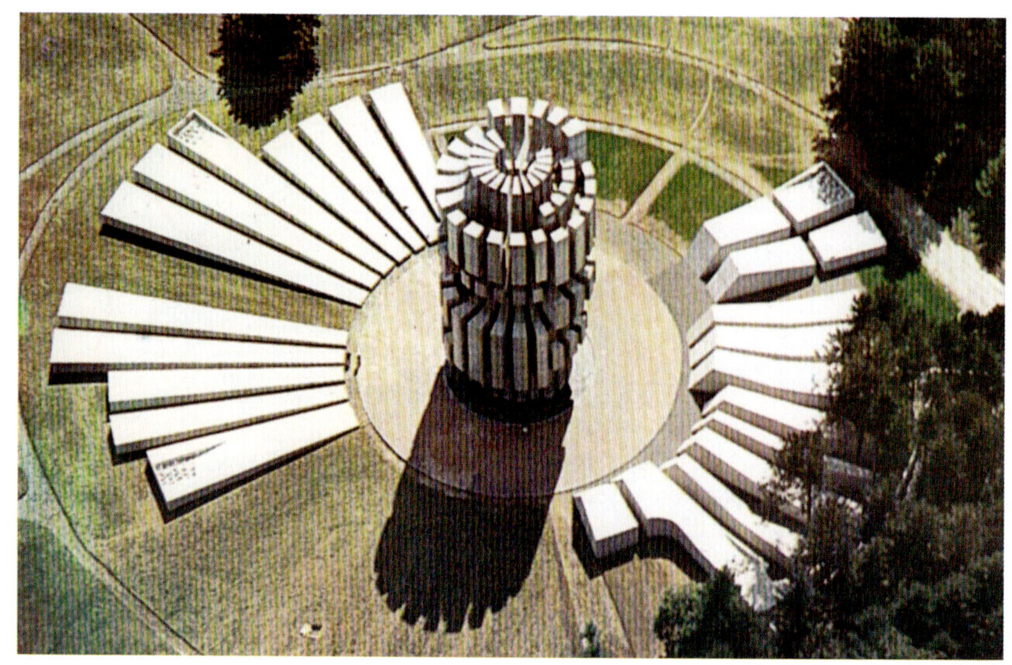

the fascist Axis powers. Behind the spomenik stands a 4-metre-high memorial wall, on which dozens of bronze plaques bear the names of the 9,921 fallen partisan soldiers.

Just below the brow of the hill, built into the hillside, is a small museum, also designed by Džamonja. It displays photographs, documents and articles testifying to the horrors endured by both the fighters of the Kozara Offensive and the local civilian population.

The broad concrete steps that cut through the forest from the road to the site doubled as an amphitheatre during the Yugoslav period. This feature of the spomenik complex was used by school groups to learn the history of the site.

The remote location and protected status of the monument have spared it from the destruction inflicted on many anti-fascist monuments during the fall of Yugoslavia and the Yugoslav Wars of the 1990s. Fortunately, only a series of stone panels listing donators were stolen at that time. After the wars, a Serbian Othodox cross was added to the main entrance of the complex. Accusations have been made that the museum has changed the focus of its exhibits from a stance of unity to being antagonistic towards Croatians. The director has stated that the controversial exhibits, which date from the 1990s, have not been replaced because of lack of funding.

The complex is widely advertised in the surrounding region as a significant cultural attraction. While the site is well maintained, popular and regularly used for commemorative events, it no longer unequivocally communicates the historical message of 'Brotherhood and Unity' that it once did.

above: An aerial view of the monument, 1980s
right: A postcard from the 1970s showing the attendees of a memorial event performing a kolo (circle) dance

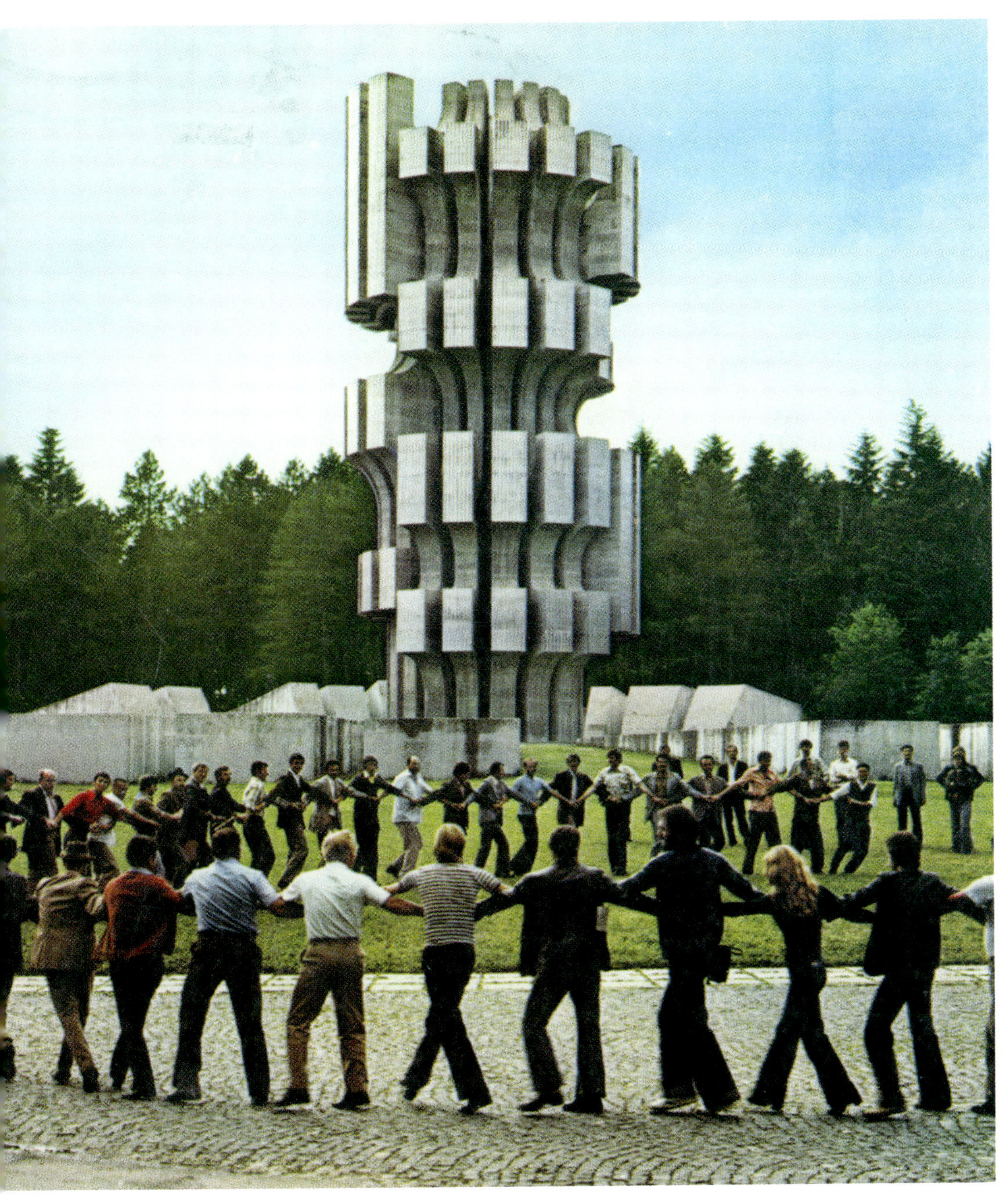

KRAGUJEVAC (krah-GOO-yeh-vats)

NAME: Šumarice Memorial Park (or Memorial Park October in Kragujevac)
LOCATION: Kragujevac, Serbia
YEAR COMPLETED: 1963
DESIGNER: Miodrag Živković
COORDINATES: N44°00'57.8", E20°53'09.1"
DIMENSIONS: 6 metres high
MATERIALS: Poured white concrete and rebar

HISTORY

In September 1941, German Wehrmacht Field Marshal Wilhelm Keitel issued a direct order from Hitler, authorising the killing of 100 civilians in retaliation for every German soldier killed, and 50 civilians for every German soldier wounded.

On 28 September, a group of partisans attacked members of the 920th Landesschützen Battalion, stationed at a schoolhouse, 40 kilometres west of Kragujevac. During this skirmish, 10 Germans were killed and 26 wounded. Enraged by this act of resistance, Franz Böhme, Wehrmacht commander of Serbia, ordered the arrest of male civilians across Kragujevac – predominately Serbs, Jews, suspected communists and anti-fascists. Struggling to meet the figures outlined in Hitler's directive, Böhme resorted to detaining students, monks and priests.

The killings took place on 21 October 1941, at the Šumarice Central Serbian Cemetery. Groups of between 50 and 100 were lined up in front of pits and shot. It is commonly held that up to 2,300 people were massacred here (Hitler's prescribed 'quota'), although some estimates range much higher. Five days later, German soldiers ordered 200 towns-people to bury the bodies in 33 mass graves. Böhme prohibited the gravesites from being marked.

After the war, Böhme was caught while escaping to Norway and tried at Nuremberg. Rather than face further trial and likely execution in Yugoslavia, on 29 May 1947, he committed suicide by jumping from the fourth-floor window of his prison cell.

DESIGN AND CONSTRUCTION

Work began in 1953 to turn the Šumarice massacre site into a 340-hectare memorial park. When it opened in 1955, the park contained no substantial monuments, but consisted of paved walkways and hiking trails. Over several decades, starting in 1959, memorial sculptures by well-known

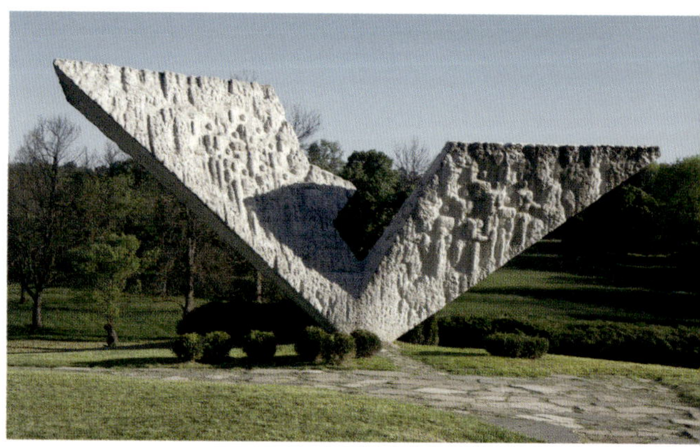

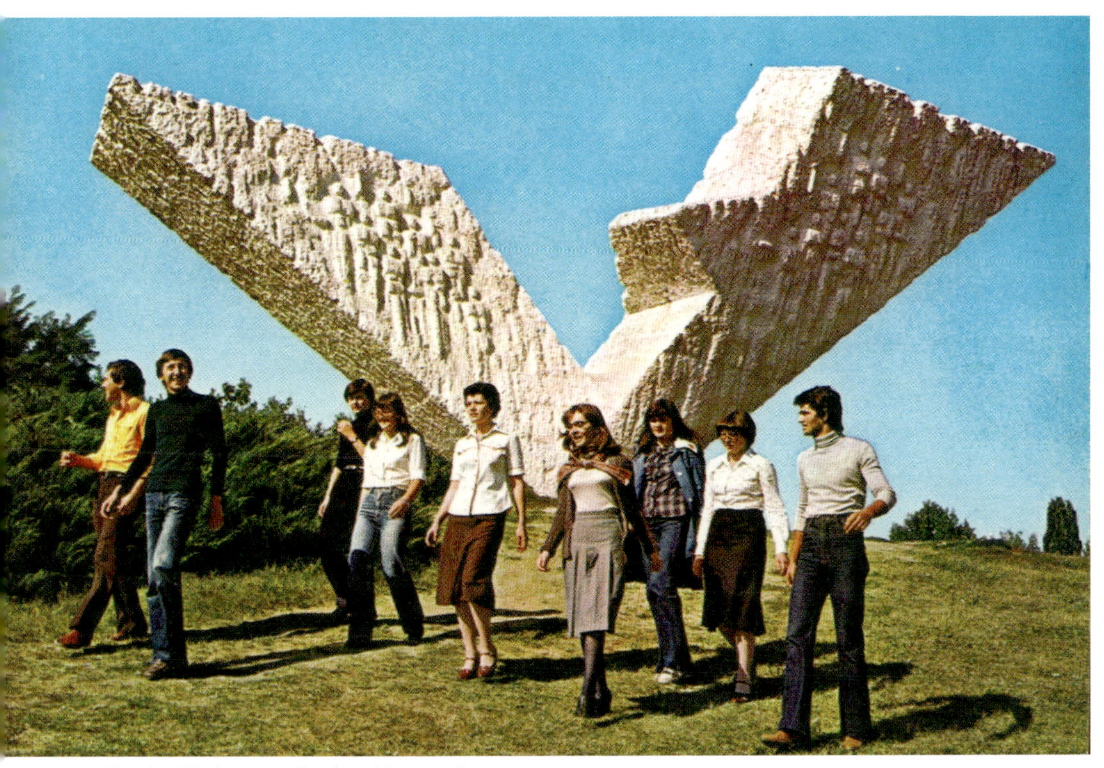

A postcard from the 1980s depicting youths in front of the spomenik

Yugoslav artists were constructed at a number of gravesites within the park. The centrepiece is the 'Monument to Executed Students' (commonly referred to as 'Interrupted Flight'), dedicated to the hundreds of students and their teachers who were massacred at this spot. Designed by sculptor Miodrag Živković, and built in 1963, it is situated where their remains are buried. It is a large asymmetrical V-shape reminiscent of a bird fallen to Earth. The front and rear surfaces are covered with low-relief ranks of human figures. The monument has become an important symbol for the city of Kragujevac and the whole of Serbia.

In 1976, the 21 October Museum was added. Designed by Ivan Antic and Ivanka Raspopović, it consists of 33 square brick columns of varying heights (4 metres to 21 metres), representing the 33 mass graves at the site.

Other monuments are scattered across the park, commemorating different aspects of the tragic events that occurred here in 1941. The most notable are listed below:

Pain & Defiance by Ante Gržetić, built in 1959. This semi-abstract sculpture depicting the anguished, twisting figures of a man and a woman was the first sculpture erected at Šumarice. It is dedicated to Nada Naumović, a student activist who worked to support partisan battle groups and who was the only woman known to be killed during the massacre. In 1951, she was recognised as a National Hero of Yugoslavia. It was at this location that the first group of citizens (including the priest Andreja Božić) were shot.

Crystal Flower by Serbian artist Nebojša Delja, built in 1968. This 7-metre-wide concrete sculpture depicts a blossoming flower split in two. It is

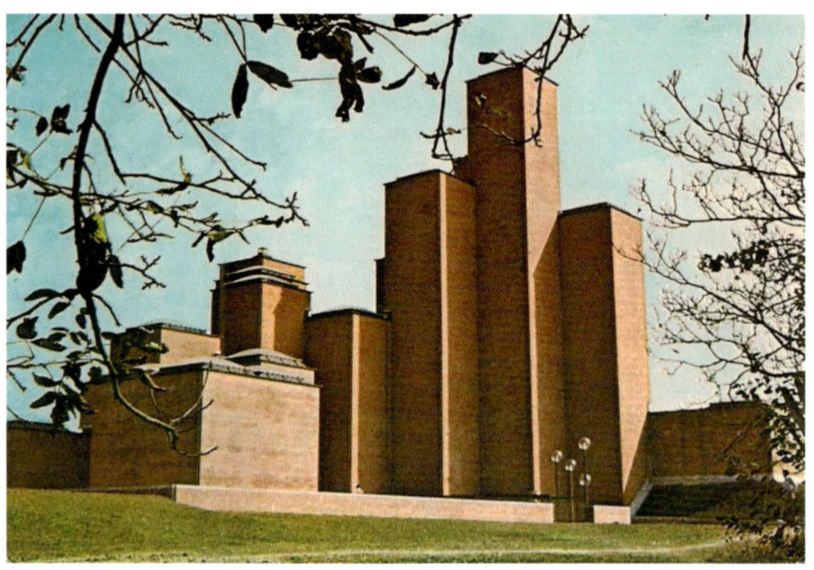

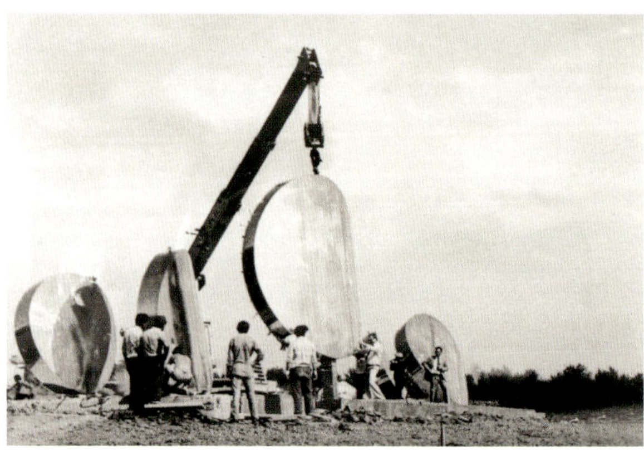

One Hundred For One by Serbian Jewish sculptor Nandor Glid, built in 1980. This 5-metre-high bronze work depicts the victims arranged horizontally above a vertical 'trunk' element so that the whole resembles a tree. The title alludes to Hitler's directive to kill 100 civilians for every German soldier.

Circles by Serbian sculptor Vojin Bakić built in 1981. This series of seven large, gently warped steel discs marks the site of several mass graves on this hillside. It was constructed as a gift to Kragujevac from the Socialist Republic of Croatia.

Monument to Resistance and Freedom by sculptor Ante Gržetić, built in 1963. A slim, tapering, Y-shaped concrete form, 12 metres tall, with a bronze semi-abstract sculpture of a wounded figure in front of it. Its position marks a number of mass graves from the massacre.

dedicated to a fifteen-year-old Roma boy who was shot and buried at this location, along with a group of adults.

Stone Sleeper by Gradimir and Jelica Bosnic, built in 1970. This terraced courtyard is bordered by stout concrete blocks, punctuated by taller curved forms somewhat resembling unopened flower heads. It is dedicated to those from outlying towns and villages who were massacred here. The monument has recently undergone renovation.

top: View of the 21 October Museum, 1980s
left: Construction of the *Circles* monument in the 1980s
(image from The 21 October Museum, Kragujevac)
right: The *Circles* monument today

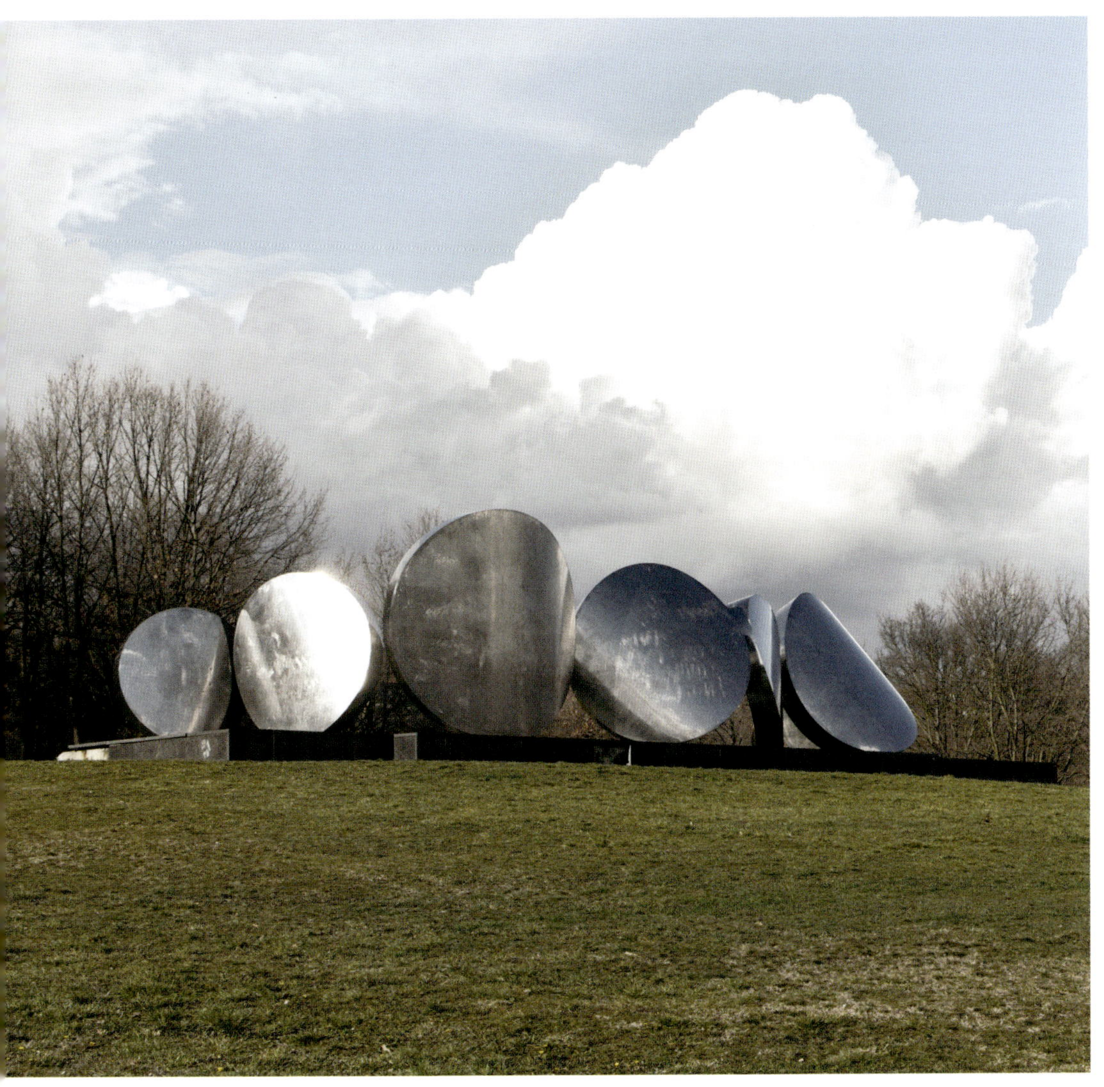

STATUS AND CONDITION

Most of the monuments are in good condition. Despite some vandalism (for instance, the eternal flame in front of the museum was extinguished a few years ago), the site is well respected, with tens of thousands of visitors every year. Since 1953, the biggest commemorative event takes place here every 21 October (a Serbian national holiday). In recent years, the televised ceremony has drawn crowds of more than 50,000 people, alongside Serbian politicians and ambassadors.

KRUŠEVO (KRU-sheh-voh)

NAME: Ilinden Memorial, also known as
'Makedonium'
LOCATION: Kruševo, Macedonia
YEAR COMPLETED: 1974 (4 years to build)
DESIGNERS: Jordan Grabul and Iskra Grabul
COORDINATES: N41°22'38.7", E21°14'54.2"
DIMENSIONS: 25 metres high
MATERIALS: Poured concrete, rebar and glass

HISTORY

The spomenik at Kruševo commemorates both the resistance fighters who took part in the Ilinden Uprising of 1903 against the Ottoman Empire and the partisan fighters of the National Liberation War (World War II).

On 2 August 1903, rebels from the Internal Macedonian Revolutionary Organisation fought Ottoman rule in present-day Kruševo. They established a provisional government and proclaimed the newly liberated region the Kruševo Republic, under the leadership of school teacher turned war hero Nikola Karev. In less than two weeks, the separatist territory was returned to Ottoman control as 176,000 Turkish soldiers crushed the uprising, massacring nearly 9,000 people in retaliation. Nevertheless, these events were a factor in the eventual collapse of Ottoman rule. The brutal way the rebellion was dealt with prompted European powers to intervene, increasing recognition of Macedonia's plight. While there are no substantial links between the uprising and the Macedonia of today, the short-lived separatist movement has been mythologised as an important part of the country's historical struggle for independence. The uprising was named 'Ilinden' because the revolt took place on 2 August, feast day of St Elijah in the Eastern Orthodox churches, 'Ilinden' being the Macedonian equivalent of 'Elijah'.

The Kruševo Partisan Detachment formed on 19 August 1942 and fought against Axis troops across Macedonia until Kruševo's liberation by Soviet-backed Bulgarians in autumn 1944. Macedonia was officially declared a nation state during the Anti-fascist Assembly for the National Liberation of Macedonia (ASNOM), held on 2 August 1944, a date chosen as a symbolic link to the Ilinden Uprising. The ASNOM considered itself the 'Second Ilinden'. This date is celebrated in Macedonia today as the Day of the Republic.

DESIGN AND CONSTRUCTION

In the early 1970s, a commission was appointed to organise the construction of a memorial complex dedicated to these events. Husband and wife artists Jordan and Iskra Grabul were chosen to collaborate on the design of the monument, but the process was fraught with disagreement: the commission wanted a more figurative memorial than the abstract form proposed by the Grabuls. Eventually, a compromise was reached and the completed complex opened on 2 August 1974, marking the 30th anniversary of

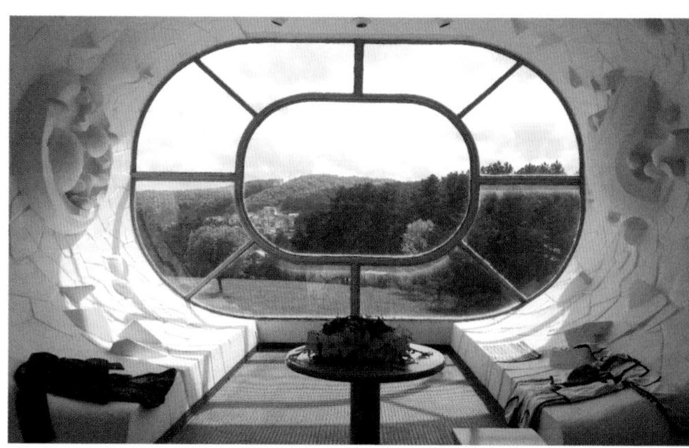

above: An interior sculpted relief
right: A postcard from the 1980s shows the amphitheatre in front of the Makedonium

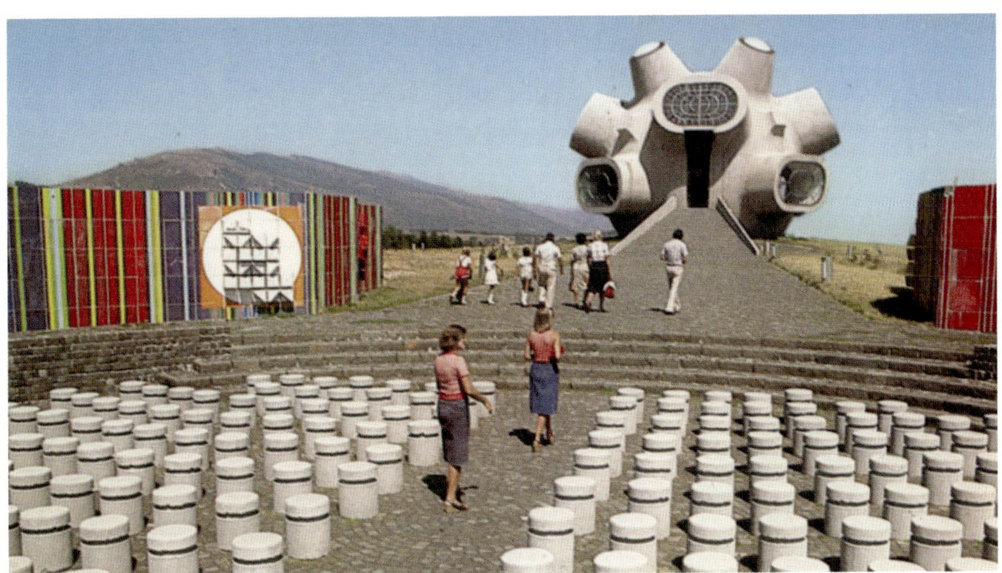

the Anti-fascist Assembly for the National Liberation of Macedonia and the 71st anniversary of the Ilinden Uprising.

Although the memorial is officially named 'Ilinden'; it is also known as 'Makedonium', after the construction company that built it. At the entrance to the complex is a series of large concrete forms resembling broken chainlinks. Along the path to the Makedonium is a crypt area where 58 tapered pillars protrude from the side of a tilted wall, each capped with a bronze plaque. The plaques bear dates and locations refering to the Ilinden Uprising of 1903. Approaching the Makedonium dome, visitors walk through a large amphitheatre containing some 200 seating bollards, flanked by two curved concrete walls decorated with colourful abstract bas-reliefs (by the painter Petar Mazev). The Makedonium itself is a 25-metre-tall concrete building resembling the head of a mace. Protruding windows admit light into the building; four of these are glazed with abstract patterned stained-glass, designed by artist Borko Lazeski, to represent the four seasons. Above these are smaller protrusions lined with sculpted reliefs intended to represent four seminal ages of Macedonia: antiquity, Turkish rule,

the time of conflict and that of independence. Centrally placed on the floor is a sculptural form evoking the 'eternal flame', which can be targeted with purpose-built lights to reveal the sunburst pattern of the Macedonian flag. Also within the Makedonium is a simple tomb for Nikola Karev, with a block inscribed with his name. Karev's remains were interred here in 1990.

Since its opening in 1974, this spomenik has been a well-maintained and popular attraction. Despite the fall of Yugoslavia, which saw many other spomeniks across the former territories destroyed, regular memorial events are still staged here. However, its popularity is largely thanks to its commemoration of the Macedonian nationalist hero Nikola Karev. It has been claimed that the monument is as anti-Yugoslav as it is anti-Ottoman, because of the strong nationalist symbolism invested in it.

In 2018, the exterior of the spomenik memorial underwent a comprehensive restoration project, with water stains removed, the structure repainted and damaged concrete repaired.

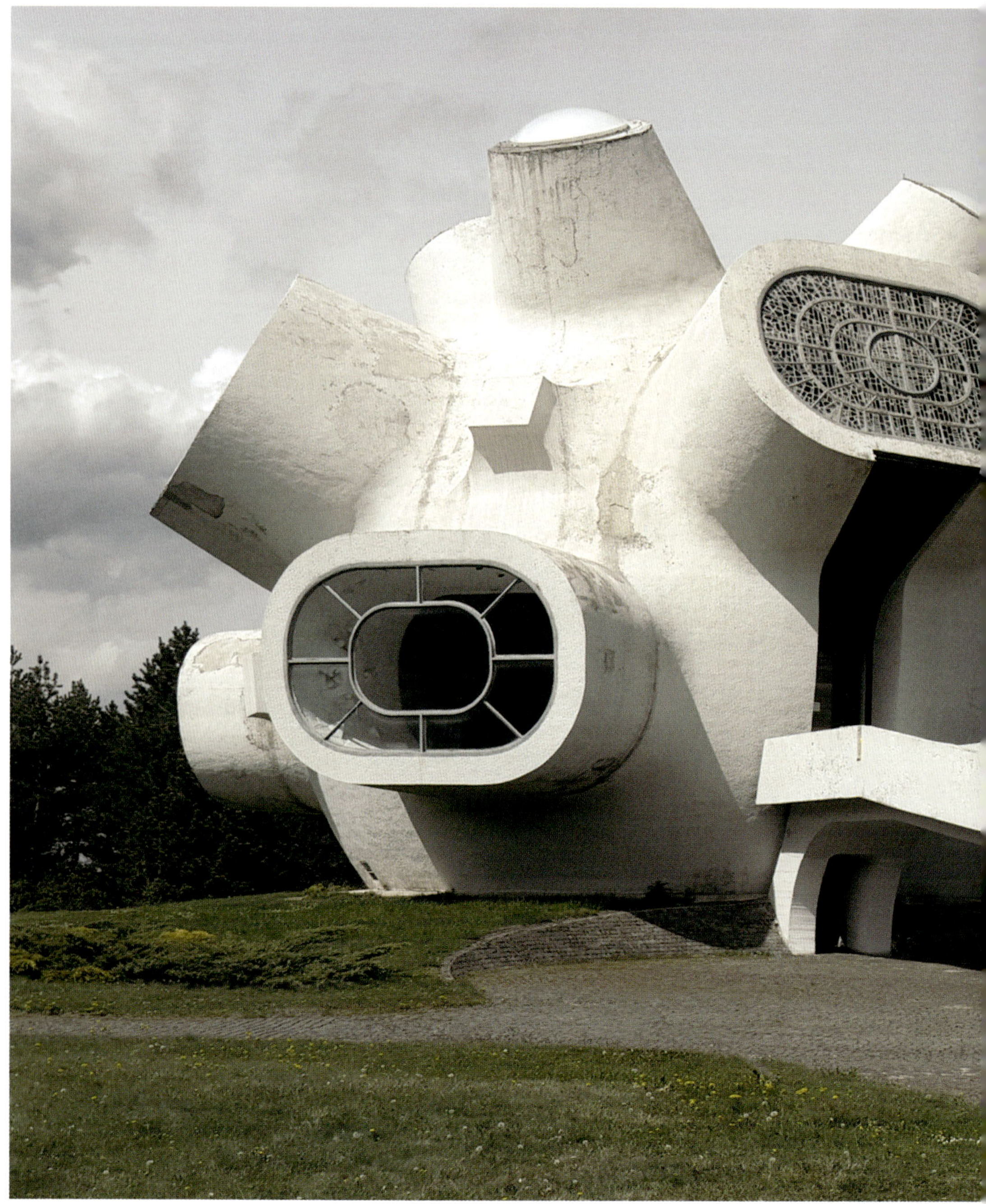

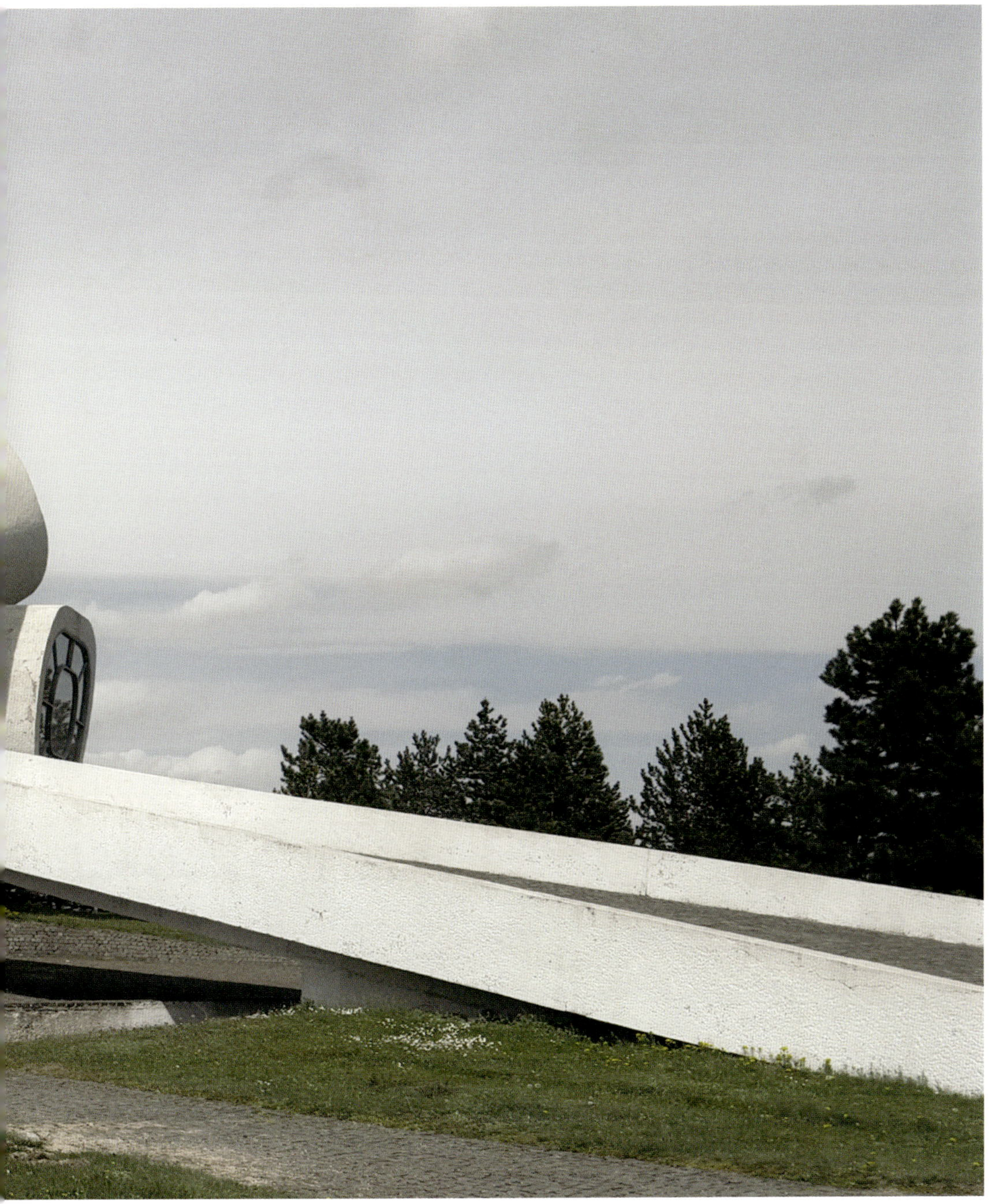

LANDOVICË (LYAN-doh-vee-tsa)

NAME: Monument to Boro Vukmirović and
Ramiz Sadiku
LOCATION: Landovicë, Kosovo
YEAR COMPLETED: 1963
DESIGNERS: Miodrag Pecić and Svetomir Basara
COORDINATES: N42°15'17.5", E20°40'55.0"
DIMENSIONS: 10 metres high
MATERIALS: Poured concrete and rebar

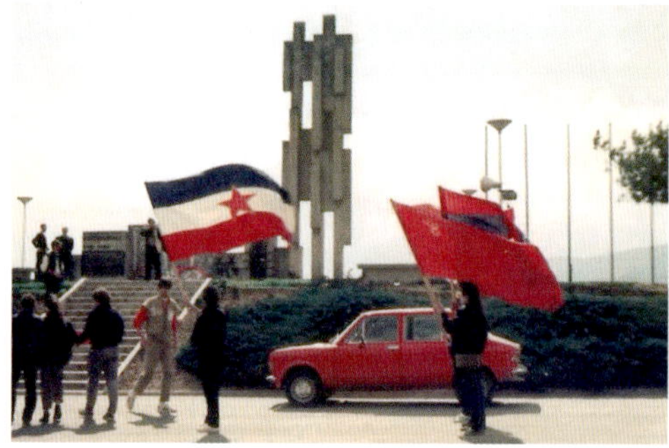
A commemoration event at the site in the 1980s
(photograph by Androvic DJ-Rale)

HISTORY

Two young members of the Communist Party of Yugoslavia, Boro Vukmirović (an ethnic-Serb) and Ramiz Sadiku (an ethnic-Albanian), became close friends as they helped the partisans to combat the Italian occupation in Kosovo and Albania in early 1941. Vukmirović spread the message of the resistance through radio broadcasts and newspapers, while Sadiku published and distributed political pamphlets condemning the Italian occupation. He also spoke at rallies, for which he was arrested several times. On 7 April 1943, while travelling together to Prizren, the pair were captured by Italian and Albanian occupation forces just east of Landovicë. When their identities were discovered, they were tortured to extract information on resistance activity. After three days of unsuccessful interrogation, preparations were made to execute the prisoners individually. However, Vukmirović and Sadiku embraced each other, refusing to be separated. They were shot together as they shouted their support for the resistance movement.

After the war, the story of their friendship became legendary and the notions of Brotherhood and Unity became the most revered guiding principles of Yugoslav society. The story of two young men, a Serb and an Albanian, becoming the best of friends and refusing to be separated in the face of death, evolved into one of the most evocative examples of that concept. They were both posthumously granted the Order of the People's Hero award.

DESIGN AND CONSTRUCTION

In the early 1960s, a memorial was proposed to commemorate Boro Vukmirović and Ramiz Sadiku at the site where they were executed. Designed by Miodrag Pecić and Svetomir Basara, with additional artistic elements by Hilmija Ćatović,

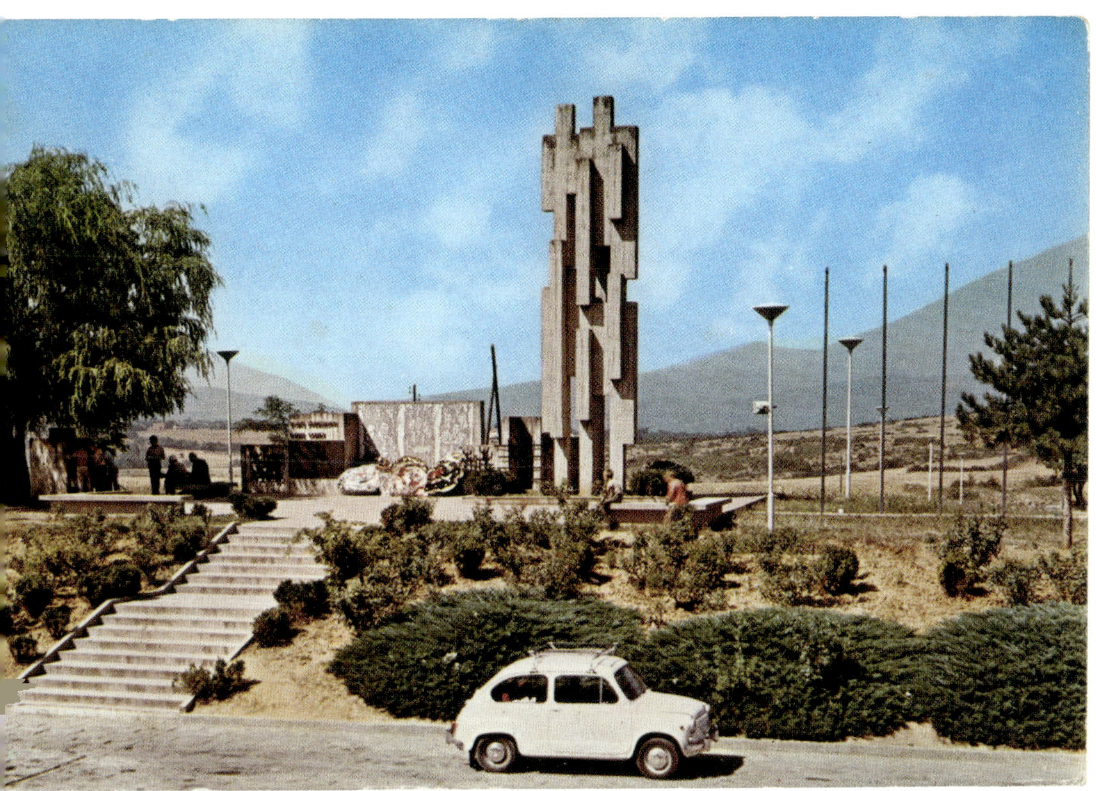

A postcard from the 1960s of the Landovica spomenik

the monument was a 10-metre-tall sturdy, rectilinear, interlocking form, intended as an abstract rendering of Vukmirović and Sadiku's embrace. In front of this, a large mosaic created by Ćatović depicted their execution.

The monument was officially opened on 30 November 1963. The event was attended by President Josip Tito and included a reading by Albanian poet Adem Gajtani of his famous work about the two friends, 'Boro dhe Ramiz'. (The poem became a standard text, recited and memorised by Yugoslav schoolchildren.)

STATUS AND CONDITION

As Yugoslavia disintegrated in the early 1990s, so the memorial fell into disrepair. In 1999, after the Kosovo War, the new government of Kosovo decided to demolish the spomenik complex. In its place they built a Martyrs' Cemetery for Kosovo Liberation Army (KLA) soldiers who had died during the Battle of Jeshkovës in March 1999. Other memorials to the two friends have suffered similar fates.

Today, the KLA Martyrs' Cemetery has undergone significant expansion, and no traces of the original spomenik remain.

LEPOGLAVA (LEH-poh-glah-vah)

NAME: Lepoglava Memorial Graveyard
LOCATION: Lepoglava, Croatia
YEAR COMPLETED: 1981
DESIGNER: Stevan Luketić
COORDINATES: N46°13'00.6", E16°01'46.0"
DIMENSIONS: 5 metres high
MATERIALS: Aluminium

HISTORY

At the end of World War I, after the fall of Austro-Hungary and the creation of the Kingdom of Yugoslavia, the Lepoglava prison continued to house political prisoners: in the 1930s, Josip Tito, who would later become President of the Socialist Federal Republic of Yugoslavia, was incarcerated here, accused of communist agitation. With the invasion of the Kingdom of Yugoslavia by Axis powers in April 1941, Lepoglava became part of the Axis-controlled Independent State of Croatia (NDH). The Ustaše (an ultra-nationalist NDH militia) began to use the prison to house anti-fascist rebels and communist dissidents.

On 10 July 1943, communist partisans from the 12th Slavonian and Kalnikov units attacked the prison. Losing only 26 fighters, they freed over 800 prisoners, around 100 of whom joined the resistance movement. In December 1943, the Ustaše converted the prison into a death camp and renamed it the Lepoglava Workers' Camp for Men, Women and Children. While exact figures are unknown, some sources estimate that more than 5,000 people were killed here. One of the most infamous examples of mass murder occurred on 30 April 1945. Fearing the town might soon be liberated by partisan fighters, the Ustaše commander of all NDH concentration camps, Maks Luburić, ordered the killing of Lepoglava's remaining inmates. About 960 prisoners, mostly youths and elderly civilians, were reported to have been executed at a small forest clearing just north of the town and their remains buried in a pit. It is also alleged that several hundred other prisoners were transported to Jasenovac death camp, where the majority were also murdered. In May 1945, less than a week after these events, the NDH government and Ustaše withdrew from the region to escape advancing partisan armies.

Luburić fled to Spain, where in 1957 he founded the Croatian National Resistance (which followed the same ideology as the Ustaše). In 1967, he was assassinated on behalf of Yugoslav State Security by an Ustaše radical infiltrator.

DESIGN AND CONSTRUCTION

In the 1970s, a mother petitioned the Lepoglava authorities to find the body of her daughter, who was killed at the camp during the war. Although the body was never found, a number of mass graves were discovered. Lepoglava's Alliance of Anti-Fascist Fighters proposed a memorial to commemorate these victims and gave the commission to Montenegrin artist Stevan Luketić. The memorial was officially opened on 10 July 1981, exactly 38 years after the partisans' liberation of the prison at Lepoglava. The central element of the memorial complex is a 5-metre-tall faceted, geometric abstract aluminium sculpture. It stands in a circular red brick-paved courtyard dotted with stone markers commemorating those interred here, both murdered civilians and partisans killed in the 1943 attack on the prison.

STATUS AND CONDITION

Since the breakup of Yugoslavia in the 1990s and the subsequent independence of Croatia in 1991, the memorial complex has fallen into disrepair, with many elements damaged. While the central sculpture in still intact, it is weather-stained and scratched with graffiti. Despite the poor overall condition of the site, annual commemorative events are still regularly held here. Lepoglava prison continued to operate through the Yugoslav era and is still in use today. Directions to the site are well signposted (although there is no information at the site itself). Some restoration has taken place, but the municipality concedes there is more to be done, as the spomenik is an attraction that regularly features in local media.

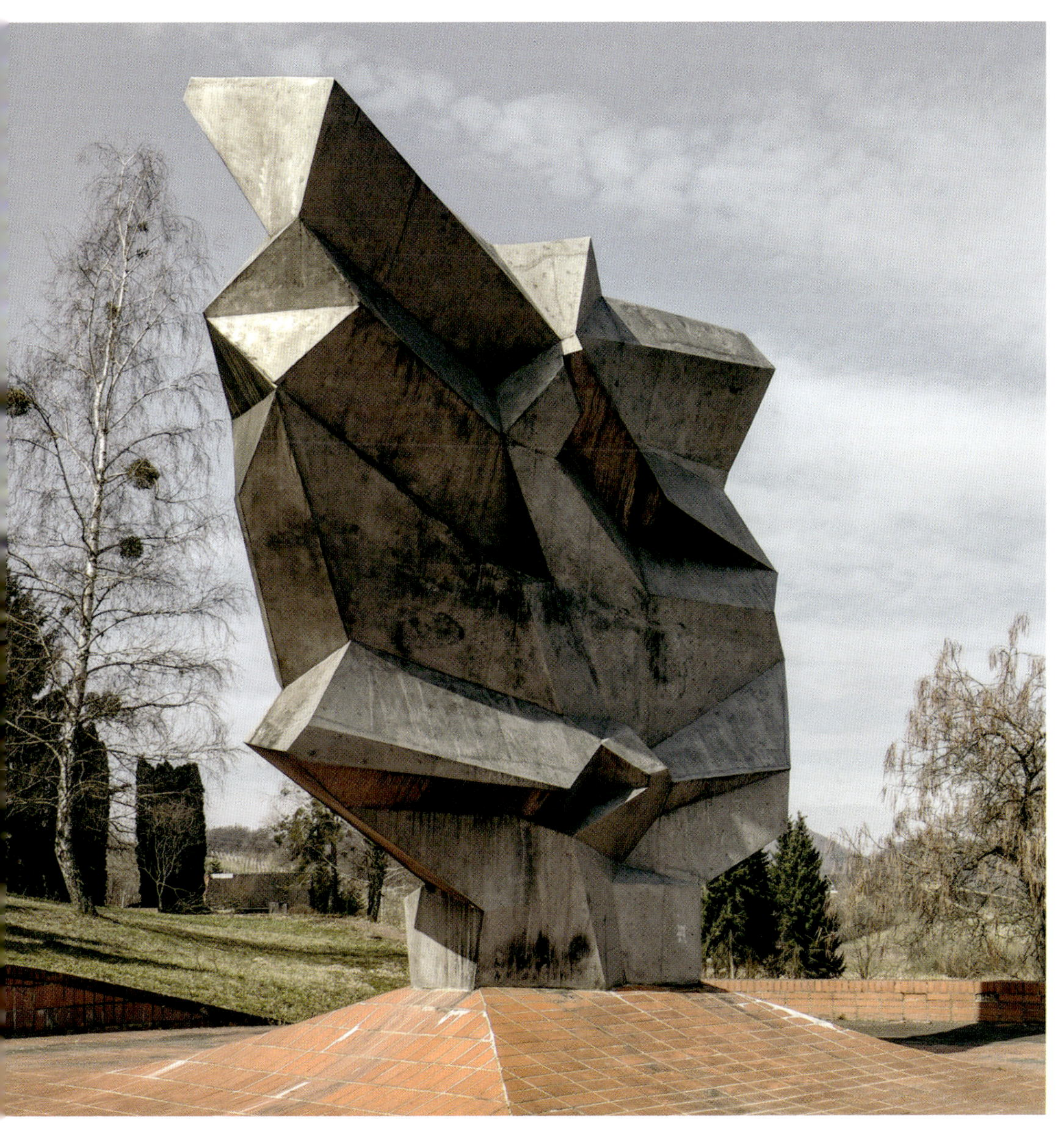

LESKOVAC (LES-koh-vats)

NAME: Monument to the Revolution
LOCATION: Leskovac, Serbia
YEAR COMPLETED: 1971
DESIGNER: Bogdan Bogdanović
COORDINATES: 42°58'59.0"N 21°56'34.2"E
DIMENSIONS: 12 metre high monolith
MATERIALS: Stone blocks and bronze

The Leskovac partisans fought continuously at great cost to both the rebel fighters and civilians. The city changed hands several times until, in 1944, the partisans began to push the German forces out completely. However, the Allies believed the Germans were still hiding in Leskovac, so on 6 September 1944, 50 US B-29s bombed the city centre. Some German forces were destroyed, but more than 1,840 of the city's buildings were levelled and between 2,500 and 4,000 civilians were killed. On 11 October 1944, during Operation Niš, the Partisan Army's 15th Serbian Brigade (with assistance from Soviet and Bulgarian forces) freed Leskovac for the last time.

HISTORY

After their invasion and occupation of the Kingdom of Yugoslavia in April 1941, the Germans established the Territory of the Military Commander in Serbia, controlled by the puppet Government of National Salvation and its appointed prime minister, the Serbian Nazi-collaborator Milan Nedić (see page 104). The brutal German occupation reserved especially harsh treatment for communist-Serbs, Jews and Roma civilians, many of whom were sent to concentration camps.

By July 1941, a partisan and Chetnik uprising had spread across Serbia, with hundreds of Leskovac citizens organised into armed rebel units, ensconced in the wooded outskirts of the city. The Germans' superior firepower necessitated that the rebels use guerrilla tactics to attack their enemy, which the Germans responded to by carrying out reprisals against the population of Leskovac. In December 1941, following the killing of three German officers by rebel fighters, the Germans rounded up over 300 civilians (mainly Roma) and transported them to nearby Hisar Hill, where they were executed. While such actions did not deter the partisan resistance, the Chetniks did not want to provoke further civilian killings. In part this led to their withdrawal from the resistance movement, and their eventual collaboration with Axis forces. Despite this, and the continued executions, the partisan-led resistance in Leskovac continued to grow.

DESIGN AND CONSTRUCTION

In 1964, Serbian architect Bogdan Bogdanović was commissioned to create a spomenik complex on Hisar Hill in honour of the many civilians who had been killed there. After seven years of planning and construction, the memorial was opened by former prime minister Petar Stambolić on 4 July 1971 (40 years since the Serbian uprising against Axis forces).

The primary element is a chimney-like construction, narrowed at its waist and made of stone blocks. It is often referred to as 'The Goddess of Victory', but originally named 'The Forest Goddess' by Bogdanović. It is 12-metres-tall, and is topped by a large symmetrical bronze form simultaneously throne-like and reminiscent of an ancient regal crown. Originally, this element had four heavy, beaded forms suspended from it, but these disappeared during the 1980s. In front of the Goddess sculpture is a small sunken amphitheatre, around which are arranged 34 stone blocks (reminiscent of ancient stećak stones), ranging from 1 to 2.5 metres tall. Fourteen of them are engraved with the names of local folk heroes. At the north entrance to the site, a 450-metre- long, stone-paved path leads up the hill to the memorial.

Along the pathway, small markers commemorate fallen partisan fighters. At the base of the hill Bogdanović created the Arapova Dolina memorial, dedicated to the group of civilians killed by German soldiers on 11 December 1941.

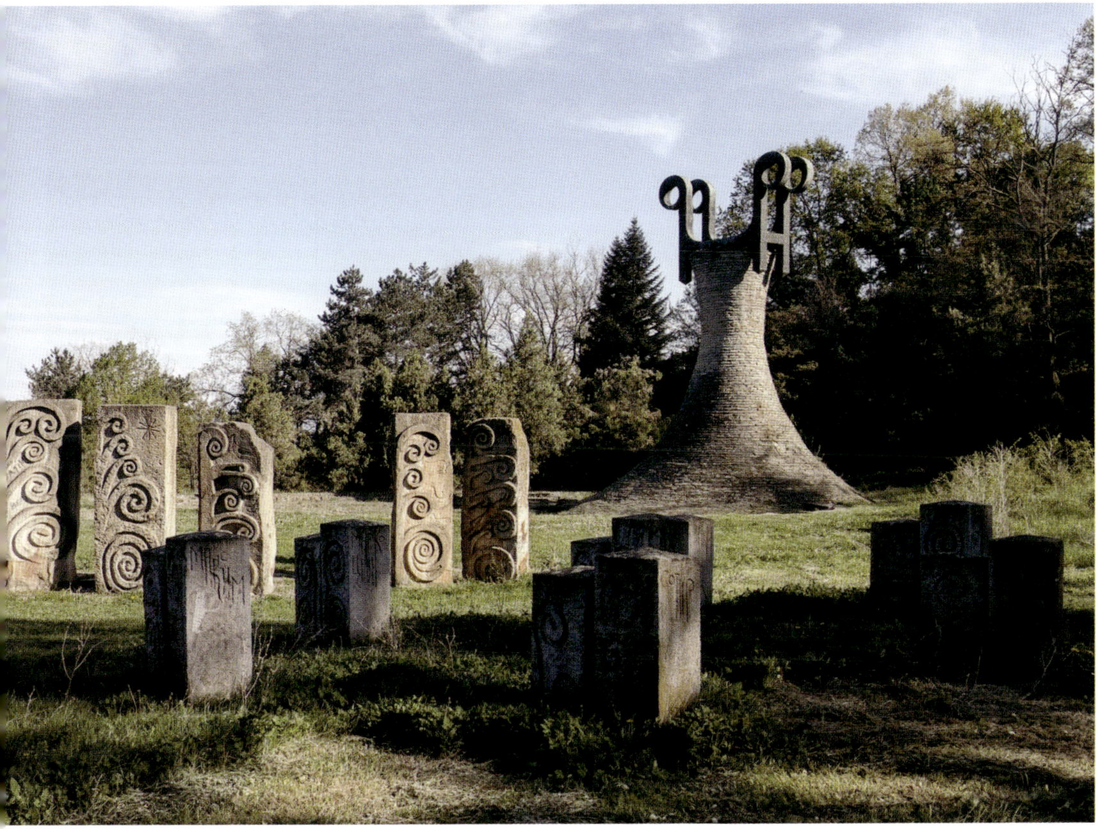

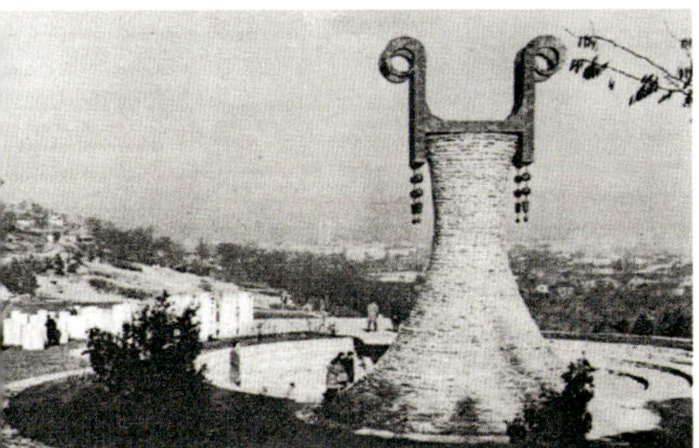

A photograph taken shortly after construction showing the original hanging bead forms (image from *Spomenici Narodnooslobodilačka Borbe Revolucije SR, 1941-1945*, Razumenka Popović Zuma, 1981)

During the 1990s, this complex fell into a general state of neglect, though most of the individual sculptural elements survive in reasonable condition. In 2015, the Leskovac municipality proposed a 16,700 Euro restoration of the spomenik park. Most of the graffiti has since been cleaned away and the landscaping has been improved. Additional efforts are also underway to restore the park's lighting systems and to recreate the decorative metal entrance gates, which were stolen in the 1990s. Currently this work is still to be completed. Today, the spomenik park receives many visitors and hosts a number of annual commemorative events.

LUKOVDOL (LUK-ov-dul)

NAME: Monument to Ivan Goran Kovačić
LOCATION: Lukovdol, Croatia
YEAR COMPLETED: 1964
DESIGNER: Vojin Bakić
COORDINATES: N45°25'43.8", E15°07'34.0"
DIMENSIONS: 4 metres high and 3 metres wide
MATERIALS: Stainless steel

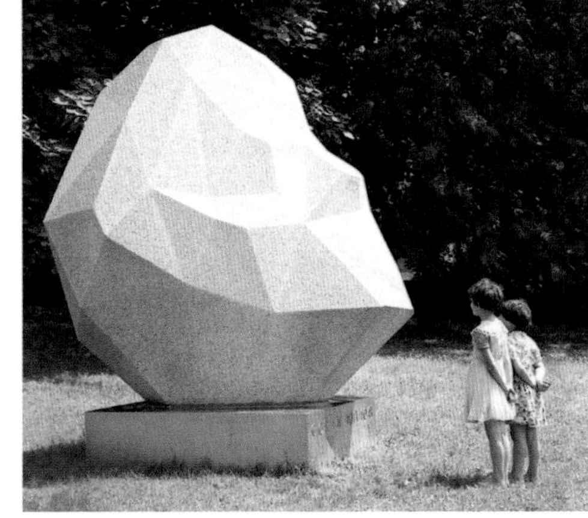

The stone version of the spomenik in Ribnjak Park, Zagreb, 1964
(image from the Tošo Dabac Archive, Museum of Contemporary Art, Zagreb)

HISTORY

Born on 21 March 1913 in the village of Lukovdol, Ivan Kovačić was an accomplished writer. His first collection of poetry, titled *Lirika* (*Lyrics*), was published in 1932. He adopted the nickname Goran, meaning 'mountain-man', in reference to the Gorski Kotar mountain region where Lukovdol is located.

A staunch supporter of the Croatian Peasant Party, Kovačić joined the partisan resistance soon after the invasion of the Kingdom of Yugoslavia by Axis forces in April 1941. While fighting with the partisans across Bosnia, he wrote extensively of the horrors inflicted by the Axis-aligned Ustaše military forces of the Independent State of Croatia (NDH). Kovačić wrote his most famous poem, *Jama* (*The Pit*), between 1942 and 1943, after witnessing such atrocities. Its title is in large part a reference to the karst pits of the Herzegovina region where his partisan unit discovered the bodies of the large number of ethnic-Serb civilians disposed of by Ustaše forces.

Kovačić was killed by Chetniks on 13 July 1943, while fighting with his unit in the village of Vrbica near the present-day town of Foča, Bosnia. *Jama* was published in the following year to widespread acclaim, was taught to schoolchildren throughout socialist Yugoslavia after the war, and became one of Croatia's most celebrated poems.

DESIGN AND CONSTRUCTION

In the early 1960s, Croatian sculptor Vojin Bakić was commissioned to create a memorial in Lukovdol, next to the writer's childhood home. He had been working on sculptures of Kovačić since 1946, after Yugoslavia's split with the USSR, these were becoming less Soviet realist in style and more abstract.

The central element of the memorial complex is a 4-metre-tall, semi-abstract stainless steel sculpture, whose facets are suggestive of human facial features. (A stone version of this sculpture, produced by Bakić at the same time, stands in Zagreb's Ribnjak Park.) There is also a large outdoor amphitheatre and other smaller sculptural elements. The opening on 21 March 1964 (the 51st anniversary of Kovačić's birth) included the first Goran's Spring competition for young writers and poets, an annual event at the site.

STATUS AND CONDITION

The Kovačić memorial site is in good condition and is much visited by tourists. Its commemorative events are well attended by the local populace, although in 2017, for the first time in 54 years, the Goran's Spring event could not be held due to lack of funding from the Croatian Ministry of Culture.

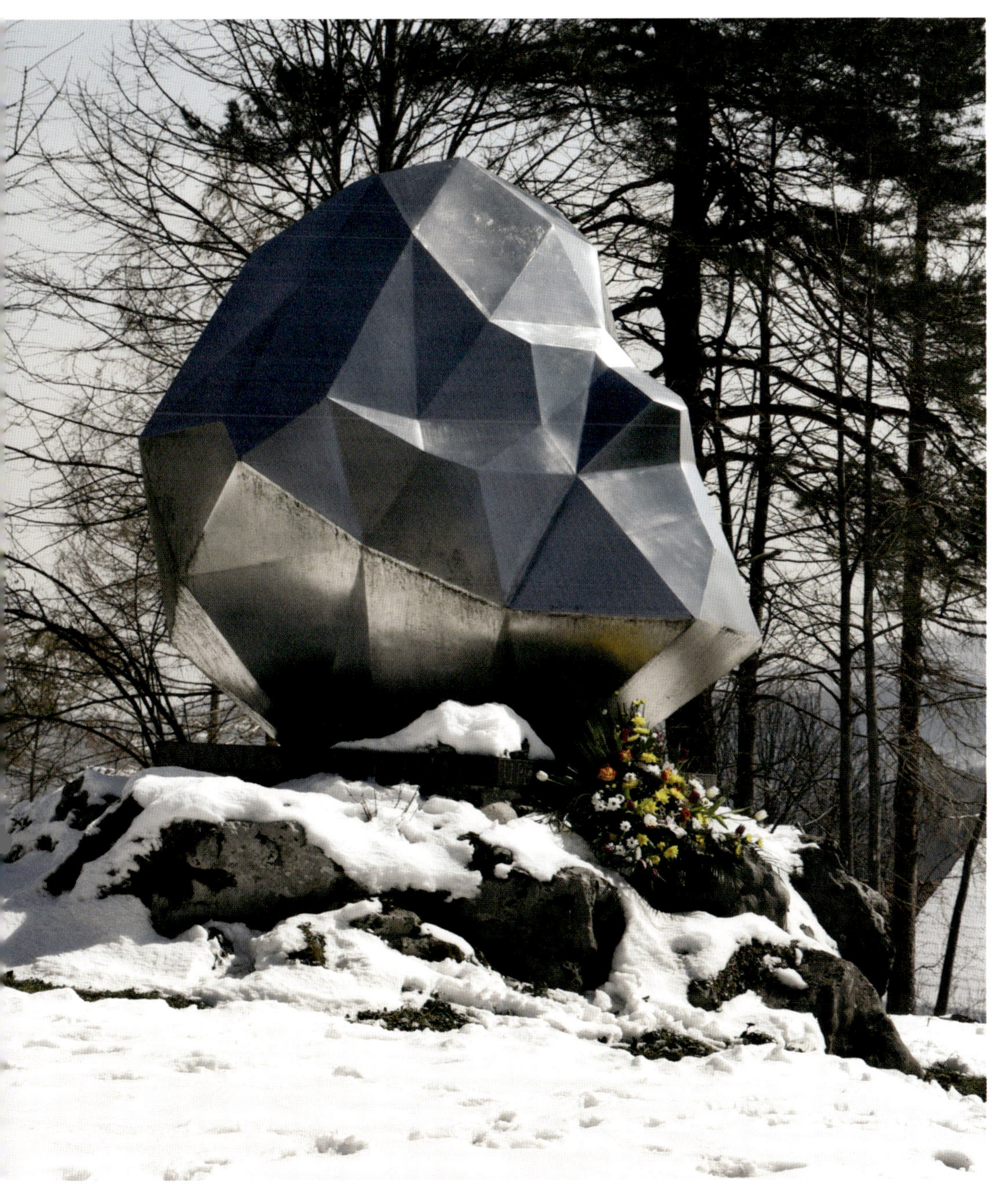

MAJDANPEK (MAHY-dan-pek)

NAME: Monument to the Liberators of Majdanpek
LOCATION: Majdanpek, Serbia
YEAR COMPLETED: unknown
DESIGNER: unknown
COORDINATES: N44°25'43.3", E21°56'34.4"
DIMENSIONS: 20 metres high
MATERIALS: Poured concrete and rebar

HISTORY

After their invasion and occupation of the Kingdom of Yugoslavia in April 1941, German forces established the Territory of the Military Commander in Serbia. Comprising roughly the same area as that of the country today, it was controlled by the puppet Government of National Salvation, with the Serbian Nazi-collaborator Milan Nedić as its appointed prime minister (see page 100).

The famous copper-mining and metallurgy town of Majdanpek, nestled in the Serbian Homolje Mountains, had all its resources seized by the German Army. They forced the miners to continue working, using the material they produced to benefit their war effort.

In July 1941, a Serbian resistance movement started in Bela Crkva, and spread across much of the country. Majdanpek citizens began to join organised resistance movements such as the communist-led partisans and the Serbian royalist Chetniks, but their attempts to gain control of the town failed. The Germans continued to extract valuable deposits from the mines at Majdanpek and at the nearby city of Bor, using thousands of prisoners as forced labour. As the end of the war approached, many of these prisoners were murdered. Majdanpek was finally liberated in late 1944 during the Belgrade Offensive, when Red Army troops freed towns from German control as they made their way to Belgrade.

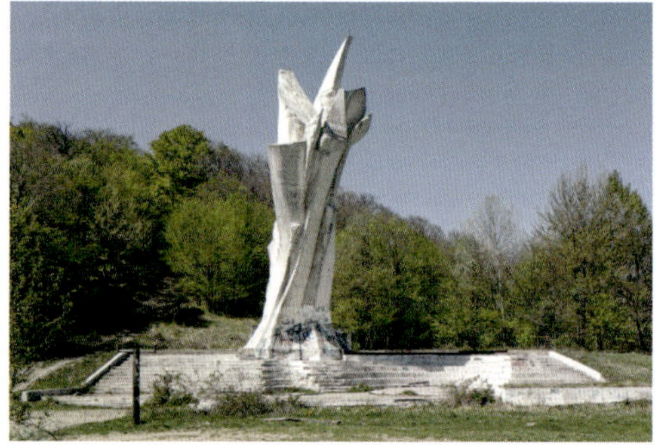

DESIGN AND CONSTRUCTION

This monument commemorates the fallen soldiers and civilians from the region who perished during the National Liberation War (World War II). Its concrete construction and surrounding paved terrace appear to date from the 1970s, although no definite information could be found.

STATUS AND CONDITION

The memorial does not appear to have suffered any major damage, although it has been heavily graffitied, as have the elements associated with it. The site appears completely abandoned and there is no evidence that commemorative events are held here.

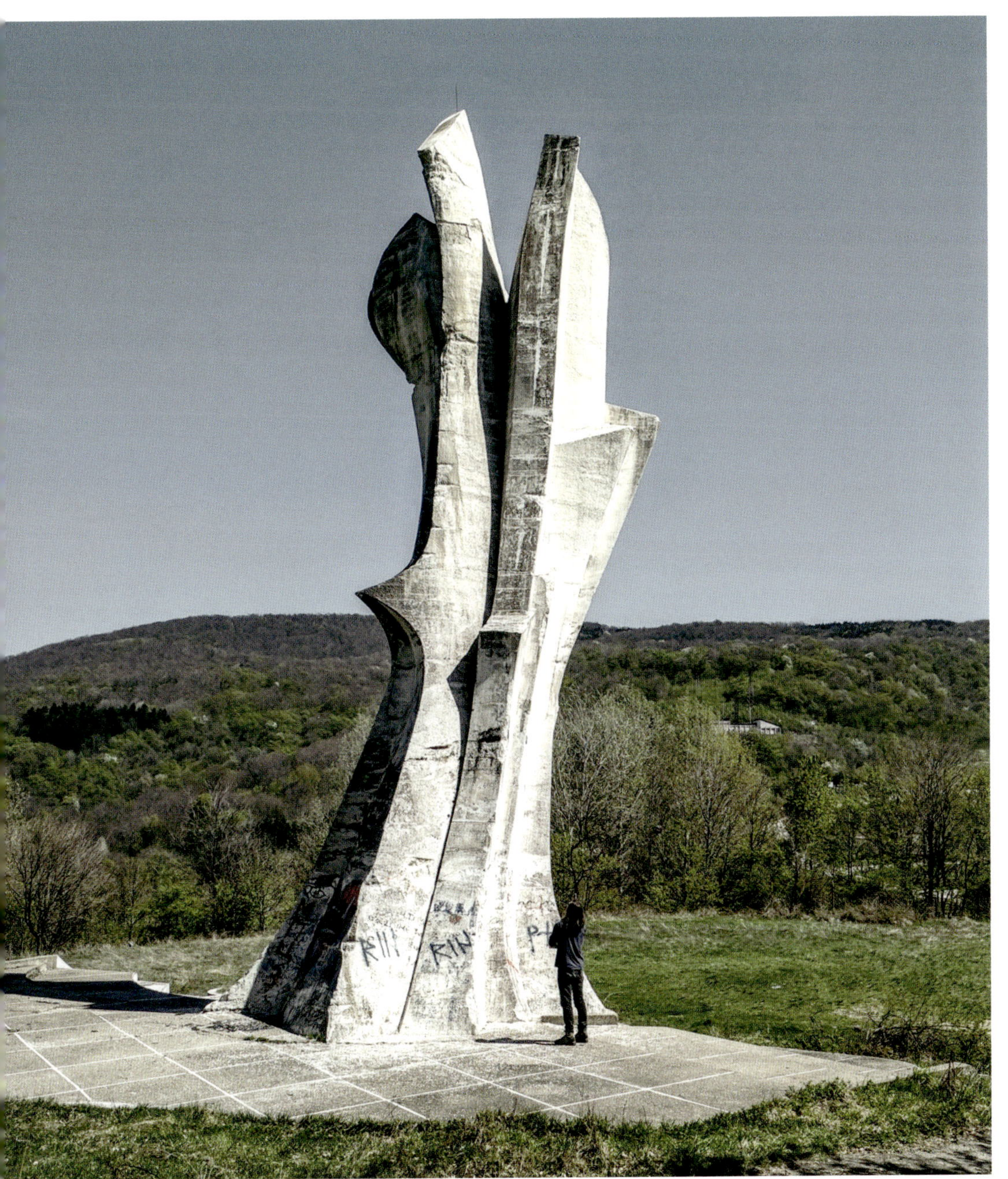

MAKARSKA (MAK-ar-skah)

NAME: Monument to the Revolution
LOCATION: Glavica Hill in Makarska, Croatia
YEAR COMPLETED: 1974
DESIGNERS: Matija Salaj and Šime Vulas
COORDINATES: N43°17'45.7", E17°00'59.1"
DIMENSIONS: Eleven vertical fins, 3–10 metres high
MATERIALS: Poured concrete and rebar

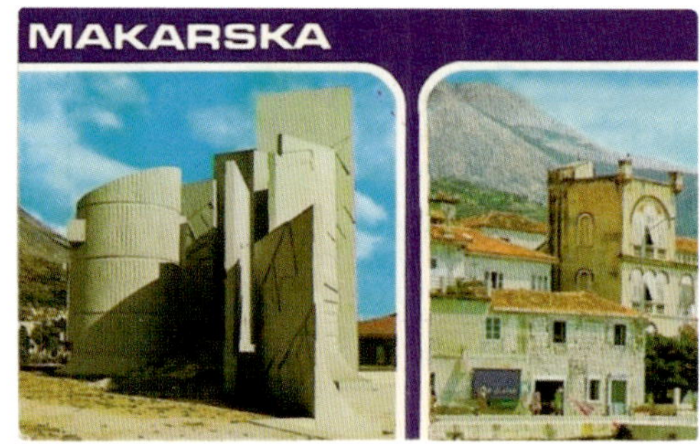

A postcard showing the rear tower before its conversion into an observatory

HISTORY

Soon after the Axis invasion of the Kingdom of Yugoslavia in April 1941, the seaside town of Makarska was integrated into the Independent State of Croatia (NDH), a newly formed Axis-controlled puppet state. At the start of the war, the town served as headquarters for the NDH's Central Adriatic Naval Command, making it the focus of military activity on the Croatian riviera. This angered locals, who began to organise themselves against the occupation. Two partisan naval brigades were formed, named 'Biokovo' after a local mountain range. Turning their fishing boats into makeshift gunships, the Biokovo Partisans waged guerrilla offensives against Italian and NDH vessels from 1942 onwards, sinking and capturing dozens of Axis military craft.

In August 1942, General Renzo Dalmazzo, commander of the Italian 6th Corps, initiated Operation Albia, with the objective of destroying all partisan resistance along the Makarskan coast. Dalmazzo convinced Serbian royalist Chetnik fighters to assist his troops (a controversial act for the NDH leadership, who had little interest in using Serbian forces to fight in their territory).

During the operation, hundreds of civilians were massacred and their homes burnt to the ground. Nearly 1,000 partisan fighters across the Makarska/Biokovo region were killed, with the loss of only 17 Italians. In response, a formal Partisan Naval Headquarters was established in the nearby coastal city of Podgora. From here, the maritime offence against Italian and NDH forces continued until the liberation of the Dalmatian Adriatic in October 1944.

DESIGN AND CONSTRUCTION

The spomenik complex was constructed in 1974 to honour the fighters and civilians who died during the war. Designed by celebrated architect Matija Salaj alongside sculptor Šime Vulas, the monument consists of eleven vertical, white concrete fins bearing low-relief designs, ranging in height from 3 to 10 metres. The combined silhouette of all the fins is reminiscent of the local Biokovo Mountains. In front of the fins is a paved courtyard with a small central fountain. Behind them stands a 9-metre- tall cylindrical tower.

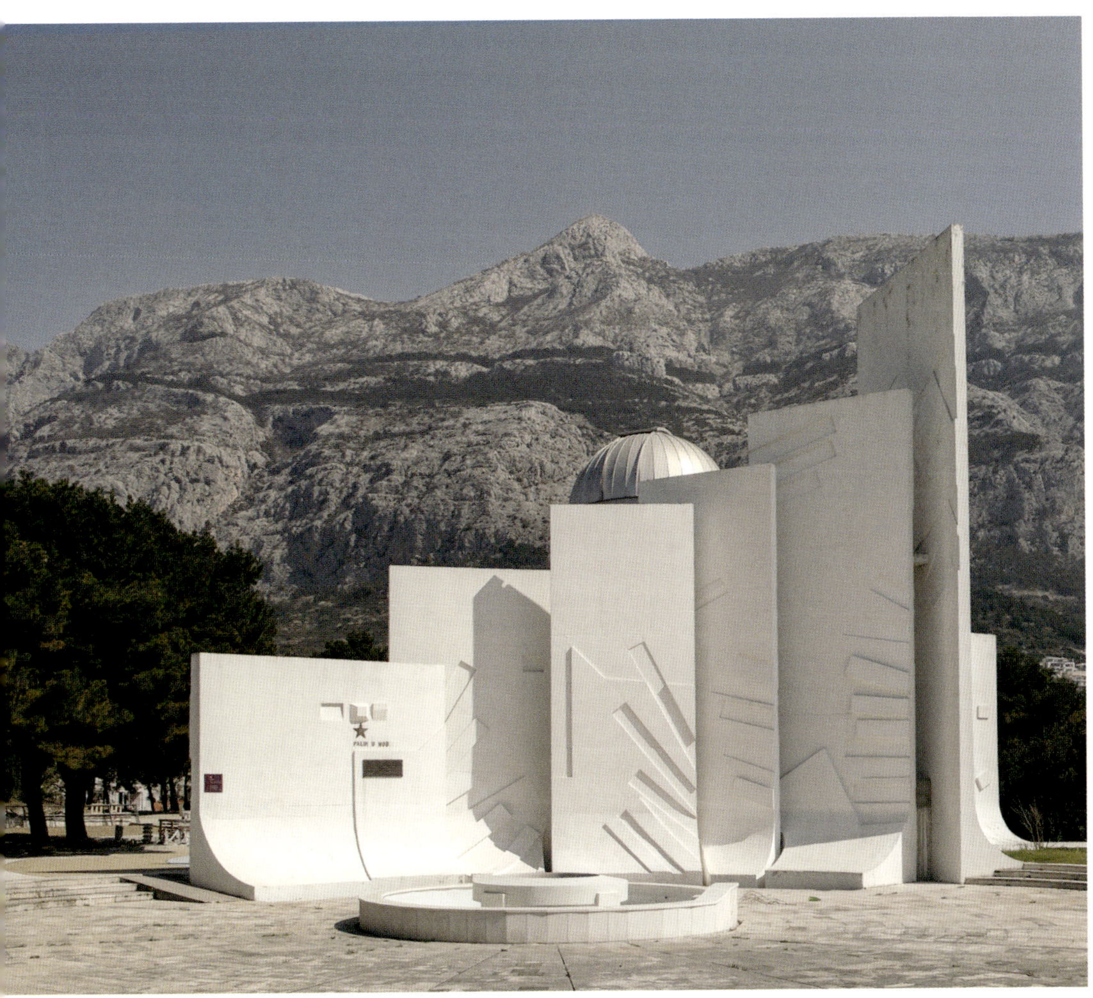

STATUS AND CONDITION

Once a revered landmark, by the early 1990s, with the onset of the Yugoslav Wars and Croatian independence, the monument was in disrepair. The electricity supply was cut off and the site became a haunt for drug addicts and vagrants.

In 2003, work began to turn the cylindrical tower of the spomenik into an observatory. In 2009, the adapted tower was opened to the public, complete with telescope. The monument itself is still undergoing renovation to transform it into an extensive 'Astro-Park', with the majority of its original elements being preserved and maintained. The complex is well visited and annual commemorative events are now held here again.

MAKLJEN (MAK-lyen)

NAME: 'The Poet' or 'The Fist' or Monument to the Battle of the Wounded or the Battle of Neretva
LOCATION: Mount Makljen, FBiH, Bosnia and Herzegovina
YEAR COMPLETED: 1978 (2 years to build)
DESIGNER: Boško Kućanski
COORDINATES: N43°50'33.9", E17°35'49.8"
DIMENSIONS: 14 metres high and 12 metres wide
MATERIALS: Poured concrete and rebar

HISTORY

In winter 1942, Hitler feared possible defeat in North Africa and at the Battle of Stalingrad. If this happened, he believed there would be an Allied invasion of Yugoslavia. In preparation, he ordered his commander-in-chief in southeast Europe, Alexander Löhr, to plan the complete elimination of partisan resistance. Löhr created 'Operation Case White', which began on 20 January 1943, with the additional objective of capturing partisan leader Josip Tito.

Tito and his partisan central command unit were able to evade the pursuing German Army throughout February. However, at Jablanica, on the eastern side of the Nevetva River valley, they found themselves in a critical situation. With Axis-Chetnik forces on the eastern bank of the river and German divisions approaching from the west, the Partisan Central Hospital was under immediate threat. Tito sent fighters over the strategically important Makljen Pass, and they successfully pushed back German forces at Gornji Vakuf. The Germans assumed he would continue this advance, but Tito, realising this would exchange one crisis for another, implemented a bold misdirection strategy. Instead of continuing across the Neretva, he ordered all the bridges over the river to be destroyed. The Germans redeployed their troops, expecting the partisan forces to head north, but Tito made makeshift repairs to one of the bridges and sent fighters across to clear the remaining Chetnik units on the east bank and establish a bridgehead. Fighting off a powerful

German advance and aerial bombardment from the Luftwaffe, the partisans (along with 4,000 wounded from the evacuated Central Hospital), were able to cross the river. The makeshift bridge was then destroyed to prevent pursuit. The partisans viewed this escape as a victory, as they had outmanoeuvred the larger and better-equipped German Army. Moreover, Tito had saved the wounded soldiers from being shot (as had occurred in Zlatibor in 1941), thus keeping his promise never to leave them behind.

These events were portrayed in the Yugoslav film *The Battle of Neretva* (1969), one of the most expensive films ever produced in the country. It was nominated for an Oscar in the category of Best Foreign Language Film at the 1969 US Academy Awards.

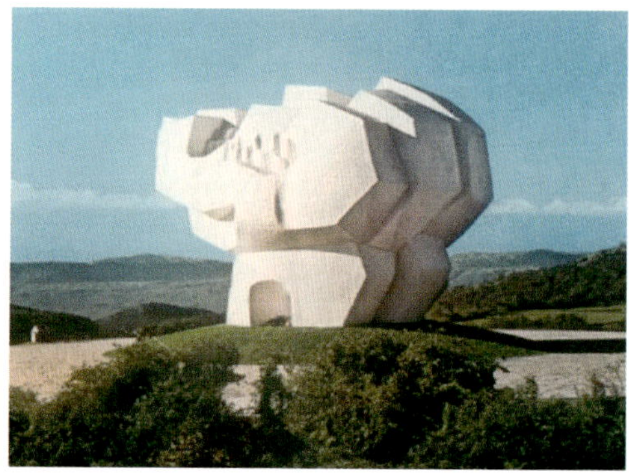

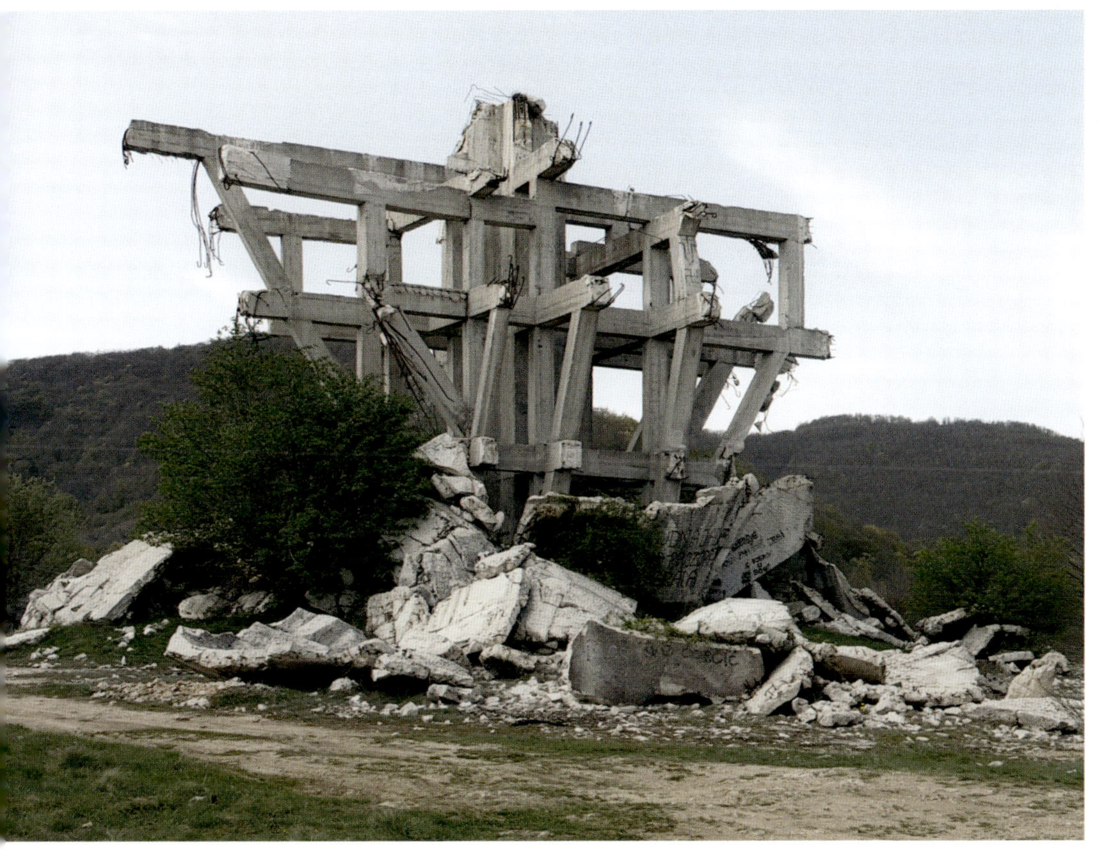

left: A view of the Makljen spomenik in the 1980s; *above*: All that remains of the monument after its destruction in 2000

DESIGN AND CONSTRUCTION

The sculptor Boško Kućanski was chosen by a national panel to create a monument commemorating the Battle of Neretva. Construction took two years, with a budget of 8.7 million Euros. The complex was inaugurated by Josip Tito on 12 November 1978. The central memorial was a 14-metre-tall, abstract concrete shape. Kućanski named this monument 'The Poet', although it was also referred to as 'Pesnica' – Bosnian for 'The Fist' (which it slightly resembles) – as an allusion to the strength of Tito. A large amphitheatre was situated 150 metres north of the main monument.

STATUS AND CONDITION

A popular spomenik during the Yugoslav era, Makljen was visited by the UK's Prince Charles in 1978. Every 4 July, tens of thousands would celebrate The Day of the Fighter National Holiday here. In the early 1990s, as the Yugoslav Wars began, the monument fell into disrepair. After Yugoslavia fell, The Day of the Fighter was delisted as a national event (it is now recognised only in Bosnia and Herzegovina). On 12 November 2000, the monument was dynamited by vandals, leaving only the framework standing. Despite being listed in 2010 as a protected cultural heritage site, to date there are no official plans for repair.

MARIBOR (MAHR-ee-boor)

NAME: Maribor Liberation Monument
LOCATION: Freedom Square, Maribor, Slovenia
YEAR COMPLETED: 1975
DESIGNER: Slavko Tihec
COORDINATES: N46°33'37.8", E15°38'56.7"
DIMENSIONS: 7 metres high
MATERIALS: Bronze

HISTORY

In 1900, the majority of Maribor's inhabitants were Austrian Germans. This situation changed after the fall of the Austro-Hungarian Empire in 1918. However, despite a policy of mandatory cultural assimilation, 25 per cent of the population remained ethnic-German. As the threat of World War II approached, the city – located on the Kingdom of Yugoslavia's northern border, directly adjacent to the expanding territory of the Greater German Reich – abandoned this policy in an attempt to advance diplomatic relations with Nazi Germany. Following the Axis invasion in April 1941, Germany annexed Maribor and the surrounding region. Immediate action was taken to Germanise the city: native Slovenes were expelled (to Croatia, Serbia and, later, to concentration camps), Slovene culture was marginalised, and ethnic Germans resettled in the territory. Many Slovenes organised themselves into resistance groups – such as the Liberation Front and the Slovene Partisans – to fight this oppression and ethnic cleansing. These movements were particularly strong in Slovenia as the country's very identity was under threat – not just from Germany, but also from Italy in the west and Hungary in the east. Despite the fact that the resistance were under-equipped and hugely outnumbered, the Germans found it difficult to deal with their tactics of sabotage and crude guerrilla warfare. The Nazis resorted to taking prominent locals hostage, warning that further attacks would result in their execution. Despite this, the attacks continued, so the threat to kill the innocent hostages was carried out, either by mass public hangings or firing squads.

To gain maximum impact, these killings were often made wilfully macabre. By the end of the war, 667 Slovene hostages had been murdered.

Several German munition plants and factories were located in Maribor, making it a target for Allied bombing. Over two dozen raids killed hundreds of civilians and levelled nearly half the city. When it was finally liberated on 9 May 1945, more than 2,600 of its residents had been killed.

After the war, any remaining ethnic-German civilians were expelled from Slovenia. Many partisan groups (particularly the anti-communist Slovene Home Guard) executed hundreds of Slovenes who had collaborated with the Nazis. These post-war extra-judicial killings were not discussed in public in Yugoslavia until 1975.

DESIGN AND CONSTRUCTION

The municipality commissioned native Maribor sculptor Slavko Tihec to create a memorial to the hostages and rebels killed by German forces. Located in Freedom Square, the monument was officially unveiled on 27 November 1975, on the 30th anniversary of the city's liberation. It is a 7-metre-tall, bronze and steel, slatted curvilinear sculpture, reminiscent of a medieval helmet, a bell, or a swiftly rising bubble before it breaks the surface. Between the slats is a deeper-set layer on which appear images – in the style of two-tone photographs – of partisan and Yugoslav heroes. The sculpture sits on an inscribed circular bronze platform: one of the inscriptions reproduces a letter written by Maribor resident Jože Fluks to his family, just before his execution in 1942.

STATUS AND CONDITION

A popular tourist attraction, the spomenik is in excellent condition. It is well publicised and remains one of the central landmarks of Maribor. However, there is no multi-lingual signage and it could not be verified if any official memorial events are held here. Locals have nicknamed the spomenik 'Kojak', because of its resemblance to the bald head of actor Telly Savalas, who played the detective in the eponymous 1970s television crime drama.

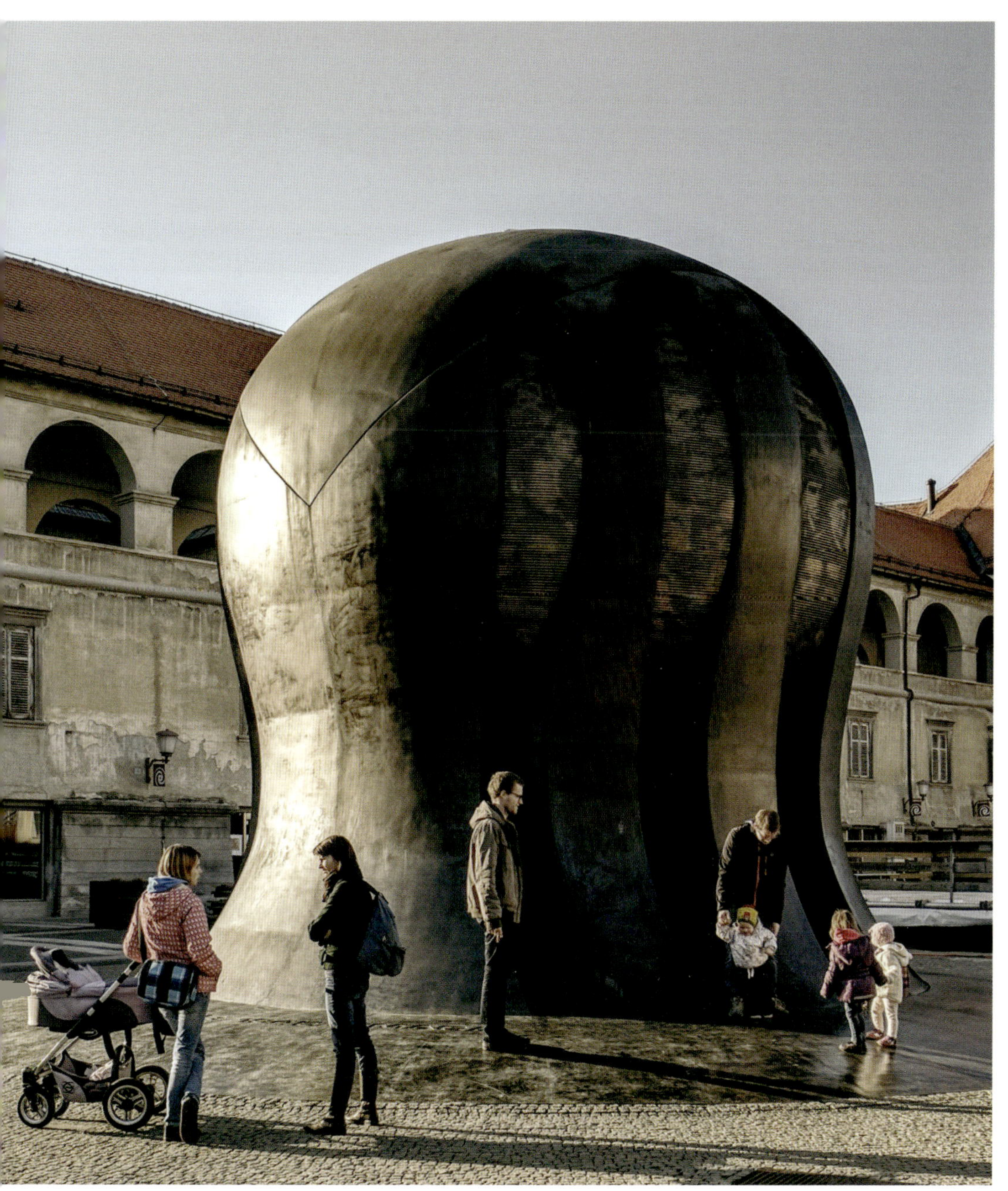

MEDENO POLJE (MEH-dee-noh POH-lyeh)

NAME: Monument to the Partisan Air Squadron
LOCATION: Medeno Polje, FBiH, Bosnia and
Herzegovina
YEAR COMPLETED: 1982
DESIGNER: unknown
COORDINATES: N44°34'18.7", E16°17'23.1"
DIMENSIONS: 8 metres high
MATERIALS: Poured concrete and rebar

HISTORY

In 1941, the Kingdom of Yugoslavia was invaded by Axis forces, giving the German Luftwaffe complete control of the skies.

This continued until the surrender of Italy in 1943 allowed the partisan resistance an opportunity to counter the situation using captured planes and other aircraft supplied by the Allies.

The first airfield was established in February 1944, on the outskirts of Medeno Polje (in present-day Bosnia). Rudimentary in nature, its grass runways were lit by gas torches, while a large bonfire on the summit of nearby Mount Oštrelj acted as a directional beacon for planes flying night missions. Relatively few sorties were flown from Medeno Polje (most were directed from the main partisan air command in Bari, Italy). The airfield's primary function was therefore the evacuation of wounded soldiers and civilians.

With Commander Josip Tito's partisan operation headquarters in nearby Drvar, only 30 kilometres south of the airfield, the location of Medeno Polje was of great strategic importance. It was also a vital staging point from which humanitarian and military aid from Bari could be

distributed across occupied Yugoslavia. Operation Manhole was one of the first such supply missions. On 23 February 1944, three gliders flown by the US 51st Troop Carrier Wing successfully landed 4,500 kilograms of arms and 30 Allied military advisors at the airfield. During May 1944, the US 60th Operation Group flew more than 1,000 people from the airfield, including some 700

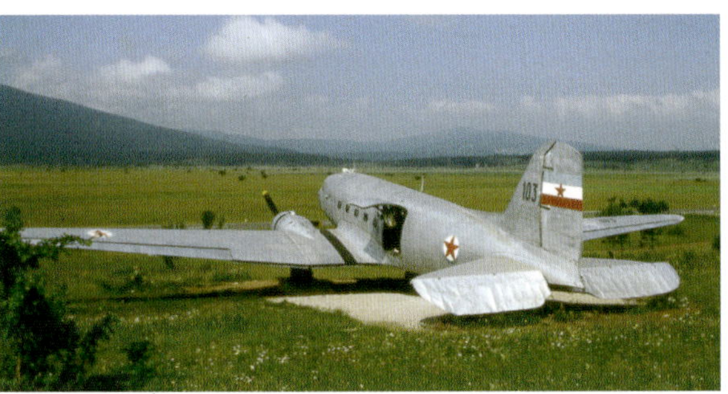

wounded partisan fighters. In total more than 2,000 wounded would be evacuated from Medeno Polje during the course of the war.

The Balkan Air Terminal Service, tasked with improving airfields behind enemy lines, was able to create a dozen additional airstrips across the Medeno Polje valley. These expansions more than doubled troop-carrier missions into the valley by the US 60th Group.

The airfield also acted as an extraction point for US airmen who had been shot down during the 1944 Oil Campaign raids on the Ploieşti oil fields of Romania, the source of more than 25 per cent of Germany's petroleum.

Medeno Polje operated almost continuously until 25 May 1944, when the partisans were driven out by German forces as part of Operation Knight's Leap, the offensive aimed at seizing Drvar and eliminating Tito.

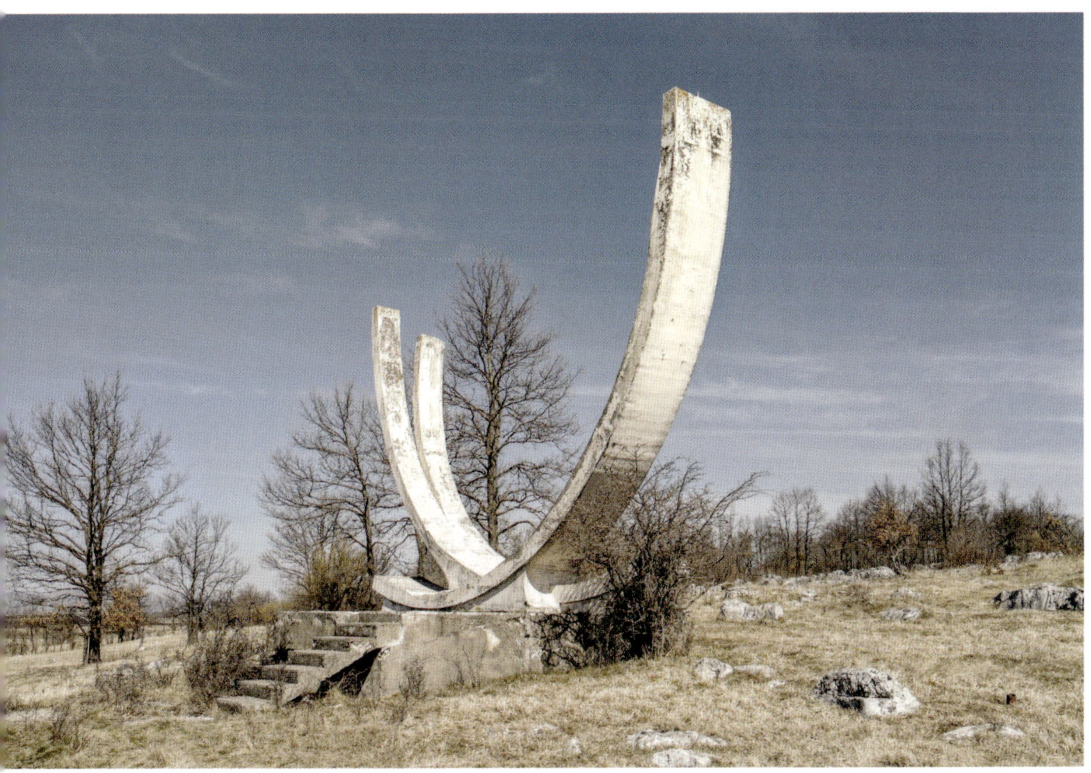

left: The Douglas C-47 Skytrain transport plane before its destruction in 1996, (photograph by Jacques Verlaeken)

DESIGN AND CONSTRUCTION

This spomenik commemorates local fallen fighters of the National Liberation War (World War II), as well as the inception of the Partisan Air Force. Little is known about its design. The monument consists of three partially intersecting concrete arcs, around 8 metres in height, reminiscent of the ribs of a beached ship or whale.

If the monument was built in 1982, at the same time as the DC-47 monument on the same site (see below), then its construction may well have been influenced by the 1979 film *Partizanska eskadrila* (*Partisan Squadron*), dramatising the events that took place at Medeno Polje airfield during the war.

STATUS AND CONDITION

The monument is in very poor condition, with many of its engravings and commemorative plaques destroyed. While the concrete super-structure is relatively intact, its base is cracked and chipped. Adjacent to the primary monument stood a Douglas C-47 Skytrain military transport plane, used during World War II by the Partisan Air Force. Originally open to the public, this fell into disrepair during the Yugoslav Wars of the 1990s, and in 1996 it was destroyed with explosives. Today only the concrete wheel-blocks remain. The site does not appear to be maintained; there is no evidence of regular visits or that commemorative events are held here.

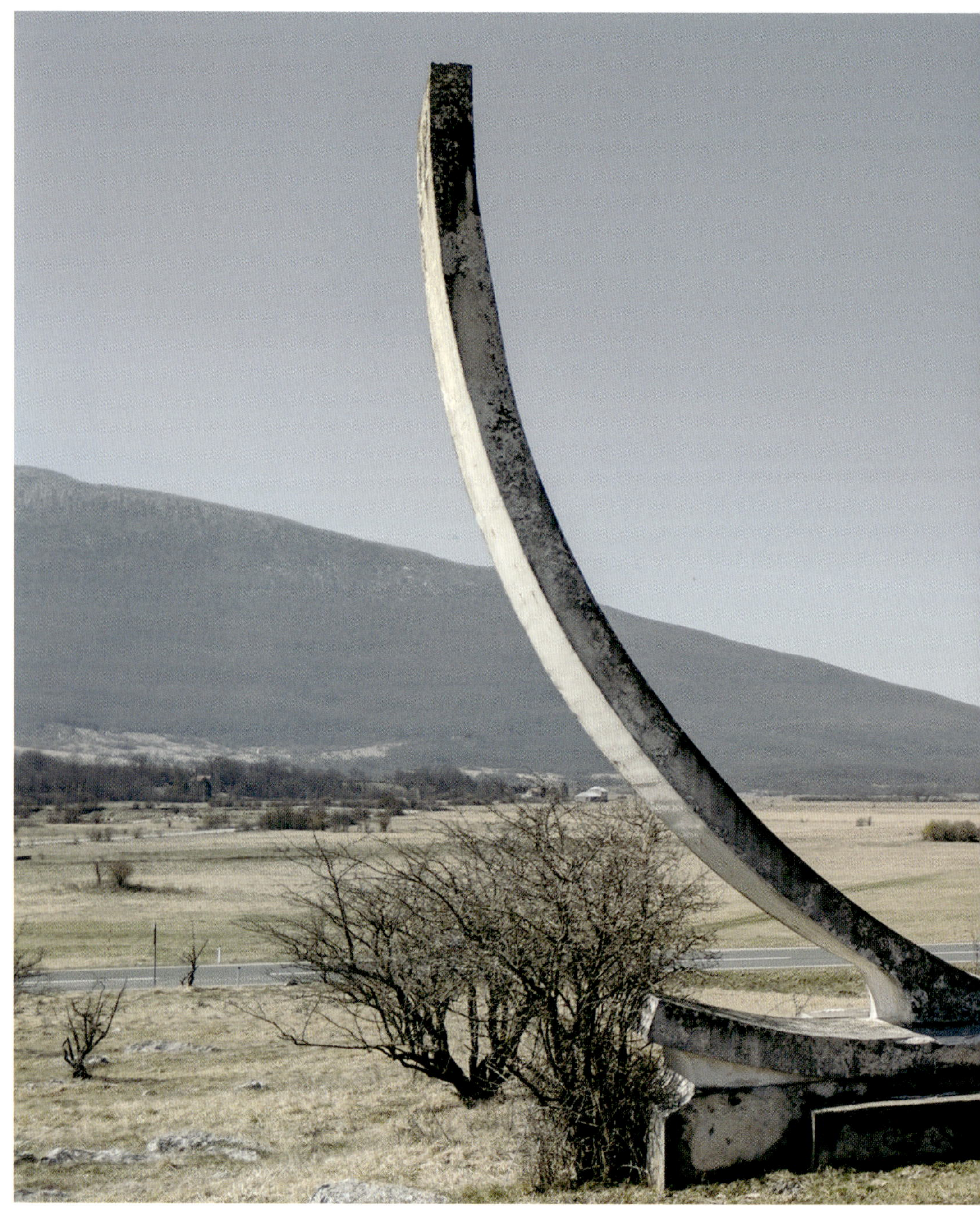

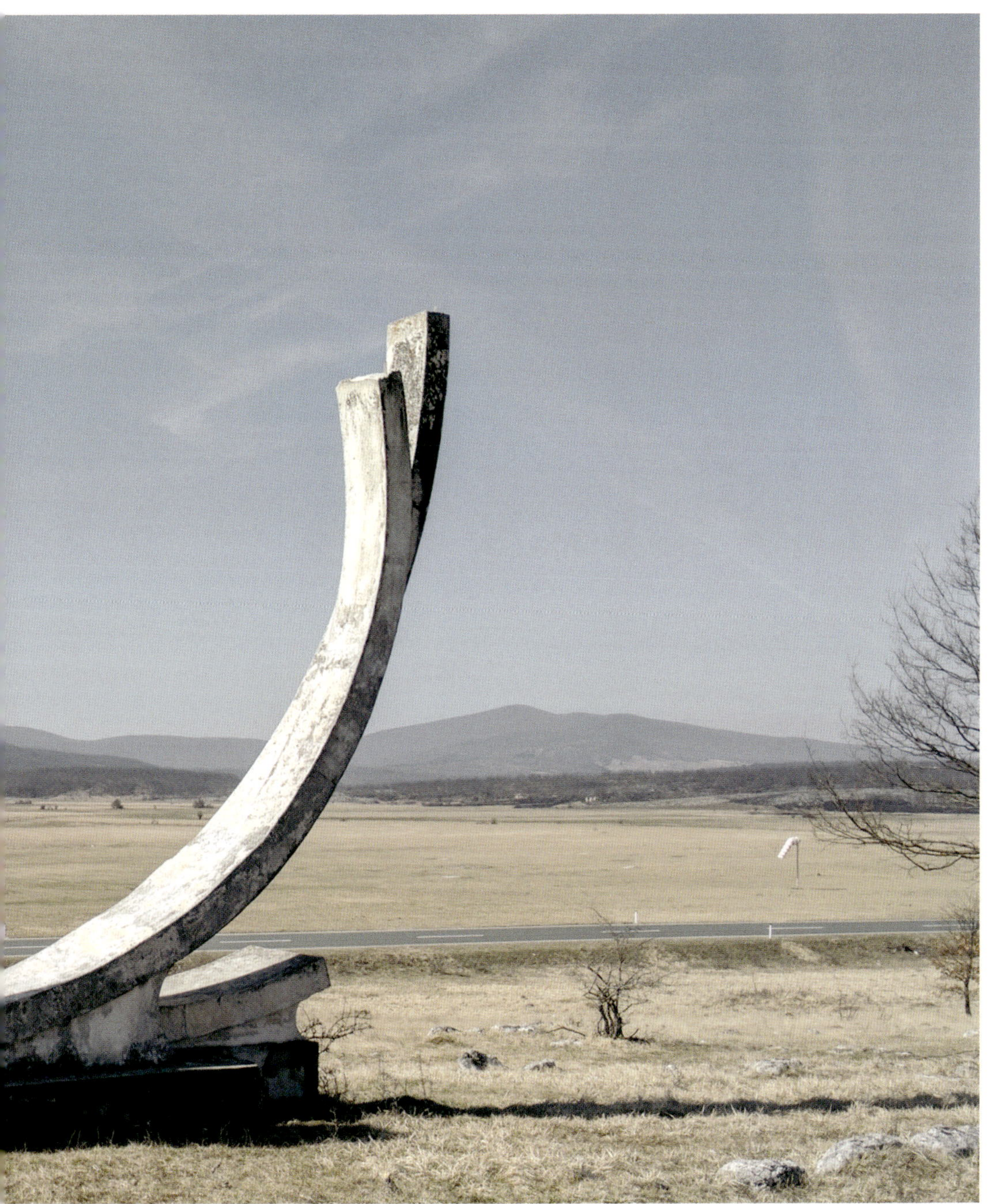

MITRAŠINCI (MEE-trah-sheen-tsee)

NAME: Monument to Partisan Detachments
at Mitrašinci
LOCATION: Mitrašinci, Macedonia
YEAR COMPLETED: 1974
DESIGNERS: Radovan Rađenović
COORDINATES: N41°46'40.3", E22°45'09.7"
DIMENSIONS: 10 metres high
MATERIALS: Concrete

HISTORY

After the Axis invasion of the Kingdom of Yugoslavia in April 1941, much of present-day Macedonia was renamed 'Vardar Macedonia' and occupied by Axis-aligned Bulgarian forces. While resistance in the region began as early as October 1941, it wasn't until Italy's capitulation in September 1943, and Bulgaria's switching of sides to join the Allied forces in 1944, that the partisan movement could make real progress.

The small village of Mitrašinci was a centre for resistance activity. On 17 September 1944, more than 1,000 partisans gathered in the hills to the east of the village to form the formidable 50th Macedonian Partisan Division. Made up of fighters from several smaller units, including the 4th, 13th and 14th Macedonian Brigades, the division was jointly commanded by Toše Jordanov and Boro Pokov.

This composite division immediately engaged German troops from Army Group E, who were retreating north from Greece. By October, the division had control over the towns of Strumica and Kočani. By the end of November, they had expelled Axis forces from Štip and Tetovo, as well as the capital city of Skopje.

The 50th Maedonian Division proved to be one of the most significant domestic units fighting to free the wider Vardar Macedonia region from Axis control during the final months of the war. Following the liberation of the Macedonian region, many fighters from the division continued to pursue retreating German forces, engaging them until the end of the war at such locations as the Sremski Front, Slavonski Požega and Zagreb.

DESIGN AND CONSTRUCTION

In the early 1970s, Macedonian architect Radovan Rađenović was commissioned to produce a memorial to the 50th Macedonian Partisan Division. Situated on a small hill to the east of the village of Mitrašinci, the monument was officially opened on 17 September 1974, on the 30th anniversary of the formation of the division.

The main memorial is a 10-metre-tall, semi-abstract, concrete sculpture resembling an upward-grasping hand or a rectilinear flower with a pistil at its centre.

STATUS AND CONDITION

Following the dismantling of Yugoslavia in the 1990s, the memorial site fell into disrepair. Today it is overgrown and crumbling, and it is apparent that many of its original features are now missing. In addition, a large metal-framed communications tower has been erected in close proximity to the monument, with no regard for the original purpose of the site.

However, two new plaques have recently been fixed to the base of the sculpture (replacing lost originals) and modest commemorative events are still held here on 17 September. Despite this, the site is not signposted and seldom visited.

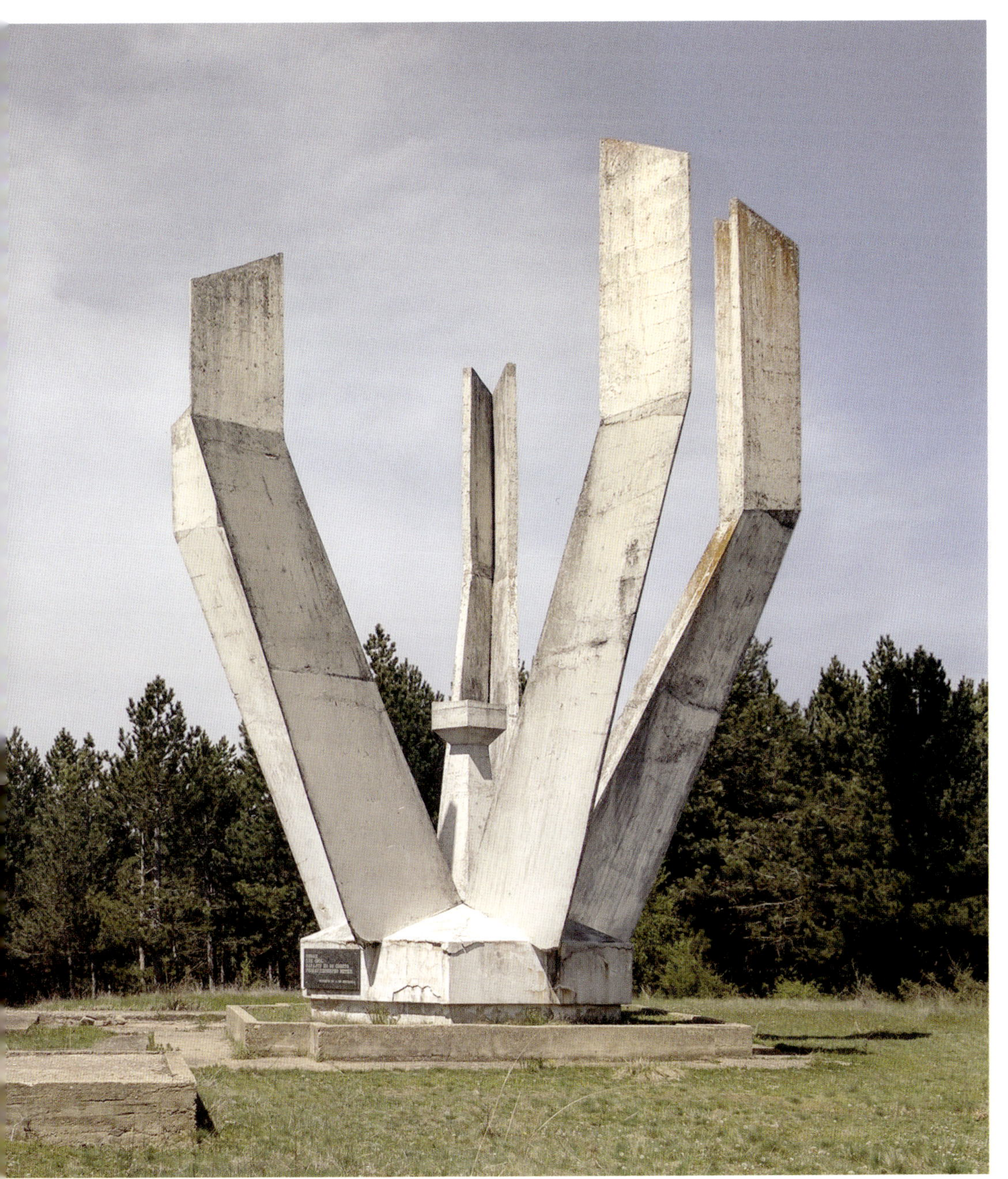

MITROVICA (mee-troh-VEE-tsah)

NAME: Shrine to the Revolution or Monument to Fallen Miners
LOCATION: Partisan Hill in Mitrovica, Kosovo
YEAR COMPLETED: 1973
DESIGNER: Bogdan Bogdanović
COORDINATES: N42°53'45.3", E20°51'36.4"
DIMENSIONS: 19 metres high
MATERIALS: Poured concrete, rebar and copper

HISTORY

In 1941, with the region of present-day Kosovo occupied by Axis forces, the highly productive Trepča mines of Mitrovica were placed under the direct control of Nazi leader Hermann Goering. Every day, more than 500 tons of zinc and lead were shipped from the mines to Germany, where they were used in armaments. To boost production, the Germans placed the miners under constant armed guard and established a forced labour camp within Trepča, using prisoners as slave workers in the pits.

The miners quickly began to plan an uprising against the Nazis, forming the partisan-aligned Miners' Troop. On 30 July 1941, workers detonated backpacks full of dynamite on Pillar 17 of the mine's cable-car system, effectively halting production in all mines. Subsequently, the Miners' Troop headed north to join forces with the Kopaonik Partisan Detachment.

This action severely impacted on Nazi Germany's capacity to source the raw ore that was vital to their campaign. The mine was one of the most productive in Eastern Europe; its Stari Trg section supplied the Germans with more than 40 per cent of their lead ore and also produced the batteries used by their submarines. During the miners' rebellion, and over the course of the struggle against the German occupation, hundreds of miners lost their lives. The city of Mitrovica was eventually liberated by partisan forces on 23 November 1944.

DESIGN AND CONSTRUCTION

In 1959, the architect Bogdan Bogdanović was commissioned by the Yugoslav government to produce a monument complex on Miners' Hill in Mitrovica, to commemorate those fighters who participated in the Miners' Troop. While the planning process for this memorial began in 1959, it was not completed until 1973.

The design consisted of a 19-metre-tall trilithon structure, with two large conical fluted concrete columns supporting a concrete element reminiscent of the kind of ore-carts used in the mines. The two vertical columns were intended to symbolise Serbs and Albanians working together, both in the mines and in their fight against the German occupiers. The horizontal cart-like form was once encased in copper plates, but most of these have since fallen off or been stolen. At the base of the monument are several limestone plaques under which are buried the remains of fallen soldiers from the Miners' Troop. Constructed around 1959, these pre-date the main monument.

Once opened, this was one of the most popular cultural and historical attractions in the region, visited by thousands of people every year from across the country. The spomenik complex was particularly popular with the Young Pioneer movement whose members learned about the Partisan Revolution by travelling on pilgrimages to various historic sites around Yugoslavia.

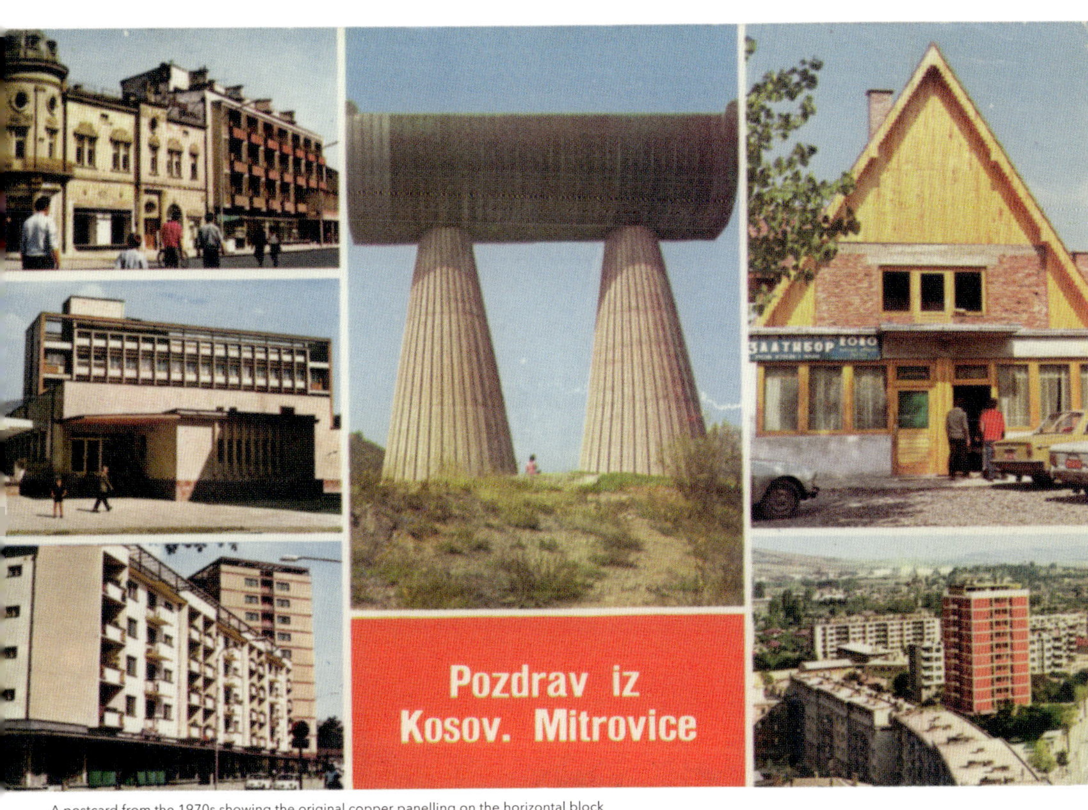

A postcard from the 1970s showing the original copper panelling on the horizontal block

STATUS AND CONDITION

After the Yugoslav Wars of the 1990s, the number of visitors to the monument fell considerably. The subsequent separation of Kosovo from Serbia in 2008 has left the region in a turbulent situation. The monument stands on the ethnic Serb-majority side of the Ibar River, where tensions between Serbs and Albanians can run high. Both sides appear largely indifferent or even antagonistic to the monument and the ideas behind it, giving it the nickname 'the barbecue'.

There are no signs of regular maintenance or security at the site and the memorial itself is not protected, although some graffiti on the lower sections has been painted out. While its structure is in decent order, showing little sign of damage or weathering, only a few small sections remain of the original copper panelling that once covered the horizontal block. In addition, many of the limestone plaques have been destroyed or stolen in recent years.

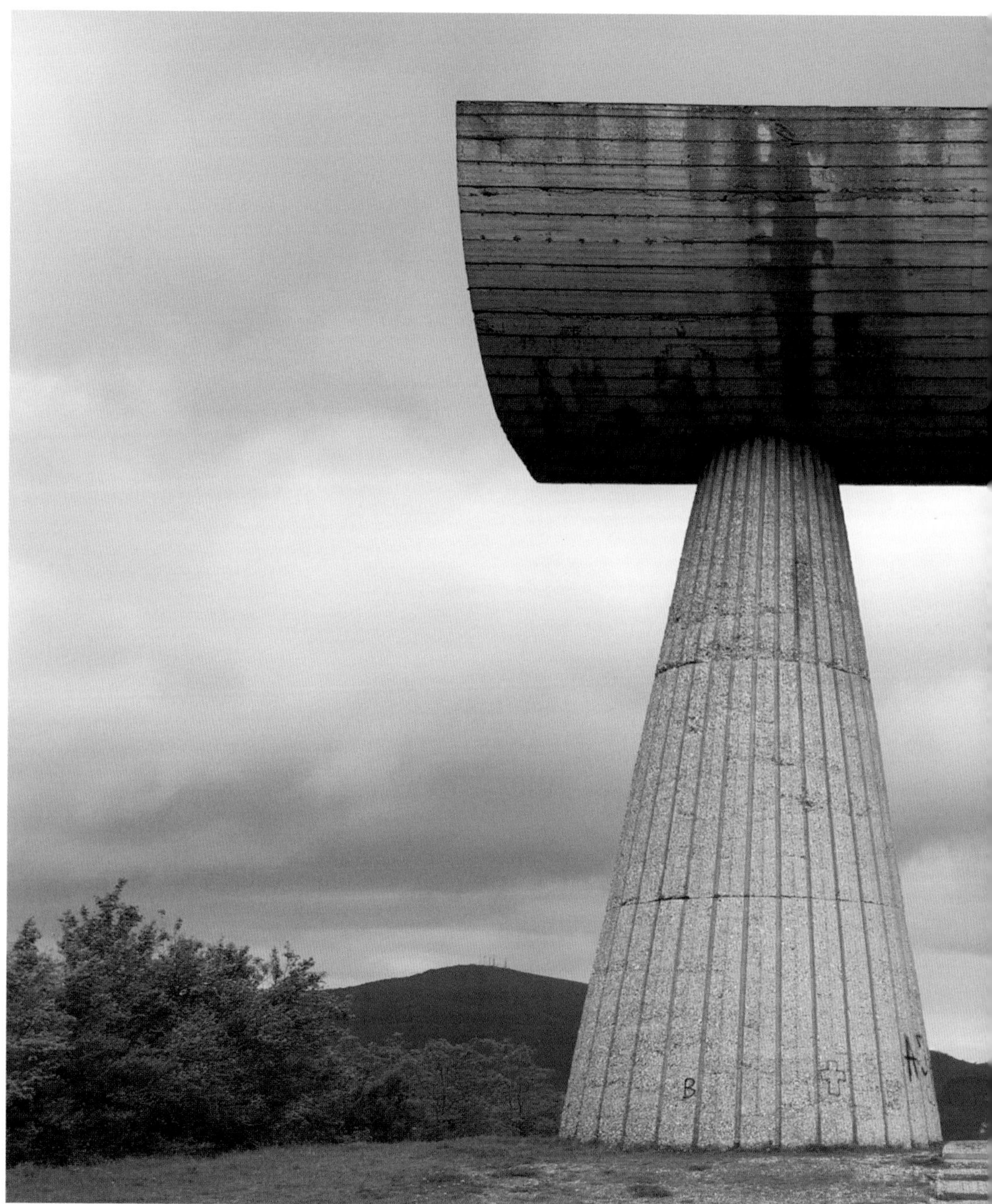

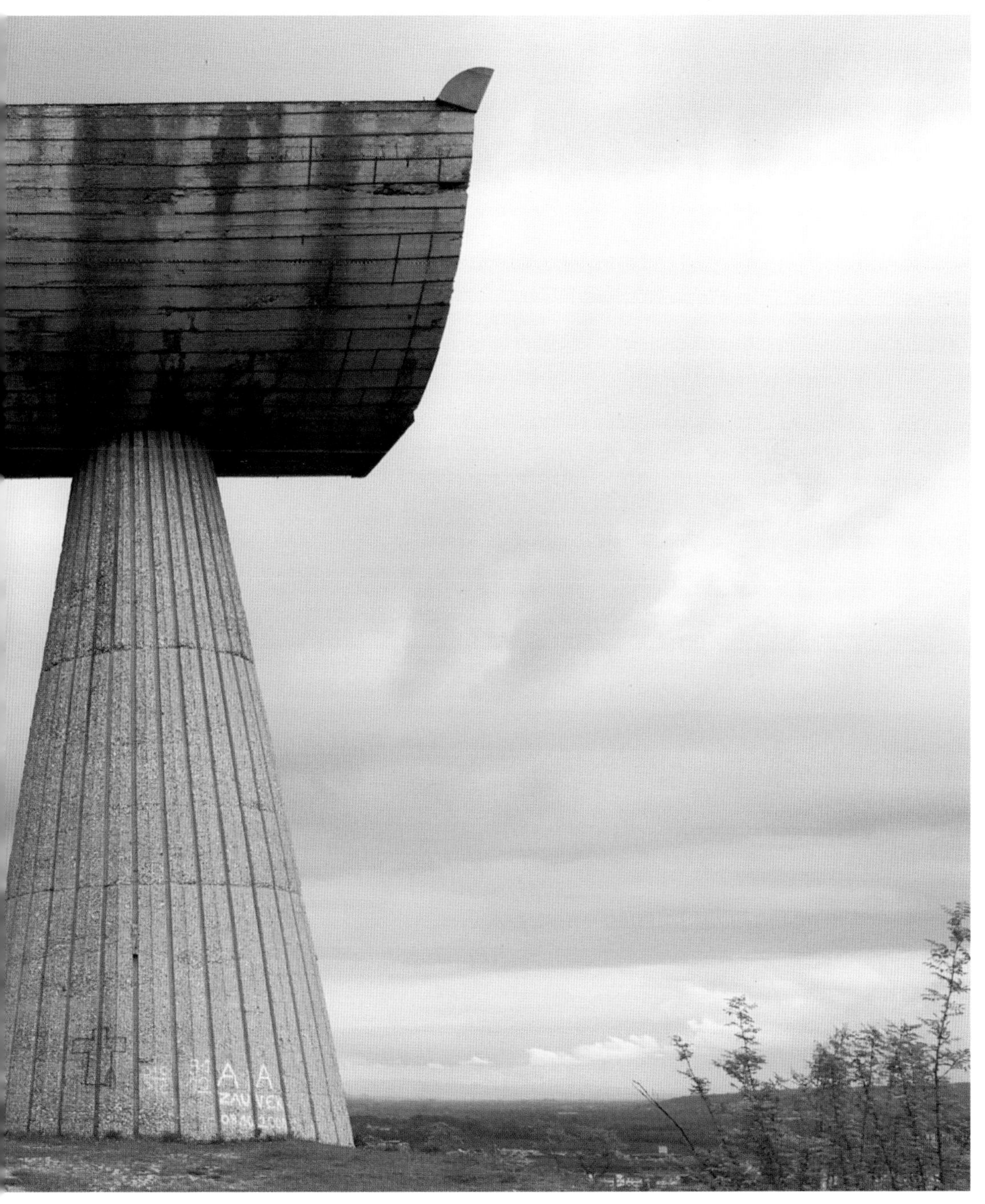

MOSTAR (MOH-star)

NAME: Partisan Memorial Cemetery in Mostar
LOCATION: Mostar, FBiH, Bosnia and Herzegovina
YEAR COMPLETED: 1965 (5 years to build)
DESIGNER: Bogdan Bogdanović
COORDINATES: N43°20'28.1", E17°47'46.1"
DIMENSIONS: 5,000 square meters of terraced hillside
MATERIALS: Poured concrete, rebar, paving stones and rubble

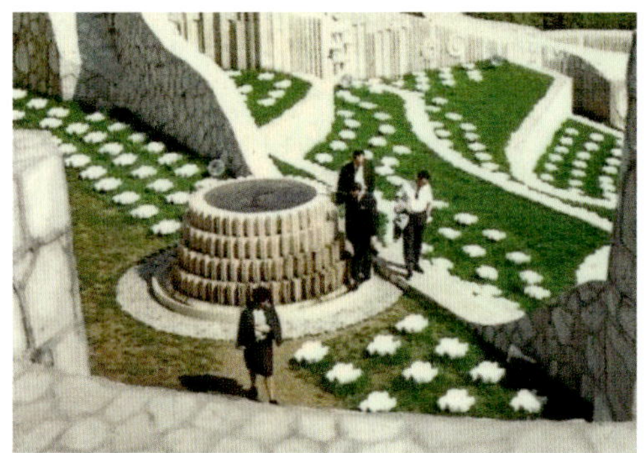
The Mostar spomenik in the 1970s

HISTORY

After the Axis invasion of 1941, Mostar found itself occupied by German, Italian and Ustaše units. During this period, many atrocities were committed against civilians by these Axis forces and their collaborators. By August 1941, organised armed resistance against the occupation had strengthened, with many joining partisan rebel groups. Mostar was the centre of a robust anti-fascist resistance, earning it the nickname 'The Red City'. Participation in the movement crossed both ethnic and religious lines.

In May 1942, partisans killed local Ustaše leaders Stjepan Barbarić, Sulejman Bašagić and Vinka Malvić. Retaliations for such actions were savage - the Ustaše routinely took civilians hostage, then executed them in a public area. By the end of the war, more than 1,000 civilians had been killed in this way. After Mostar was liberated on 14 February 1945 by the 8th Dalmatian Partisan Corps, partisans scoured the city, hunting down and executing those they viewed as collaborators, including several Franciscan monks.

DESIGN AND CONSTRUCTION

In 1959, the government commissioned architect Bogdan Bogdanović to create a memorial complex on Biskupova Glavica Hill, on the southern outskirts of the city, to commemorate Mostar's significance as an anti-fascist stronghold. Bogdanović intended to create not just a memorial, but an entire necropolis complex, comparable to those found in the Middle East or at Etruscan sites. Work began in 1960, with huge areas of the hillside being dynamited to form terracing. In other areas material was added - including leftover rubble from the city's devastation during World War II. Josip Tito, then president of Yugoslavia, inaugurated the monument's opening in 1965.

Two symmetrical, curved cobblestone walk-ways (emulating those found in Mostar) wind their way up the hill, the space between them forming a cascading water feature (no longer in operation). They lead to five tiers of wide terraces (reflecting the steep and dramatic hillsides of the Neretva Valley that surround the city), separated by vertical wavy columns of concrete. The terraced areas are dotted with 630 individual stone markers, engraved with the names of fallen soldiers. Around 560 of these are for partisan fighters whose remains are physically interred at the site. The remaining 70 are symbolic, representing those Mostar partisans whose bodies were never found. The names testify to the wide range of ethnicities - Serb, Croat, Bosnian, Jewish, etc. - of those who fought in the partisan movement.

In the middle of the top terrace, in front of an irregular circular cosmological motif set into the wall, stands a large, round concrete fountain. Originally water flowed from it along a narrow groove, collecting in a large pool at the bottom of the hill. This feature was intended to represent the splitting of Mostar by the Neretva River.

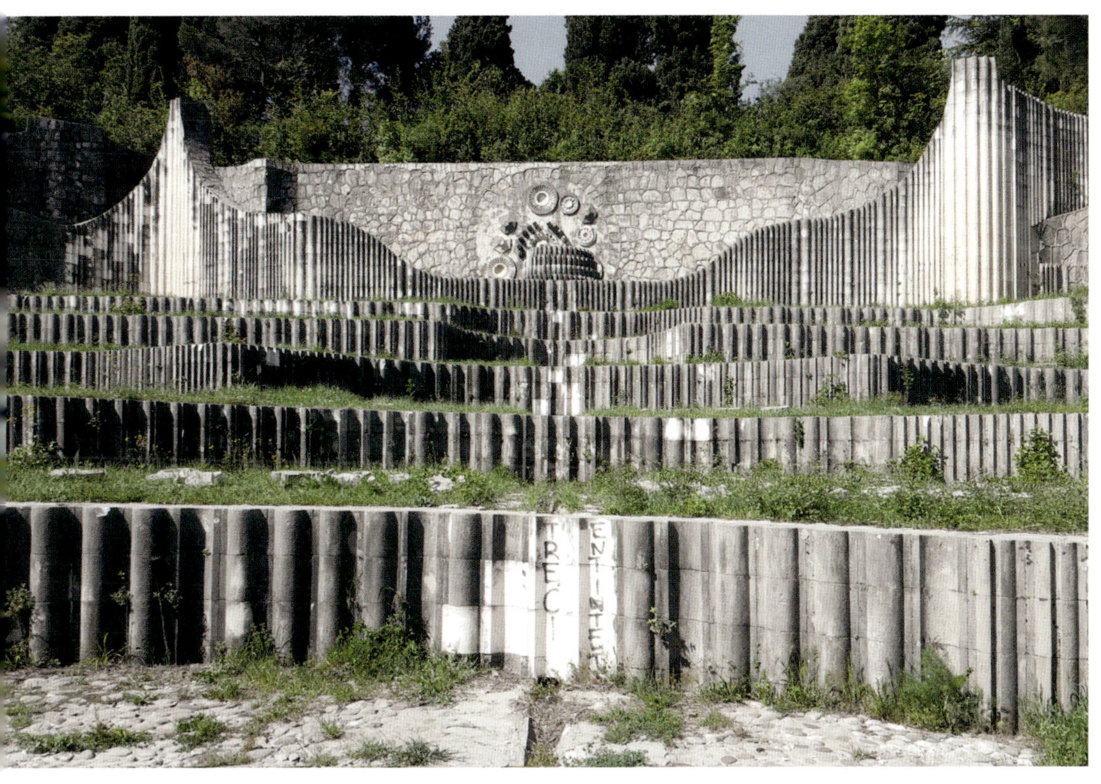

This popular memorial was visited by large numbers of tourists during the Yugoslav era, particularly in 1984, when the Olympics were held in Sarajevo. However, with the fall of Yugoslavia and ensuing Yugoslav Wars of the 1990s, the monument fell into disrepair, being bombed, set on fire, looted and vandalised. Perhaps most damage occurred after the wars, because of the spomenik's status as a symbol of Yugoslav ethnic co-operation and unity, ideals opposed by many post-Yugoslav ethnic nationalist movements.

The site was declared a national monument by the Bosnian government in 2006, but despite a number of attempts at restoration, it remains in very poor condition. The rubbish-strewn paths are overgrown and the walls are covered in graffiti. None of the fountain elements work and many of the stone markers have been smashed. Some of the graffiti relates to the ongoing ethnic tensions between Catholic Croatians on the west of the Neretva River (where the monument is sited) and Muslim Bosniaks on the east – tensions made more complicated by disagreements over the legacy of the many wars that plagued this area during the 20th century. In November 2017, a number of student visitors to the site were attacked by a group of masked assailants – it is therefore not advisable to visit without the assistance of a local guide. Although the site is still used for commemorations, there is no public information about it in the city and direction signs have been stolen, making it difficult to visit.

NIKŠIĆ (NIK-sheech)

NAME: Monument to Fallen Fighters of World War II
LOCATION: Nikšić, Montenegro
YEAR COMPLETED: 1987
DESIGNER: Ljubo Vojvodić
COORDINATES: N42°45'47.2", E18°57'34.6"
DIMENSIONS: 20 metres high
MATERIALS: Poured concrete and rebar

HISTORY

In July 1941, the Communist Party of Yugoslavia sent dissident Milovan Đilas into Italian-occupied Montenegro to organise armed resistance. He quickly united communist, nationalist, partisan and Chetnik Montenegrins to fight against the occupation. Italian forces were unprepared and within three weeks the resistance had almost re-taken the entire country. However, within a further three weeks, the Italians regrouped and, using a force of 67,000 troops, put down the uprising. The resistance was destroyed, with nearly 10,000 rebels killed across Montenegro and more than 20,000 interned in camps. Partisan attempts at massing forces to counterattack failed. Many Montenegrin nationalists and Chetniks who participated in the resistance movement wanted to abandon the fight, believing that their action had been futile and had caused the deaths of too many civilians. But the communist-led partisans wanted to continue. This difference of opinion caused a spilt in the movement, resulting in the Chetniks and nationalists changing sides to become Axis collaborators. In January 1942, fighting broke out between Chetniks and partisans. Although outnumbered 5,000 to 8,000, by May, Italian support had enabled the Chetniks to drive the partisans out of Montenegro.

During the retreat, 32 partisan fighters were captured by Chetnik and Italian forces as they attempted to escape Nikšić. In retaliation for their losses during the battle, the Italian commanders ordered them to be put to death. On 9 May 1942, the 32 men were taken to Trebjesa Hill, where they were shot and thrown into a mass grave. One of the executed fighters was Ljubo Čupić, an American university student, caught up in the occupation resistance movement of 1941. He had reached the position of commissioner of the partisan movement in Nikšić before being captured by Chetniks in April 1942. Josip Tito posthumously awarded him the 'Order of the People's Hero' medal on 10 July 1953.

In 1943, following the Italian surrender at the Armistice of Cassibile, partisans re-entered the region to battle against the Chetniks, who this time were assisted by the Germans. By the beginning of 1944, the Chetniks and Germans began to retreat, with Nikšić finally being liberated in December. During the war, more than 1,000 fighters and civilians from the Nikšić region were killed by Axis occupiers.

DESIGN AND CONSTRUCTION

In the late 1970s, Yugoslav architect Ljubo Vojvodić was commissioned by regional and national government organisations to construct a spomenik complex commemorating both the civilians and fighters of the Nikšić region killed during the war and the 32 partisans shot by firing squad at this site. Completed in 1987, this imposing, abstract, rather griffin-like or sphinx-like monument was a popular attraction during the Yugoslav era, but fell into disrepair when the country broke up in the early 1990s.

STATUS AND CONDITION

Today, the spomenik structure itself is in good condition (such a large concrete mass would be difficult to damage). However, many other elements have been vandalised. While some annual ceremonies are still held here (particularly on 9 May), the monument is largely disused.

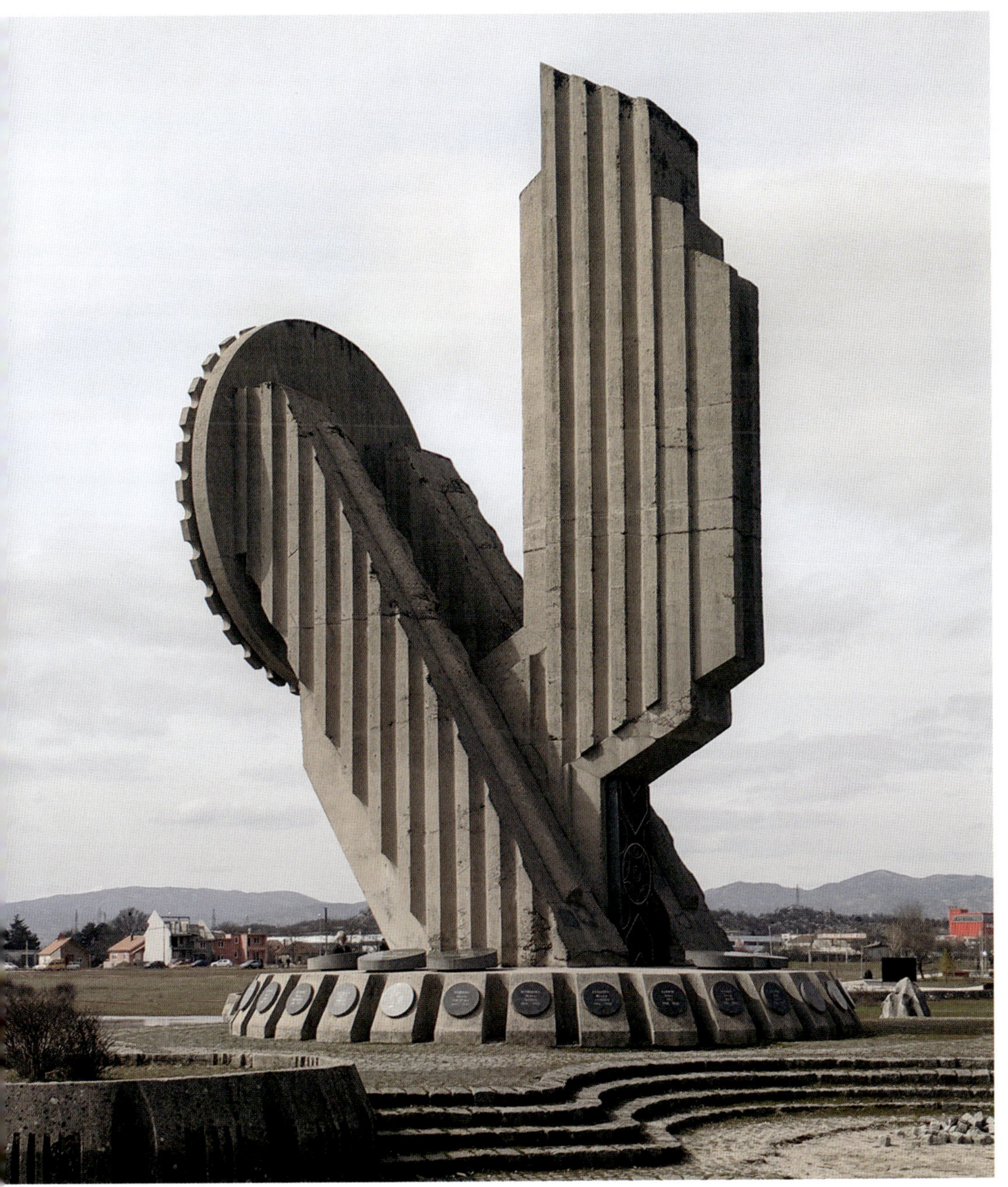

NIŠ (NEESH)

NAME: Bubanj Memorial Park, 'The Three Fists'
LOCATION: Niš, Serbia
YEAR COMPLETED: 1963
DESIGNERS: Ivan Sabolić and Mihajlo Mitrović
COORDINATES: N43°18'18.2", E21°52'21.9"
DIMENSIONS: Three monoliths, 18–23 metres high
MATERIALS: Poured concrete and rebar

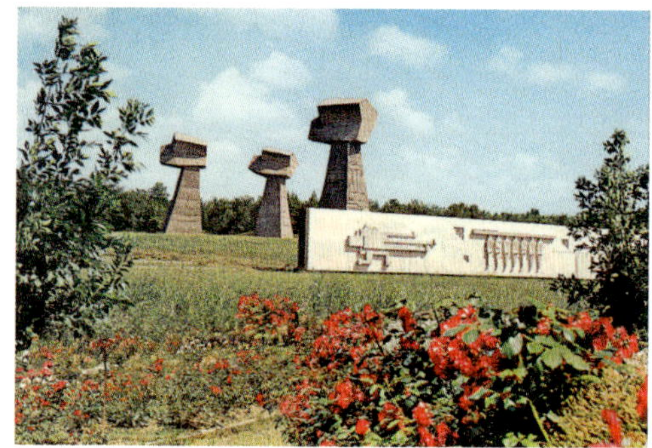
A postcard from the 1960s with the memorial wall in the foreground

HISTORY

After the German invasion and occupation of Serbia in April 1941, a prison camp named Red Cross was established in the city of Niš to detain dissidents, Jews and Roma. On 12 February 1942, 105 inmates made one of the first successful concentration camp escapes of World War II. During the escape, eleven German guards were killed. Five days later, retaliatory executions of prisoners began on the outskirts of Niš. Initially just over 1,000 were killed, but more followed, carried out at night to make it easier for the Germans to conceal their actions. The victims were forced to dig the pits in which they were then shot and buried. It is estimated that between 10,000 – 11,000 Serbs, Jews and Roma were killed here, though the real figure could be higher – the bodies were bulldozed into large trenches, some of which may remain undiscovered. In addition, the Germans spent the last weeks of the war excavating and burning decomposed remains in an effort to destroy evidence of their crimes. Niš was finally liberated by partisans and the Bulgarian Army on 14 October 1944, when the 7th German SS Division were driven out of the city.

DESIGN AND CONSTRUCTION

The first monument commemorating the killings that took place on this site was a small stone pyramid built in 1950. In 1958, a competition was announced for the design of a new, more substantial monument complex at this location. After a long selection process, the commission was awarded to Croatian artist Ivan Sabolić and architect Mihajlo Mitrović. Construction of the monument began in 1962 and the complex was officially opened on 14 October 1963, the 19th anniversary of the liberation of the city from German forces. In 1979, the Serbian Parliament declared the memorial complex a cultural heritage site of exceptional importance.

Set in a meadow in the middle of a large wooded park, three monoliths, topped with rectilinear clenched fist shapes, defiantly reach skywards. They are three different sizes to acknowledge that not only men, but also women and children lost their lives here. A large, open-air amphitheatre stands at one end of the complex. At the opposite end, five bas-relief panels mounted on a 23-metre-long marble wall bear witness to the massacres.

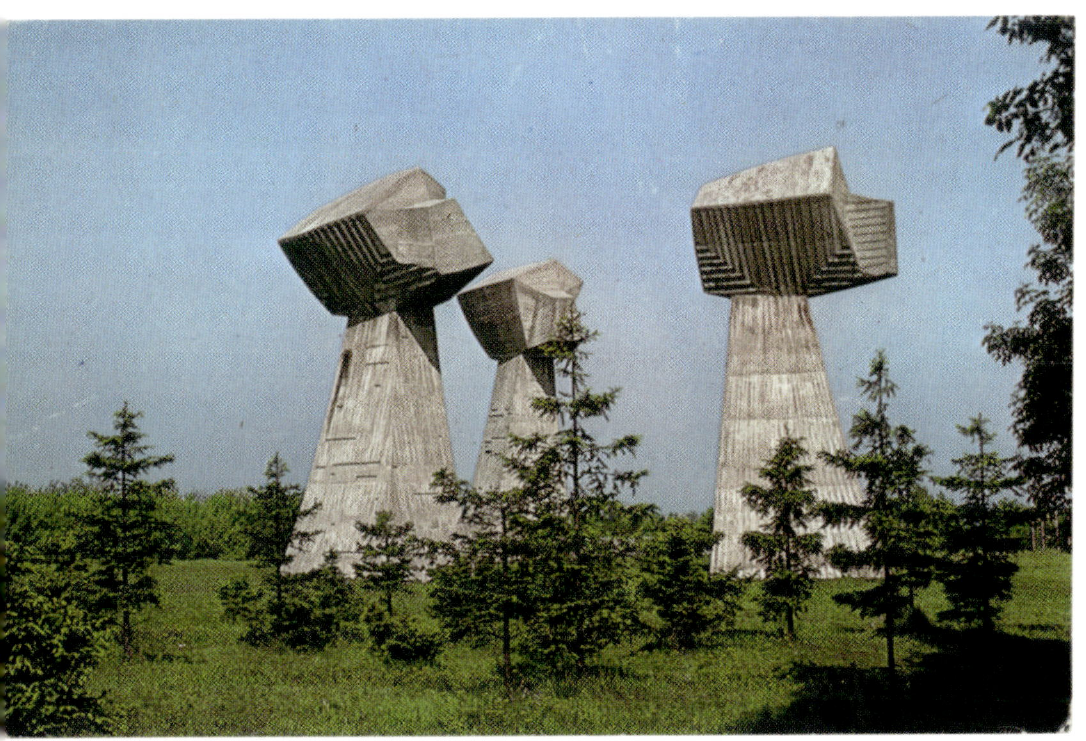

A postcard from the 1970s showing the concrete relief design

The site is also a popular city park, so the complex is well maintained, with graffiti being successfully removed in most instances. In 2004, a glass chapel sculpture, created by artist Alexander Buđevac, was added to the park and in 2009, the entire complex underwent renovation.

An annual ceremony is held at the monument on 14 October to celebrate the liberation of Niš. In July 2016, there was controversy over the use of the amphitheatre to host a classical music concert. Public opinion was divided as to whether the complex should only hold events directly related to the memorial. In 2017, it was announced that 170,000 Euro had been set aside to restore the site, this work is in progress. The monoliths are in good condition and the amphitheatre has recently been repaired. Furthermore, the city government and thousands of local volunteers continue to make considerable efforts to maintain the complex.

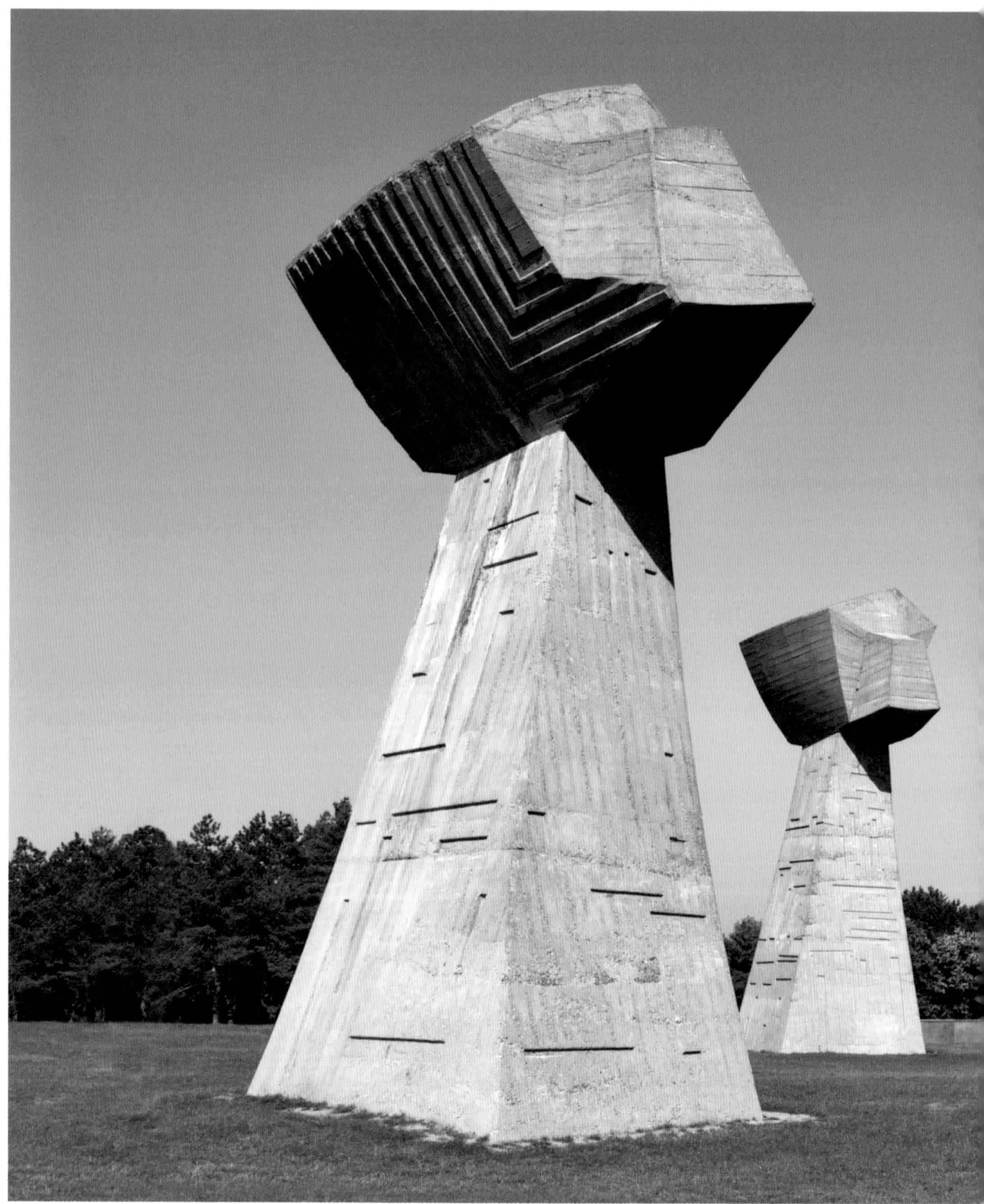

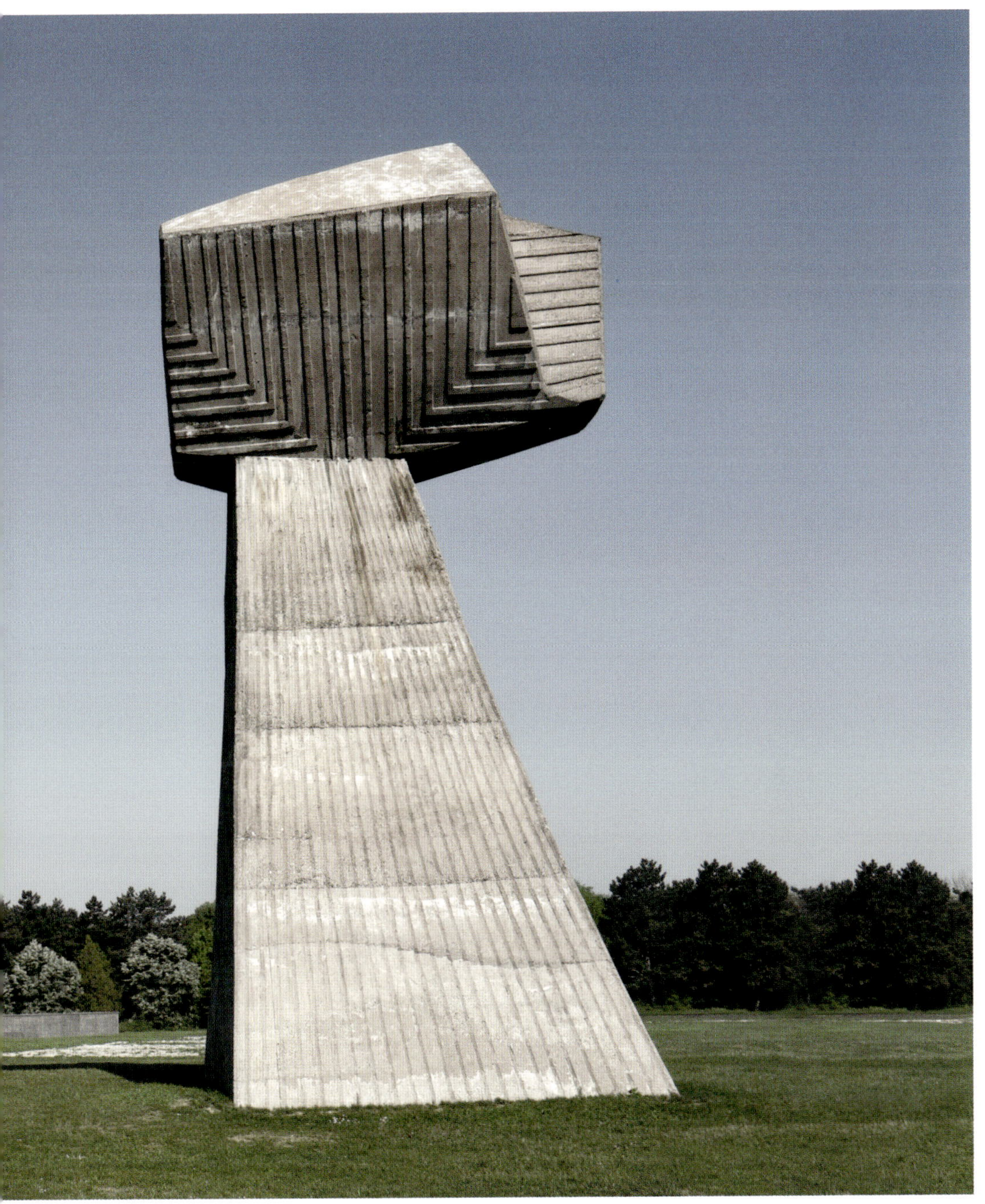

NOVI TRAVNIK (NO-vee TRAV-nik)

NAME: Necropolis for the Victims of Fascism
LOCATION: Čamića Brdo, a hill just northeast of Novi Travnik, FBiH, Bosnia and Herzegovina
YEAR COMPLETED: 1975 (4 years to build)
DESIGNER: Bogdan Bogdanović
COORDINATES: N44°11'47.6", E17°41'28.3"
DIMENSIONS: Twelve monoliths, 3–4 metres high
MATERIALS: Bihacite stone blocks

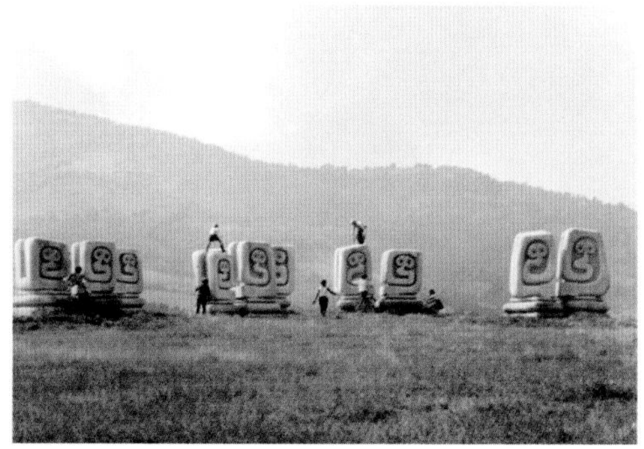

Children climbing on the stone monoliths, late 1970s
(image from the ArchitekturZentrumWein, Bogdanović Archive, Vienna)

HISTORY

Following the occupation of 1941, Ustaše troops of the Axis-aligned Independent State of Croatia (NDH) embarked on a campaign of ethnic cleansing against Serbs in what is present-day Bosnia. Thousands were arrested, deported, imprisoned and killed. Of those arrested, many were sent to prisons at Gospić in Croatia, from which they were later taken to be liquidated at the Jadovno death camps, usually by being pushed into deep ravines located nearby. On 1 August 1941, the Ustaše leadership issued directive 105/41, authorising the arrest and elimination of communists in the municipality. In addition, the directive noted that if the suspects were Jews or ethnic-Serbs, no evidence was required to make an arrest. Over several days, around 700 ethnic Serbs were rounded up by the Ustaše near the town of Novi Travnik. Instead of being transported to death camps, they were marched en masse to the top of a nearby hill – Čamića Brdo – to the east of the town. Here they were separated into smaller groups, made to dig a large pit, and shot by firing squad.

The Travnik region remained under Ustaše control until it was liberated by the 4th Partisan Division on 19 February 1945.

DESIGN AND CONSTRUCTION

In 1971, the mayor of Novi Travnik invited Serbian designer Bogdan Bogdanović to create a memorial complex for the town to commemorate the slaughter at Čamića Brdo. The completed memorial was opened on 30 February 1975, 30 years after the liberation of the town. Bogdanović says he used the 'universal symbols of the sun, planets and moon. The monument speaks to everyone, and succeeds in becoming an authentic component of the space.'

The central element is formed of 12 sandstone monoliths of between 2 and 3 metres in height. Standing on stone pedestals, they are arranged in pairs around the apex of the hill. Each of the double-sided monoliths bears a sinuous, large-eyed, snake-like design, carved by stonemasons from the town of Pirot in Serbia. Underneath the monoliths lies a crypt, where the remains of the victims are now interred.

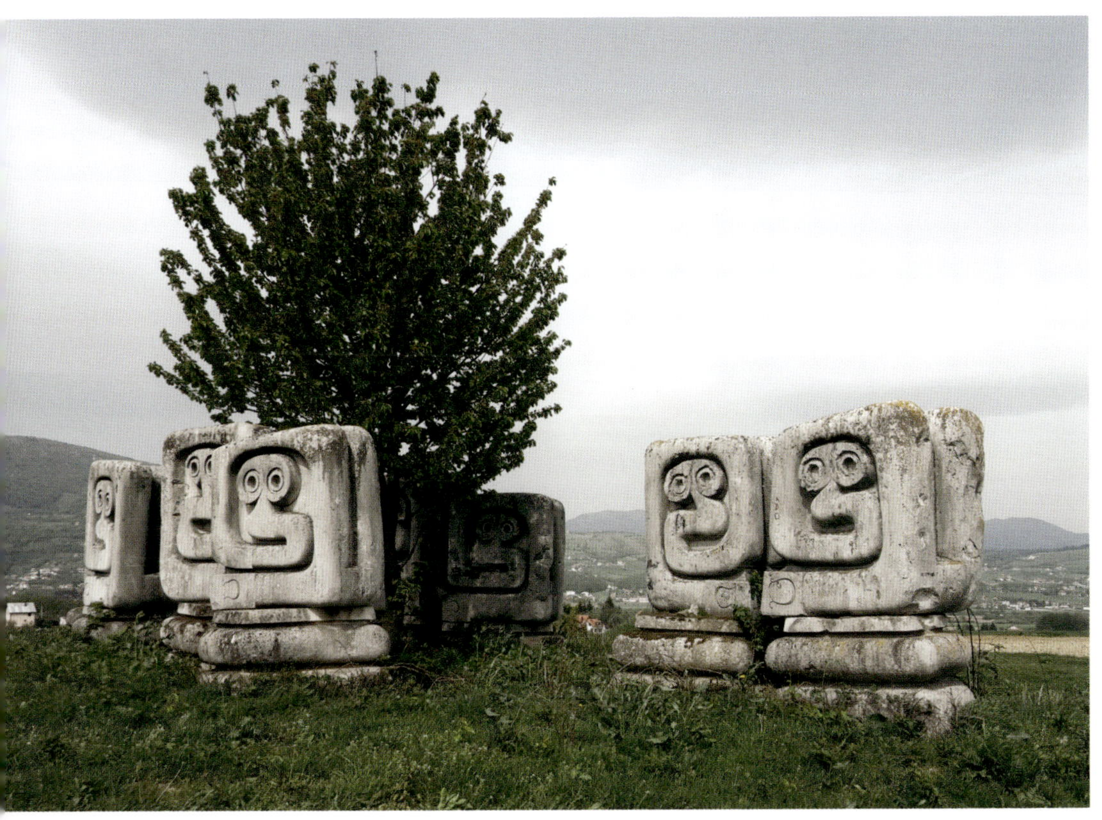

Following construction, the memorial was much visited. However, with the onset of the Yugoslav Wars in the early 1990s, this area became the front line for many brutal conflicts. One monolith was completely destroyed in the fighting, while others were scarred by gunfire. In addition, landmines were planted in the area, many of which may well still be present and dangerous.

Though officially taken under the aegis of the Bosnian Commission to Preserve National Monuments in 2012, the spomenik remains in poor condition. No repairs have been made and much of the complex's original grounds are now used as farmland. A wreath-laying ceremony takes place annually on 9 May.

OBADOV BRIJEG (OH-bah-dov BREE-yeg)

NAME: Monument on Obadov Hill
LOCATION: Obadov Hill, Danilovgrad, Montenegro
YEAR COMPLETED: 1974
DESIGNER: Slobodan Vukajlović
COORDINATES: N42°34'49.6", E19°03'12.7"
DIMENSIONS: 4 metres high and 5 metres wide
MATERIALS: Concrete

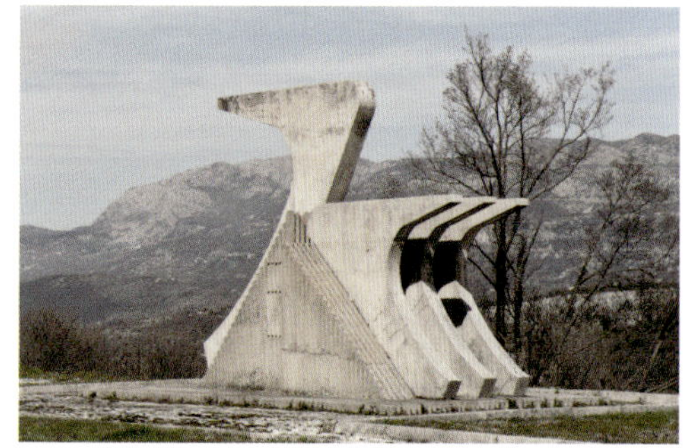

HISTORY

The 500-strong partisan 6th Montenegrin Strike Brigade was formed near Kolasin, Montenegro, on 14 November 1943. The unit primarily fought German and Chetnik troops, as well as Muslim militias. Throughout September 1944, the brigade participated in the final liberation of both the Nikšić and Grahovo regions. Following these successes, they fought against the remaining Axis forces in the Danilovgrad region.

In late October, the German 21st Mountain Corps, led by Commander Ernst von Leyser, pushed north through the Danilovgrad region in an attempt to retake the town of Nikšić from partisan control. On 13 November 1944, several partisan units (including the 6th Montenegrin Brigade) engaged the Germans to prevent them from crossing a mountain pass on Obadov Hill. British forces from the Middle East Command provided artillery support, while Allied planes targeted German columns along the road.

The bloody battle lasted thirteen days before the partisans forced the Germans to retreat east, away from the pass. Partisan commander Josip Tito personally congratulated the 6th Montenegrin Brigade on their success during this battle.

DESIGN AND CONSTRUCTION

Nikšić architect Slobodan Vukajlović was commissioned by local government and SUBNOR veterans to create a spomenik for the 6th Montenegrin Strike Brigade at Obadov Hill. The monument was opened in November 1974, on the 30th anniversary of the battle.

The spomenik is a 4-metre-tall, abstract concrete sculpture – with smooth curved parts and ribbed triangular slabs – suggestive of a swimming bird. The monument is the centrepiece of a small memorial complex at the Obadov Hill pass, a short distance from the main road between Nikšić and the capital Podgorica (named Titograd during the Yugoslav era).

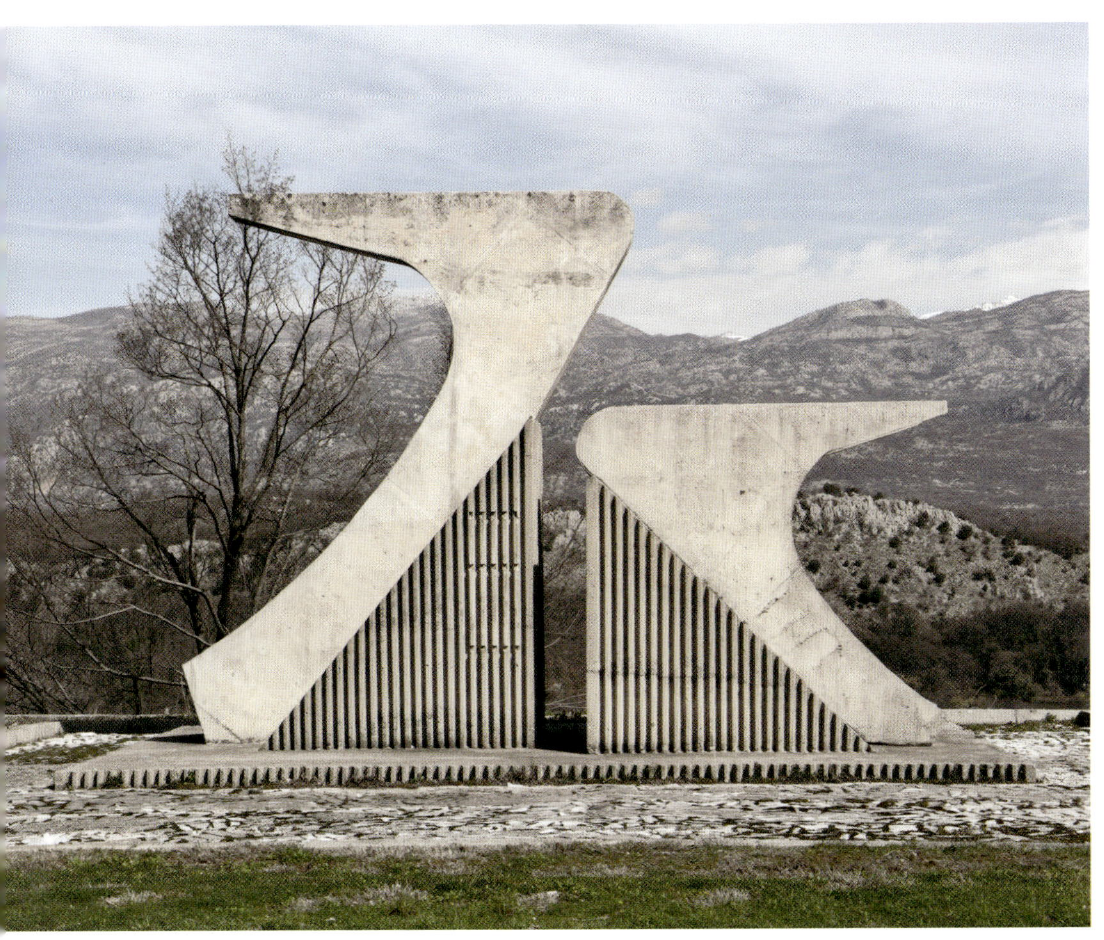

Since the break up of Yugoslavia, the spomenik complex has fallen into decay. The central memorial is still relatively intact, but the plaque attached to it is missing and the site itself is completely neglected. It is not signposted and there is no information about the monument at the site. As far as can be determined, no commemorative events are held here.

OSTRA (OH-strah)

NAME: 'Courage': A Monument to the Fallen
Soldiers of the Čačak Partisan Detachment
LOCATION: Ostra, Serbia
YEAR COMPLETED: 1969 (2 years to build)
DESIGNERS: Miodrag Živković and Svetislav Ličina
COORDINATES: N43°54'41.5", E20°30'59.7"
DIMENSIONS: 10 metres high and 17 metres wide
MATERIALS: Poured concrete, steel frame and
aluminium panels

HISTORY

On 7 July 1941, a Serbian uprising against occupying Axis forces took place at Bela Crkva. Five days later, the Čačak Partisan Detachment was formed. Initially commanded by partisan commander Momčilo Radosavljević and Chetnik leader Predrag Raković, this anti-fascist, communist and Serbian nationalist (Chetnik) group was one of the first armed and organised resistance units in Serbia. They immediately began to attack German units and infrastructure.

On 24 September 1941, along with twelve other partisan detachments and their Chetnik partners, the Čačak Detachment took part in the liberation of the Serbian towns Čačak and Užice and the surrounding region. This brief liberation, one of the first in occupied Europe, allowed the establishment of the Republic of Užice.

However, within five weeks, Germans had retaken the area, forcing the defeated partisan detachments to retreat into neighbouring Bosnian and Sandžak territory. During the fighting, Predrag Raković and his Chetnik fighters betrayed the partisans over internal disputes, siding with the German troops on the eve of the fall of Užice.

In the process of their hurried retreat, the Čačak Detachment was forced to leave eight wounded members behind in Zlatibor, expecting them to be taken as POWs by their pursuers. Instead, the German troops executed them, along with the wounded from other partisan detachments. For months, the surviving members of the Čačak Partisan Detachment evaded the Chetniks, who were now working on behalf of Axis forces. In spring 1943, under the command of Radiše Poštića, 25 fighters of the detachment made a renewed attempt to liberate Čačak. On 5 March, during the course of their trek to Čačak, they were ambushed in the small village of Ostra by more than 400 Chetnik fighters. Fourteen fighters were killed, including Poštića, and the detachment was defeated.

While this bid to free the city was a failure, Yugoslav partisans were ultimately successful in liberating Čačak when the last German troops were driven out of the city on 4 December 1944, with the assistance of the Soviet Red Army and Western Allies.

DESIGN AND CONSTRUCTION

Construction of this memorial to the Čačak Partisan Detachment (who were all from the nearby city of Čačak) began in 1967. Designed by artist Miodrag Živković and architect Svetislav Ličina, it was officially unveiled in 1969. The 10-metre-tall, sharply angled, aluminium monolith bursts from the ground, dramatically suggesting the sacrifice, suffering and valour of the fallen fighters. Its fractal motifs and stylised semi-abstract, angular human faces are typical of Živković's work. On the paved approach, a text on a low triangular wall relates the story of the battle.

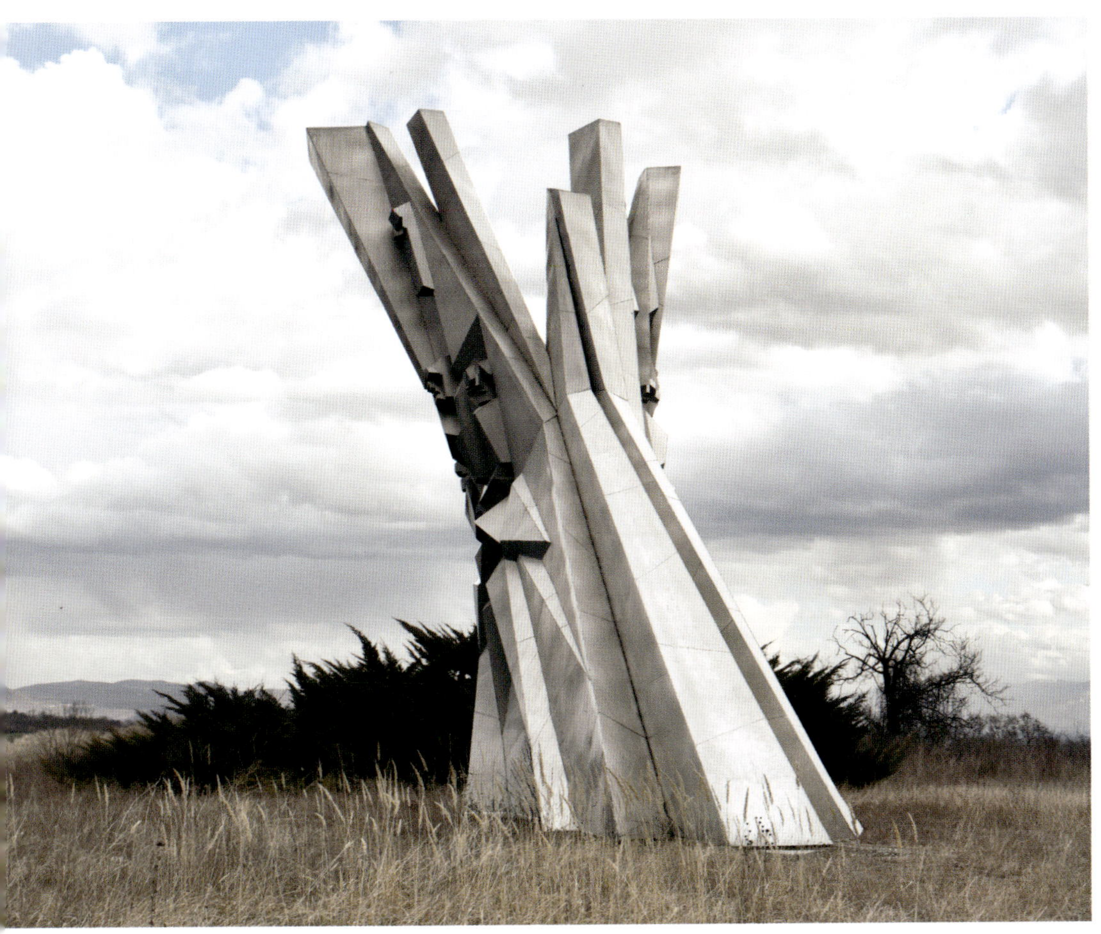

The monument was regularly visited until the break up of Yugoslavia in the early 1990s, at which point it fell into disrepair. Today, the memorial entrance wall has crumbled and is no longer legible. Nearly all the concrete structures, surfaces and walkways are overgrown with weeds. However, the central aluminium monolith is still in reasonable condition: no panels are missing or seriously damaged (although many are covered in graffiti).

In the late 2000s, the unusual decision was made to site the Serbian Orthodox church of St Petka adjacent to the spomenik. The inclusion of St Petka's (completed in 2014) within the monument complex was controversial: it was opposed by Živković, the partisans and later the Serbian government were ambivalent towards it, and its position – directly between the entrance and the monument significantly changes the intended design of the complex.

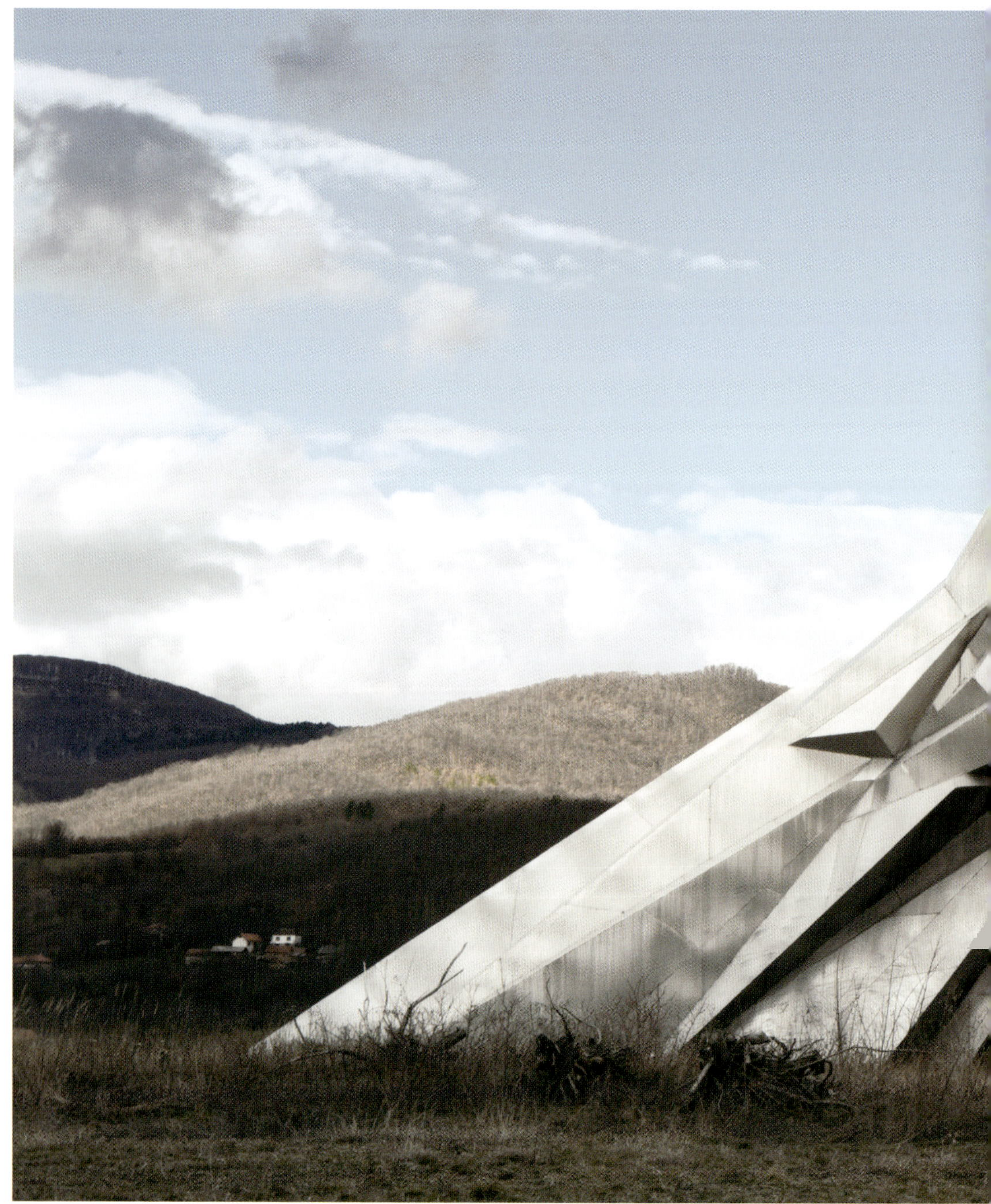

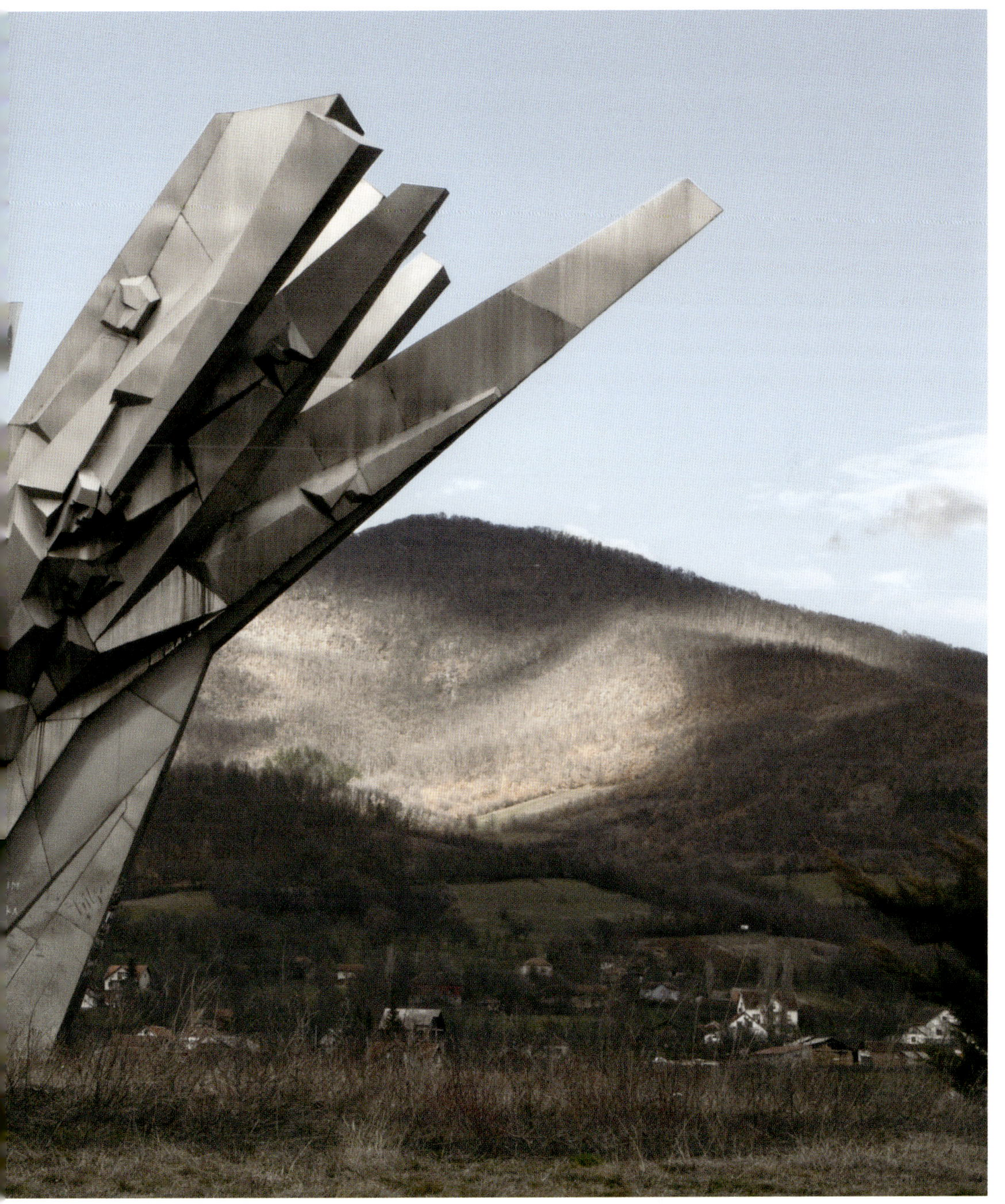

PETROVA GORA (PEH-troh-vah GAR-ah)

NAME: Monument to the Uprising of the People of
Kordun and Banija
LOCATION: Petrova Gora National Park, Vojnić,
Croatia
YEAR COMPLETED: 1981 (10 years to build)
DESIGNERS: Vojin Bakić and Berislav Šerbetić
COORDINATES: N45°18'58.6", E15°48'17.6"
DIMENSIONS: 37 metres high and 40 metres wide
MATERIALS: Poured concrete, rebar, steel frame and
stainless-steel plates

HISTORY

In summer 1941, Ustaše militiamen across the
newly created Independent State of Croatia (NDH)
began forcibly to deport ethnic-Serbs to Serbia,
assigning their homes to Axis-friendly Slovenes.
Ethnic-Serbs of the Kordun and Banija regions
had witnessed this situation unfold in the Plivitice
area and were afraid of suffering the same fate.
When the communist fighters of the 2,500-strong
Kordun Partisan Detachment learned of this, they
infiltrated these heavily occupied regions and
convinced hundreds of ethnic-Serbs to join in
organised resistance against the Ustaše.

They established a headquarters near the
summit of Mali Petrovac Hill in the Petrova Gora
mountain range, from which they co-ordinated
their collaborative partisan/ethnic-Serb resistance.
Fortifications were laid, infrastructure created,
and an underground hospital complex built.
Around 15,000 people from the surrounding area
spent the winter under the protection of this
partisan stronghold.

The Kordun resistance fighters made repeated
raids on the surrounding towns, increasing
tensions with Axis forces. On 19 March 1942, the
Ustaše instigated Operation Petrova Gora, with
the objective of eradicating all ethnic-Serb and
partisan resistance from the region. But the
offensive only succeeded in escalating ethnic-
Serb anger, allowing the partisans to grow

stronger by rallying more peasants to their cause.
However, during a sudden breach of defences
in April 1942, Ustaše forces stormed partisan
positions around Petrova Gora. Taken completely
by surprise and armed only with pitchforks and
other crude weapons, hundreds of peasants who
had sought refuge on the mountain charged
towards them. But they stood little chance against
the trained soldiers and more than 300 ethnic-
Serb peasants were killed.

By May 1942, the Petrova Gora range was
under the control of the Ustaše. Of the hundreds
of ethnic-Serb peasants captured by them, those
not immediately killed were sent to concentration
camps across the region, mainly Jasenovac. Over
the course of the war, around 27,000 people from
the Kordun region lost their lives (approximately
30 per cent of the pre-war population).

DESIGN AND CONSTRUCTION

The importance of the Mali Petrovac site (the
tallest summit in the Petrova Gora range) was
recognised directly after the war. In 1946, a
cornerstone was laid here in anticipation of a
monument to the ethnic-Serb peasants who died
fighting the Ustaše militia.

However, it was only in 1970 that a new
initiative to build a memorial (predominantly
funded by public contributions from the people
of Karlovac) led to a design competition.
From the seventeen proposals submitted, the
commission was awarded to a young architect,
Igor Toš, with a design by sculptor Vojin Bakić as
runner-up. As the project proceeded, it became
apparent that the designs of both Toš and Bakić
would be too costly to build, so construction was
abandoned. After a second competition in 1974,
a new, more practicable design was submitted

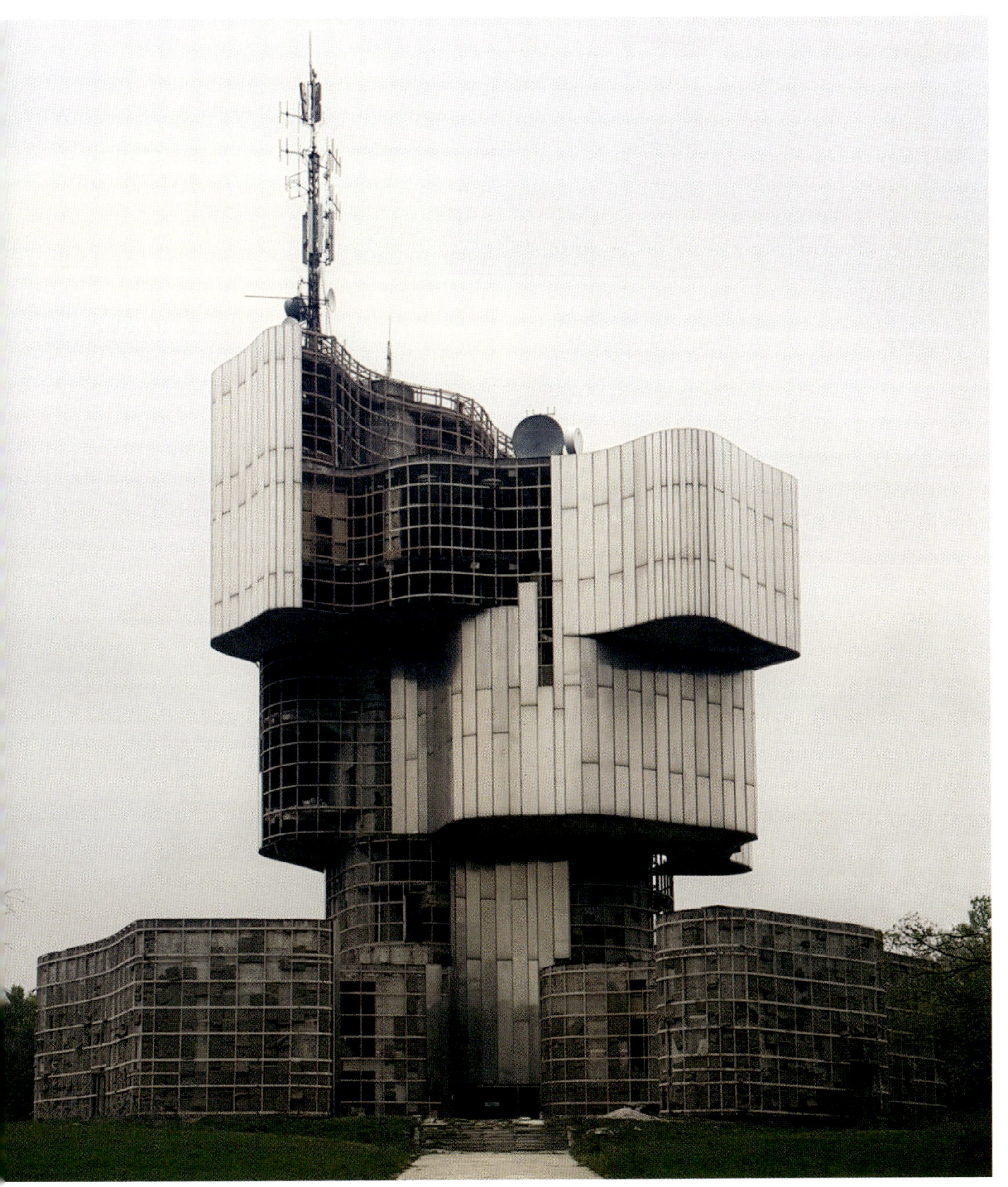

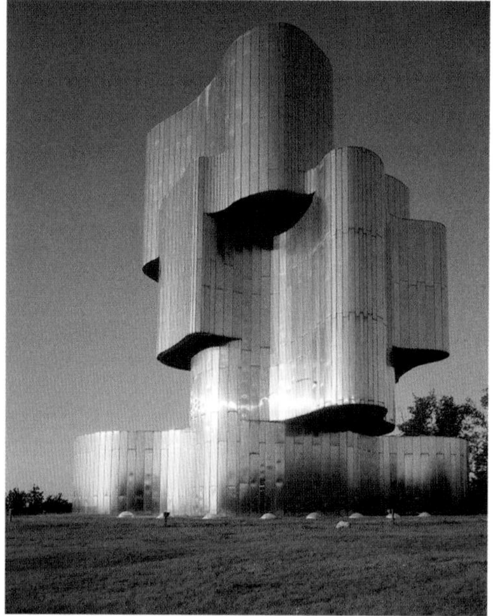

Petrova Gora in the 1980s with the covering panels intact
(image from the Museum of Contemporary Art, Zagreb)

by Bakić , who was assisted by architect Berislav Šerbetić. He dedicated the monument to his four brothers, all of whom died at the Jadovno death camps in 1941.

But even this concept was complicated to construct – requiring electricity, water and infrastructure. Although work began immediately, the deadline of 4 July 1981 (the 40th anniversary of the National Liberation movement) was not met. The official opening ceremony took place on 4 July 1982.

The finished memorial building, perched on top of Mali Petrovac, dominates the landscape for miles around. Constructed from stainless-steel panels cladding a concrete structure, it stands 37-metres-tall and is arranged over five storeys with undulating walls. From a large visitors' centre, a long stairway leads up to the main spomenik structure. Originally this contained a 250-seat congress hall, a library, a reading room, a café and a museum that housed hundreds of documents and artefacts relating to the battle and to the history of ethnic-Serb struggles.

With the onset of the Yugoslav Wars in 1991, the monument fell into disrepair. Then in 1995, the interior museum was also destroyed. One reason the site has been so substantially damaged is because of its importance to the region's ethnic-Serbs. This has made it a target for Croatian nationalists, particularly following the conflicts over the breakaway Republic of Serbian Krajina (RSK), a self-proclaimed Serb state within Croatia, that lasted from 1991 to 1995. The Petrova Gora site fell within the territory of the RSK, and its ownership is still unclear today.

Despite protests from a number of anti-fascist organisations, little effort has been made to prevent further damage or to punish those responsible for it. Today the spomenik is a hollow shell held in place by a massive concrete skeleton, defaced, looted and partially dismantled. Most of the stainless-steel panels have been removed and sections of rotted insulation material are scattered inside and around the monument. Although the entrance to the building is fenced off, holes have been made in the fencing, allowing access to the structure. Many parts of the interior are dangerous and unstable. The basement level is flooded and inhabited by animals and the elevator shafts are open. The visitors' centre at the base of the monument complex is completely derelict. As a final indignity, communications towers have been mounted on the top of the spomenik. Despite this situation, modest commemorative events are still occasionally held here.

Efforts are being made to preserve the monument as a historical site for ethnic-Serbs and as part of the artistic legacy of Vojin Bakić. But repair work has been hindered because the site is technically under the jurisdiction of three separate municipalities, none of which are prepared to accept ownership and subsequent responsibility for its maintenance. It is estimated that it would cost tens of millions of Euros to restore the monument fully.

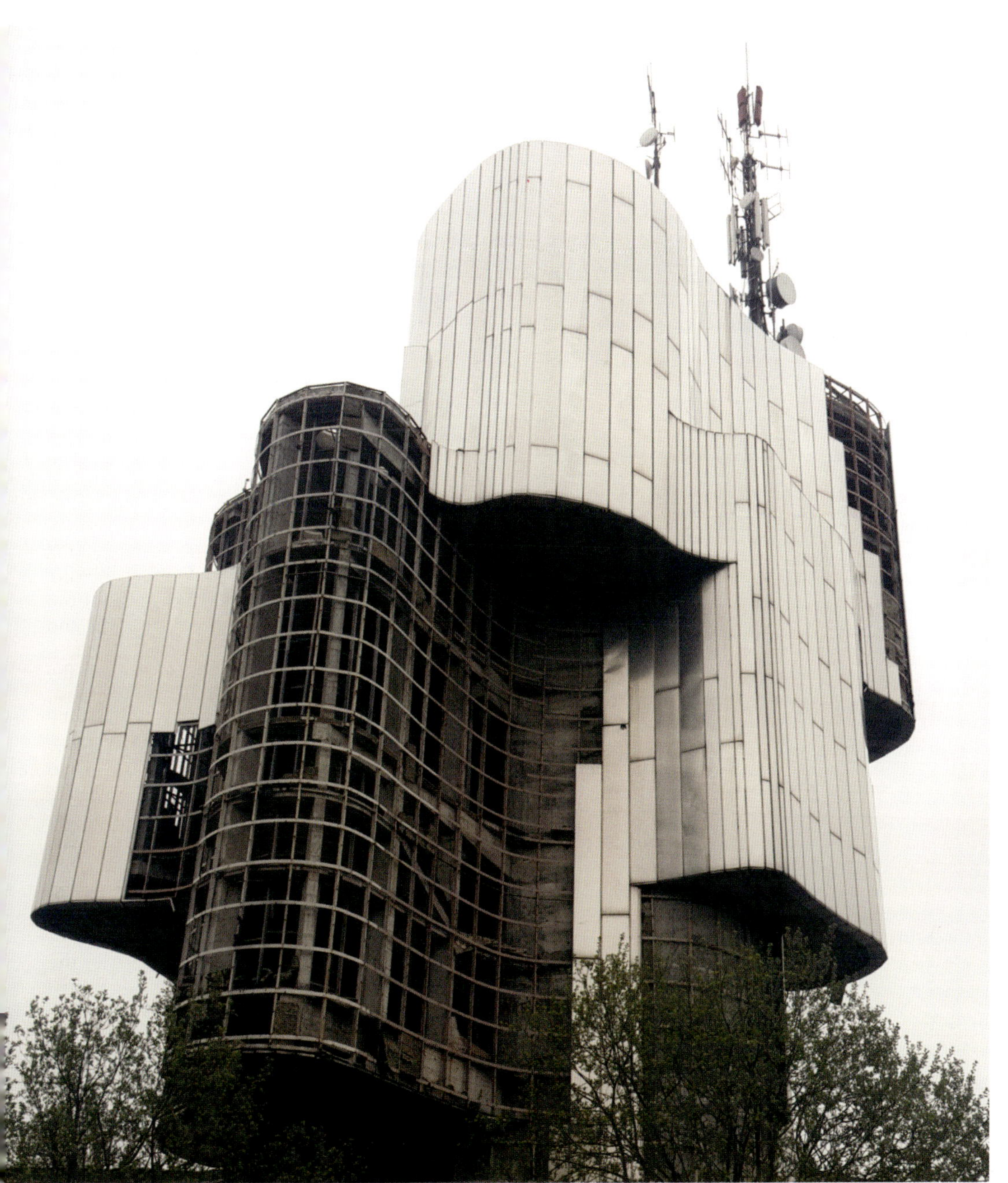

PLESO (PLEH-soh)

NAME: Broken Ring
LOCATION: Pleso (suburb of Zagreb), Croatia
YEAR COMPLETED: 1978
DESIGNER: Marijan Burger
COORDINATES: N45°43'51.6", E16°03'53.3"
DIMENSIONS: 8 metres high and 8 metres wide
MATERIALS: Poured concrete and rebar

HISTORY

In April 1941, German and Italian forces entered the Zagreb region, appointing the city as capital of their newly created puppet regime, the Independent State of Croatia (NDH). Ruthless occupation followed, with the passing of race laws that resulted in the persecution, torture and execution of ethnic minorities. By May, partisan resistance movements had formed in the region. Initially these groups worked to sabotage networks and infrastructure important to Axis communication and supply. In December 1943, members of the Turpolje Partisan Unit attacked Axis-controlled airports in the Pleso and Kurilovec areas of greater Zagreb, leaving the former damaged and the latter all but destroyed. These raids were part of the partisan plan to break the defensive circle formed by Ustaše and German troops around the city. Between February 1944 and March 1945, the American 15th Air Force flew twelve bombing sorties over Zagreb, targeting the airports at Pleso and Borongaj and further weakening the Axis grip on the city.

On 5 May 1945, the final battle for Zagreb began, with Axis forces facing the advancing partisan Yugoslav 1st Army. The next day, with the partisans in a strong position, the NDH government fled the city towards Austria. On 7 May, German troops in Zagreb surrendered unconditionally. However, victory for the Yugoslav 1st Army had come at great cost. The day was the bloodiest they had ever experienced, with more than 158 killed and 358 wounded. Finally, on 8 May, the partisans entered Zagreb with little resistance, capturing more than 15,000 Axis troops in the process.

Over the course of the war, tens of thousands of Zagreb residents perished as a result of executions, reprisal killings, concentration camp deportations and resistance against Axis forces.

DESIGN AND CONSTRUCTION

In the mid-1970s, politicians and veterans' groups commissioned the Croatian artist Marijan Burger to create a spomenik complex in the Pleso area to symbolise the breaking of the Axis ring around Zagreb, and the partisans who fell in the liberation of the city. It was opened on 8 May 1978, 32 years after the liberation.

The spomenik is an 8-metre-tall, 8-metre-wide monument suggestive of a huge ring that has been snapped and pulled apart.

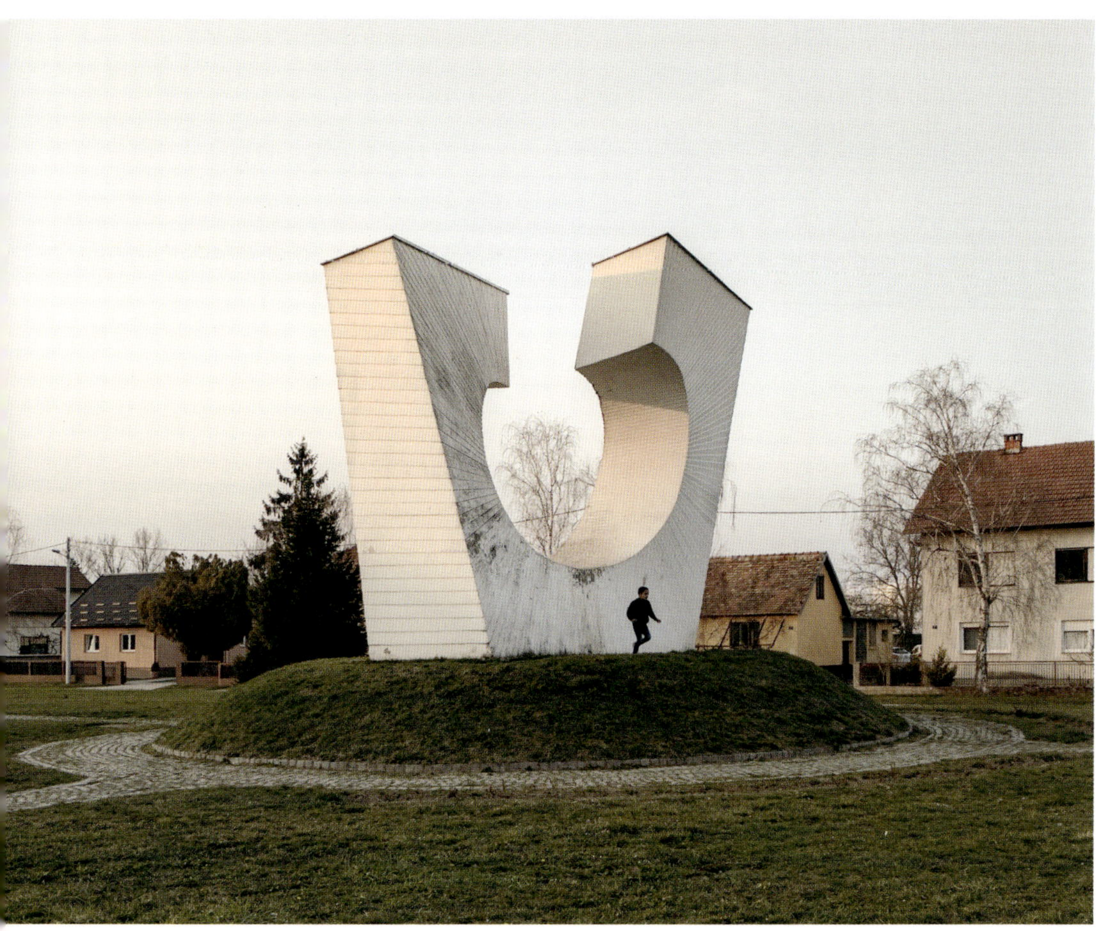

Between 1991 and 1995, Zagreb was significantly affected by the Yugoslav Wars and the Croatian War of Independence. Bombing and rocket attacks by the breakaway Republic of Serbian Krajina (RSK) were common. The most significant took place on 2 May 1995, when RSK forces fired M-87 Orkan rockets directly into the city centre, resulting in seven deaths. These attacks were retaliation for the RSK's loss of territory to the Croatian Army during their Operation Flash offensive. Thousands of Croats were killed during the war for their independence. In 1997, a small plaque was added to the Pleso spomenik commemorating two local men who fought and died during that war (the addition of Yugoslav War-era commemorative plaques to World War II monuments is not unusual).

Today, the memorial and its surroundings are in good condition. Although many tributes are left at the monument, they are clearly left on the plaque for the Croatian Independence fighters, not that of the partisan fighters.

PLOVANIJA (ploh-VAH-nee-yah)

NAME: Monument to Fallen Soldiers and Victims of Fascism
LOCATION: Plovanija, Croatia
YEAR COMPLETED: 1981
DESIGNER: Aleksandar Rukavina
COORDINATES: N45°27'02.7", E13°38'07.1"
DIMENSIONS: 12 metres high
MATERIALS: Poured concrete, rebar and mosaic tiles

HISTORY

Following the invasion of the Kingdom of Yugoslavia by Axis forces in April 1941, the Istrian peninsula, where the village of Plovanija is located, was occupied by Italian troops.

Many Croats and Slovenes fled. Those who remained were subjected to violent oppression. Thousands of Italians were moved into the region and Italian became the official language, while the Slavic language was outlawed. Underground resistance movements sprang up across Istria throughout 1942 and into 1943, though they were no match for the strength of the Italian Army. However, once Italy had surrendered to the Allies in September 1943, partisan forces were able to liberate the region.

On 13 September 1943, in the town of Pazin, 50 kilometres southeast of Plovanija, the partisan rebels held an Anti-Fascist Council, which determined that Istria would be totally separated from Italy and incorporated into Croatia. However, German forces quickly occupied the areas formerly held by the Italians, resulting in the loss of much of the partisans' freed territory in Istria. The partisans battled on, and on 9 May 1945, Plovanija was liberated. It is estimated that in Plovanija and the surrounding area, more than 50 homes were burnt to the ground and 200 local people killed during the course of the war.

In the months after World War II, thousands of Italians who had settled in Istria during the 'Italianisation' of the territory were forcibly deported. A number of Italians in the greater Plovanija region (and elsewhere in Istria) were killed in retaliation for the brutal occupation. Later known as the Foibe massacres, estimates of the number of victims range from hundreds to thousands. After the war, Plovanija did not immediately become part of Yugoslavia. Instead, it was integrated into a provisionally independent Free Territory of Trieste, an area administered by the United Nations. This was intended to ease post-war ethnic tensions and quell rival territorial claims between Italy and Yugoslavia. In 1954, Plovanija became part of Yugoslavia, with the disputed territorial claims finally settled in 1975.

DESIGN AND CONSTRUCTION

In the late 1970s, local government and veterans' groups planned a spomenik to commemorate the civilians and fighters of Plovanija who had died in World War II. The Croatian sculptor and painter Aleksandar Rukavina was commissioned to design the complex, which was officially unveiled on 22 June 1981, marking the 40th anniversary of the Croatian partisan uprising. Located in the centre of the village, the primary monument is a 12-metre-tall, concrete structure made up of three curved fins (possibly echoing the three ethnicities of the area – Croats, Slovenes and Italians) set very close to each other and tapering towards the ground. On the concave surface of each fin is a mosaic frieze depicting one of three scenes: Tradition (represented by a folk dance accompanied by traditional instruments); Labour (represented by oxen pulling a laden cart); Resistance (represented by fighters defending a group of women and children).

STATUS AND CONDITION

The spomenik is in a fair condition, though over time it has suffered from weathering and the mosaics have lost many of their tiles. The Istrian peninsula was comparatively unaffected by the Yugoslav Wars of the 1990s, so this monument was spared the mistreatment endured by many others across the former Yugoslavia. This site still receives regular visitors, and commemorative ceremonies continue to be held here annually.

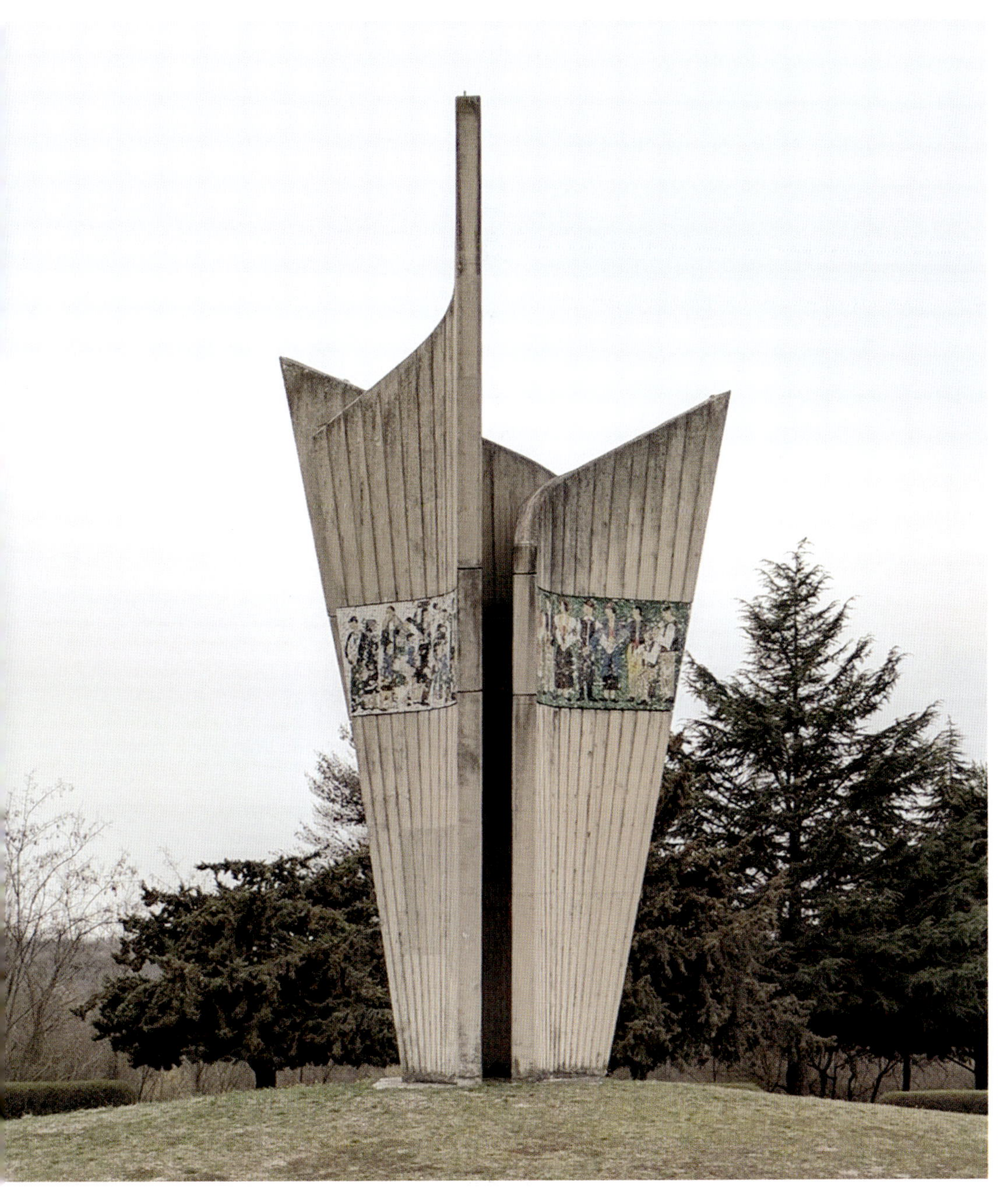

PODGARIĆ (POHD-gar-eech)

NAME: Monument to the Revolution of the People of Moslavina
LOCATION: Podgarić, Croatia
YEAR COMPLETED: 1967 (2 years to build)
DESIGNERS: Dušan Džamonja and Vladimir Veličković
COORDINATES: N45°38'27.0", E16°46'39.6"
DIMENSIONS: 10 metres high and 20 metres wide
MATERIALS: Poured concrete, rebar, aluminum sheets

HISTORY

In April 1941, following victory by Axis forces over the army of the Kingdom of Yugoslavia, the Moslavina region (along with the rest of present-day Croatia) was integrated into the Independent State of Croatia, a new Axis puppet state. The country was now controlled by the oppressive military rule of the Ustaše, who targeted ethnic-Serbs, Jews, Roma and Croat rebels with the intention of creating a compliant and ethnically pure Croatian state. As a consequence, many in Moslavina began to organise themselves against the persecution. On 22 June 1941, rebels near the town of Sisak initiated an uprising – the first armed resistance movement against Axis occupation during World War II. Quickly spreading across Moslavina and into large areas of occupied territory, many rebels coalesced around the communist partisan army of Josip Tito.

For the rest of the war, the area around the Moslavina village of Podgarić became a significant centre of partisan revolt and a hub of activity for the Croatian Communist Party's Central Committee. On the hillsides above the village, hospital complexes such as Stara Konspiracija and Novo Konspiracija were constructed. Housing hundreds of troops, medical personnel and workshops, they treated thousands of war casualties, both fighters and civilians.

DESIGN AND CONSTRUCTION

In the mid-1960s sculptor Dušan Džamonja and architect Vladimir Veličković were commissioned to create a spomenik complex to mark Podgarić's significance in the fight against Ustaše forces. It was unveiled on 7 September 1967, at a grand ceremony attended by Josip Tito.

The primary element of the complex is a winged abstract sculpture, approximately 10 metres tall and 20 metres wide, with a central convex 'eye' covered in aluminium-plate segments. According to Džamonja, the monument was intended to represent the 'wings of victory' – an allusion to the triumph of the partisan rebels over the occupying Axis forces.

The approach pathway houses a crypt containing the remains of some 900 partisan soldiers who died in the surrounding hillside hospitals. Above ground, the pathway is punctuated by a dramatic, angular, ribbed-concrete arch, at the base of which is an engraved bronze memorial plaque. A small artificial lake was created in the valley below the complex by damming the Kamenjače River. This was intended to enhance the beauty of the view, while also acting as a tourist attraction for the Vila Garić resort hotel at the lake's south end.

right: Podgarić spomenik in the early 1970s

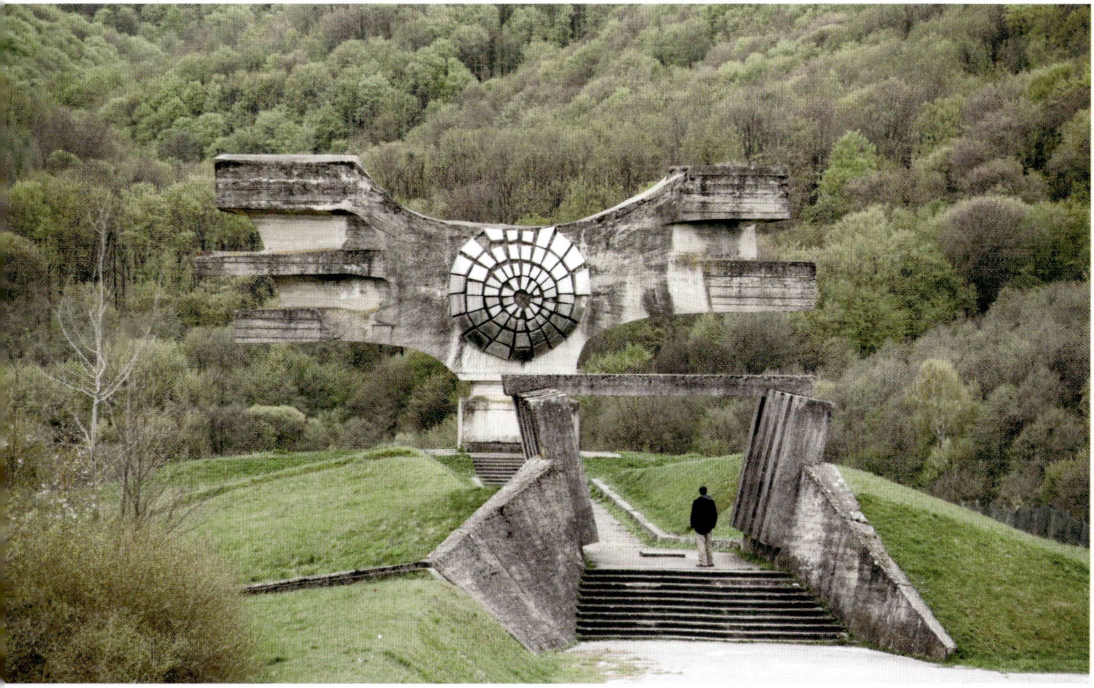

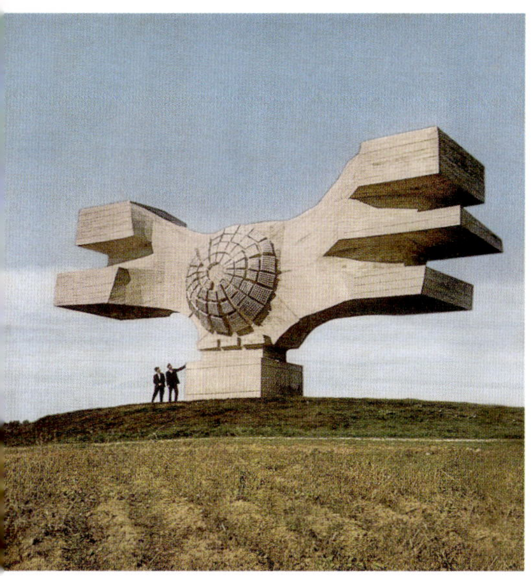

The site became a popular cultural, historical and tourist destination. However, following the breakup of the country in the early 1990s, the Yugoslav Wars and subsequent Croatian independence, interest dropped considerably. Today visitor numbers are very low, however modest commemorative events are still held at the site. The monument itself is in reasonably good condition, with few signs of serious structural damage.

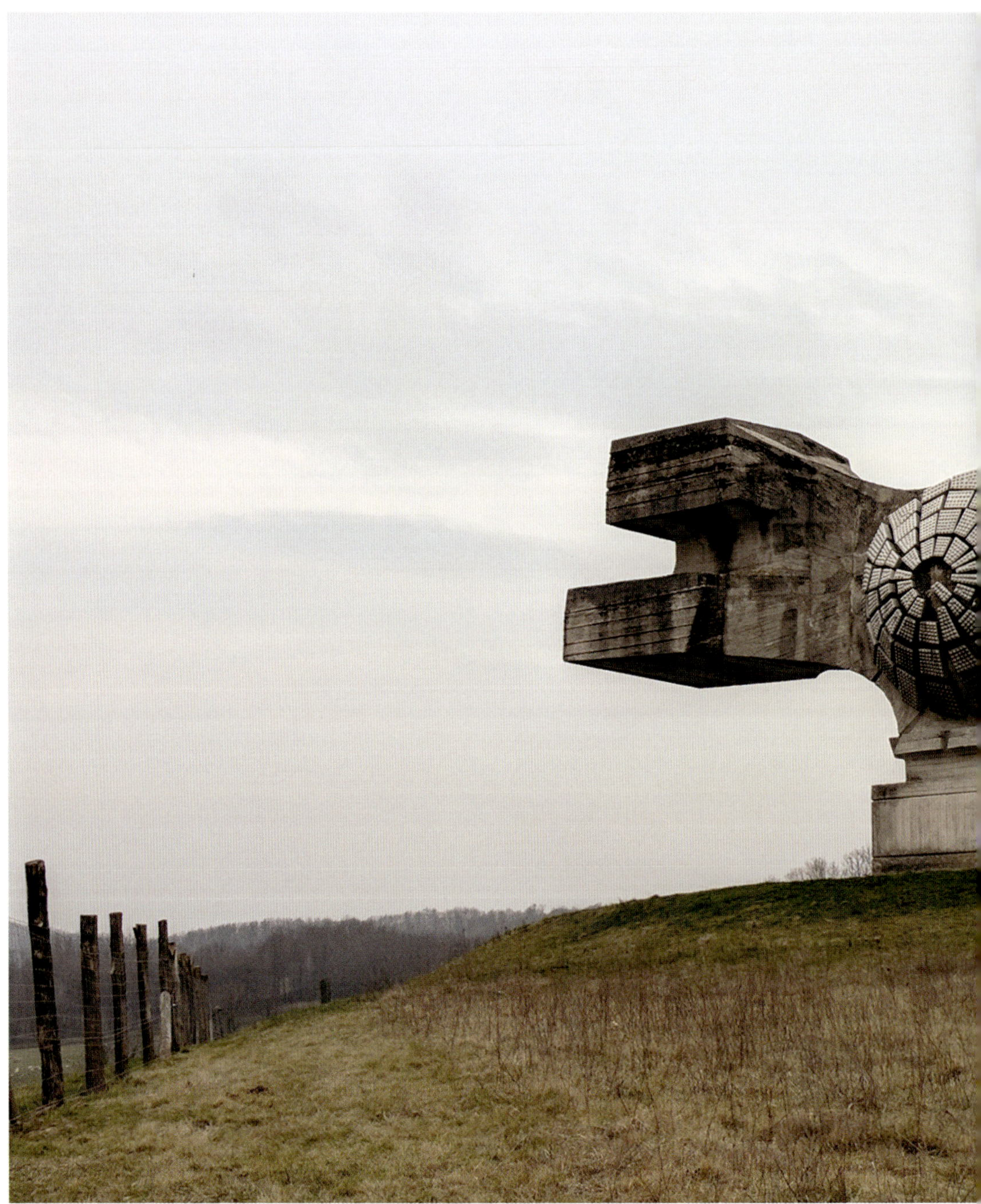

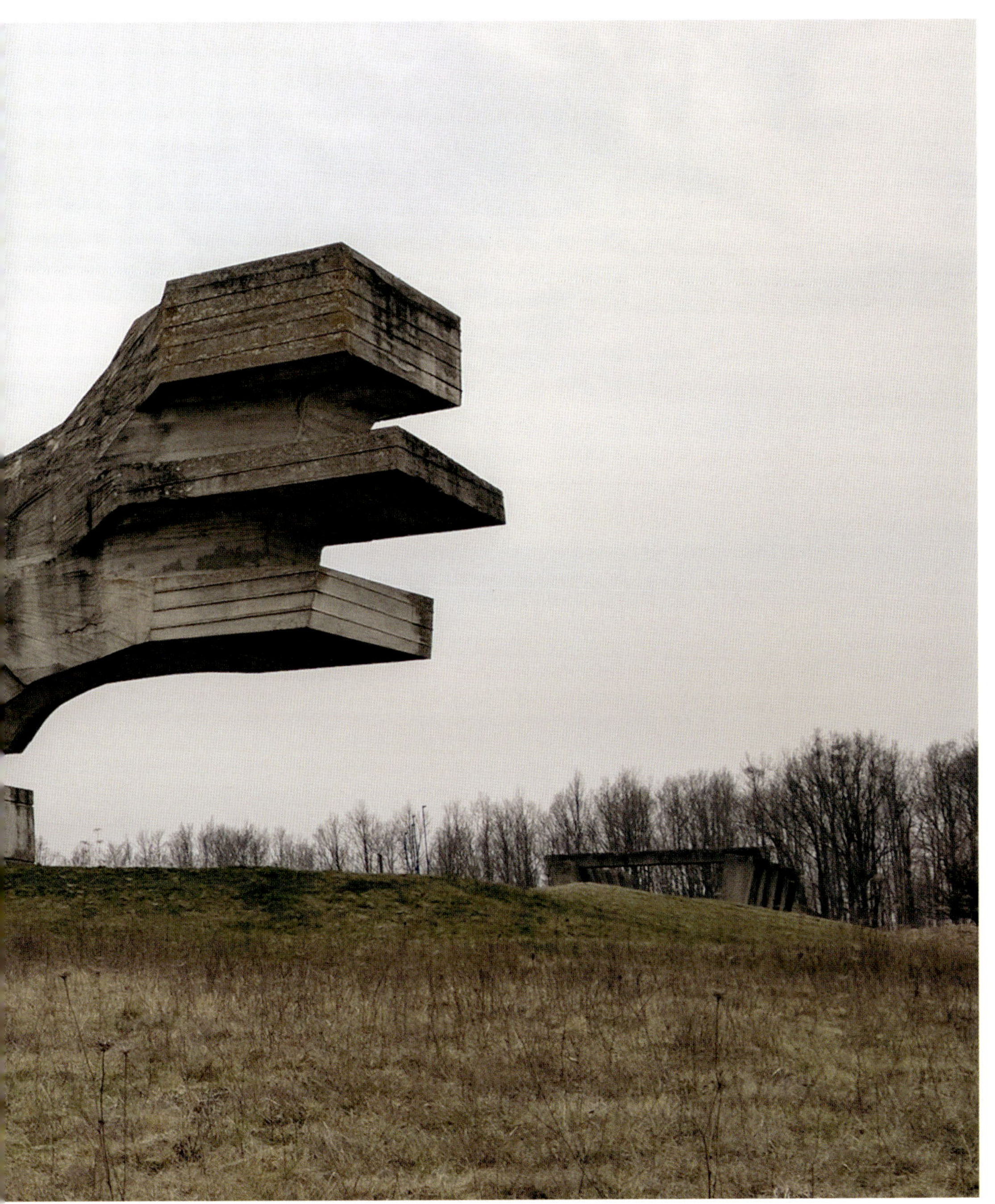

PODGORA (POHD-gor-ah)

NAME: Seagull Wings Monument
LOCATION: Podgora, Croatia
YEAR COMPLETED: 1962
DESIGNER: Rajko Radović
COORDINATES: N43°14'44.6", E17°04'13.9"
DIMENSIONS: 60 metres high
MATERIALS: Poured concrete, rebar and marble

HISTORY

In the aftermath of the Axis invasion of the Kingdom of Yugoslavia in April 1941, the Dalmatian coast fell under the control of the Italian Army and Ustaše. In August 1942, following months of guerrilla attacks by partisan units, General Renzo Dalmazzo of the Italian 6th Corps initiated Operation Albia, a campaign to rid the Biokovo region of rebel fighters. By the end of the operation, nearly 1,000 partisans had been killed, with the loss of only 17 soldiers from the Italian ranks. In addition, hundreds of local civilians were deliberately murdered and their homes razed to the ground.

In September, Biokovo partisan commanders met with Marshal Josip Tito to conceive a response. It was decided that a Partisan Naval Headquarters would be established in the nearby town of Podgora, from which naval offensives against Italian forces could be organised.

Initially, this partisan 'navy' consisted of only around 150 local fishermen and their boats, who did what they could to disrupt attacks by Italian vessels. However, by the end of the war it numbered more than 16,000 sailors, with a combined force of over 500 assorted ships, spread across several units including the Prekomorske (Overseas) Fleet and the 26th Dalmatian Division. They successfully carried out smuggling operations, blockade-running and even direct attacks on Italian ships. However, they suffered significant losses, with nearly 600 sailors losing their lives over the course of the war.

DESIGN AND CONSTRUCTION

In the early 1960s, plans were made to build a spomenik complex overlooking the Adriatic to commemorate the inception of the region's partisan naval force. Serbian sculptor Rajko Radović was commissioned to create the monument, which was unveiled by Josip Tito on 10 September 1962, this date marked the 20th anniversary of the formation of the first Partisan Naval Detachment.

Standing on a hillside overlooking Podgora, it consists of two large concrete 'gull wings' set on a polished-marble panelled platform, with a large amphitheatre built into the hillside, where presentations and historical lectures were once given to visitors. One 'wing' extends 60 metres vertically in a shallow curve, symbolising partisan successes over fascist naval forces. The other 'wing' is bent horizontally at a height of 20 metres, to represent those fighters who died in battle.

STATUS AND CONDITION

The monument complex is in good condition and reasonably well maintained, having escaped much of the vandalism inflicted on similar monuments after the Yugoslav Wars. Although the number of visitors has dropped considerably since the 1990s, the monument is promoted as a tourist attraction in the town of Podgora, with multi-lingual signs at the site describing the location's cultural and historical significance. The site still hosts annual commemorative events.

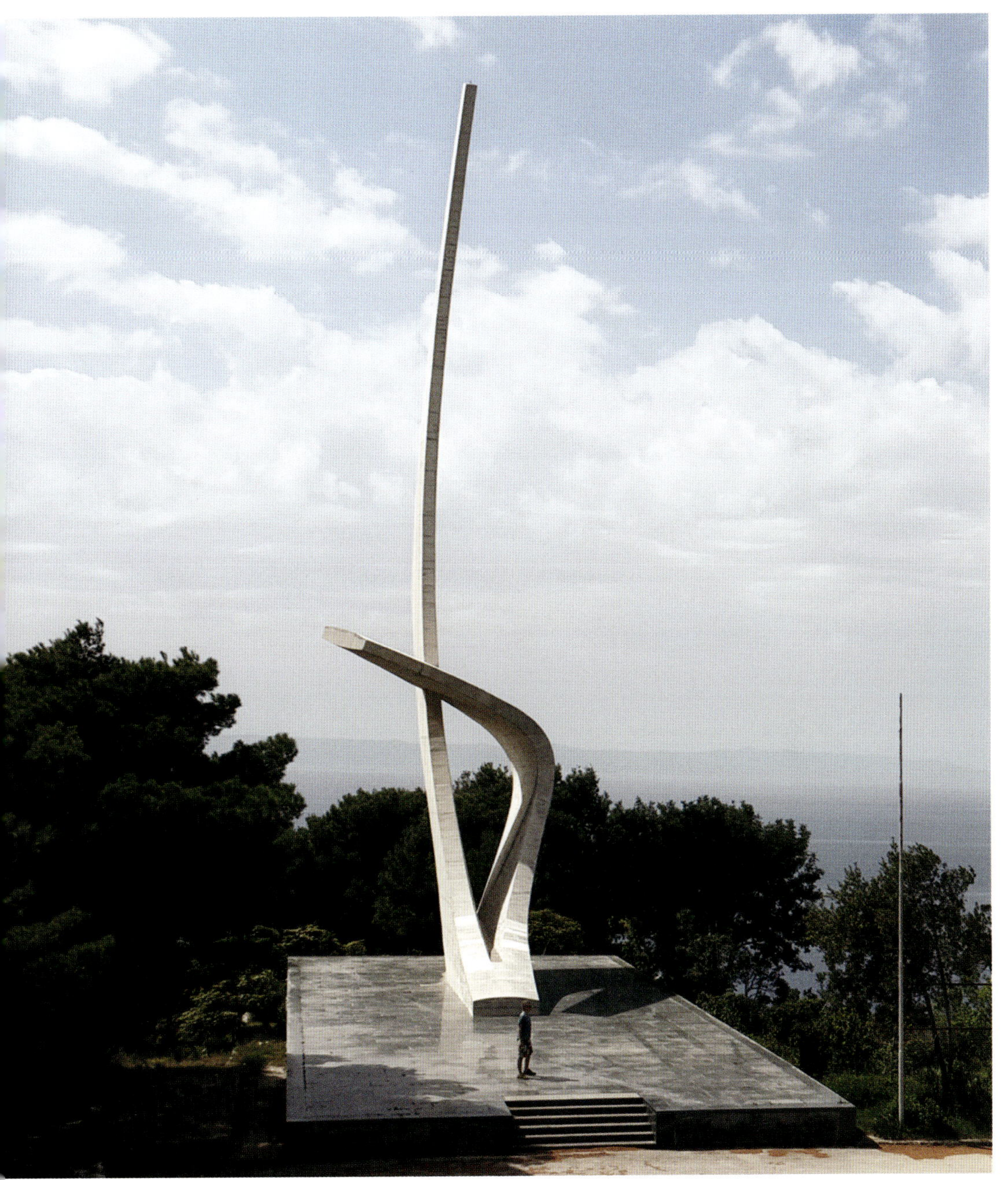

PODHUM (POHD-hoom)

NAME: Monument to the Victims of Fascism
LOCATION: Podhum, Croatia
YEAR COMPLETED: 1970
DESIGNERS: Šime Vulas, Duško Rakić and
Igor Emili
COORDINATES: N45°22'31.9", E14°29'49.6"
DIMENSIONS: 22 metres high
MATERIALS: Poured concrete and rebar

HISTORY

When Yugoslavia and its Istrian peninsula were invaded by Axis powers in April 1941, the small town of Podhum was occupied by Italian forces, under the administration of the Italian province of Carnaro. Within a few months of occupation, organised resistance movements were formed, and by early 1942, Italian control over the peninsula was being threatened. The Prefect of Carnaro ordered harsh reprisals to be carried out in any towns and villages refusing to co-operate with the Italian authorities. In July 1942, sixteen Italian soldiers were killed by resistance fighters in Podhum. The reprisal took place on 12 July, when 250 Italian soldiers, under the command of Waffen-SS Major Armando Giorleo, entered the town and rounded up 91 males of military age. Fourteen of these resisted arrest and were shot immediately. The rest were marched to an open field south of the town, where they were shot in groups of five and thrown into a pit. (The precise number of deaths is unknown. Some estimates put the figure at 130.) Following the massacre, the soldiers burned the town and deported the remaining women and children to concentration camps in Italy. Podhum was eventually liberated in May 1945.

DESIGN AND CONSTRUCTION

Immediately after the war, makeshift crosses and other grave-markers were erected by locals to commemorate those killed during the Italian occupation. In the late 1960s, the government, alongside veterans' organisations, made plans to create a more substantial spomenik complex. The famous Croatian sculptor Šime Vulas was commissioned to design the monument, with landscaping and architecture by Duško Rakić and Igor Emili. Officially unveiled in July 1970, the central element of the park is a 22-metre-tall concrete pillar, broadening out towards the top, with its surface modulated by 91 curved shapes, one for each of the victims. To the north of this monument are two sunken amphitheatres and two grids containing several dozen square concrete markers. The whole complex is surrounded by a tall, curved stone wall, on the inside of which hang a number of additional commemorative markers.

STATUS AND CONDITION

The spomenik complex is well maintained. It is still visited, and commemorative events are held here every year.

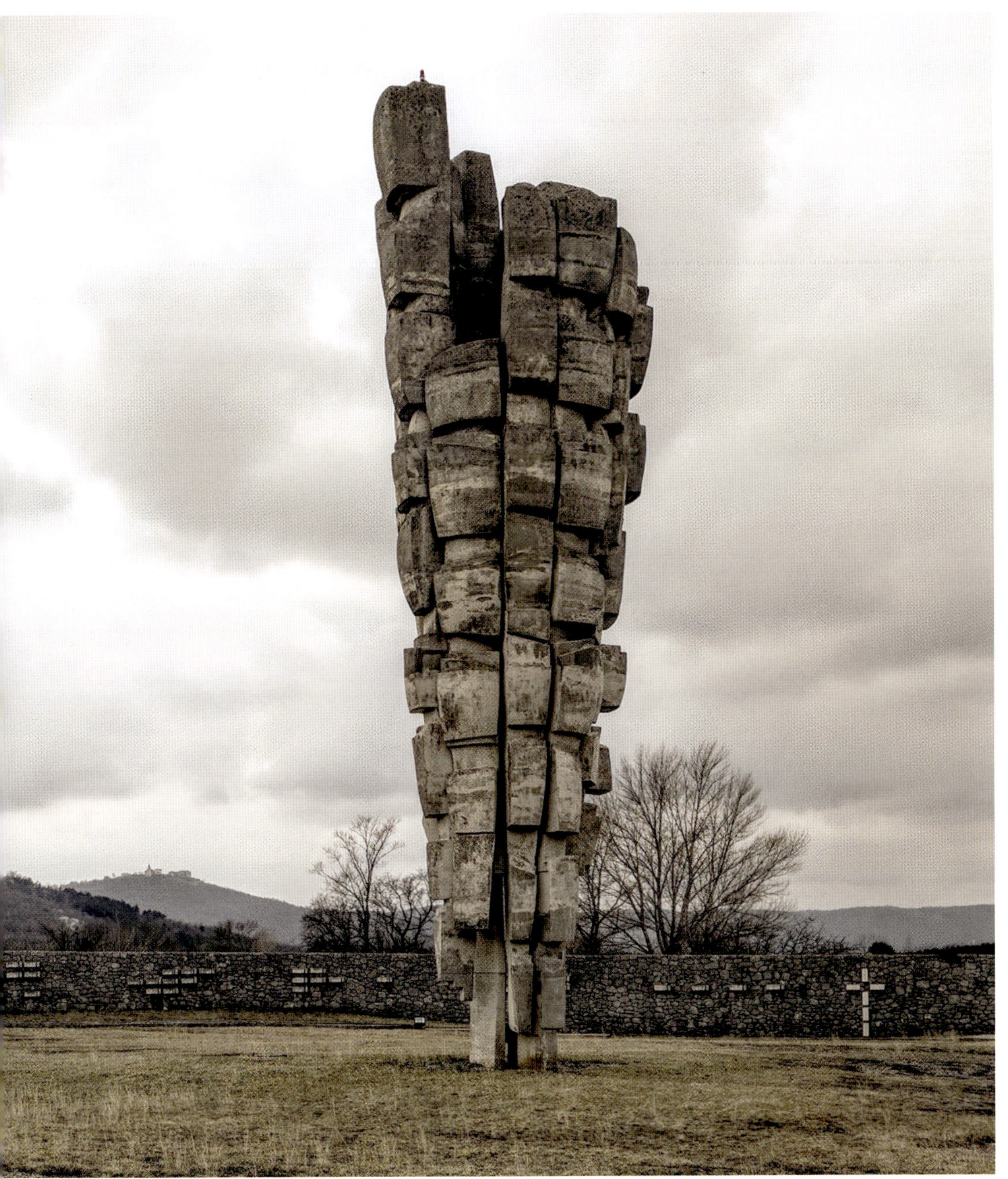

POPINA (POH-pee-nah)

NAME: Popina Monument Park or Mausoleum to the Fallen Insurgents against Fascism or 'The Sniper'
LOCATION: Štulac, Serbia
YEAR COMPLETED: 1981 (3 years to build)
DESIGNER: Bogdan Bogdanović
COORDINATES: N43°37'48.9", E20°57'29.6"
DIMENSIONS: Three monoliths, 10–18 metres high, set in a 12 hectare park
MATERIALS: Gabbro stone blocks

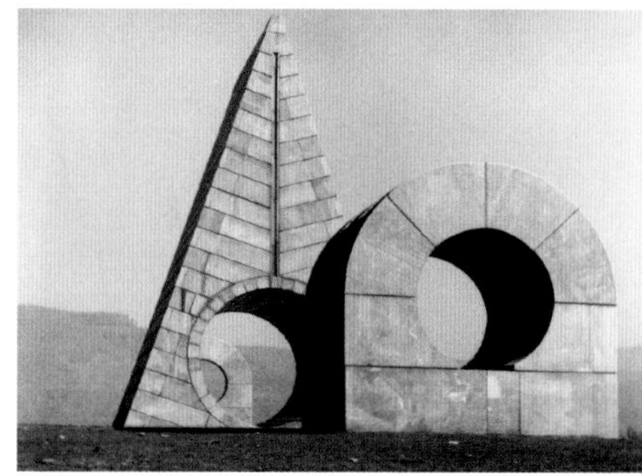

Popina spomenik in the mid-1980s
(image from the ArchitekturZentrumWein, Bogdanović Archive, Vienna)

HISTORY

In late September 1941, Tito's Partisan Army liberated a significant area of western Serbia, formerly under the control of German forces. This territory, which was named the Republic of Užice, was the first in Europe to be freed from Axis control. The city of Užice became the new capital of the Republic, with Tito relocating his partisan headquarters here from Belgrade. German troop movement was disrupted by the insurrection in western Serbia, prompting the first German counter-insurgency campaign. In what became known as Operation Užice, commander Franz Böhme dispatched 80,000 soldiers to recover the situation, instructing them to employ brutal methods to discourage future uprisings.

On 12 October, as the 1,000-strong, well-armed 717th German Infantry Division travelled towards Užice along the West Morava Valley, they encountered the Trstenički Partisan Unit, consisting of 300 fighters, who were patrolling the borders of the Republic of Užice. Fighting began the following day, with a four-hour battle taking place on a hillside to the east of Štulac. What would become known as 'Popinski Bitka' (the Battle of Popina) was the first frontal assault between German troops and partisan rebels. The Germans began before dawn, using heavy artillery to target rebel positions near the West Morava River. Eventually, they drove the partisans out, killing more than 40 of their number in the process. By December 1941, Tito's partisan resistance had been expelled from the Užice region and the freed territory they had previously held had been firmly restored to Axis control.

DESIGN AND CONSTRUCTION

As a means of stimulating the tourist industry in the area, in 1977, the local authorities of Vrnjačka Banja and Trstenik allocated funding for a memorial to honour the partisan fighters of the Battle of Popina (supplemented with donations from across Yugoslavia). Renowned architect Bogdan Bogdanović was commissioned to work on the project. Bogdanović had already retired, and agreed to accept the commission only after he had been granted full creative control over the construction.

Over a period of three years, he created a memorial complex consisting of four main elements: a commemorative block and three monoliths made from gabbro stone blocks. The monument is devoid of the elaborate ornamentation or engravings that characterise

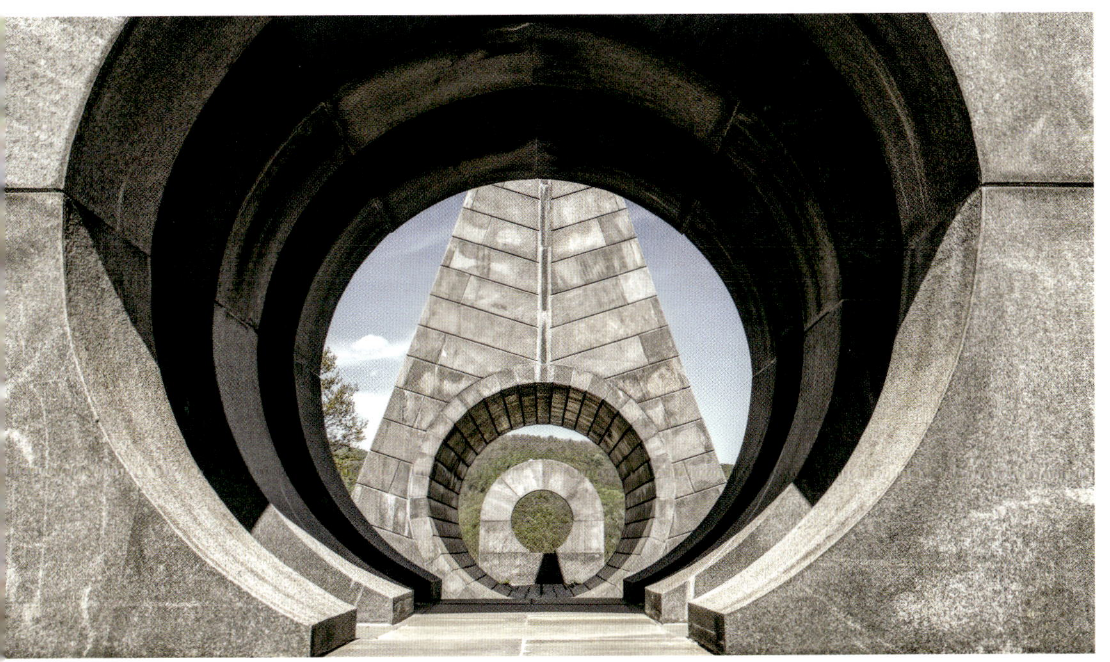

almost all Bogdanović's spomenik complexes. The monoliths are evenly spaced, connected by a straight, 100-metre-long, paved pathway. The central monolith is triangular and 18 metres high; those at each end are cylindrical and 10 metres high. Running through the middle of each block is a large round opening. These all align, incidentally creating what has popularly become recognised as a gun-barrel effect, giving the spomenik its nickname of 'The Sniper'. Bogdanović was appalled to learn of this epithet, and that his creation was being likened to a weapon of war.

He had originally proposed a more extensive scheme for the site, including a motel, sports facilities and an elaborate cascading fountain. However, with costs spiralling out of control, these plans were left unrealised. It is not clear to what degree the complex was ever a viable tourist attraction, even during the Yugoslav period, when such monuments were widely celebrated.

The monument is in very good condition. Although the site receives little maintenance, the stone blocks show minimal discoloration or deterioration. The complex has suffered little vandalism or graffiti. Perhaps the major factor in its preservation is its remote location – aided by the fact that it is not promoted by the local authorities, or even signposted.

In 2011, a ceremony was held at the spomenik to commemorate the 70th anniversary of the Battle of Popina. However, such events are not regular occurrences. In 2016, the Institute for the Protection of Monuments in Kraljevo made plans for a complete restoration to commemorate the 75th anniversary of the battle. In 2017, a grant was agreed by the Serbian Ministry of Labour, Employment and Social Policy, and restoration work started. Considerable progress has been made in improving the condition of the spomenik and the surrounding trails and infrastructure.

PRILEP (PREE-lep)

NAME: Burial Mound of the Unbeaten or Prilep
Partisan Necropolis
LOCATION: Park of the Revolution, Prilep, Macedonia
YEAR COMPLETED: 1961
DESIGNER: Bogdan Bogdanović
COORDINATES: N41°20'03.6", E21°33'16.2"
DIMENSIONS: Eight monoliths, 3–5 metres high
MATERIALS: White marble blocks

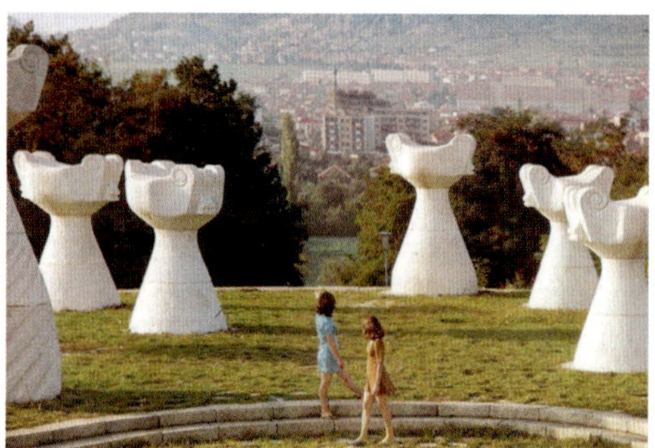

Prilep spomenik in the 1960s with the city in the background

HISTORY

Almost immediately after Prilep was occupied by
Axis German and Bulgarian forces in April 1941,
resistance groups planned an armed uprising.

The first resistance action took place on 11
October 1941, when 60 fighters from the local
Youth Communist League attacked an Axis-run
police station in the town centre, cutting phone
lines and collecting weapons. The Bulgarian Army
and police reacted by arresting more than 1,000
Prilep residents, many of whom were beaten,
tortured or killed.

Consequently, the city rose up against the Axis
occupation, with hundreds of local citizens joining
newly established partisan units and proceeding
to carry out both direct attacks and acts of
sabotage against Bulgarian forces.

On 2 August 1944, the partisans drove the
Bulgarians out, only to have their city retaken
nine days later by German soldiers. However, on
3 November, the Germans were expelled and
the city was finally liberated.

Over the course of the war, nearly 700 Prilep
resistance fighters were killed. Fifteen of those
who fell in combat were posthumously named
Yugoslav National Heroes. Of Prilep's pre-war
population of 25,000, over 8,000 participated in
the armed resistance. In the early 1960s, Prilep
was designated a Partisan City, in honour of its
resistance legacy. And in recognition of the
courage of its citizens, on 7 May 1975, Prilep was
awarded Yugoslavia's highest honour by being
named a People's Hero City.

DESIGN AND CONSTRUCTION

To commemorate Prilep's 1960s Partisan City
designation, architect Bogdan Bogdanović was
commissioned to create a monument to those
who died liberating the city. His Park of the
Revolution complex opened on 11 October 1961,
marking the 20th anniversary of Macedonia's anti-
fascist uprising (instigated in Prilep).

Further elements were added in 1962. Once
completed, the park consisted of four main parts:
a burial mound, a small amphitheatre, the Alley
of Heroes, and eight stone columns. The burial
mound is a semi-circular embankment containing
the remains of 462 partisan resistance fighters
who died during the occupation and liberation
of Prilep. Dotted around on a paved area in front
of the mound stand the eight columns, ranging
from 3 to 5 metres tall, bulbous in profile with
simple scrolled capitals that resemble ancient
drinking vessels or thrones. The Alley of Heroes
is a row of ten bronze busts mounted on plinths,
leading from the entrance to the park.

STATUS AND CONDITION

In the years following the breakup of Yugoslavia,
the site was neglected. However, in 2007-08,
70,000 Euros were spent on a complete
restoration. Unfortunately the amphitheatre has
since been vandalised. Today, this spomenik
complex is well promoted by the municipality
and attracts many visitors. Numerous annual
commemorative events are held here.

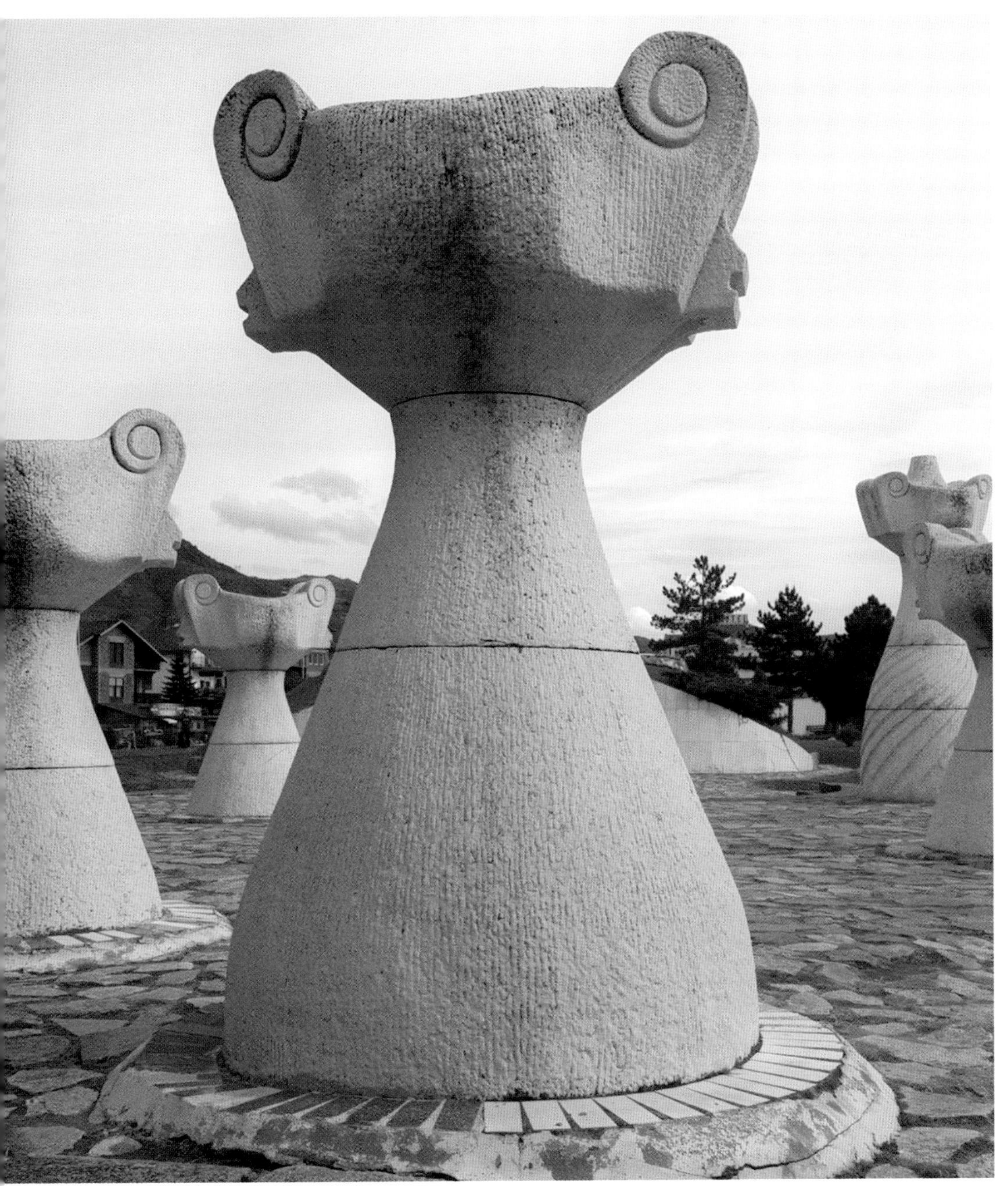

SANSKI MOST (SAN-ski MOST)

NAME: Šušnjar Memorial Complex
LOCATION: Sanski Most, FBiH, Bosnia and
Herzegovina
YEAR COMPLETED: 1970
DESIGNER: Petar Krstić
COORDINATES: N44 45 44.1, E16 41 02.2
DIMENSIONS: 15 metres high and 5 metres wide
MATERIALS: Stainless-steel panels over a steel frame

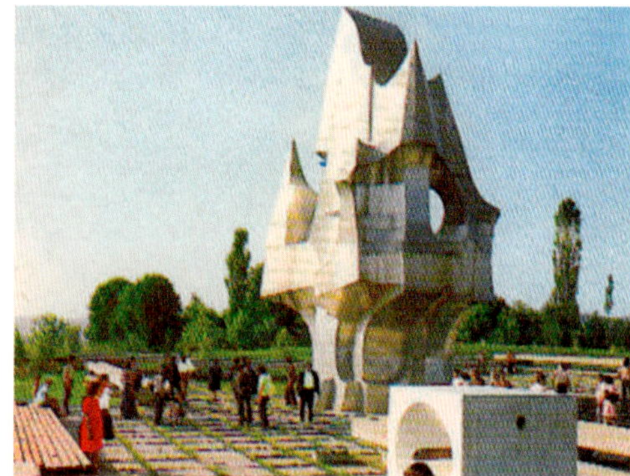
A postcard from the 1970s showing visitors at the Sanski Most spomenik

HISTORY

On 6 May 1941, just a few weeks after the fall of the Kingdom of Yugoslavia and the creation of the Axis puppet regime of the Independent State of Croatia (NDH), peasants from the town of Sanski Most revolted against the NDH's Ustaše military forces. This was the first all-out hostility against Axis/Ustaše forces in Bosnia. The community uprising began when mostly Muslim Ustaše instigators disrupted ethnic-Serb civilians during their celebration of St George's Day (Đurđevdan). During the hostilities, Ustaše forces killed dozens of civilians and arrested dozens more. On 9 May, the rebellion was finally put down with the help of a German unit from Prijedor. In retribution, the regional Ustaše commissioner Viktor Gutić ordered the execution of 27 ethnic-Serb male civilians accused of participating in the unrest. Serb and Jewish prisoners were forced at gunpoint to hang the dead bodies from trees in the town centre, as a warning to others. After three days, the bodies were buried in a mass grave at Šušnjar, to the east of the town.

The killings were not only an effort by Ustaše forces to prevent further uprisings, but part of a co-ordinated Ustaše campaign to eliminate completely ethnic-Serb and Jewish populations from the Bosanska Krajina region. On 28 May,

Gutić addressed a rally of 4,000 people in Sanki Most declaring: 'I have published drastic laws for their [the ethnic-Serbs] complete economic destruction, and new laws will follow for their complete extermination. Don't be generous toward any of them. Bear in my mind that they were always our gravediggers, and destroy them wherever they may be found.' On 2 August 1941, during the St Elijah's Day celebrations, thousands of ethnic-Serb and Jewish civilians were arrested and marched across the town to various killing fields, where they were brutally murdered and tossed into pits. Some accounts state that prisoners who converted to Catholicism were spared. The exact number killed is unknown, but estimates range from 2,000 to 10,000. In August 1942, all the Jews still residing in Sanski Most were arrested and transported to the death camps at Jasenovac.

At the end of the war, Gutić fled the Balkans. He was recognised in Venice and extradited to Yugoslavia in 1946 by Italian war-crimes investigators. During his trial, he denied all charges, but this did not prevent a guilty verdict. He was sentenced to death and executed in 1947.

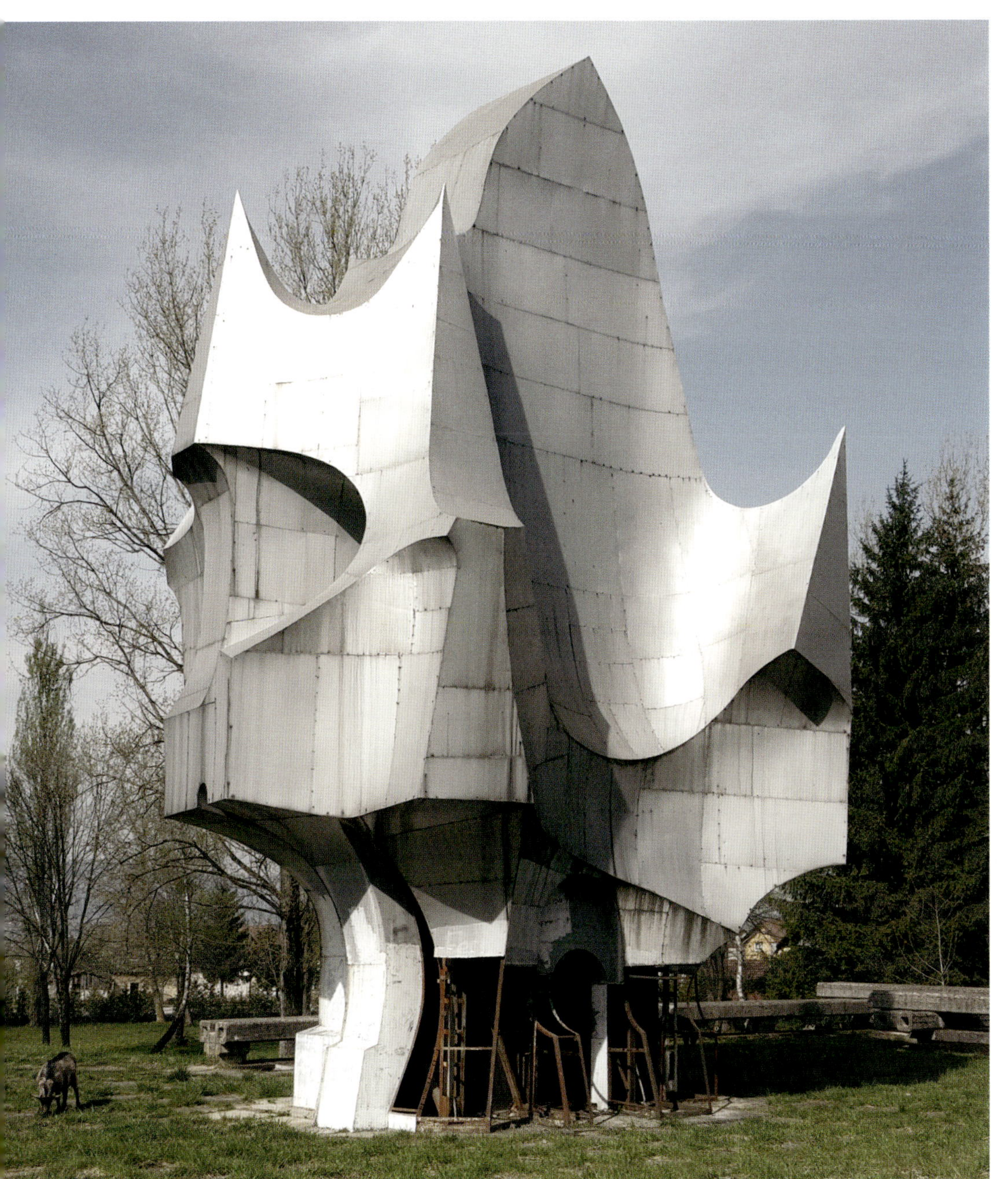

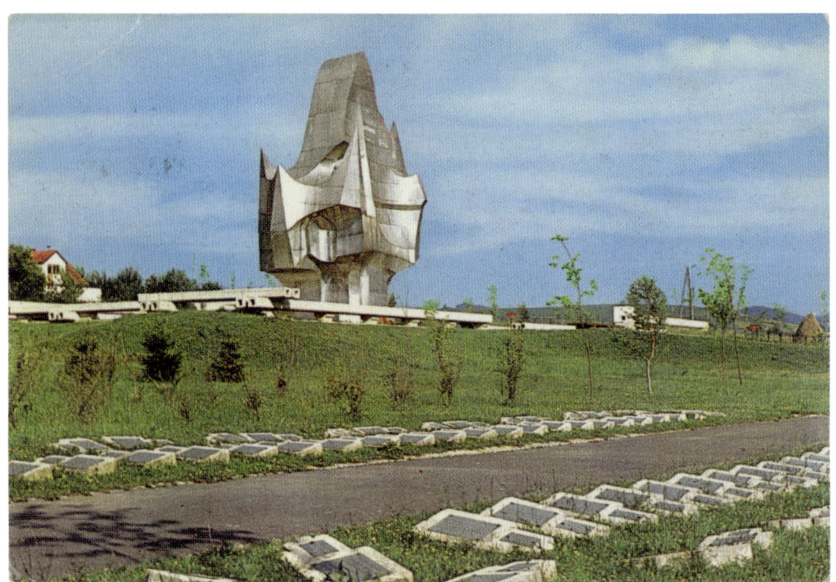

A postcard showing the approach path lined with stone blocks, c.1970

DESIGN AND CONSTRUCTION

In late 1968, three acclaimed designers were considered to create a spomenik memorial on the site. Belgrade architect Bogdan Bogdanović proposed a 'Tower of Babel' structure, while Croatian designer Vanja Radauš suggested a bone-shaped construction. Both were rejected, as the purpose of the memorial was reconciliation rather than antagonism.

The project was finally awarded to Sarajevo architect Petar Krstić. His irregular and luminescent form, completed in 1970, and made from stainless steel, resembles a flame, symbolising the light of life and victory over fascism. Approach paths lined with stone blocks commemorate the victims, while the monument itself is surrounded by concrete beams, which act as seating for visitors and students. Krstić wanted the sculpture to mark not only the suffering of the people of the town, but also that of people throughout the ages. His original design called for sounds and lights to be emitted from the memorial, but this element proved to be prohibitively expensive.

STATUS AND CONDITION

After the fall of Yugoslavia, the memorial complex fell into disrepair. In 1992, a Bosnian Serb veterans' group built a large concrete cross within the grounds. Bosnian Serbs controlled the area until 1995, when the Dayton Agreement granted it to the Federation of Bosnia and Herzegovina. Some local Muslims still find the addition of a cross anathema. In addition, the plaque for partisan Muslim veterans was previously removed. Around 20 to 30 tiles commemorating partisan soldiers killed in the rebellion are also missing, leaving only tiles relating to Jewish and ethnic-Serb civilians, many of which have, also been desecrated. Despite the site being protected by the Bosnian government as part of its national heritage, it would require significant investment to restore it to its original state.

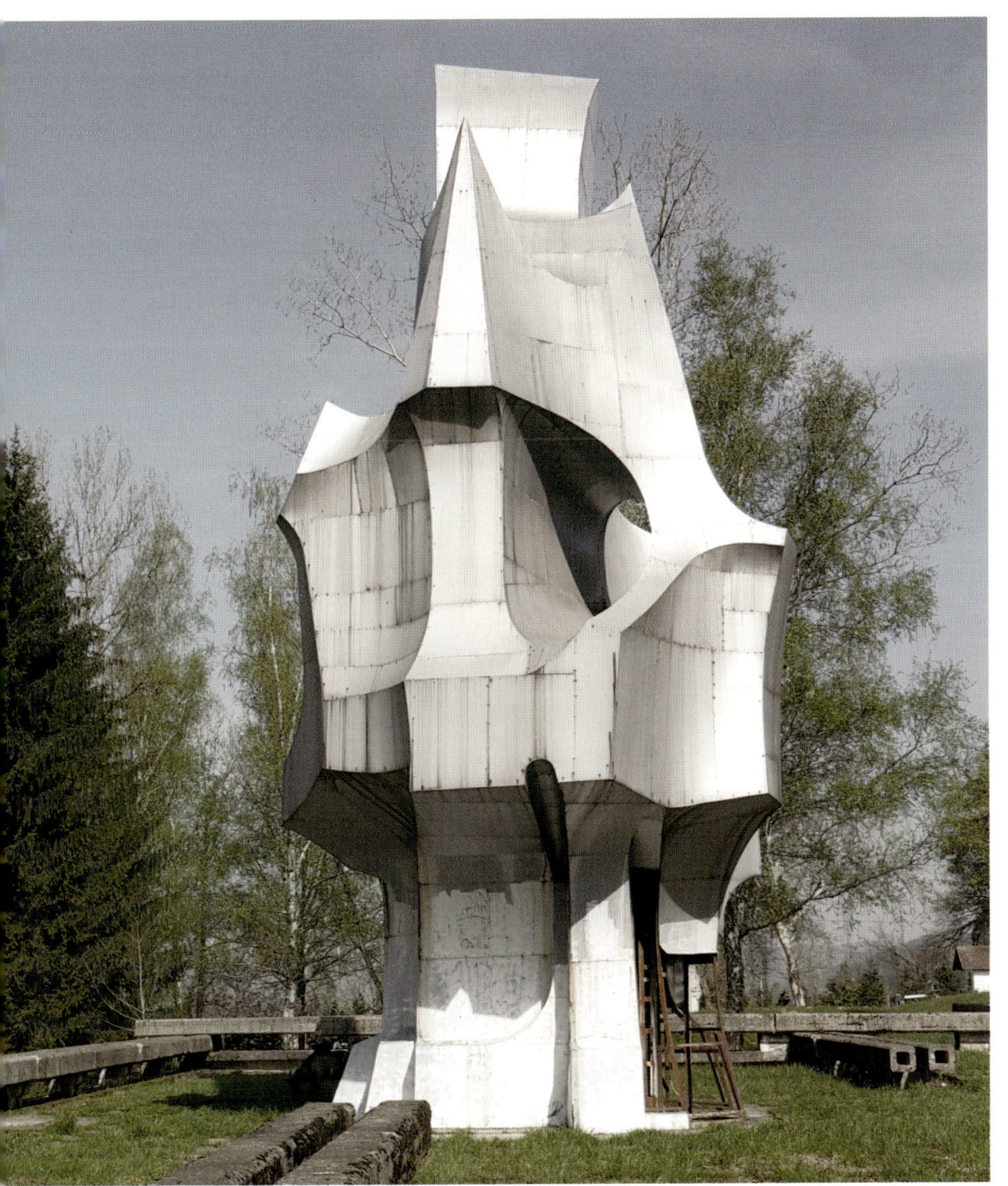

SINJ (SEE-nya)

NAME: Memorial to the Executed Captured Soldiers
of the First Split Partisan Unit – Ruduša
LOCATION: Sinj, Croatia
YEAR COMPLETED: 1962
DESIGNER: Vuko Bombardelli
COORDINATES: N43°41'54.1", E16°37'31.0"
DIMENSIONS: 5 metres high and 8 metres wide
MATERIALS: Poured concrete and rebar

HISTORY

In April 1941, the Croatian city of Split was occupied by Italian forces. By August, Yugoslav partisan recruiters Pavle Pap Šilja and Mirko Kovačević had formed a resistance movement – the Split Partisan Detachment – consisting of three separate units.

On 11 August, the detachment left Split under cover of darkness to join other partisan units at Dinara, a mountain 80 kilometres further north, near the Bosnian border. During the course of this night-time journey, the 1st Unit of the Split Partisan Detachment, commanded by Mirko Kovačević, became disoriented in the mountains. On 14 August, two members of the group entered the village of Košute (see page 82) looking for directions and supplies. The villagers immediately alerted nearby Italian and Ustaše NDH militiamen. A battle ensued in which four partisans were killed, twenty-eight were captured and thirteen escaped. In Sinj, a court of Ustaše military judges sentenced twenty-one of the captured partisans to death. On 26 August, these partisans were taken to a wooded area called Ruduša (just outside Sinj), where they were shot by Italian soldiers. This was one of the first instances of captured resistance fighters being shot for their actions.

DESIGN AND CONSTRUCTION

In the early 1960s a design competition was held for a spomenik at the site where the partisans of the 1st Split Partisan Detachment were shot. Construction was funded by the municipalities of Sinj and Split, alongside the RNK Split Football Club (many members of the detachment had played for the team before the war). The commission was given to Split architect Vuko Bombardelli, whose design was unveiled on 26 August 1962, exactly 21 years after the date of the executions.

The memorial is a 5-metre-tall, open tent-like tripod structure, with three large triangular legs, connected to a smaller triangle set horizontally at its top. A separate spomenik complex in the village of Košute, marked where the inital battle had occurred. Built the year before, it was also designed by Bombardelli. The events of this battle and the fate of the partisan soldiers were depicted in the 1972 film *Prvi Splitski Odred* (*First Split Detachment*), directed by Croatian film-maker Vojdrag Berčić.

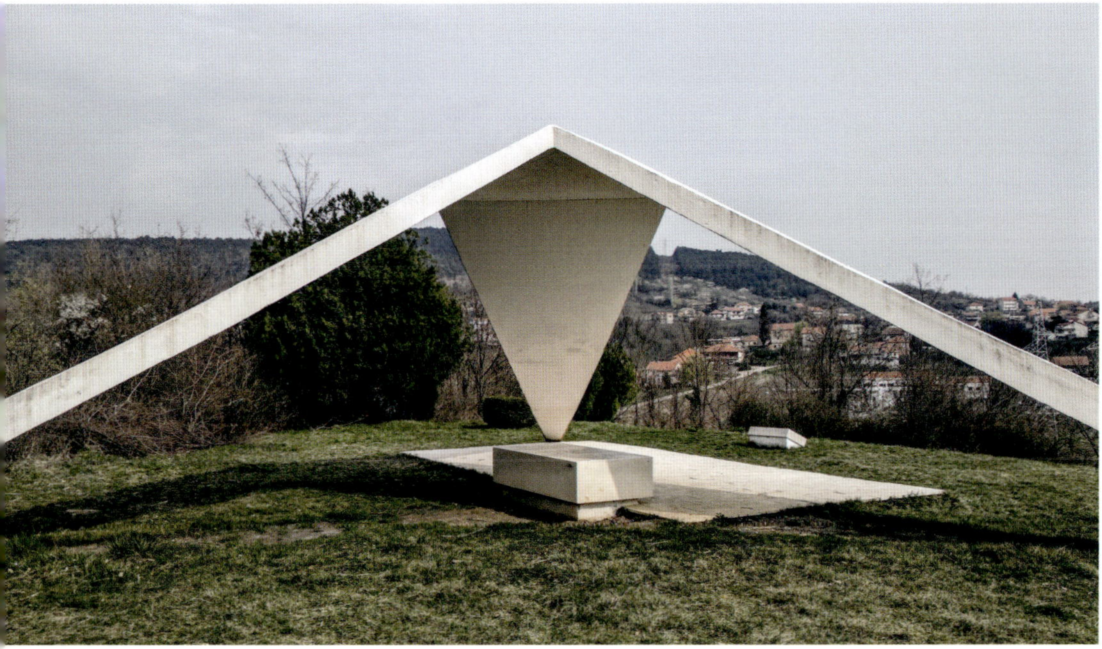

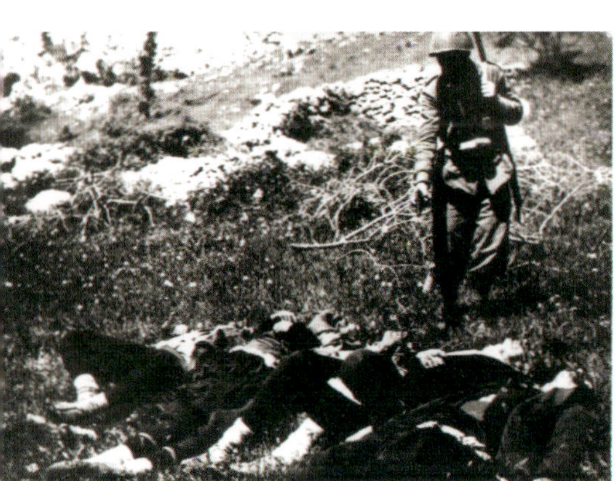

Split partisans are shot by an Italian soldier at Sinj, 1941

STATUS AND CONDITION

In the 1990s, as Yugoslavia broke up and Croatia moved towards independence, commemorative ceremonies were discontinued at the Sinj spomenik and it fell into disrepair. However, in 2008, members of the RNK Split Football Club restored the site to its original state. On 21 August 2009, the memorial was re-inaugurated during a well-attended ceremony, marking 68 years since the 1941 killings. Ceremonies are now held here annually.

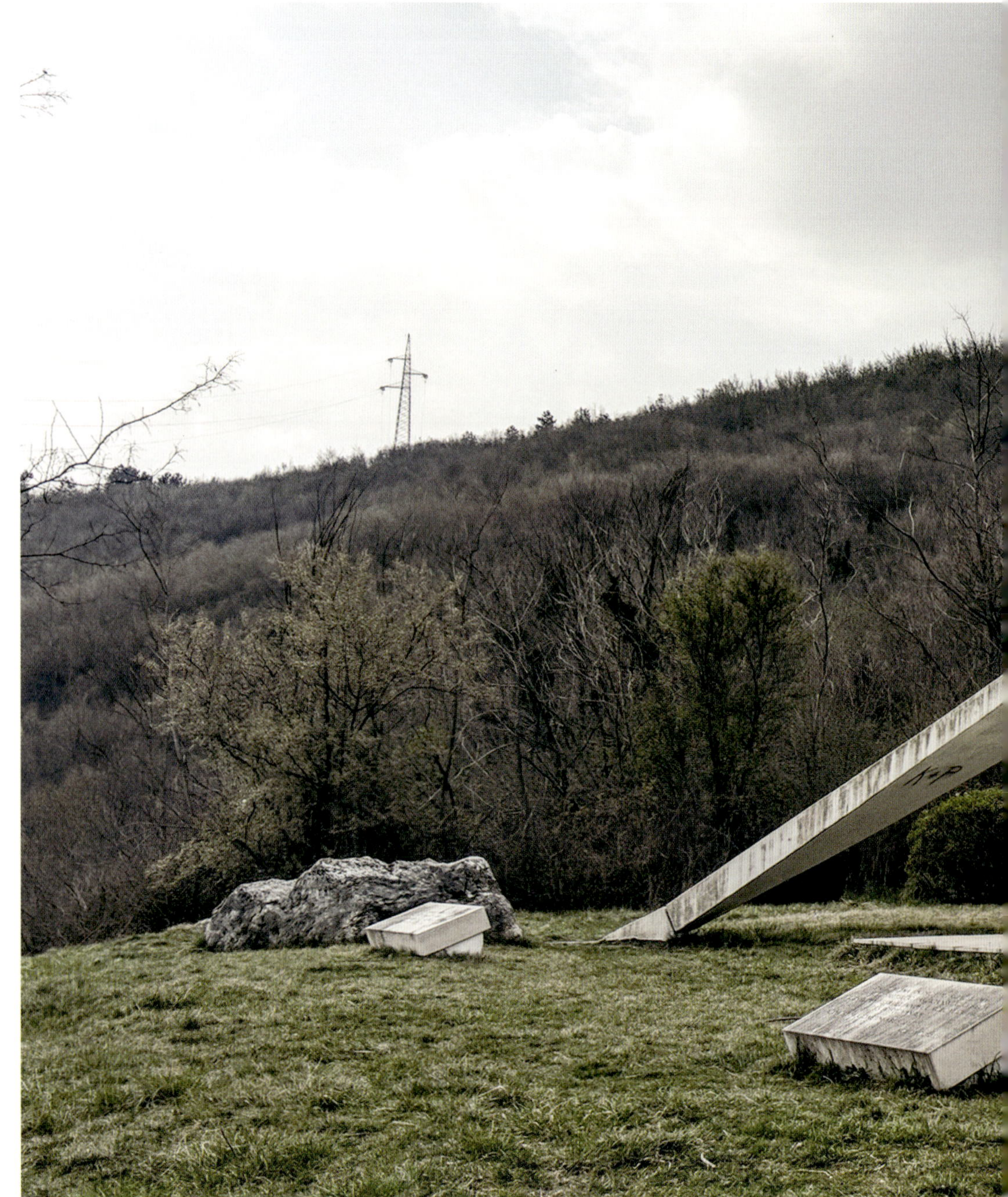

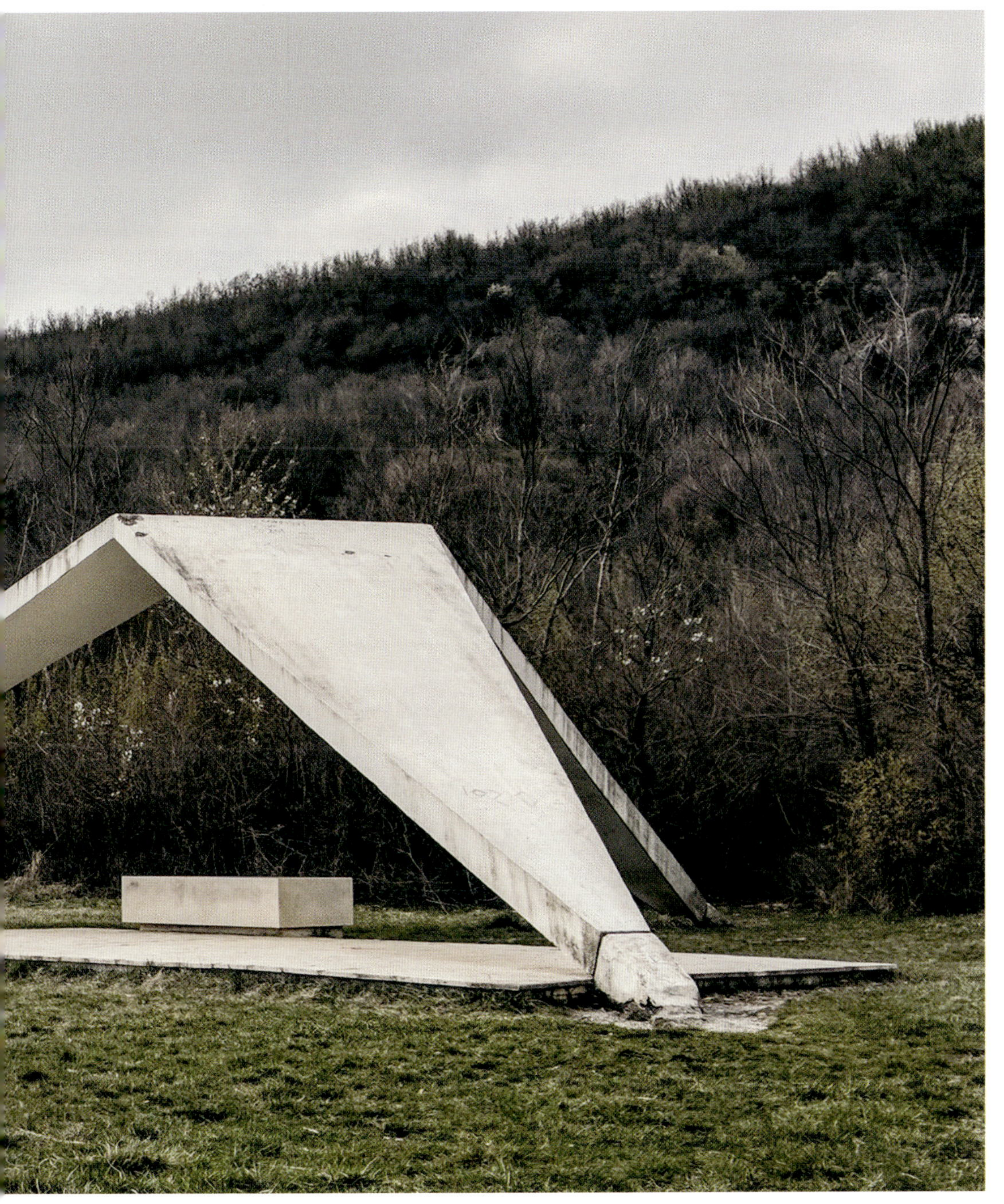

SISAK (SIH-sak)

NAME: Monument to the Detachment in Brezovica Forest or Brezovica Spomen-Park
LOCATION: Novo Selo Palanječko, Croatia
YEAR COMPLETED: 1981
DESIGNER: Želimir Janeš
COORDINATES: N45°30'09.6", E16°27'30.2"
DIMENSIONS: 20 metres high
MATERIALS: Poured concrete and rebar

HISTORY

From April 1941, Axis forces had been in control of the former Kingdom of Yugoslavia, where their puppet government – the Independent State of Croatia (NDH) – was brutally oppressing ethnic-Serbs, Jews, Roma, communists and anyone suspected of being a dissident. On 22 June 1941, in violation of the 1939 Molotov–Ribbentrop non-aggression agreement, Nazi Germany began Operation Barbarossa: the invasion of the Soviet Union. On hearing this dramatic news and fearing for their own safety, ten members of both the Yugoslav Communist Party and the Communist Youth League of Yugoslavia immediately left Sisak for the nearby forests of Brezovica. Angered by continued oppression from the NDH, they are said to have gathered under the cover of a large elm tree, where they made the decision to form the 1st Sisak Partisan Detachment. This group is often referred to as the first armed organised resistance unit in Europe intent on combating occupying Axis forces - marking the beginning of the National Liberation Movement in Yugoslavia.

Commanded by Vlado Janić and Commissar Marijan Cvetković, the detachment enlisted around 80 young fighters from Sisak. They immediately began to attack the NDH's Ustaše militiamen, while also engaging in sabotage missions against strategic railway lines and depots. In response, over 500 Ustaše militiamen were assigned to intercept and eliminate the rebels. Following several disastrous encounters with much better equipped Ustaše fighters, in September 1941 the Sisak Detachment retreated south across the Sava River. Later that month, the detachment merged with other partisan fighting brigades and was renamed the Banija Partisan Unit (by now numbering several hundred fighters), while continuing under the command of Janić.

DESIGN AND CONSTRUCTION

Directly after the end of World War II, a small plaque was erected underneath the large elm tree in the Brezovica forest to commemorate the formation of the 1st Sisak Partisan Detachment. In the 1970s (long after the elm had fallen), it was decided that a more substantial memorial should be built. Designed by Croatian architect Želimir Janeš, the spomenik was unveiled on 22 June 1981, the 40th anniversary of the event.

The central element is a 20-metre-high, white-finned, concrete tower, an abstract version of the original elm tree. Adjacent to the spomenik are several other memorial elements: a concrete plinth; a small wall bearing an engraved plaque; and a bronze statue called 'Uprising' created by Croatian artist Frano Kršinić.

STATUS AND CONDITION

The general condition of the memorial complex is good, but the bronze 'Uprising' statue had suffered significant damage before being stolen in May 2014. It was recovered several months later, when police apprehended the thieves attempting to sell it for scrap metal. Restoration of the statue was to have started in 2016, but to date no work has commenced.

Recently, some Croatian academics have questioned the formation of the Sisak Partisan Detachment in the Brezovica forest, arguing that the recognition of the holiday should cease. However, Anti-Fascist Struggle Day continues to be celebrated at the site on 22 June every year and is attended by delegations of high-ranking national officials.

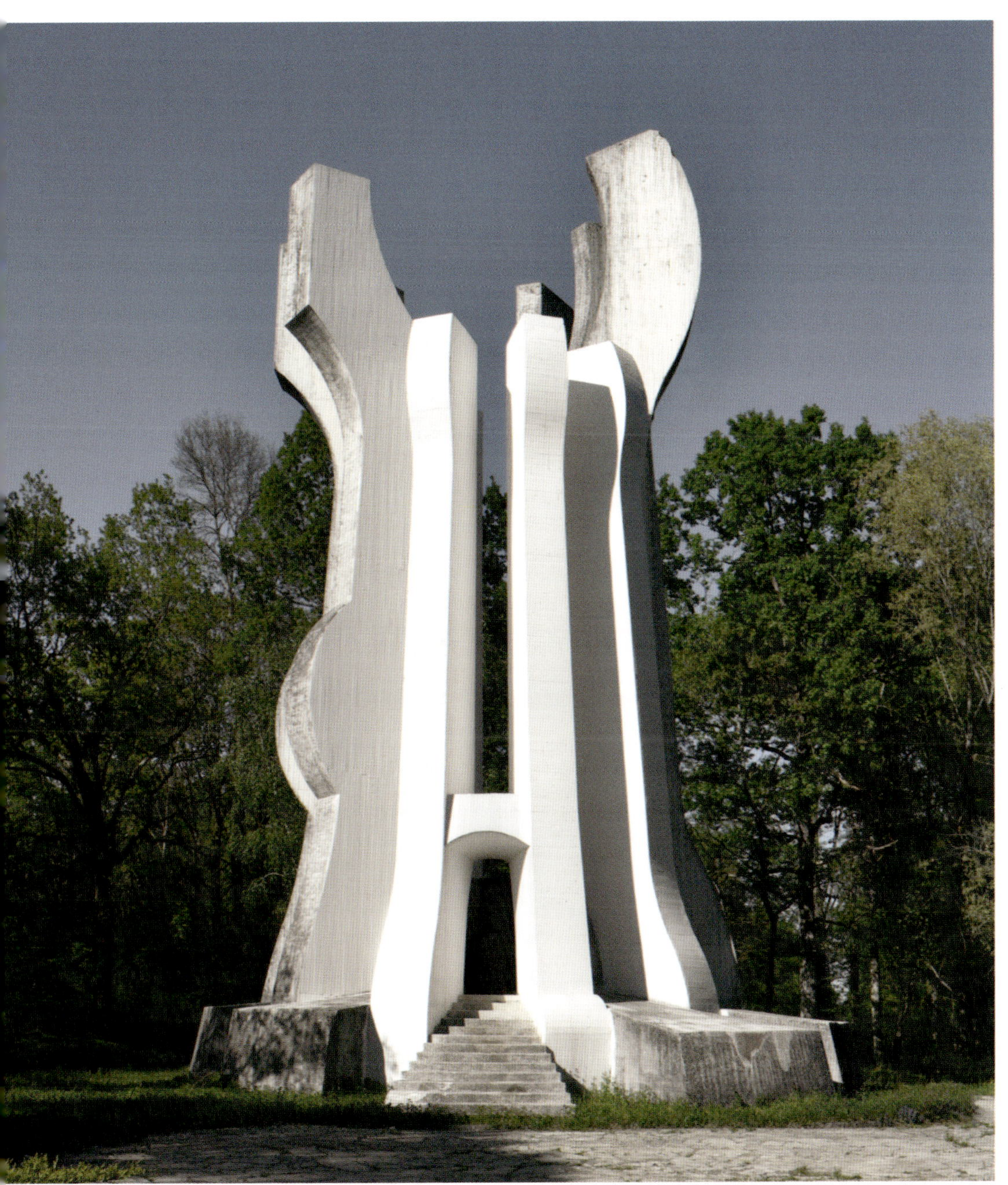

SLABINJA (SLAH-bee-nyah)

NAME: Monument to Fallen Fighters and Victims
of Fascism from Slabinja
LOCATION: Slabinja, Croatia
YEAR COMPLETED: 1981
DESIGNER: Stanislav Mišić
COORDINATES: N45°12'36.9", E16°40'09.5"
DIMENSIONS: 15 metres high
MATERIALS: Poured concrete, rebar and
stainless steel

HISTORY

In April 1941, Axis forces invaded the Kingdom
of Yugoslavia and established the puppet
Independent State of Croatia (NDH). The village
of Slabinja fell under the control of the nationalist
Ustaše militia.

Given a mandate to expel ethnic-Serbs from
the region, the Ustaše quickly set to work. Those
who failed to escape were either executed or
sent to the region's many death camps, such as
Jasenovac (see page 60), less than 25 kilometres
east of Slabinja. Other Slabinja residents took up
arms against the Axis forces, with many joining
the communist-led partisan resistance movement.
They would take part in numerous anti-Axis
offensives across the region, most notably the
Battle of Kozara in 1942 (see page 84).

In 1943, with the surrender of the Italians to
the Allies, the territory experienced a lull in the
fighting. Consequently, many of the town's
refugees returned to their homes and attempted
to rebuild their lives. It was at this time that they
erected a small monument to the victims of Ustaše
violence. However, it was not long before Axis
forces returned, driving the populace out again
and killing many in the process. The violence
finally ended with liberation by partisan forces in
May 1945. Of Slabinja's original 1,100 inhabitants,
only 495 remained at the end of the war. The rest
had either been killed or displaced.

DESIGN AND CONSTRUCTION

The village council chose Zagreb sculptor Stanislav
Mišić to create a monument commemorating
soldiers and civilians of the village who were
killed during World War II. The spomenik was
symbolically unveiled on 30 May 1981, the 40th
anniversary of the Yugoslav people's uprising
against oppression. Thousands attended the
event, which included music, plays and readings
by the writer Đorđe Đurić.

The central element is a 15-metre-tall spire,
clad in stainless steel, impaling a 7-metre-tall,
red painted concrete triangle, with one corner
touching the ground. Arranged around the
monument are five engraved stone markers telling
the story of Slabinja from 1941 to 1945.

STATUS AND CONDITION

Initially, the spomenik was a popular attraction
for the village – well visited and maintained.
However, in the 1990s, with the onset of Croatia's
struggle for independence and the ensuing
Yugoslav Wars, this situation changed. Still largely
comprised of ethnic-Serbs, the area around
Slabinja became part of the separatist Republic
of Serbian Krajina (RSK), an unrecognised rebel
state which, between 1991 to 1995, attempted
to break away from newly independent Croatia.
The spomenik was neglected and damaged
during this period, and it is still in a very run-
down condition – with evidence of the monument
having been shot at on at least one occasion.
There are no current plans for repair, and there
is no sign that commemorative events are held
at the site.

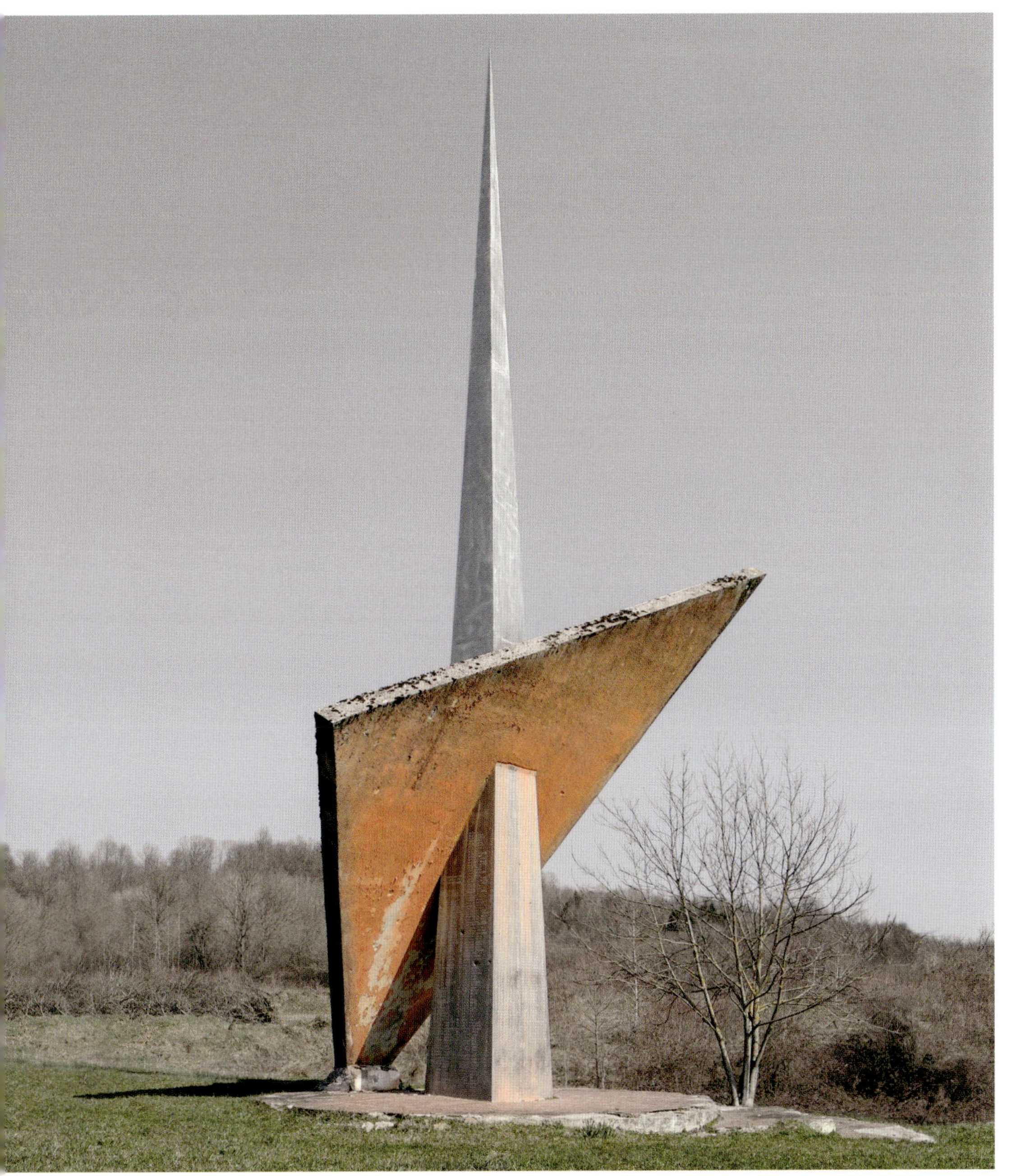

SREMSKA MITROVICA

(SREM-skah MEE-troh-vee-tsah)

NAME: Necropolis at Sremska Mitrovica
LOCATION: Sremska Mitrovica, Vojvodina, Serbia
YEAR COMPLETED: 1960, reopening in 1981
DESIGNER: Bogdan Bogdanović
COORDINATES: N44°58'36.0", E19°36'22.7"
DIMENSIONS: 7-metre-high monument in a
12-hectare complex
MATERIALS: Bronze

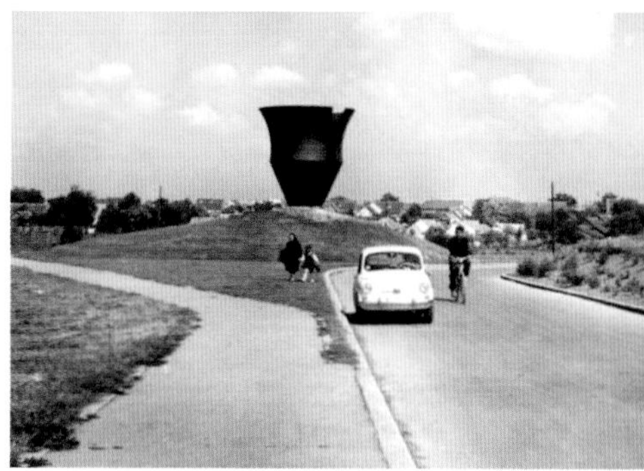

Sremska Mitrovica spomenik in the 1960s

HISTORY

When Axis forces invaded the Kingdom of Yugoslavia in April 1941, the city of Sremska Mitrovica was incorporated into the newly created Axis puppet state named the Independent State of Croatia (NDH).

One of the primary goals of the NDH was to create an ethnically and culturally 'pure' Croatia. This led to a campaign of ethnic cleansing against Serbs, Jews and Roma across the territory. In July 1941, as resistance groups instigated uprisings against the NDH's Ustaše forces, attacks on ethnic targets intensified. However, reprisal killings of civilians were not yet a common occurrence in Sremska Mitrovica. This situation changed on 26 August 1942, with the arrival of Ustaše Provost Marshal, Viktor Tomić, who had already overseen the execution of hundreds of innocent civilians in Vukovar (see page 192). Following the sabotage of local rail and communication lines by partisans, Tomić issued orders for the arrest and execution of civilians across the city.

The majority of killings took place in open fields adjacent to the city's Serbian Orthodox cemetery. Prisoners were shot in the head and dropped into the pits they had been forced to dig. After just two weeks under Tomić's control, more than 10,000 civilians from the region had been arrested (mostly Serb, Jewish and Roma). All of them were tortured, executed or shipped to nearby concentration camps. This period is often referred to as the Srem Bloody Summer. It is estimated that by the end of the war, between 7,000 and 12,000 civilians, dissidents and soldiers had been liquidated at these killing fields.

The town was finally liberated on 1 November 1944 by the partisans' 6th Proletarian Division, assisted by the Soviet Red Army. The war took a heavy toll on Sremska Mitrovica: its population declined from pre-war numbers of more than 16,000 to around 9,000.

Tomić escaped to Italy, where in 1947, he was apprehended by war-crimes investigators and imprisoned in Rome. Informed that he would be extradited to Yugoslavia to face trial, he committed suicide by slitting his wrists.

DESIGN AND CONSTRUCTION

Directly after the war, the location of the mass killings was marked with a modest stone cross. In the late 1950s, the Yugoslav government and veterans' groups from Sremska Mitrovica organised the creation of a more expansive spomenik park. Officially named the Necropolis at Sremska Mitrovica, it was designed by architect Bogdan Bogdanović. The initial unveiling took place on 4 July 1960, with further elements being added until October 1981.

The primary element is a 7-metre-tall sculpture resembling an ancient bronze beaker that has

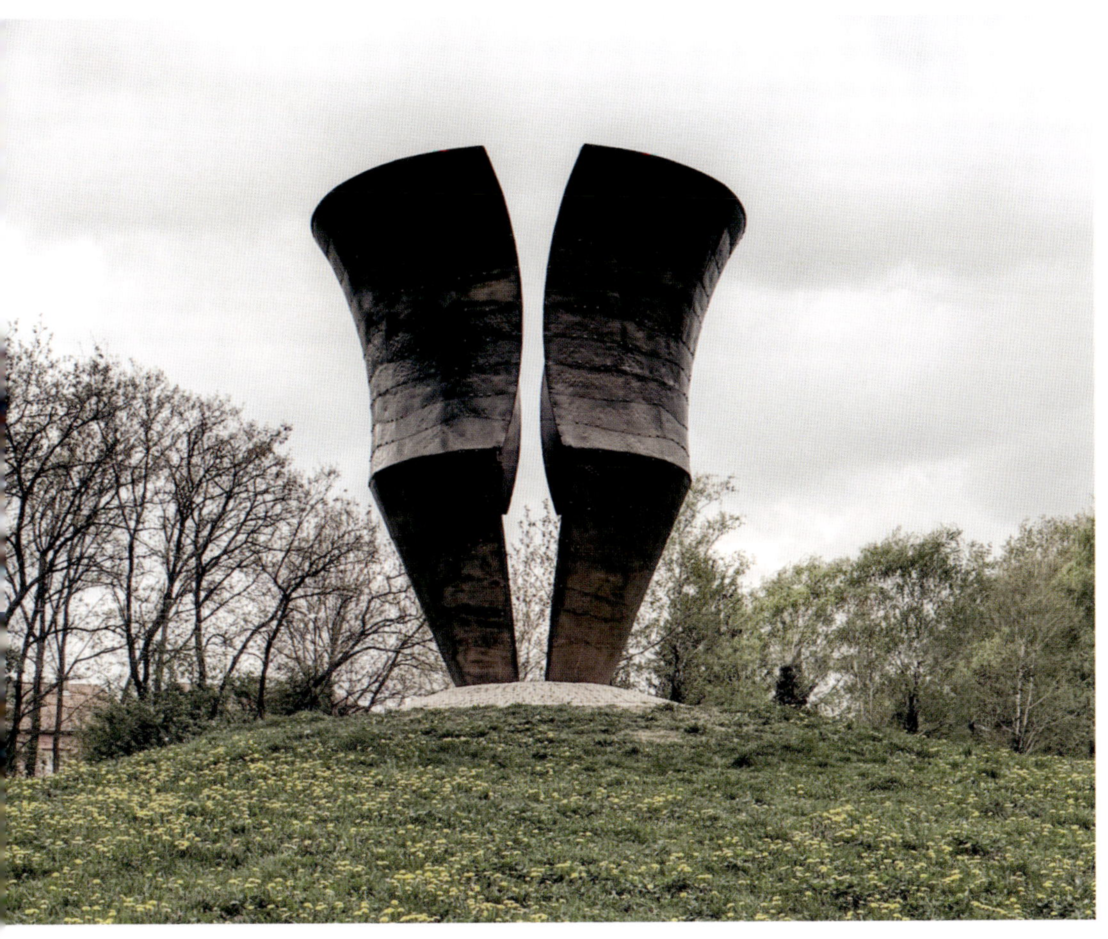

been hacked down the middle. This was located at the eastern entrance to the park.

To the west of the park, the Alley of Heroes pathway incorporates eight burial mounds, with a 2-metre-high bronze flame sculpture on top of each. (The original design contained only six mounds, each symbolising a Yugoslavian republic. However, in 1974, Kosovo and Vojovodina were granted increased levels of autonomy, and two mounds were duly added in 1979.)

STATUS AND CONDITION

Following the fall of Yugoslavia, this spomenik complex became neglected and vandalised. Many of the bronze flame sculptures were destroyed, while the main spomenik was badly damaged. In 2012, the Institute for the Protection of Cultural Monuments of Sremska Mitrovica began an 83,000 Euro programme of restoration on both the spomenik complex and the park as a whole. Today, it is in good condition, is well visited and hosts numerous commemorative ceremonies.

STRUGA (STRUH-gah)

NAME: Monument to the Revolution
LOCATION: Struga, Macedonia
YEAR COMPLETED: 1974
DESIGNER: Vojislav Vasiljević
COORDINATES: N41° 10'39.6", E20° 40'46.2"
DIMENSIONS: 15 metres high
MATERIALS: Poured concrete and rebar

HISTORY

On 6 April 1941, the Kingdom of Yugoslavia was invaded by the German Army, with Axis troops (Germans, Italians and Bulgarians) reaching Macedonia by the end of the month. The town of Struga and the surrounding Debar region were integrated into the Kingdom of Albania, an Italian controlled puppet state. Italian forces occupied the town, with the aid of local ethnic-Albanian collaborators.

By October 1941, a number of armed resistance movements organised by communist-led partisans had been established across Macedonia, but the Italian forces were vicious in their suppression of the partisans, whose successes in the face of such hostility were minimal. As the Italian surrender to Allied forces drew near (3 September 1943), more of the region was freed from occupation. Struga became the southern-most part of a large liberated territory that stretched as far north as Gostivar. However, only a few weeks later, German and Bulgarian troops arrived to fill the power vacuum and prevent the sabotage of Axis communication lines between Skopje and Greece. On 9 September 1943, German troops, alongside Albanian Balli Kombëtar nationalist forces, defeated partisan resistance fighters to re-occupy the town.

In September 1944, following its invasion by the Red Army, Bulgaria changed sides and joined forces with the Soviet Union. Over the following two months, encouraged partisans fought to free the region of Struga in a series of bloody battles.

On 6 November 1944, the 48th Macedonian Partisan Division initiated the ultimate battle for Struga. After two days of close combat, the partisans were able to drive German forces out of the area, liberating Struga for the last time. Of the 3,000 Macedonian fighters who took part in the National Liberation War (World War II), 335 were from Struga (182 Macedonians, 128 Albanians, 17 Vlachs, 4 Turks and 3 Roma).

DESIGN AND CONSTRUCTION

A monument to the fighters from Macedonia who gave their lives in the National Liberation War was first planned in 1971. Architect Vojislav Vasiljević was commissioned to design the monument, which was located in the centre of Struga, by Marshal Tito Square.

The monument was unveiled on 8 November 1974, the 30th anniversary of the liberation of Struga. The main element is a large, irregular, concrete, stalagmite-like structure, about 15 metres tall. On one side of its base is an engraving depicting five armed partisans (one of whom is female) charging into battle carrying the Yugoslav flag. The monument is surrounded by contoured steps, seating and an amphitheatre.

STATUS AND CONDITION

Until recently, the spomenik has been subject to vandalism and decay. However, in January 2016, the town allocated 30,000 Euros for the restoration of the site, with the intention of attracting local residents to it.

A significant amount of this work has been done so far, although there are currently no directional signs or information at the site. However, remembrance ceremonies are held here every 11 October to mark the anniversary of the town's anti-fascist uprising.

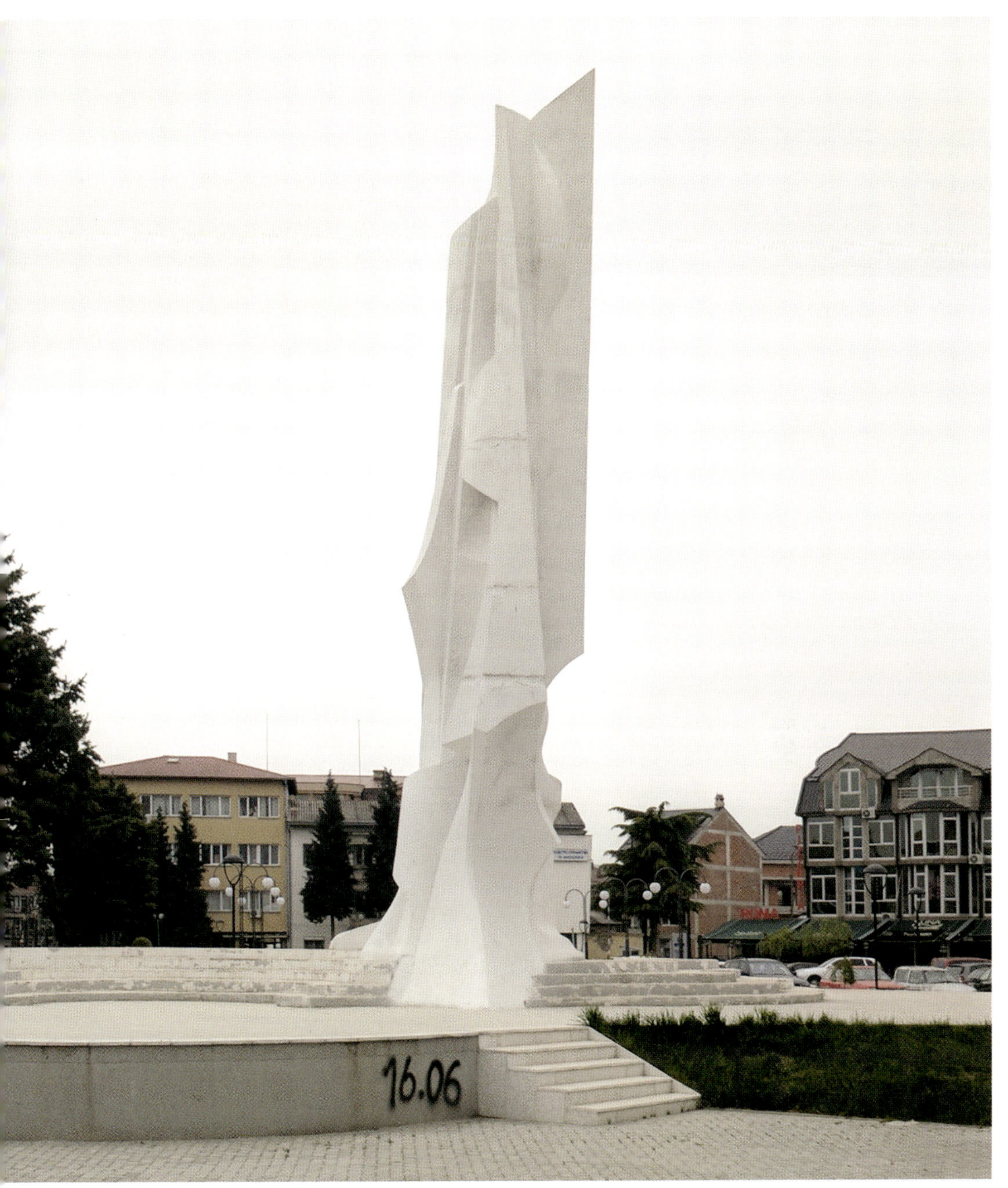
16.06

TITEL (TEE-tell)

NAME: Monument to Fallen Soldiers and Victims
of Fascism
LOCATION: Titel, Vojvodina, Serbia
YEAR COMPLETED: 1970s
DESIGNER: Jovan Soldatović
COORDINATES: N45°12'18.4", E20°18'42.8"
DIMENSIONS: 9 metres high
MATERIALS: Concrete

HISTORY

On 13 April 1941, the Serbian Bačka region in which Titel is situated was invaded and occupied by Axis-aligned, Hungarian Honvédség forces. They proceeded to carry out brutal repressions of the population, directed particularly at the ethnic-Serbs and Jews.

As a result, many Titel locals joined the anti-Axis resistance partisans fighting against the Hungarian occupation. The Honvédség then began to take retaliatory action against the partisans. On 8 January 1942, on the second day of the Orthodox Christmas, Honvédség forces entered Titel, arrested between 60 and 80 ethnic-Serb and Jewish townspeople, forced them out on to the frozen Tisa River on the eastern side of the town, and then shelled the river to break the ice, causing their deaths.

Similar raids occurred across Hungarian occupied Bačka, notably in the towns of Novi Sad, Gospođinci, Žabalj, Mošorin and Temerin. Ultimately, between 3,000 and 4,000 people were killed in this way (see page 34). While the majority of victims were ethnic-Serbs, several hundred Jews, Roma and anti-fascist dissidents were also among the dead.

DESIGN AND CONSTRUCTION

The early 1970s saw the construction of a series of monuments across the Bačka region commemorating those who died during the 1942 raids. The Titel monument, which also honours local fighters, was built as part of this initiative. Created by local Novi Sad sculptor Jovan Soldatović, it is situated on the west bank of the Tisa River, close to the site of the massacre.

The central element of the site, set next to a small concrete stage, is a 9-metre-tall concrete sculpture, suggestive of an upturned claw or skeletal hand, with each of its three digits made of four tapered and angled blocks, the topmost of which almost touch at a central point.

STATUS AND CONDITION

The monument is in good condition. Ceremonial events continue to be held at the site, often attended by politicians and community figures. The stage next to the monument is also well used. Graffiti is a constant problem, and is regularly addressed by the local municipality.

There are no directional signs to the site or information at the memorial itself.

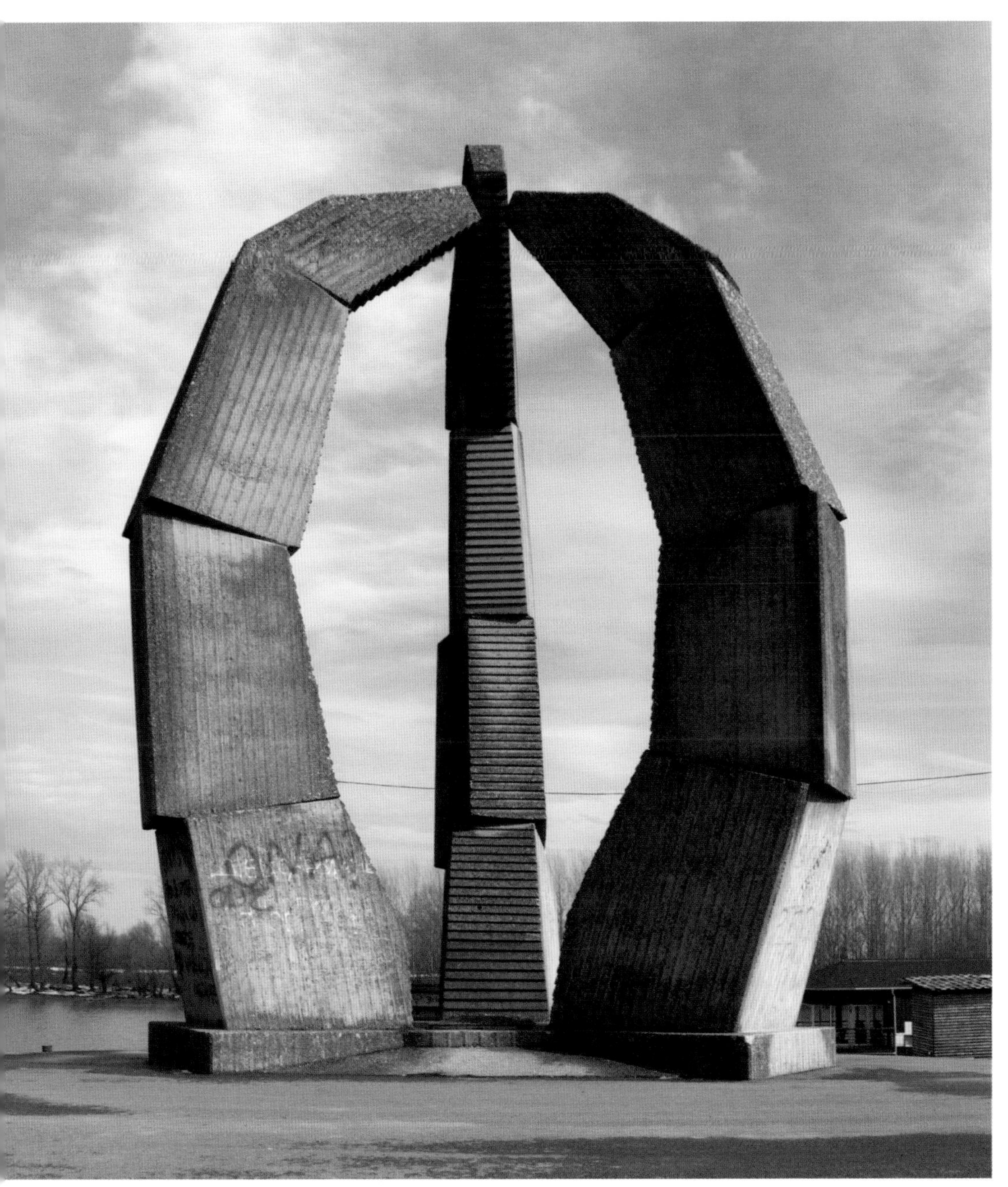

TJENTIŠTE (TYEN-teesh-teh)

NAME: Battle of Sutjeska Memorial Monument
Complex in the Valley of Heroes
LOCATION: Tjentište, Republic of Srpska,
Bosnia and Hercegovina
YEAR COMPLETED: 1971 (7 years to build)
DESIGNERS: Miodrag Živković and Ranko Radović
COORDINATES: N43°20'46.0", E18°41'12.6"
DIMENSIONS: 15 metres high and 25 metres wide
(variable)
MATERIALS: Poured concrete and rebar

HISTORY

Almost immediately after Axis powers took control
of the Kingdom of Yugoslavia in April 1941, the
German and Italian armies encountered armed
uprisings organised by local resistance groups,
primarily Josip Tito's communist partisan army.

The partisans' guerrilla tactics made them
difficult for the Axis command to deal with. In an
attempt to decapitate the partisan leadership and
destroy the movement, the German Army devised
a series of operations specifically targeting Tito.
The first, named Operation Case White, and later
referred to by Yugoslavians as the Battle of
Neretva, took place in January 1943. The offensive
ended when Tito used dramatic tactics to inflict
a humiliating strategic defeat on the Germans.

In May 1943, Axis powers launched Operation
Case Black, massing 127,000 troops against
22,000 partisans. German forces encircled the
partisans in the Durmitor and Zelengora
Mountains, forcing them to engage in a fierce
month-long battle. In early June, Tito's partisan
group was surrounded near the small village of
Tjentište in the Sutjeska River valley. Hitler ordered
their complete annihilation, resulting in the
desperate Battle of the Sutjeska, in which more
than 7,000 partisans were killed. However, Tito
and his surviving fighters broke through the
German lines and escaped into eastern Bosnia.
This was a pivotal moment for the partisans,
cementing their reputation as a viable fighting
force. The legacy of their victory - self-sacrifice,
suffering and moral virtue in the face of overwhelming odds - became an intrinsic part of
Yugoslavian post-war mythology.

These heroic deeds were chronicled in the
government-funded feature film *Battle of Sutjeska*,
with Hollywood superstar Richard Burton playing
the part of Josip Tito. Unsurprisingly, Tito was
personally involved in various aspects of the
production, which on its release in 1973, was the
most expensive film the country had ever made.

DESIGN AND CONSTRUCTION

The first memorial to mark the Battle of the
Sutjeska was built in the 1950s on this site, a
hillside near the village of Tjentište, where most
of the fighting took place. It consists of a large
stone altar standing over a tomb containing
the remains of 3,301 partisan soldiers killed in
the battle. Construction of the fractal-wall
monument by sculptor Miodrag Živković (who
created a number of spomeniks throughout his
career), began in 1964 and was finally completed
in 1971. A further museum called 'Spomen-dom'
(Memorial House), designed by architect Ranko
Radović was opened in the valley below the
monument in 1975. The interior of the large
angular Spomen-dom museum has a series of
skylights that dramatically cast daylight on to walls
engraved with the names of more than 7,000
partisan fighters who died in the Battle of Sutjeska.
Interspersed between the names are a dozen
frescoes painted by Croatian artist Krsto
Hegedušić with the assistance of historian Dusan
Plenča. They depict various macabre scenes of
suffering inflicted on the region's people by the
fascist Axis forces during the time of the National
Liberation War (World War II).

A further 79 smaller-scale memorials were also
constructed across the forests and mountains of
Sutjeskta National Park, two of which (at Ljubin
Grob and Lake Donje Bare) are designed by
Živković in a similar abstract style.

Throughout the Yugoslav era, this memorial

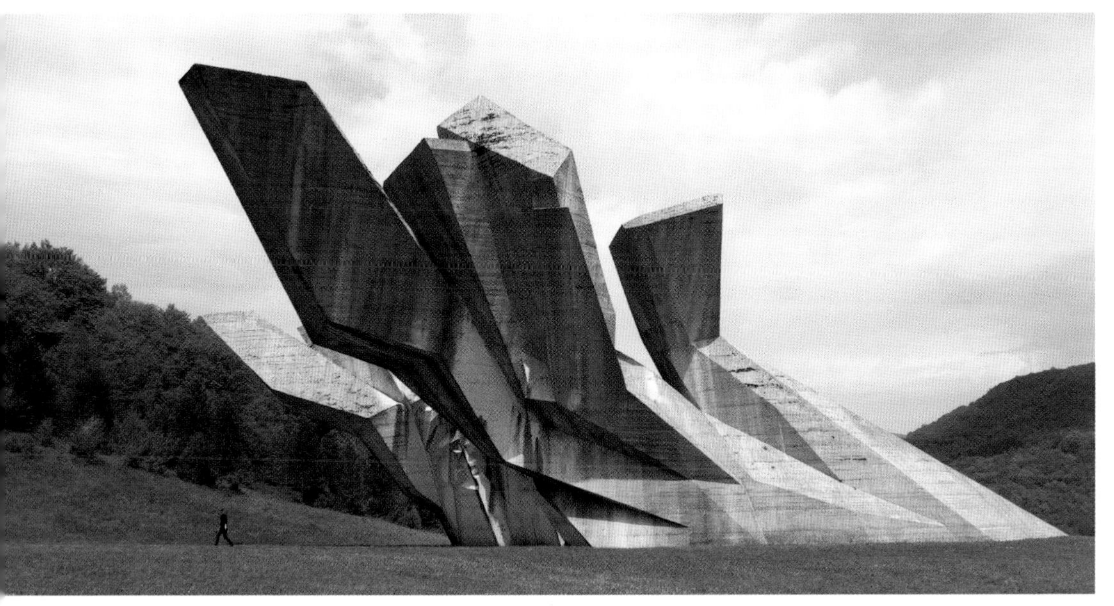

complex was one of the most popular attractions in Bosnia, with hundreds of thousands of students, youth groups and tourists visiting to pay their respects and to learn about the harrowing events that occurred here.

The soaring concrete monument is intended to represent the 'wings of victory', overcoming the oppression inflicted by German and Italian occupying forces. The site of the sculpture is significant – positioned on the foothills in such a way that it can be seen from almost every part of the valley, it acts as a focal point to commemorate the dead of the battle. Živković stated: 'The idea is that of breakthrough and victory. The two blocks with the figures inside represent the breaking of the circle created around the partisan forces.'

The German historian Dr Heike Karge criticises the monument's apparent celebration of war: 'What is missing is the senselessness of dying... the pain of those waiting for help which never arrived. That is not in this monument. [Instead] it is victory, it is heroes giving their lives purposefully for the "new project".'

A popular attraction during the Yugoslav era, the complex fell into disrepair with the breakup of the country and the Yugoslav Wars of the early 1990s. Between 1992 and 1995, the Bosnian Serb Army (VRS) destroyed parts of the complex, including many of the museum exhibits. In the years after the wars, the monument was relatively unvisited. In 1973, 80,000 people celebrated the 13th anniversary of the Battle of Sutjeska here, but these commemorations ceased until 1998 and have only grown in popularity again since 2004.

After a period of neglect, today the monument is in a reasonable state of repair. In 2011, the Spomen-dom complex underwent a UNESCO-funded refurbishment, the frescoes inside are still being worked on. Recently the spomenik's lighting was repaired and plans are being made to use the monument as a backdrop for events.

In 2018 an extensive cleaning process was completed, revealing bright concrete that had been hidden by years of weather staining. In the same year a substantial landside struck the hillside site, this damage has since been repaired.

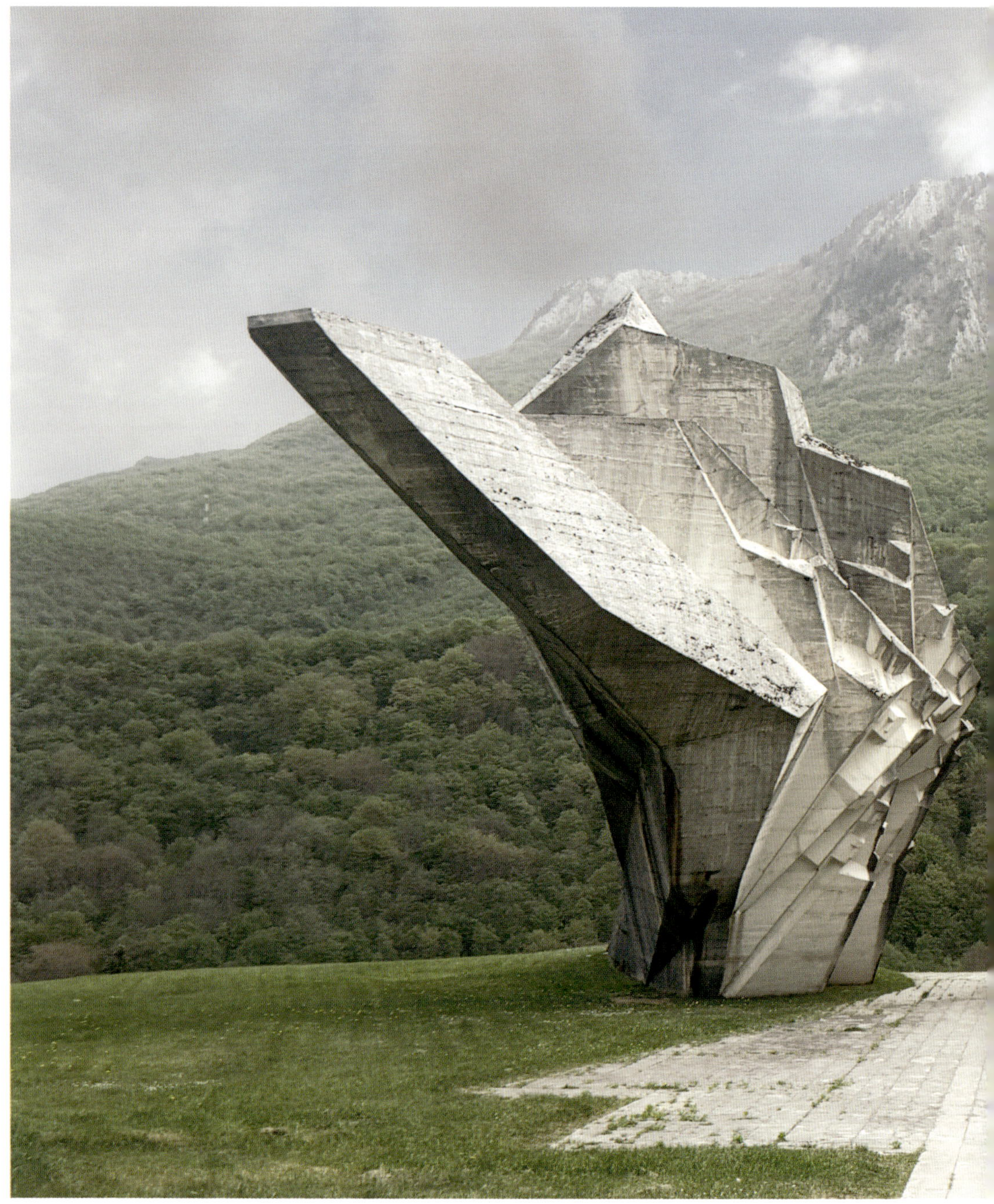

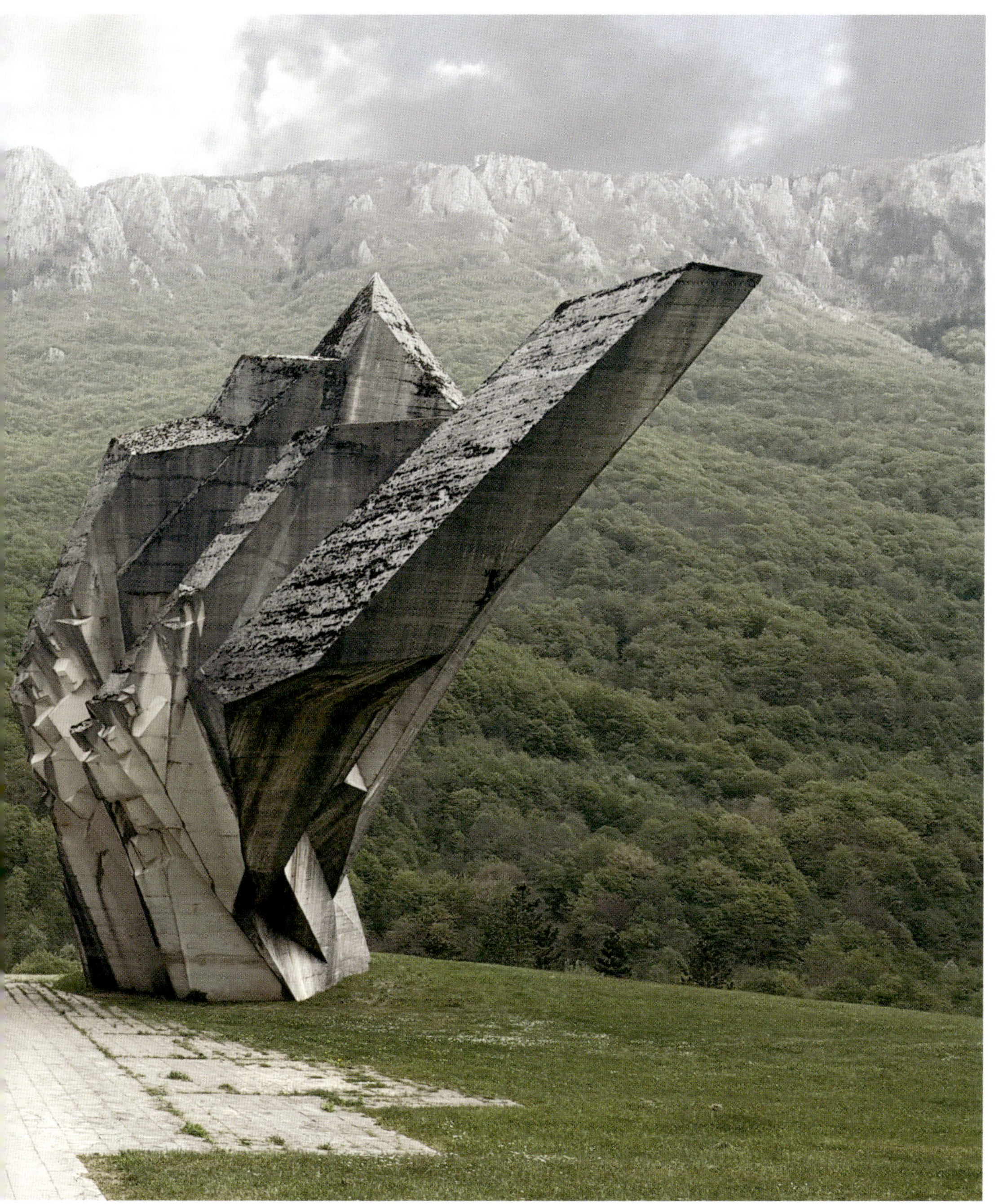

ULCINJ (OOL-tseen)

NAME: Freedom or Liberty Monument
LOCATION: Ulcinj, Montenegro
YEAR COMPLETED: 1985
DESIGNERS: Miodrag Živković and Đorđe Zloković
COORDINATES: N41°55'25.8", E19°12'20.6"
DIMENSIONS: 12 metres high and 15 metres wide
MATERIALS: Poured concrete and rebar

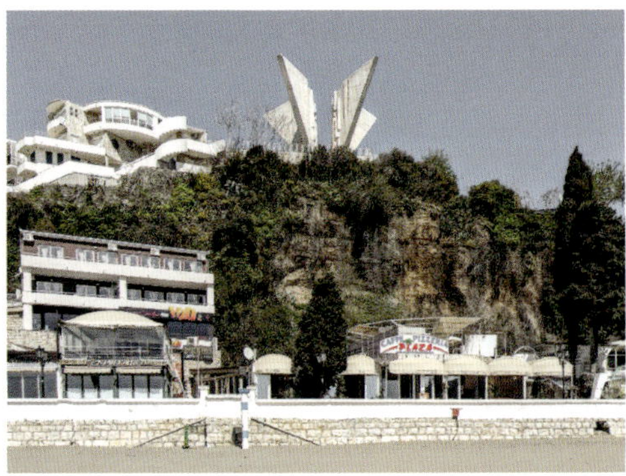

HISTORY

Following the invasion and occupation of the Kingdom of Yugoslvia by Axis forces in 1941, the town of Ulcinj was integrated into the adjacent Kingdom of Albania, a puppet state created by Italy after its invasion of the Albanian region in 1939. The Italians initially anticipated few problems (Italian Queen Elena was the daughter of Montenegrin monarch Nicholas I), but the people of Montenegro were soon angered by the occupation (see page 12). Ulcinj residents were particularly dismayed by the Italians' annexation of the town's salt-producing facilities, which were crucial to the local economy. The Italians had originally planned to establish a 'Kingdom of Montenegro', but this aim was quashed as Montenegrins sided with the communist-led partisan movement and fought to overthrow their occupiers. Mussolini responded by sending a force of 90,000 troops to regain control. Nearly 10,000 were killed across Montenegro and more than 20,000 interned at camps. Following the Italian surrender in 1943, German forces replaced the Italians in Ulcinj (and all other parts of Montenegro and Albania). The town was finally liberated on 26 November 1945. Ulcinj was then officially integrated into Montenegro, which itself became part of Tito's Republic of Yugoslavia.

A number of sources state that this memorial also commemorates the Royal Yugoslav Air Force during World War II. Following the 1941 invasion, any Royal Yugoslav Air Force resources were appropriated by Axis powers. Although the partisans formed a number of small air units using captured Croatian planes, these constituted no great threat to the enemy. However, on 1 June 1944, a number of former Royal Yugoslav pilots were enrolled into the Balkan Air Force in Bari, Italy.

The BAF, comprising 100 aircraft under the command of British RAF Air Marshall Sir William Elliot, provided air support for partisan operations across occupied Yugoslavia. On 15 July 1945, with the formation of the Republic of Yugoslavia Air Force, the BAF was disbanded. During its short life, it had flown more than 38,000 missions, dropping at least 6,000 tons of bombs, and evacuating some 19,000 wounded.

DESIGN AND CONSTRUCTION

Officially opened in 1985, the monument was created by sculptor Miodrag Živković and architect Đorđe Zloković. Overlooking the popular Mala Plaza beach, the imposing concrete structure, suggestive of aircraft tail-fins, stands 12 metres tall and 15 metres wide and is visible from much of the town's waterfront. Original plans included a public square and amphitheatre, with associated restaurants and hiking trails. However, with the breakup of the country shortly after the monument was completed, these plans were never realised.

While some experts contend that in addition to fallen partisan fighters, the spomenik is also a tribute to the victims of Kragujevac (see page 88); others assert that the monument's wing-like shapes honour Yugoslavia's wartime pilots.

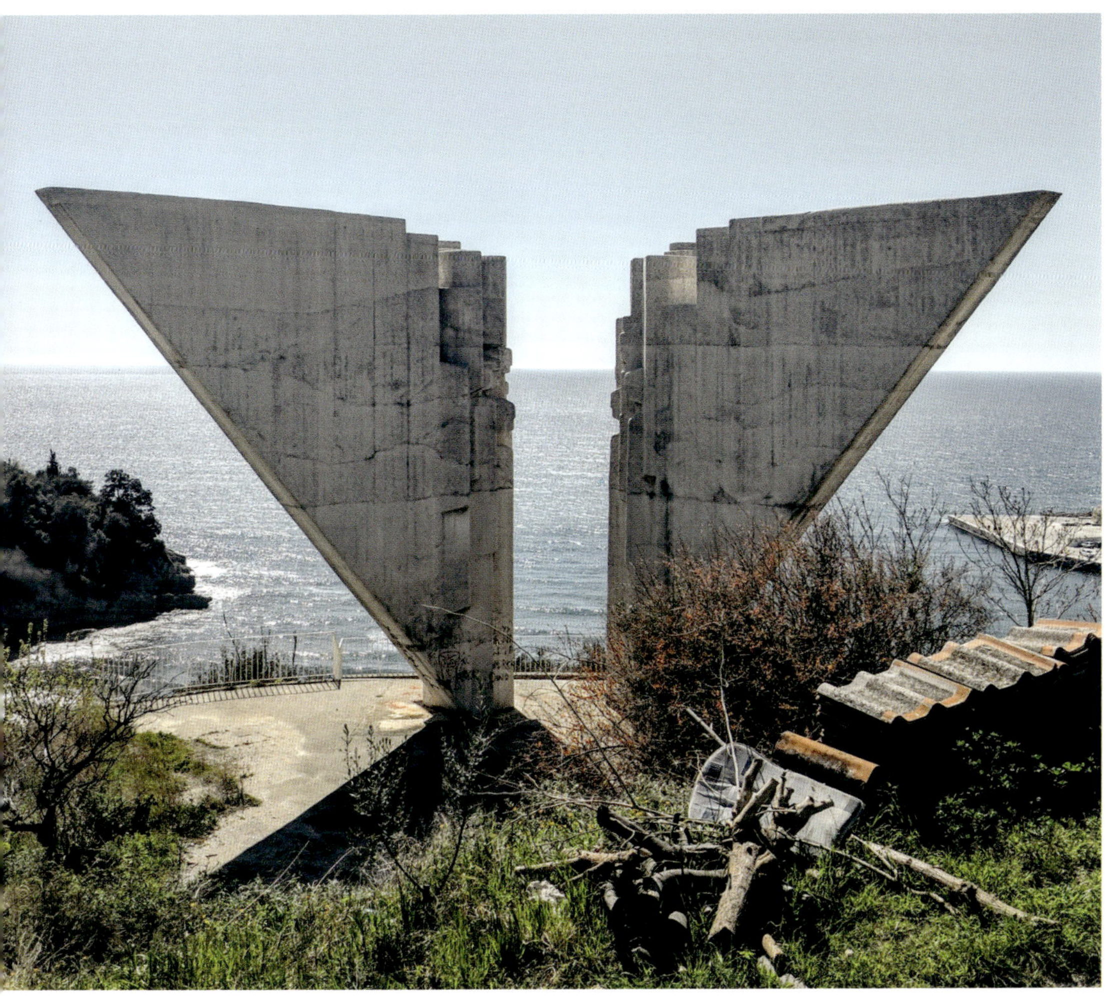

Today, the spomenik is showing signs of decay and is covered in graffiti. It sees few visitors, and no commemorative events are held here. The political climate may affect the monument's future: ethnic-Albanians, who make up 60 per cent of the town's population, argue that Ulcinj was given to Montenegro on a 100-year accord during the London Conference of 1912, and that since that time has now expired, the town should become Albanian territory once more. This could threaten the future of the spomenik, as resentment is felt by many ethnic-Albanians towards relics of the Yugoslav era – particularly following the ethnic cleansing of Albanians in Kosovo by the People's Army of the Federal Republic of Yugoslavia (Serbia and Montenegro) in the late 1990s.

VELANIJA (veh-lah-NEE-yah)

NAME: Partisan Martyrs Cemetery
LOCATION: Matičansko Hill, Velanija, Priština, Kosovo
YEAR COMPLETED: 1961
DESIGNER: Svetislav Ličina
COORDINATES: N42°39'31.8", E21°10'31.8"
DIMENSIONS: 3-hectare monument park
MATERIALS: Poured concrete and rebar

HISTORY

In April 1941, Axis forces invaded and occupied the Kingdom of Yugoslavia. The Kosovo region was integrated into an Italian protectorate called the 'Kingdom of Albania'. Many anti-Yugoslav, ethnic-Albanian nationalists viewed the Italians as liberators, but for others – Jews, Serbian royalists and communist dissidents – their occupation was brutal. To prevent possible uprisings, the Italians attempted to turn all ethnic groups (Serbs, Albanians, etc.) against each other. By contrast, Josip Tito's communist-led partisan resistance sought to unite these diverse ethnicities against the occupation.

In late 1941, armed uprisings took place in Priština. In retribution, the Italians killed both rebels and civilians. The vast majority of victims were communists and ethnic-Serbs. Although some fled to avoid persecution, many remained, continuing to fight alongside anti-Axis ethnic-Albanians. In August 1942, the Kosovo Partisan Unit began organised offensives against the Italians. This escalation led to the arrest of hundreds of Priština citizens, who were then executed or sent to concentration camps.

In September 1943, the Italian forces surrendered to the Allies, but their withdrawal from Kosovo was followed by an equally brutal German occupation. In May 1944, the 21st Waffen Mountain Division of the SS (mostly consisting of ethnic-Albanian Axis collaborators) arrested 281 Jews in Priština and transported them to Bergen-Belsen concentration camp. In July, a special camp was established for partisan and anti-fascist sympathisers. In a single day, more than 100 prisoners detained there were shot. Despite this oppression, the partisan resistance movement continued. Priština was freed from Axis control on 19 November 1944, as the 25th Serbian Partisan Brigade entered the city.

During the war, Tito promised ethnic-Albanians that the Kosovo region could democratically decide whether they wished to be part of Albania or the new Yugoslavia. In January 1944, with the Resolution of Bujan, ethnic-Albanians chose to join Albania. After the war, Tito, recognising that Serbia would not accept this, reneged on his offer – instead integrating Kosovo into the new Socialist Republic of Serbia, one of the six republics of the new Socialist Federal Republic of Yugoslavia.

DESIGN AND CONSTRUCTION

In 1960, famous Serbian architect Svetislav Ličina was commissioned to create a memorial complex named 'The Martyrs' Cemetery' in Velanija, to commemorate the local partisans and civilians who died in World War II. Located in a hilltop park, this popular complex was opened in November 1961. It consists of a central globe-like form made from metal struts, bordered by eight curved concrete walls which appear to be made of individual pillars packed together like giant sets of teeth. Set into their inner concave faces were 220 medallions representing those killed during the war, whose remains are interred in a crypt beneath the monument.

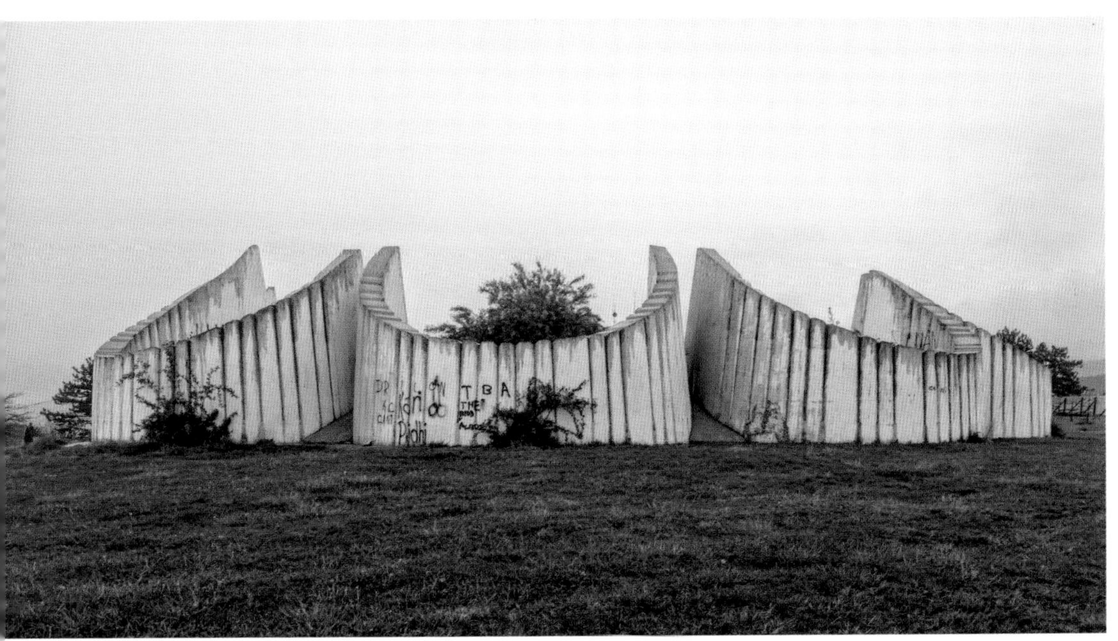

During the Yugoslav Wars of the 1990s, the complex was vandalised and elements were stolen. In 1992, Kosovo declared itself the independent Republic of Kosova, electing Ibrahim Rugova as its first president. In 1998, increasing tensions resulted in the Kosovo War between the Kosovo Liberation Army (KLA) and the Federal Republic of Yugoslavia. In 1999, at the end of the war, the Republic of Kosovo became a de facto independent nation, separate from Serbia. The area surrounding the spomenik was used as a makeshift burial ground for KLA casualties, angering many ethnic-Serbs, who felt this was disrespectful to the memory of the partisans. Parts of the complex were redeveloped, including the central sphere, which was stripped to its horizontal ribs and mounted on a circular podium.

In 2006, following the death of Ibrahim Rugova, an area of the spomenik park was used to create a tomb for his remains. Some members of the KLA were outraged by the burial of a non-veteran in the Martyrs' Cemetery, particularly as Rugova's non-violent approach to Kosovar independence was in direct contrast to that of the KLA.

Today the spomenik is in a poor state of repair. All its commemorative medallions have been stolen and its concrete structures are covered in graffiti. In 2013 plans were approved to demolish the monument and replace it with a memorial dedicated to Ibrahim Rugova. Although anti-fascist veteran associations are opposing the scheme, the construction of an amphitheatre adjacent to the partisan cemetery, has already been completed.

In May 2015, the bodies of nine ethnic-Albanian insurgents killed in a shootout with police in Kumanovo, Macedonia, were buried in the KLA cemetery within the grounds. While the cemetery is regularly visited by local Kosovars, there are no indications that commemorative events take place at the spomenik itself.

VELES (VEH-les)

NAME: Memorial Ossuary to the Heroes of World War II
LOCATION: Veles, Macedonia
YEAR COMPLETED: 1979 (3 years to build)
DESIGNERS: Ljubomir Denković and Savo Sugotin
COORDINATES: N41°43'24.0", E21°47'21.4"
DIMENSIONS: 10 metres high and 15 metres wide
MATERIALS: Poured concrete and rebar

HISTORY

On 6 April 1941, the city of Veles sustained relentless bombing by the German Luftwaffe, as Axis forces began their campaign to invade the Kingdom of Yugoslavia. The Royal Yugoslav Army quicky capitulated and Axis command handed over the eastern two-thirds of modern-day Macedonia (where Veles is situated) to Bulgarian control. Using brutal tactics – deportation, looting, torture, murder – Bulgarian forces subdued the population. Jews and Roma were particularly targeted, alongside communists, dissidents and those opposing the occupation.

In late 1941, small groups of anti-fascist rebels attempted to organise armed resistance units in Veles, but participants were quickly rooted out by Bulgarian forces and either imprisoned or executed. Spring 1942 saw tensions rise within the population. High-school students and women's groups protested in the streets against the heavy-handed tactics. It was this spirit, alongside other resistance efforts, that led to the organisation of several new partisan detachments in the Veles region. Perhaps the most important and accomplished of these was the Pere Toshev unit. This detachment was successful in three separate battles against Bulgarian police squads (at Mount Lisec, Kriva Krusha and Vojnica). These crucial victories led to the creation of the Veles-Prilep Partisan Detachment. When first formed in April 1944, it consisted of only 30 fighters, but by September, its ranks had swollen to more than 500.

In early November, the Veles-Prilep partisans descended on Bulgarian forces in Veles. A two-day battle followed, with the partisans finally liberating the city at 4am on 9 November 1944. After the war, Veles renamed itself Titov Veles in gratitude to the partisan leader Josip Tito, reverting to its original name only in 1996, to align itself within the newly formed independent state of Macedonia (FYROM).

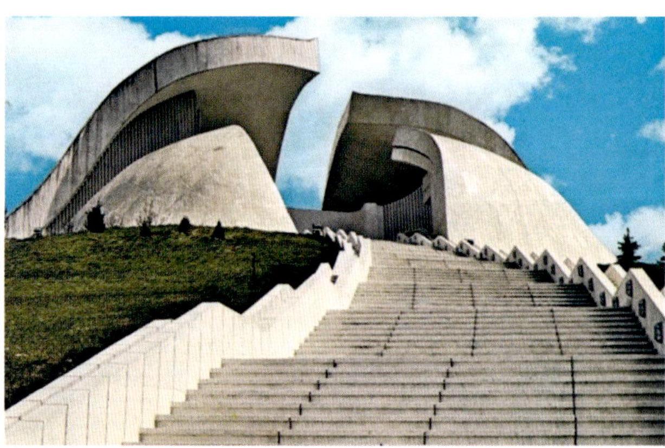

A postcard from the 1980s of the Veles spomenik

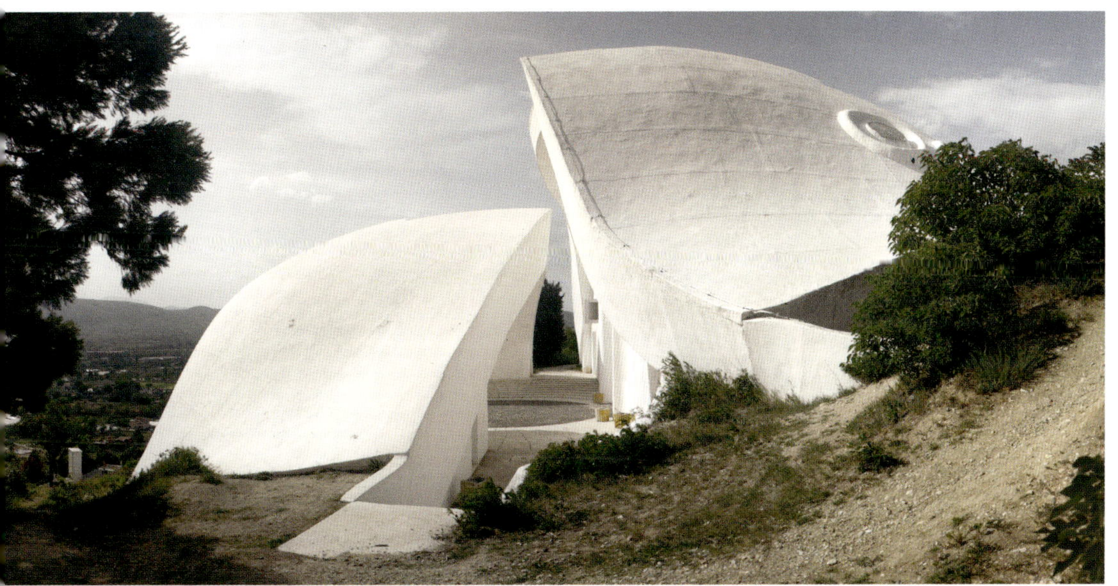

DESIGN AND CONSTRUCTION

The idea of a monument commemorating these events was put forward almost as soon as the city of Veles was liberated. However, construction didn't begin until 1976. Designers Ljubomir Denkovik and Savo Sugotin created a monument in the shape of an inverted poppy flower. The four 'petals' of the building form two distinct halves. One is an open-air chamber, originally containing copper memorial plaques, since stolen. The other houses a small museum and a five-piece mosaic by artist Peter Mazev. Covering 220 square metres, the work depicts the history of the country and is often called the 'Guernica of Macedonia', in reference to Picasso's masterpiece.

The underground ossuary holds the remains of 87 partisans from Veles who took part in the battle to liberate the city. One of these fighters was poet Kočo Racin, a significant figure of modern Macedonian literature. The complex, named 'Spomenik Kosturnica' (Memorial Ossuary), was opened in 1979, with an inaugural address given by General Costa Niki, president of the Association of Yugoslav Fighters.

STATUS AND CONDITION

With the breakup of Yugoslavia in the 1990s, the condition of the monument deteriorated. While the art and mosaics in the museum survived almost unscathed, the copper plaques on the walls of the outside area disappeared. The façade was weather-stained, the roof leaked and the exterior concrete was cracked and graffitied. In 2003, the city received 100,000 Euros from the Macedonian Institute for the Protection of Cultural Monuments to renovate the complex and install a security system. While this solved many problems, water damage and other issues persisted. In 2015, further work was undertaken to prevent leaks and the monument was repainted. In the same year an annual poetry event, Racin Meetings, was held for the first time, in honour of Kočo Racin.

However, today the monument is still in poor condition, suffering from lack of staff, poor maintenance, recurring leaks and extended periods without electricity. The municipality of Veles is seeking new funding for additional repairs and renovations.

VOĐENICA (VOH-jeh-nee-tsa)

NAME: Monument to the Vođenica Company
LOCATION: Vođenica, FBiH, Bosnia and Herzegovina
YEAR COMPLETED: unknown
DESIGNER: unknown
COORDINATES: N44°38'04.3", E16°16'28.4"
DIMENSIONS: 6 metres high
MATERIALS: Poured concrete and rebar

HISTORY

Following the invasion of the Kingdom of Yugoslavia in April 1941, the village of Vođenica became part of the newly created, Axis-controlled Independent State of Croatia (NDH), whose orders were enforced by the Ustaše, an extremist Croatian nationalist militia group. On 27 July 1941, citizens from the surrounding villages of Suvaje, Skakavac and Brestovac formed the Vođenica Partisan Company, with the purpose of combatting the Ustaše's brutal occupation. Commanded by well-known local communist Zdravko Čelar, they ambushed Ustaše convoys and sabotaged communication lines. As their numbers grew to more than 100, they fought across the whole of western Bosnia.

In February 1942, Zdravko Čelar was promoted to commander of the 1st Krajina Brigade after stepping down as leader of the Vođenica Company. Vođenica native and decorated fighter Marko Jokić then took over the leadership. Later that year, the Vođenica Company was integrated into the larger 3rd Krajina Partisan Brigade. In November, they took part in the storming of Bihać, overpowering the German forces to create the independent territory of the Bihać Republic, which included Vođenica (see page 18). However, just two months later, the Germans recaptured the city. Vođenica and the Petrovac region were finally liberated on 1 August 1944, when, after several failed attempts, partisans drove Axis forces from their Bosanski Petrovac stronghold.

The 3rd Krajina Brigade went on to play a vital role in many battles across Bosnia, including those at Sutjeska, Drvar and Neretva. Marko Jokić, initially commander of the 1st Company of this brigade, was promoted to the 2nd Officers' Company in 1944. Later that year, during the build-up to the descent on Drvar (see page 42), Jokić was killed in action. In 1953, he was posthumously awarded the distinction of National Hero by the Yugoslav government.

DESIGN AND CONSTRUCTION

The first memorial to the fighters of the Vođenica Company was built on the road at the east side of the village in the 1950s. The current structure, which was probably erected in the 1970s, is adjacent to the original. The name of its maker and the exact date of its construction are not known. The spomenik consists of four 6-metre-tall concrete, octagonal, spoon-like forms, with their convex faces turned towards a common centre, at the foot of which is a small altar.

Originally the monument was adorned with stone panels engraved with the names of the members of the Vođenica Company and local World War II victims.

STATUS AND CONDITION

Today, the spomenik is still standing, but is severely damaged and neglected. The concrete shows signs of deterioration, and many of the original elements are missing. Most of the village of Vođenica itself is also derelict and abandoned, probably since the Bosnian War (1992–95). Of the eight panels that were once mounted on to the vertical surfaces, only the smashed fragments of the panel relating to the village of Suvaja remain at the site. The other panels would have related to the villages of Vođenica, Skakavac and Brestovac, from where the members of the Vođenica Company were drawn. Currently no commemorative events are held here.

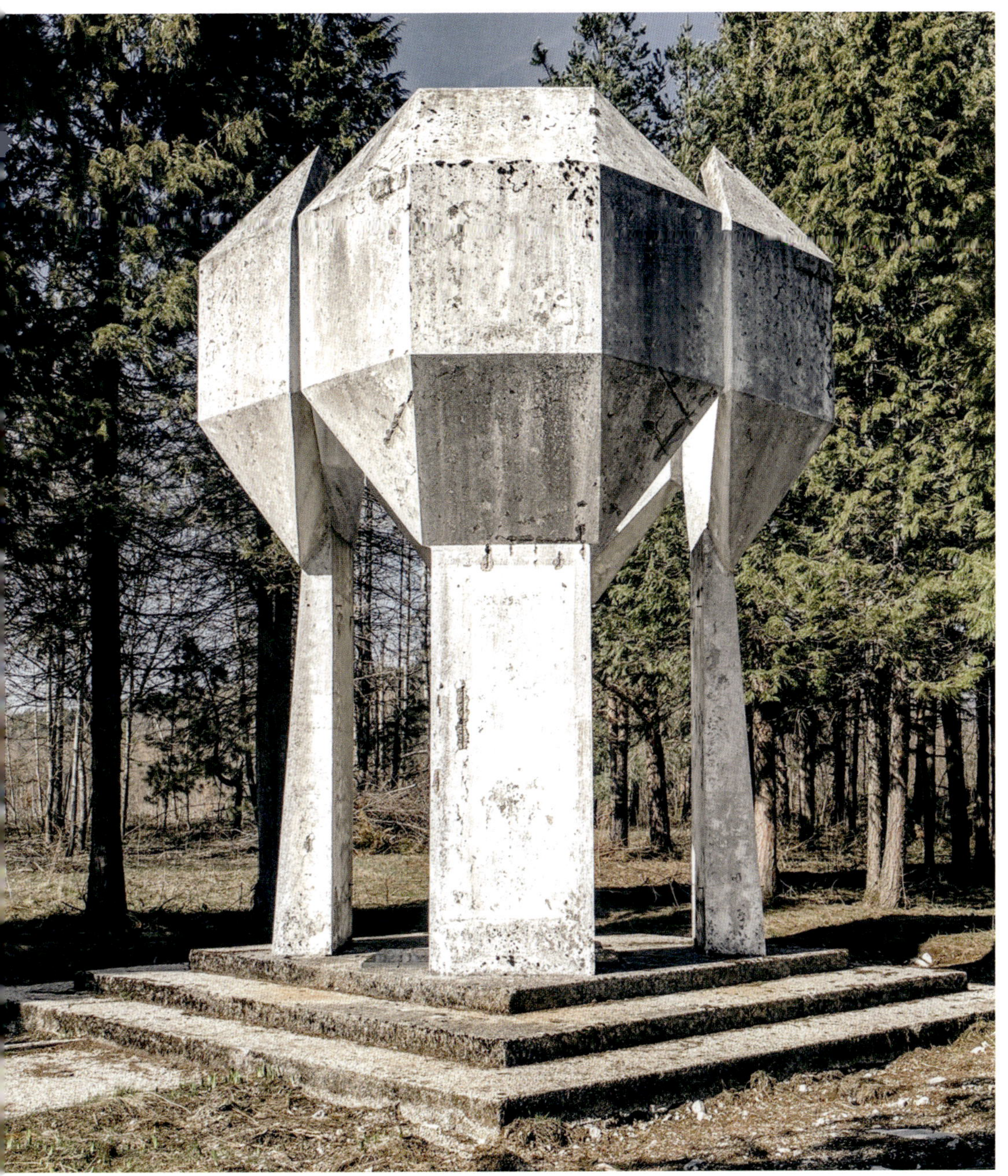

VOGOŠĆA (VOH-gohsh-chah)

NAME: Monument to the Fallen Fighters of the People's Liberation War
LOCATION: Džindino Hill, Vogošća, FBiH, Bosnia and Herzegovina
YEAR COMPLETED: 1969
DESIGNERS: Petar Krstić and Zlatko Ugljen
COORDINATES: N43°53'57.9", E18°21'00.0"
DIMENSIONS: 6 metres high and 8 metres wide
MATERIALS: Poured concrete, rebar and copper

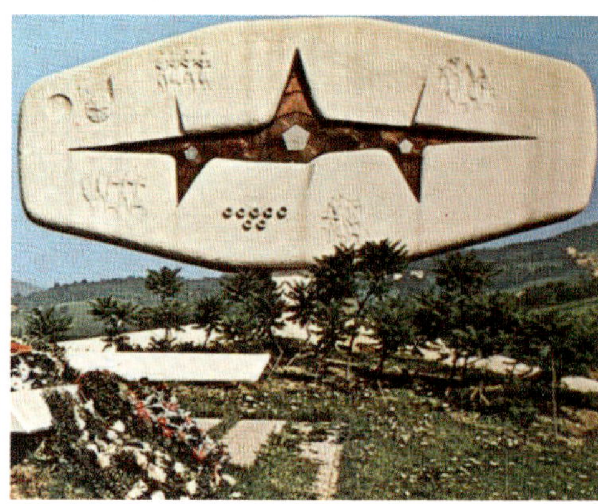

The Vogošća spomenik with commemorative wreaths, 1970s

HISTORY

On 17 April 1941, after nine days of relentless Luftwaffe air attacks, the city of Sarajevo surrendered to invading Axis troops. While the Nazi forces were accepted and welcomed by the Volksdeutsche (ethnic-Germans), many citizens of nearby Vogošća were persecuted, particularly the town's ethnic-Serb, Jewish and Roma populations. To incite greater tension between local communities, the Ustaše militia attempted to turn the Muslim population against the ethnic-Serbs, who were subsequently persecuted by some Muslims with Ustaše approval. In response, others signed the 'Resolution of Sarajevo Muslims', condemning the oppression of ethnic-Serbs. As the occupation continued, ethnic-Serbs, Jews and Roma were regularly sent to death camps and even openly killed.

In summer 1941 two sets of armed resistance movements emerged: the communist partisans, led by Josip Tito, and the nationalist Chetniks, led by Draža Mihailović. The most notable unit to form locally was the Vogošća Partisan Detachment, led by Trifko Đokić and Radovan Šućur, which disrupted Ustaše and German forces, while laying the groundwork for the eventual recapture of Sarajevo. Initially, the partisans worked together with the Chetniks, but at the end of 1941, Chetnik forces switched sides, helping the Germans to drive the partisans out of Vogošća.

However, by summer 1943, the Vogošća partisans returned, attacking the Chetniks and killing their commander, Spasu Tadića. For a time (before it was retaken by Axis forces), Vogošća became a small partisan-held territory, where the resistance movement could operate freely.

The Vogošća partisans then joined forces with the nearby Visoko-Fojnica Partisan Detachment of the 6th Krajina Brigade, fighting across the Sarajevo region. Despite Trifko Đokić being killed in a Chetnik ambush, in summer 1944 alone, Visoko-Fojnica partisans destroyed 10 German trains, 100 convoy trucks and more than 200 wagons. On 6 April 1945, Vogošća was liberated by partisans. Nearly 100 local Vogošća partisans died during the course of the war and the liberation of the town.

DESIGN AND CONSTRUCTION

On 21 July 1969, a large complex by artist Petar Krstić and architect Zlatko Ugljen was officially opened. As well as being a memorial to the fallen partisan fighters from Vogošća, it also contains a crypt where their remains are interred.

The primary element of the memorial is a large concrete slab, 8 metres wide, with engravings and bas-reliefs, supported by three central concrete legs that trail off as long, tapering 'feet'. Both sides of this slab are almost bisected by an

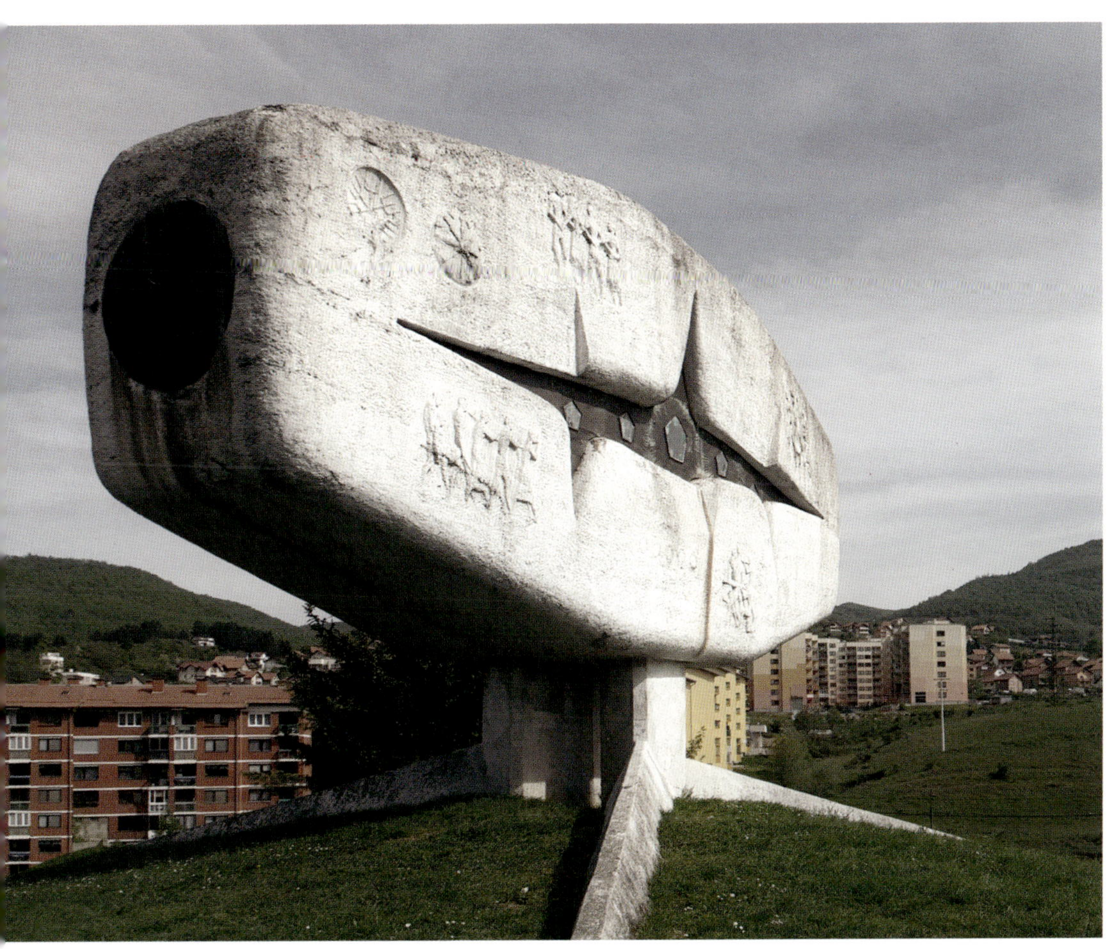

explosive, copper-lined 'wound', creating the impression of a previously rectangular shape being pushed apart from its centre.

In front of the central monument are three overlapping, horizontal concrete bars, triangular in section and engraved with the names of the 62 fallen partisan soldiers from this region, most of whom were involved in the Zvijezda Detachment, the Visoko-Fojnica Detachment and the 6th Krajina Brigade.

The site is well maintained, the monument is in reasonable condition, despite some damage to its base. There is some graffiti, but efforts have been made to remove it. The memorial is not promoted as a historical site in the town, so visitor numbers are small. However, remembrance ceremonies are held here every year on 6 April (Vogošća and Sarajevo Liberation Day), 27 July (Bosnia Uprising Day), and 24 November (Bosnia Statehood Day).

VRANJSKE NJIVE (VRAH-nyas-keh NYEH-veh)

NAME: Monument to Hanged Patriots or
'The Fork'
LOCATION: Vranjske Njive, Montenegro
YEAR COMPLETED: 1970s
DESIGNER: Svetlana Kana Radević
COORDINATES: N42°29'19.9", E19°13'27.7"
DIMENSIONS: 6 metres high
MATERIALS: Poured concrete and rebar

HISTORY

Through most of World War II, the city of Podgorica and its surrounding villages, such as Vranjske Njive, were controlled by Axis Italian forces. After their surrender to the Allies in 1943, the Italians were replaced by German troops (and their Chetnik collaborators, see page 22), who were at least as brutal as their Italian counterparts in their oppression of Montenegrin citizens.

German forces would regularly perform grisly executions such as public hangings, with the objective of terrorising the local population into submission. The victims of such killings were usually captured resistance fighters or locals who had been rounded up as hostages to be killed in retaliation for partisan attacks on German soldiers.

In December 1943, more than 100 partisan fighters were publicly executed in the Podgorica area. This number included the group of nine captured partisans commemorated by this monument, who were hanged by German and Chetnik soldiers in Vranjske Njive, at the base of Velje Hill in the Zeta River valley. The valley leads directly south towards Podgorica, making Velje Hill a strategic location that was fiercely contested by partisans, who battled to free it from German control. Partisans viewed the struggle at Velje Hill as integral to the greater fight for the liberation of Podgorica itself.

The village of Vranjske Njive, along with the rest of the Podgorica region, was finally liberated by partisan forces on 19 December 1944. It is estimated that nearly 5,000 civilians and soldiers from the region were killed during the war. On 13 July 1946, the city and region of Podgorica changed its name to Titograd in honour of partisan military commander Josip Tito. The city reverted to its original name with the breakup of Yugoslavia and the ensuing conflicts of the early 1990s.

DESIGN AND CONSTRUCTION

In the early 1970s, local authorities planned a spomenik memorial near the village of Vranjske Njive to commemorate the partisan fighters who were hanged at this location during the war.

The prominent Montenegrin architect Svetlana Kana Radević was commissioned to design the memorial, which opened in the mid-1970s (the exact date is unknown).

The primary element is a fork-like concrete sculpture; 8 or 9 metres long; which juts up and out horizontally to loom ominously overhead, like a huge, desperately outreaching hand. A small, red eternal-flame sculpture is set on an altar at the base.

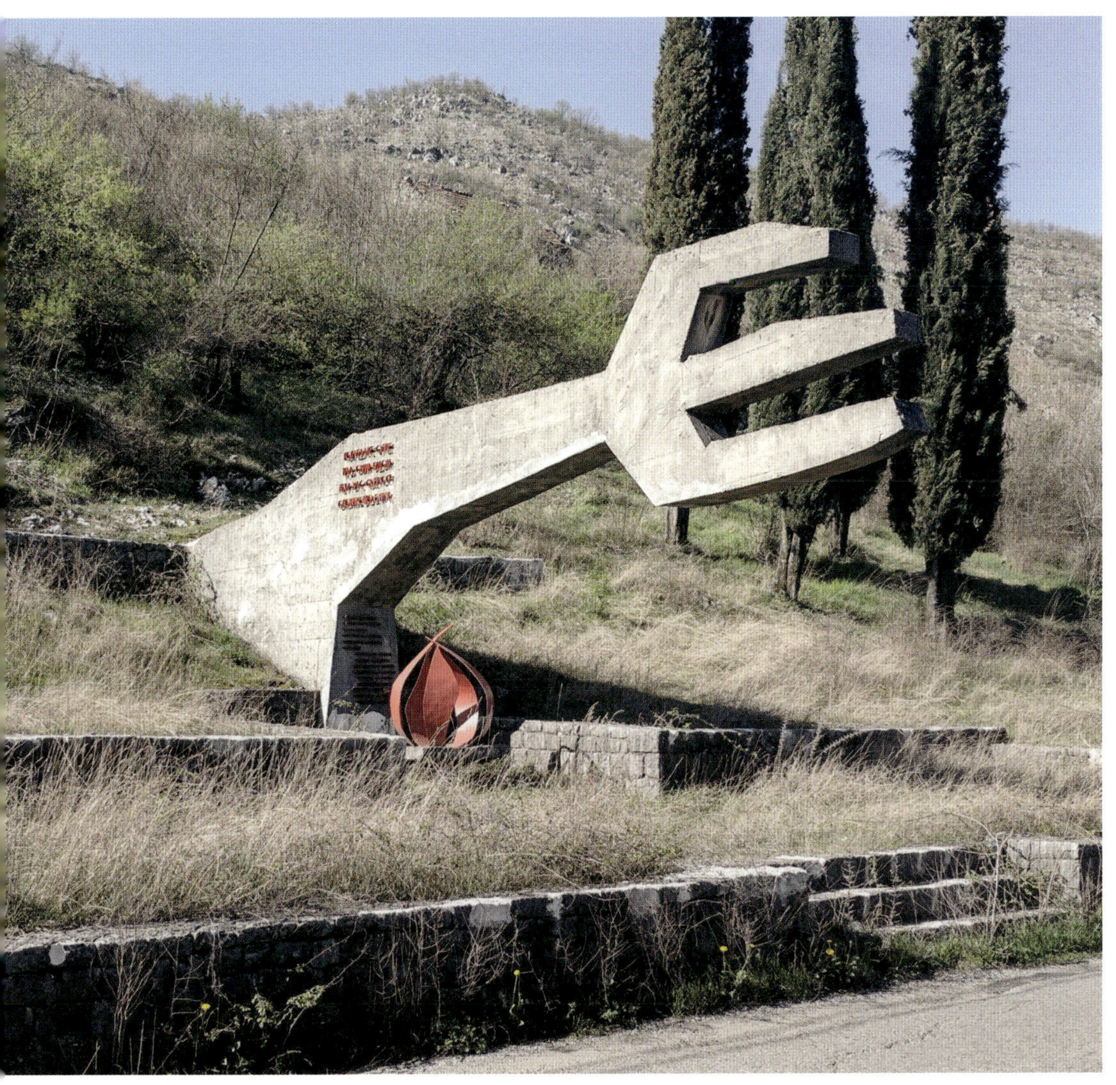

STATUS AND CONDITION

Since the dismantling of Yugoslavia in the early 1990s, the Vranjske Njive memorial has been neglected and has fallen into disrepair. Although the memorial grounds are overgrown, the spomenik itself is in relatively good condition and could easily be restored. Today, few people visit the site and there is no evidence that commemorative events are held here.

VUKOVAR (VOO-koh-var)

NAME: Dudik Memorial Park
LOCATION: Vukovar, Croatia
YEAR COMPLETED: 1980 (2 years to build)
DESIGNER: Bogdan Bogdanović
COORDINATES: N45°19'49.4", E19°01'02.7"
DIMENSIONS: Five cone monoliths, 18 metres high
MATERIALS: Diorite stone blocks, wood and copper

HISTORY

Soon after the invasion of the Kingdom of Yugoslavia by Axis forces in April 1941, the city of Vukovar was incorporated into the newly created Independent State of Croatia (NDH), a puppet state of the Axis powers. NDH laws were enforced by the brutally fascist Ustaše militia. Intent on building a racially pure Croatia, they murderously persecuted Serbs and Jews, as well as communists, dissidents and anyone else whom they deemed undesirable.

One of the most infamous mass executions in this region took place in June 1941, when, as retaliation for partisan attacks in the nearby mountains of Fruška Gora, hundreds of civilians from across the Syrmia area were arrested and transported to Vukovar. Here they were stripped of their belongings, subjected to hasty show-trials and killed in an area called Dudik – a grove of mulberry trees on the outskirts of the town. In total, 348 Serbs, 71 Croats and two Bosnians were murdered and buried in nine mass graves spread among the trees.

Despite these killings, resistance continued. NDH leaders decided that further action should be taken, and in August 1942, Ustaše Provost Marshal Viktor Tomić was sent to Vukovar with orders to expel the ethnic-Serb population and bring the situation under control. Tomić restricted

access to telephone services and imposed a curfew, making residents prisoners in their own homes, to ensure as few people as possible would witness his next actions. He proceeded to expel Serbs, Jews and other NDH undesirables, and also imprisoned, and subsequently killed, hundreds more without trial. At the end of August, Tomić was posted to the nearby city of Sremska Mitrovica (see page 170). Before leaving, he ordered all civilians still in captivity in Vukovar to be transported to the death camps at Jasenovac.

Vukovar was finally liberated on 14 and 15 April 1945, by partisan and Soviet Red Army forces.

DESIGN AND CONSTRUCTION

During war-crimes investigations after the war, some of the Dudik mass graves were excavated and the remains of around 400 bodies were found. These were re-interred at the site in a new, specially built memorial crypt. It is believed that there are more mass graves yet to be discovered.

In 1978, a committee composed of councillors and veterans commissioned Serbian architect Bogdan Bogdanović to design a monument dedicated to those killed at this site. The memorial complex, over a hectare in size, was opened to the public on 26 June 1980. The central element is a group of five 18-metre-tall cones, set within the grove of mulberry trees where the mass graves were found. The lower sections of the cones are built from diorite blocks, while the upper sections are sheet copper over a wooden framework. Bogdanović said of the design: 'It seems to me that the visitor is rather like an adventurous traveller returning to the remote past and, to his surprise, comes across the secret, unexplained mausoleum of [the Etruscan king] Lars Porsena....'

To the north of the cones lie 27 large diorite stone blocks, seemingly arranged randomly and each bearing a low-relief, semi-abstract, symmetrical image of a Šajka (a type of historic native wooden boat).

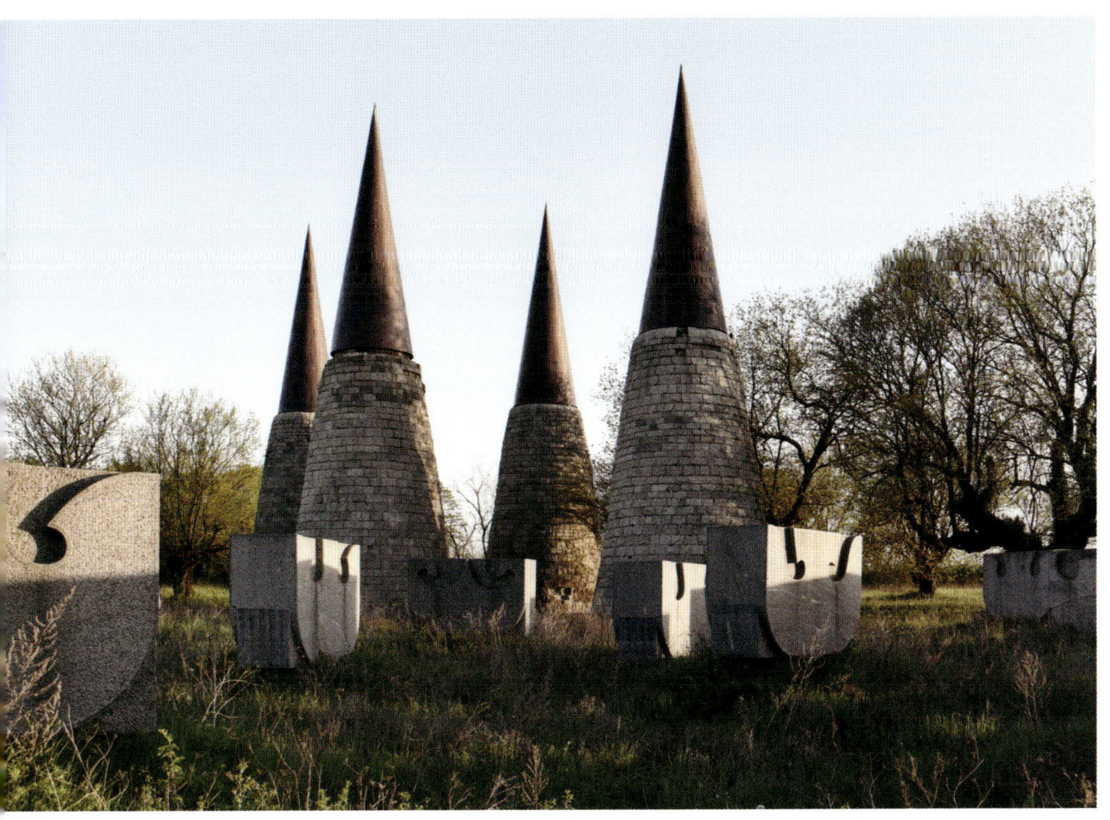

A popular memorial in the Yugoslav era, the monument began to decline at the onset of the Croatian War of Independence in 1991. On 25 August 1991, the Battle of Vukovar began. During this 87 day siege by the Belgrade-led Yugoslav People's Army, the spomenik complex was badly damaged by shells and bullets, and a number of the site's original mulberry trees were cut down. The Battle of Vukovar was the largest conflict of the Croatian Wars of the 1990s, destroying approximately 90 per cent of Vukovar, and killing more than 1,000 civilians. The city's famous water tower, struck by shells nearly 600 times, has been deliberately left in its battered condition as a symbol of the city's suffering.

The memorial remained in this ravaged state until 2014, when Croatia's Ministry of Culture allocated 40,000 Euros for repairs. This allowed the damaged cone tops to be mended and the landscaping to be restored. However, other original elements have yet to be repaired. Despite the refurbishment, the site is not promoted: Vukovar is perceived as an ethnically tense and divided city and the monument sees few visitors. While events such as Anti-Fascist Struggle Day (22 June) and Vukovar Liberation Day (10 May) are commemorated here, they attract only a few dozen people. However, the memorial's survival is significant, as few spomeniks have managed to recover from such extensive damage.

ZAGREB (ZAH-greb)

NAME: Monument to the December Victims of 1943
LOCATION: Dubrava, Zagreb, Croatia
YEAR COMPLETED: 1960
DESIGNER: Dušan Džamonja
COORDINATES: N45°49'30.9", E16°02'17.0"
DIMENSIONS: 5 metres high
MATERIALS: Concrete and wire

HISTORY

After the invasion of the Kingdom of Yugoslavia by Axis forces in 1941, the present-day countries of Croatia and Bosnia were amalgamated into the Axis-controlled Independent State of Croatia (NDH), led by Croatian nationalist Ante Pavelić. Intent on creating an ethnically pure nation of Croats, Pavelić imposed anti-Serbian and antisemitic policies, which were enforced by the NDH's brutal Ustaše militia.

Josip Tito's partisan resistance fought back, attacking Axis forces and infrastructure. The Ustaše retaliated by taking hostages and threatening to execute them if attacks continued. On the night of 18 December 1943, the Turopoljsko-Posavska Partisan Detachment, commanded by Marijan Badel, set out on an operation targeting German ammunition depots in the village of Sopnica, north of Zagreb. After disarming the guards and evacuating the villagers, they used explosives to destroy four warehouses filled with 8,500 tons of armaments and munitions.

Two days later, sixteen civilian hostages were taken from their prison cells by the Ustaše and transported to the main square of the Dubrava neighbourhood of Zagreb. The Ustaše used wooden utility poles fitted with meat hooks as makeshift gallows from which to hang the hostages. Intended to act as a deterrent to locals, the hangings had an adverse effect on German military diplomats who had been sent to Zagreb to assist the Ustaše. German Army General Edmund Glaise-Horstenau, who was stationed in Zagreb, distanced himself and his men from the action, denouncing it as 'criminal'. The hangings inadvertently aided the resistance, galvanising the conviction of those already involved and persuading witnesses to the atrocity to join their cause. The Ustaše hanged a further 25 citizens at this site, before finally fleeing Zagreb along with the NDH government when the city was liberated by partisans on 8 May 1945.

DESIGN AND CONSTRUCTION

After the war, the road on which the victims were hanged was renamed December Victims Avenue, and all sixteen were declared National Heroes by the Yugoslav government. The Macedonian artist Dušan Džamonja was commissioned to design a spomenik in Dubrava, to be unveiled on 20 December 1960, the 17th anniversary of the executions. The 5-metre-high concrete and wire monument, resembles billowing fabric or leather stretched over a fragile framework. It was viewed as groundbreaking at its installation, since such an abstract design had never before been seen in a Yugoslav war memorial, and it engendered a profusion of innovative World War II monuments across the country. Accordingly, Džamonja is often viewed as the father of abstract spomenik design.

STATUS AND CONDITION

With the breakup of Yugoslavia and the ensuing Yugoslav Wars of the 1990s, Croatian nationalism increased, resulting in dwindling interest in World War II memorials. In 1990, the December Victims Avenue was officially renamed Dubrava Avenue. Around this time, the sculpture was moved from its original prominent position to a more obscure one within the park. During this relocation, all the memorial's original signs and engravings were lost. Recently, modest remembrance ceremonies have once again been held at the site.

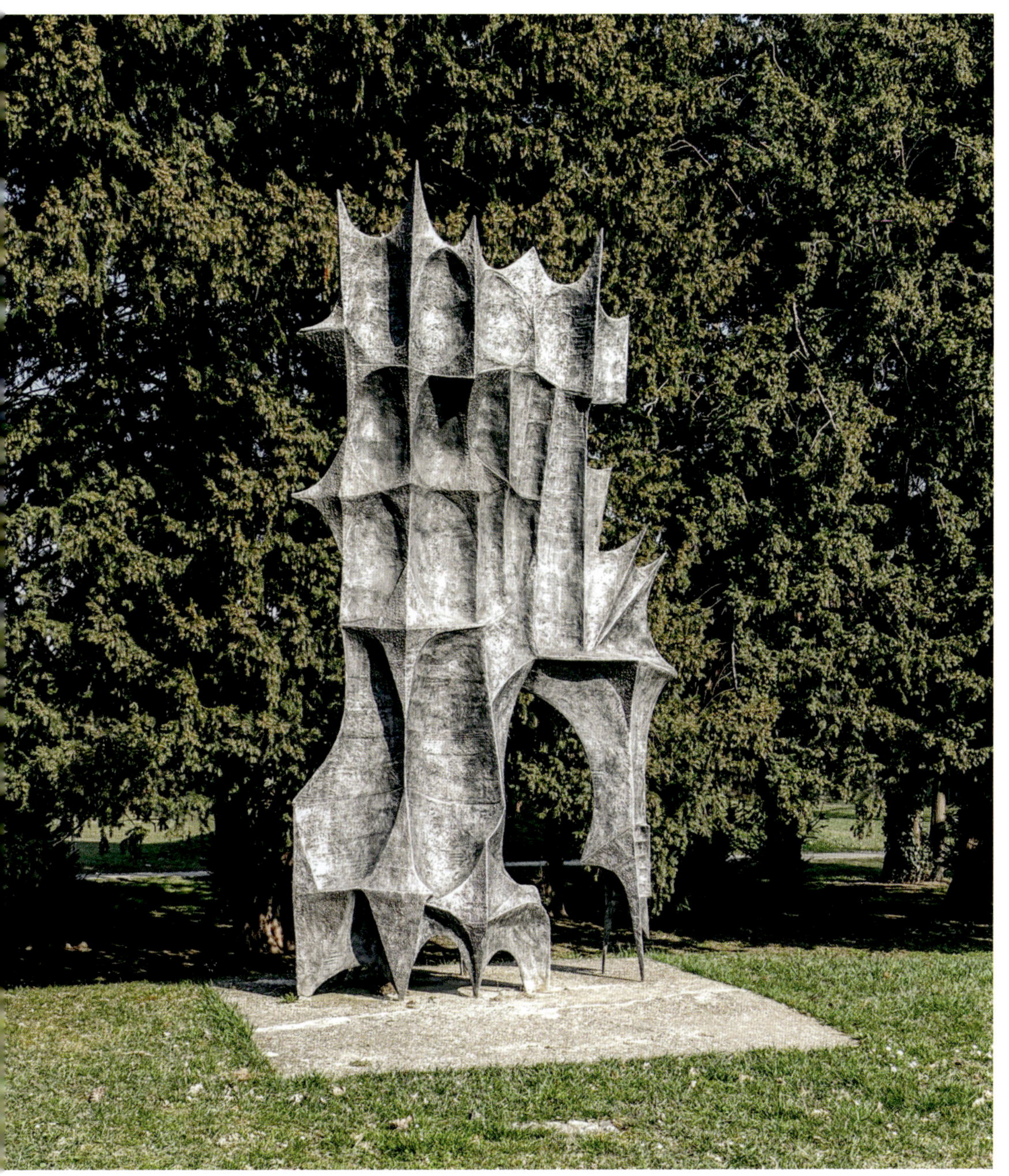

ZAJEČAR (ZAH-yeh-char)

NAME: The Gallows or Monument to the Fallen in the Liberation War and the Victims of Fascist Terror
LOCATION: Kraljevica Hill, Zaječar, Serbia
YEAR COMPLETED: 1971
DESIGNER: Vladimir Veličković
COORDINATES: N43°53'21.2", E22°15'53.6"
DIMENSIONS: Three monuments, 9 metres high
MATERIALS: Poured concrete and rebar

HISTORY

After the invasion of the Kingdom of Yugoslavia by Axis forces in April 1941, Zaječar (along with the rest of Serbia) found itself in the grip of a brutal occupation. Groups of resistance fighters across Serbia began their counter-attacks, and in July 1941, uprisings against the oppression resulted in the deaths of hundreds of Axis troops.

Franz Böhme, the Wehrmacht commander of Serbia, was so enraged he implemented Hitler's order to suppress all resistance. This authorised the killing of 100 civilians in retaliation for every German soldier killed, and 50 civilians for every German soldier wounded (see pages 56 and 88). In addition, the order stated that Jews, communists and any suspected rebels should be rounded up as hostages, to be executed if any further German soldiers were killed or attacked. A prominent victim of this crackdown was Secretary of the Yugoslavian Communist Party, Milenko Brković

Crni, who was captured on 12 September 1941 while on his way to Zaječar. On 18 September, after being tortured for six days, he and several other local Communist Party leaders were taken to Kraljevica Hill, where they were hanged. Partisan attacks in the Zaječar region continued. Accordingly, German forces took hundreds of civilians hostage, subsequently executing them at Kraljevica Hill. By the end of the war, thousands had been murdered at this location.

On 23 August 1944, King Michael I of Romania instigated a coup against the country's Nazi-aligned government run by Ion Antonescu. Zaječar was of pivotal strategic importance, as following the coup, both Axis and Allied forces were hastening to secure northeast Serbia, which was crucial to controlling the Danube River. However, the 23rd Serbian Partisan Division reached Zaječar first. On 7 September, after a day-long battle, the city was liberated from the 5,000 German and Axis-aligned Chetnik troops.

It is alleged that approximately 200 retaliatory killings took place on Kraljevica Hill after the end of the war.

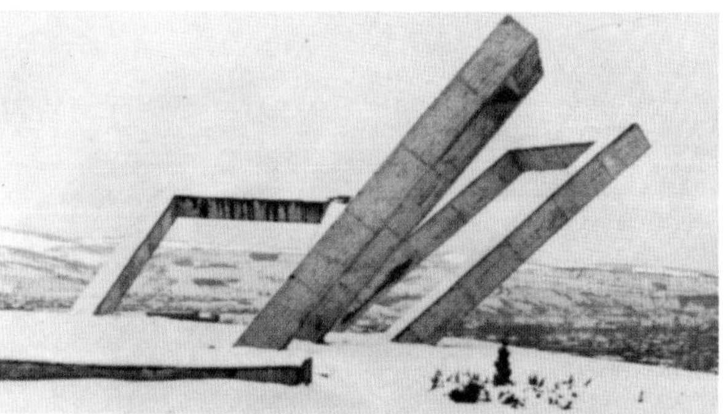

The Zaječar spomenik covered in snow, 1970s
(image from *Spomenici Narodnooslobodilačka Borbe Revolucije SR, 1941-1945*, Razumenka Popović Zuma, 1981)

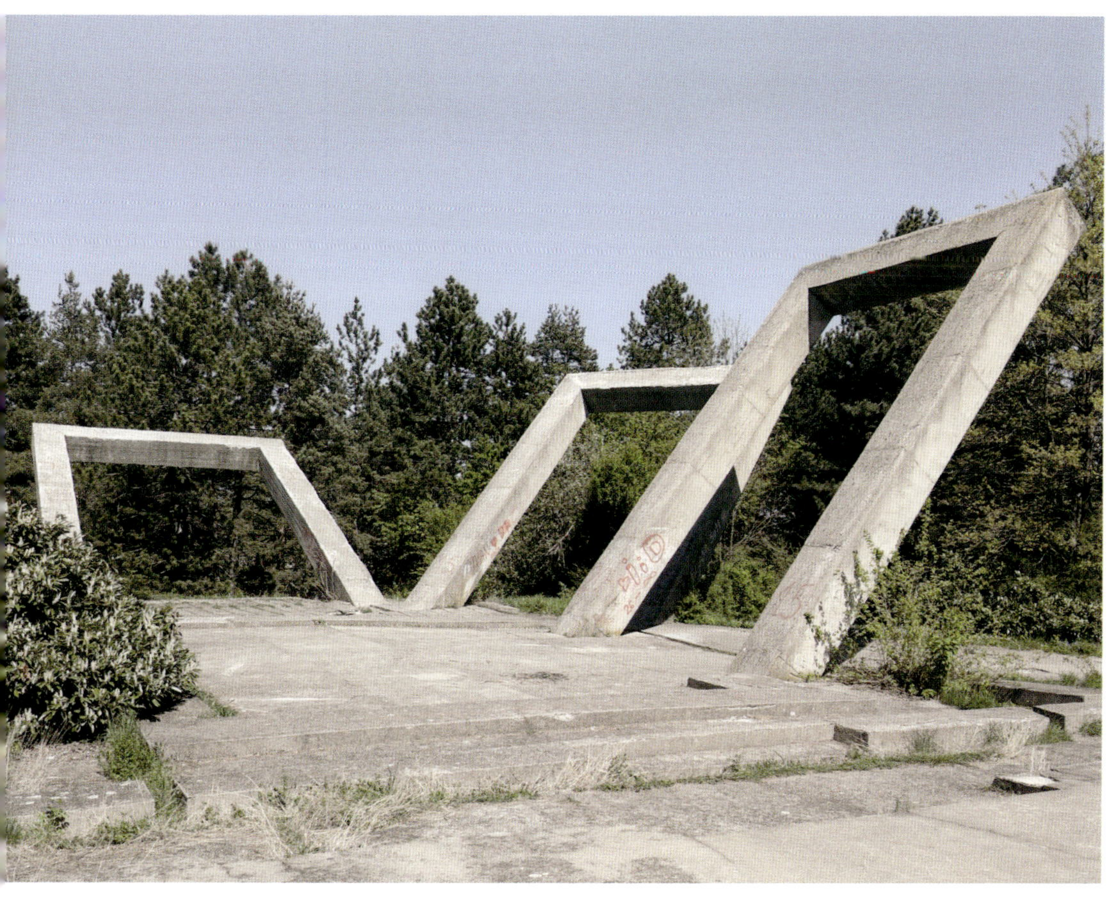

DESIGN AND CONSTRUCTION

The spomenik complex honouring the fighters and victims of World War II was unveiled on 7 July 1971, 30 years after the first Serbian uprisings against German occupation.

The primary sculpture by artist Vladimir Veličković consists of three open, rectilinear, concrete frame shapes – similar to the gallows used on Kraljevica Hill – tilted at increasingly acute angles, suggesting a sequential view of a single such form in the process of falling (or being raised up). Underneath, a crypt contains the remains of the partisans who died liberating Zaječar.

STATUS AND CONDITION

A popular tourist attraction and valued community asset during the Yugoslav era, after the wars of the 1990s, the site fell into disrepair. Today, while the structural elements are intact, they are suffering from superficial decay and graffiti. The paved memorial site has significant weather damage and is overgrown in places. The spomenik is not promoted, and the few signs at the site itself are in Serbian only. Despite this, annual commemorative events are still held here by local government and veterans' groups every 7 July (Uprising Day).

ZAOSTROG (ZAY-oh-strog)

NAME: Monument to the National Liberation War
LOCATION: Zaostrog, Croatia
YEAR COMPLETED: 1979
DESIGNER: Rudolf Matutinović
COORDINATES: N43°08'21.9", E17°16'41.9"
DIMENSIONS: 10 metres high
MATERIALS: Marble, poured concrete and rebar

HISTORY

After the Axis invasion of the Kingdom of Yugoslavia in April 1941, the Dalmatian coast fell under the control of the Italian Army and the Ustaše. Zaostrog became part of the newly formed Independent State of Croatia (NDH), a puppet state of the Axis powers under the control of the ultra-nationalist Ustaše militia. Many Dalmatian citizens, angered by the occupation, organised themselves into fighting units. Known as the Biokovo Partisans after the area where they were formed, they fought on both land and sea (utilising fishing boats to sink and capture dozens of ships in the Makarska Adriatic zone).

In August 1942, to counter partisan actions, Italian General Renzo Dalmazzo initiated Operation Albia (see pages 106 and 150), intended to eliminate resistance on the coast of Dalmatia. The Italians brought in Serbian Chetnik fighters to assist them – a contentious move for the NDH leadership, who did not want Serbian forces fighting in their territory.

On 18 August, the defensive line held by the 3rd Battalion of the Biokovo Partisans in the hills above Zaostrog was broken by Chetnik and Italian troops. Around 650 partisans fled west into the mountains but were intercepted and killed by Italian forces. For Axis troops, the destruction of the 3rd Battalion was significant, as they were known for having killed Ustaše soldiers and collaborators in nearby Vrgorac in June 1942. At the end of the operation, nearly 1,000 partisan fighters had been killed, with the loss of only seventeen Italian soldiers. In Zaostrog and other coastal towns, hundreds of civilians were killed and their homes burned to the ground.

Biokovo partisan commanders met with Marshal Josip Tito to plan a response. It was concluded that a Partisan Naval Headquarters would be established in the nearby city of Podgora, from which naval offensives against Italian forces could be organised. Partisan sailors and soldiers from Zaostrog fought until the liberation of the region in May 1945. During the course of the war, hundreds of soldiers and civilians from the Zaostrog region were killed.

DESIGN AND CONSTRUCTION

This spomenik on the Zaostrog waterfront commemorates the victims of World War II. Opened in May 1979, it was designed by Croatian sculptor Rudolf Matutinović, who was born in the town and lost many family members in the war. His father, mother and brother are listed on the engraved panels at the base of the monument. The spomenik is a 10-metre-tall concrete form resembling a torch or a sturdy flower on the point of opening its petals.

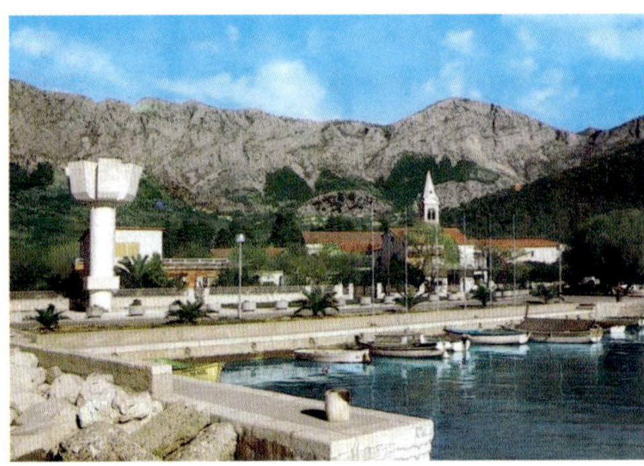

A postcard showing the Zaostrog spomenik and harbour, 1980s

STATUS AND CONDITION

Due to its proximity to the populous beach and harbour, the monument is well maintained. However, there are no signs explaining its significance, and it is not known if commemorative events are still held here.

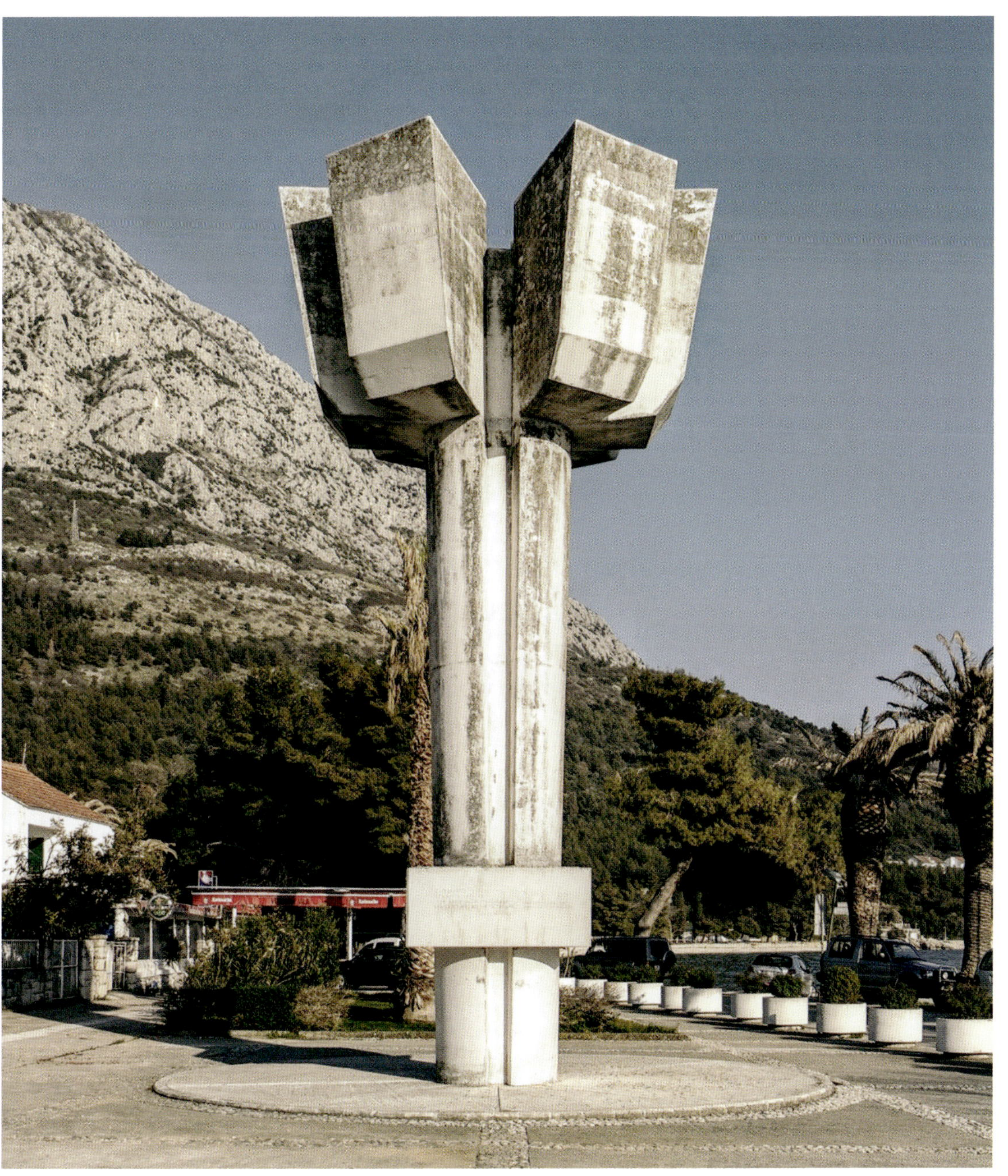

ZENICA (ZEH-nee-tsa)

NAME: Monument to the Fallen Zenica Partisan Detachment
LOCATION: Zenica, FBiH, Bosnia and Herzegovina
YEAR COMPLETED: 1968
DESIGNER: Arfan Hozić
COORDINATES: N44°14'41.1", E17°57'34.8"
DIMENSIONS: 13 metres high and 5 metres wide
MATERIALS: Steel frame with aluminium plates and marble panels

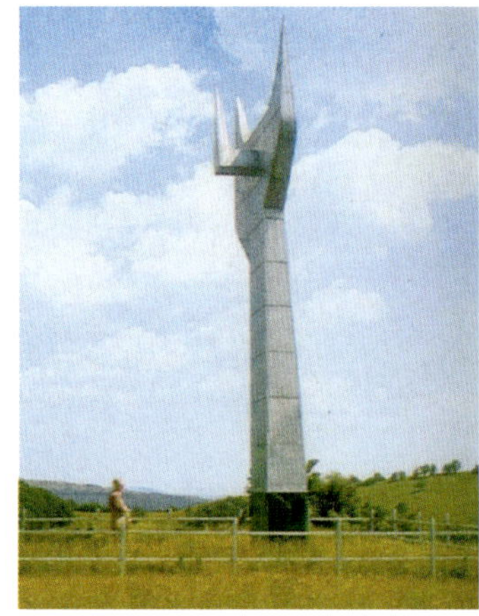

The Zenica spomenik in the 1970s
(photograph by Amy Wagner)

HISTORY

In spring 1942, Axis forces from Germany, Croatia and Italy organised a counter-insurgency plan named Operation Trio, against advancing partisans in the Bosnian region. The aim was to create a violent schism within the partisan brigades by splitting the Serb Chetniks from the communist-led partisans (who were from various ethnic backgrounds), thus undermining their opposition. This was to be achieved not only through military action, but also by using racial propaganda to exploit ethnic tensions between the more nationalistic Serb Chetniks and the communist-led partisans. Many Chetnik-led coups were instigated, resulting in the murder of large numbers of partisan soldiers. One of these coups occurred on Smetovi Hill (in the mountains to the northeast of Zenica), where disaffected Chetniks massacred 32 of their partisan allies within the 3rd East-Bosnian Strike Battalion and the Zenica Partisan Detachment. Following these coups, the Chetniks collaborated with the Axis Italians and the Ustaše regime. For the rest of 1942, they controlled eastern Bosnia, forcing partisan forces to withdraw and re-organise in western Bosnia.

DESIGN AND CONSTRUCTION

Designer Arfan Hozić was commissioned by a spomenik selection committee to construct a commemorative complex near the summit of Smetovi Hill, in the mountains northeast of Zenica, where the Chetnik massacre against partisan fighters occurred.

The monument, which was officially unveiled at a commemorative event in October 1968, is a flared, aluminium-plated obelisk with marble panels at its base. It stands on a paved stone area, protected by a modest iron fence. Approximately 30 metres to the north of the spomenik is a small amphitheatre, which was originally used for historical lessons and presentations.

STATUS AND CONDITION

The site is a popular destination for visitors because of its panoramic views of Zenica. This means that – fortuitously – the monument is in a reasonable condition. Some of the marble base sections are missing and the lower aluminium sheets are covered in graffiti. A number of tall conifers are growing within the compound, though these are not part of the original design. The amphitheatre has been destroyed, with little of its original infrastructure remaining.

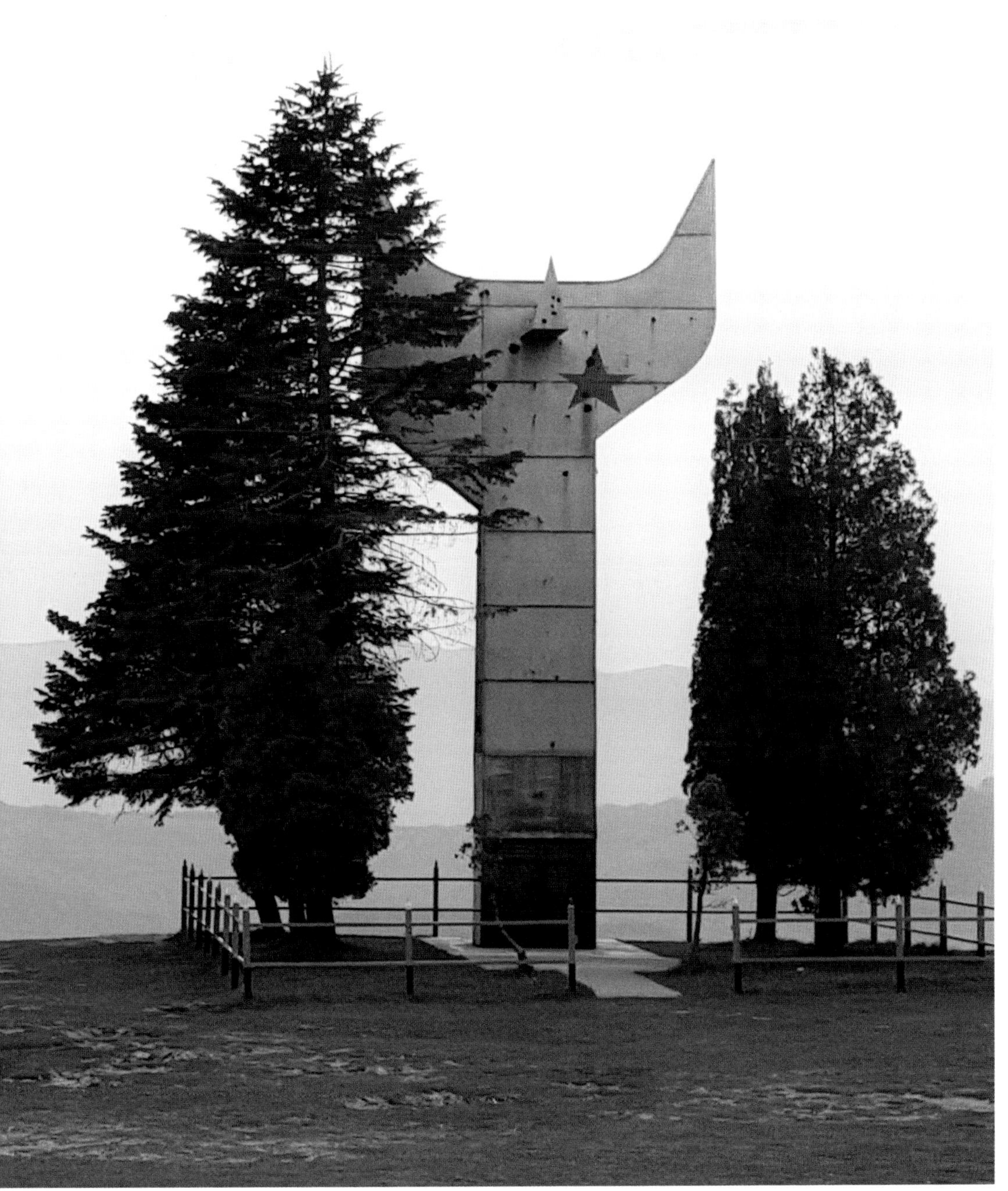

ZRENJANIN (ZREN-yah-nin)

NAME: Memorial to the Uprising in Vojvodina
LOCATION: Zrenjanin (formerly Petrovgrad and also
Bečkerek), Vojvodina, Serbia
YEAR COMPLETED: 1982
DESIGNER: Mladen Marinkov
COORDINATES: N45°22'07.3", E20°22'08.5"
DIMENSIONS: 3 metres high and 5 metres wide
MATERIALS: Bronze

HISTORY

The present-day city of Zrenjanin in Serbia was orignally known as Bečkerek. In 1934, its name was changed to Petrovgrad in honour of King Peter I of Serbia. Following the invasion of the Kingdom of Yugoslavia by Axis forces in April 1941, German occupiers changed the city's name back to Bečkerek, and made it their headquarters for the region. One of the first German actions took place on 19 April 1941, when seventeen local ethnic-Serbs, accused of being petty criminals, were executed by firing squad in the Bagljaš neighbourhood of Bečkerek. Such killings would continue for the duration of the occupation.

In response, resistance groups began to coalesce around the People's Liberation Movement of the Yugoslav communist rebels. On 23 June 1941, the day after Germany invaded the USSR, local communist party members gathered at a farm in Bagljaš. They determined to fight the Axis forces, appointing their group and its location as the Headquarters and Main Staff for the planning and operation of all partisan detachments in Vojvodina. Revolutionary fighter Žarko Zrenjanin was instrumental in the formulation of these plans. Born in the village of Izbište, he was a prominent figure in the struggle to liberate the Vojvodina and Banat regions. He was killed in action in November 1942. Another notable revolutionary was Sonja Marinković, who played an integral role in the preparation of local uprisings. She was captured by German troops on 14 July 1941, tortured, and condemned to death by firing squad along with 89 others. The sentence was carried out in Bagljaš by a unit of local Banat ethnic-German Nazi collaborators. After 1942, much of the initial partisan resistance in the area was curtailed by fierce German counter-actions and reprisal killings. It was not until 1944 that German troops were completely expelled from the region.

On 2 October 1944, Bečkerek itself was liberated. Shortly afterwards, local politicians changed the town's name once again, this time from Bečkerek to Zrenjanin in honour of the newly declared Yugoslav National Hero Žarko Zrenjanin. In addition, Sonja Marinković's father, Đorđe, was named as the first president of Zrenjanin's National Committee.

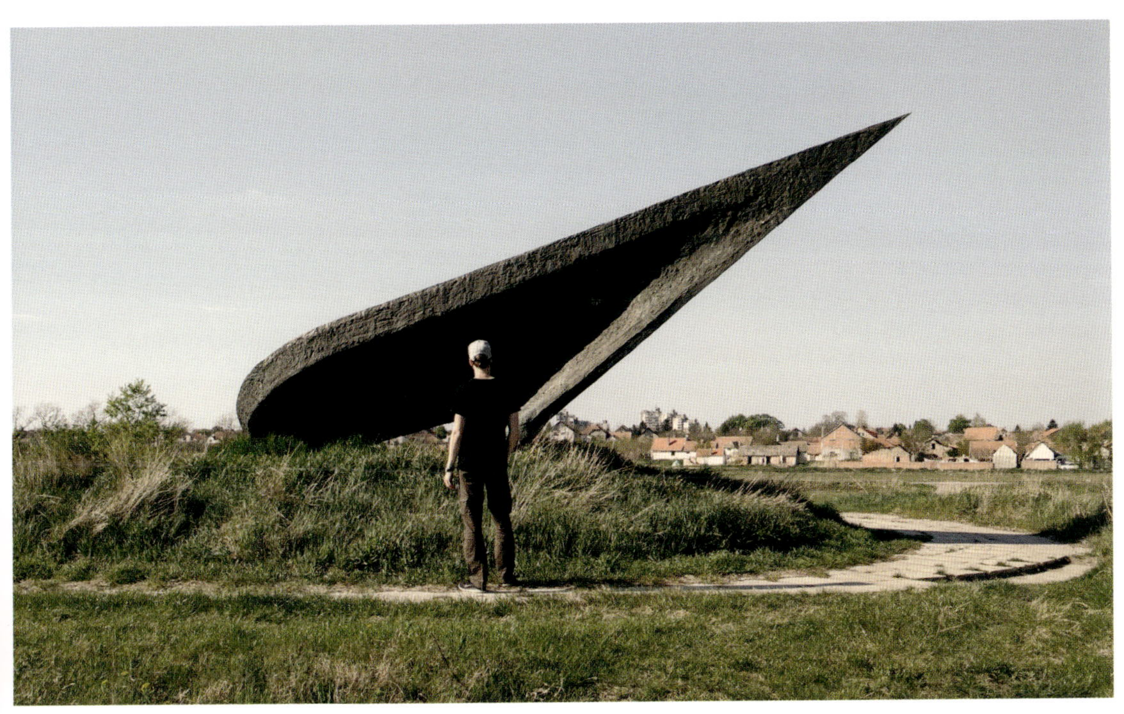

DESIGN AND CONSTRUCTION

In the late 1970s, Novi Sad artist Mladen Marinkov (who had already created a significant World War II memorial in the Bosnian town of Zavidovići) was commissioned to design a spomenik in honour of the establishment of the Main Staff Group for Vojvodina's partisan detachments. Located on the site where the group was first formed, the monument was officially opened on 23 June 1985, 44 years after that event.

Its central element is a 5-metre-long bronze sculpture resembling both the blade of a plough and a sleek jet poised for ascent. The informal name given to the monument by Marinkov was 'Raonik', (ploughshare). He said that he intended it to be seen as a form that 'aspires to the heavens'. The memorial was well received, resulting in several awards for its creator.

STATUS AND CONDITION

Since the fall and subsequent dismantling of Yugoslavia through the 1990s and 2000s, the memorial has fallen into neglect. The sculpture itself is still relatively intact, although its surface is scratched and covered in graffiti. The engraved plaque that was once in front of it is missing, and there are no other indications as to what the memorial honours. The rural location of the site means that agricultural vehicles and machinery are often driven across the grounds surrounding the spomenik. However, every 23 June, local groups still conduct annual commemorative events here.

Marinkov has stated that he would like the memorial to be moved to a more central location in Zrenjanin, although to date there are no official plans to do so.

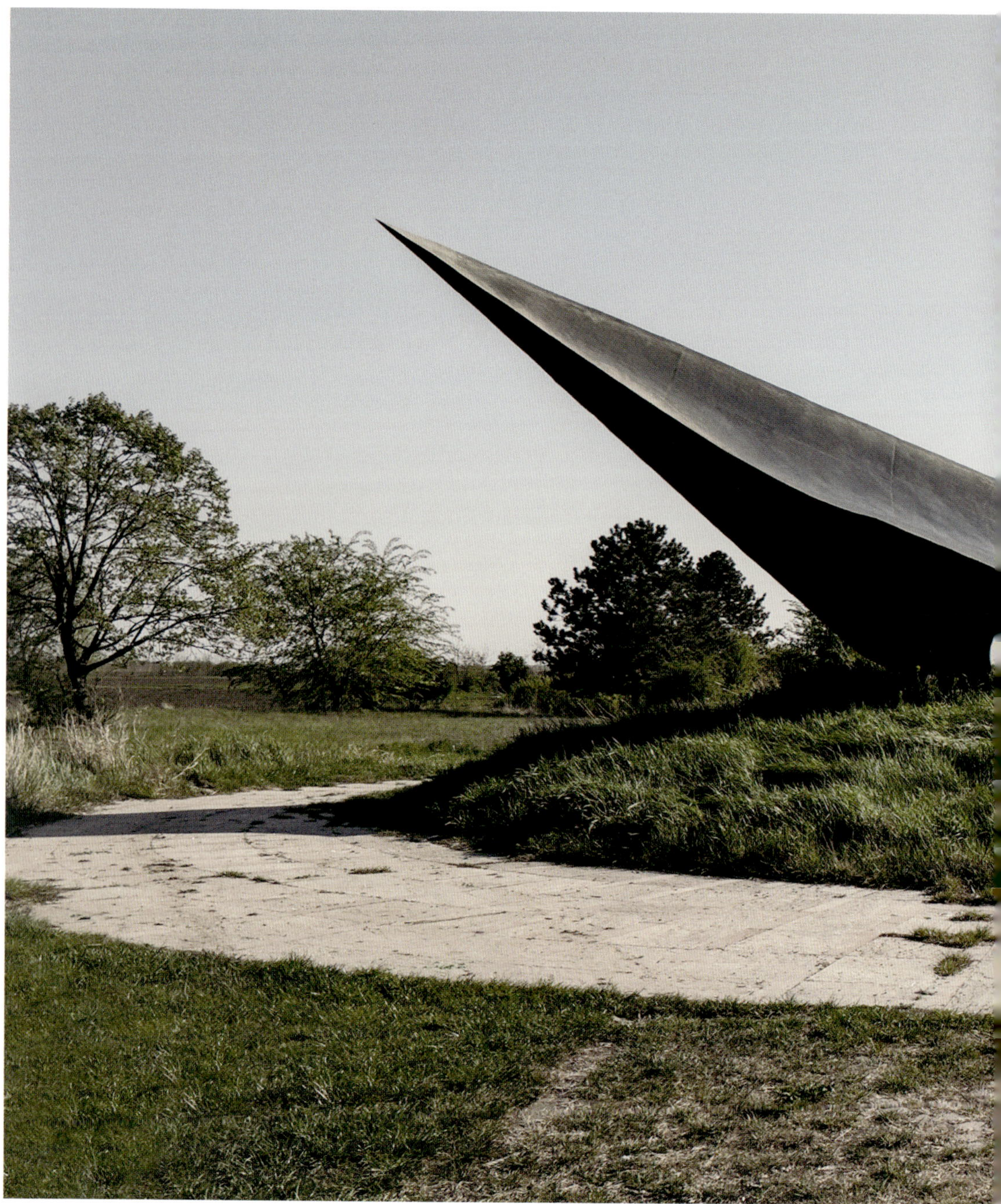

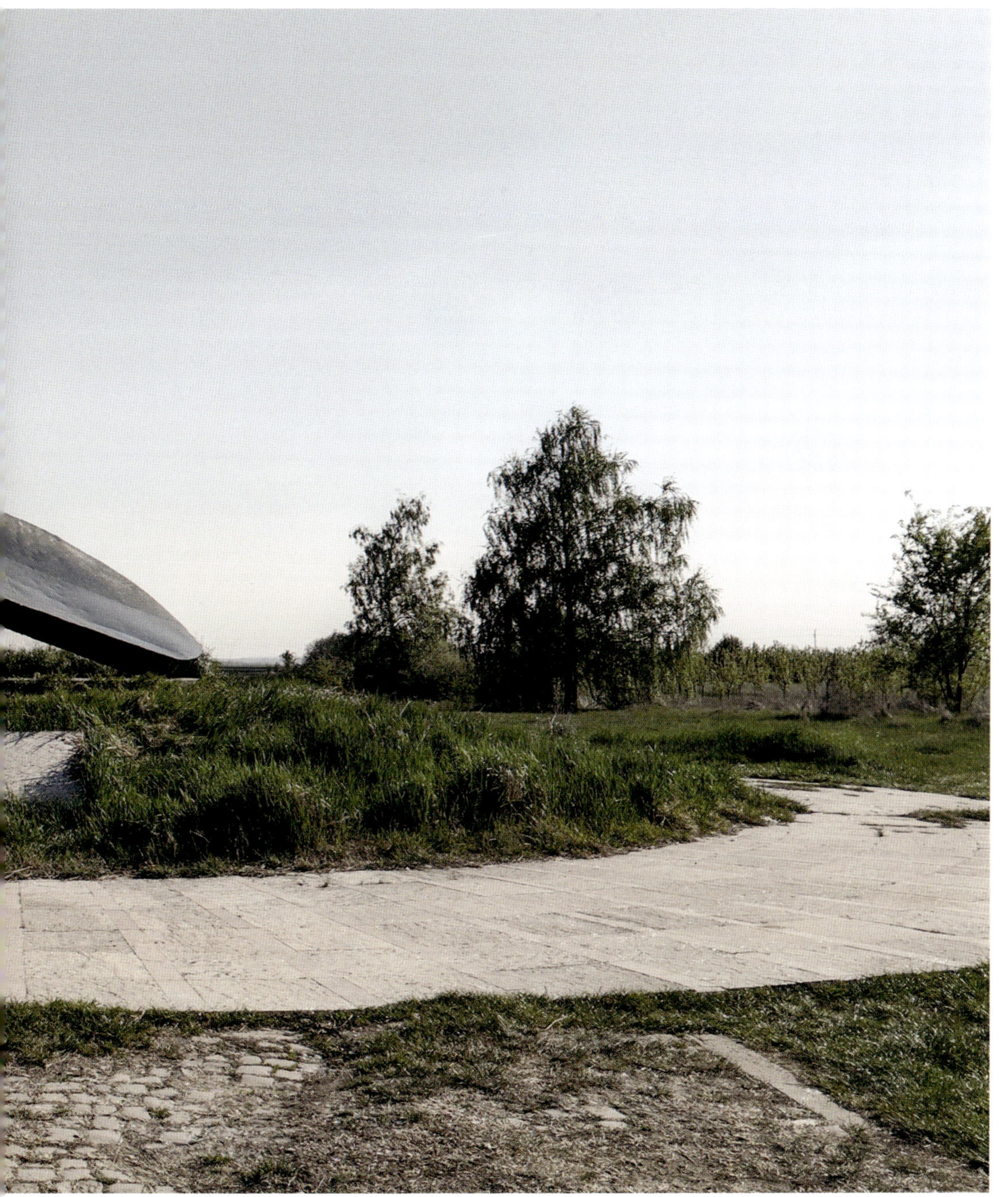

ŽUPA NIKŠIĆKA (ZHOO-pah NIK-sheech-kah)

NAME: Monument to the Fallen Soldiers
on Sutjeska
LOCATION: Župa Nikšićka, Carine, Montenegro
YEAR COMPLETED: 1984
DESIGNER: Ljubo Vojvodić
COORDINATES: N42°43'56.1", E19°04'59.4"
DIMENSIONS: 11 metres high
MATERIALS: Concrete

HISTORY

After the invasion of the Kingdom of Yugoslavia in April 1941, the Župa Nikšićka valley was occupied by Italian forces and its inhabitants subjected to brutal oppression. Consequently, many joined the partisan resistance. Italian forces responded mercilessly in an attempt to stop the rebels gaining momentum, but these actions only galvanised the resolve of the partisans and inspired others to join their cause.

In June 1942, dozens of valley citizens joined the newly formed 5th Montenegrin Proletariat Brigade, which consisted of around 900 fighters commanded by respected local revolutionary fighter Sava Kovačević. Throughout the rest of June, the unit conducted successful operations across the southern Bosnian region. However, in July they lost 600 fighters during the bloody Battle of Sutjeska in Bosnia (see page 176), including Kovačević who was killed alongside eight other Župa Nikšićka valley fighters.

In 1943, in retaliation for the continued insurrection, Italian troops entered Carine (one of twelve villages situated in the valley) and proceeded to loot and vandalise the ancient monastery complex of St Luke's (founded in 1235), burning hundreds of important religious books and documents.

The villages of the Župa Nikšićka valley were finally liberated by the 6th Montenegrin Partisan Brigade on 29 November 1944.

DESIGN AND CONSTRUCTION

Local Nikšić architect Ljubo Vojvodić was commissioned by the Župa Alliance of Veterans and the Nikšić Union of Workers to design a monument to commemorate the fighters of the 5th Montenegrin Proletariat Brigade killed in the Battle of Sutjeska in June 1943. The location (100 metres northwest of the monastery) was chosen to forestall any religious interpretation of the monument. (The majority of spomeniks follow this same precept.) The complex was officially opened with a large ceremonial event on 29 November 1984, the 40th anniversary of the liberation of the region.

The central element is an 11-metre-tall concrete monument set on an elaborate mound. While the monument broadly resembles an arrowhead, the disc at the top, the rounded extremities of the star-shaped hole in that disc, the curved forms at the base and the soft edges of the blocks from which it is made all conspire to give the impression of a robed priest.

STATUS AND CONDITION

The basic structure is in good condition, although the main memorial is chipped and cracked in several places. The grounds are well maintained, and remembrance services are still being held here. There are, however, no directional signs to the location, and the little information at the site is in Serbo-Croatian.

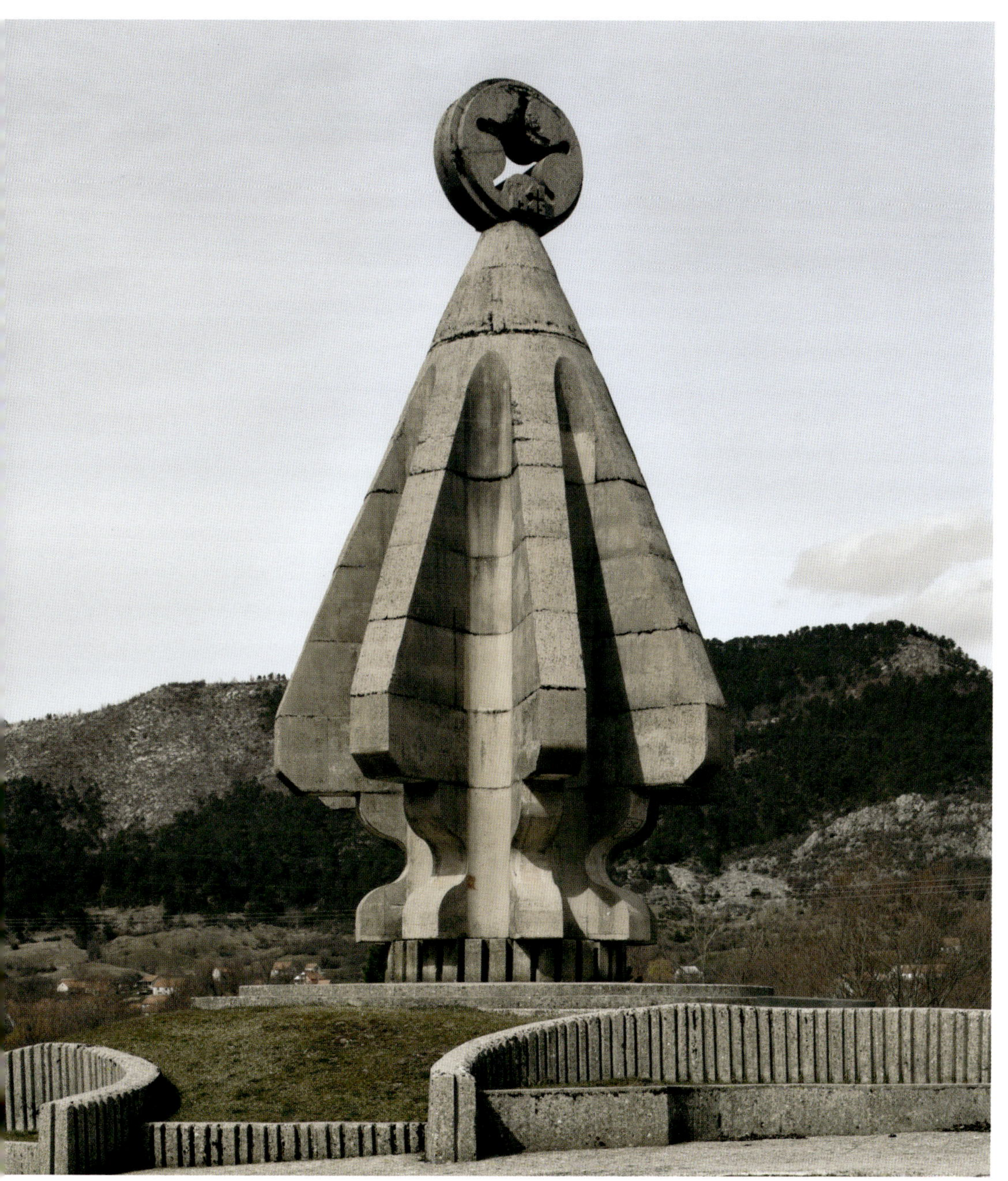

ACKNOWLEDGEMENTS

I would like to thank the following people and organisations for helping and assisting me along the way in my creation of this project and the assembly of information for this book:

Predrag Bajić (Muzej Vojvodine)
Svetomir Basara (along with Uglješa Dapčević)
Anthony Bautovich
Mark and Kirsty Bennetts (Kathmandu & Beyond)
Dragan Heingl Bugarčić (El Diablo)
Nebojša Đorđević
FUEL Design & Publishing
Gloryan Grabner (Makarska Observatory)
Sanja Horvatinčić (University of Zagreb)
Jan Kempenaers
Gal Kirn
Andrew Lawler
Mladen Marinkov
Memorial Park 'Kragujevački oktobar'
Sunny Milošević
Muzej Jablanica
Muzej Jugoslavije
Muzej Kozare
Muzej Veles
Branko Obradović (Krenjeuša.net)
Ana Pajović
Vjeran Pavlaković (University of Rijeka)
Dejan Pavlović (Sutjeska National Park)
Ivo Pejaković (JUSP Jasenovac – Memorijalni muzej)
Polimski muzej
Vladana Putnik Prica (University of Belgrade),
    (as well as Vladan)
Darmon Richter (Bohemian Blog)
Savez antifašističkih boraca i antifašista Republike
    Hrvatske
Saša Šimpraga (Virtualni muzej Dotrščina)
Enes Škrgo (Zavičajni muzej Travnik)
Edina Sprečaković (Doctor's House)
Iya Tarashkevich
Stevo Vasiljević (Mediterranean University)
Giulio Zanni
Miodrag Živković

And most of all, I would like to thank my most amazing partner, Tyler Pannell, without whom none of this would have been possible!

DONALD NIEBYL
spomenikdatabase.org

This book is not intended as an exhaustive collection of Yugoslav spomeniks, but as a selection of some of the most impressive and significant of these monuments.

Published in 2018
Reprinted in 2019, 2020, 2024, 2026

FUEL Design & Publishing
33 Fournier Street
London E1 6QE

fuel-design.com

Text © Donald Niebyl
Copy edited by FUEL and Fergal Stapleton
All photographs by Donald Niebyl except for archive images and postcards
Designed and edited by Murray & Sorrell FUEL

Distribution by Thames & Hudson / D. A. P.
ISBN: 978-0-9957455-3-7
Printed in China

EU Authorized Representative: Interart S.A.R.L.
19 rue Charles Auray, 93500 Pantin, Paris, France
www.interart.fr

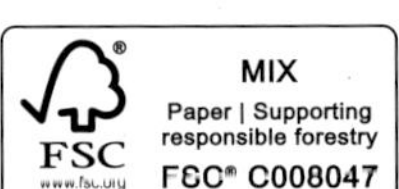

Printed with non mineral ink on FSC® (Forest Stewardship Council) certified paper, from responsibly managed forests and recycled materials, ensuring sustainable forestry practices and environmental protection.

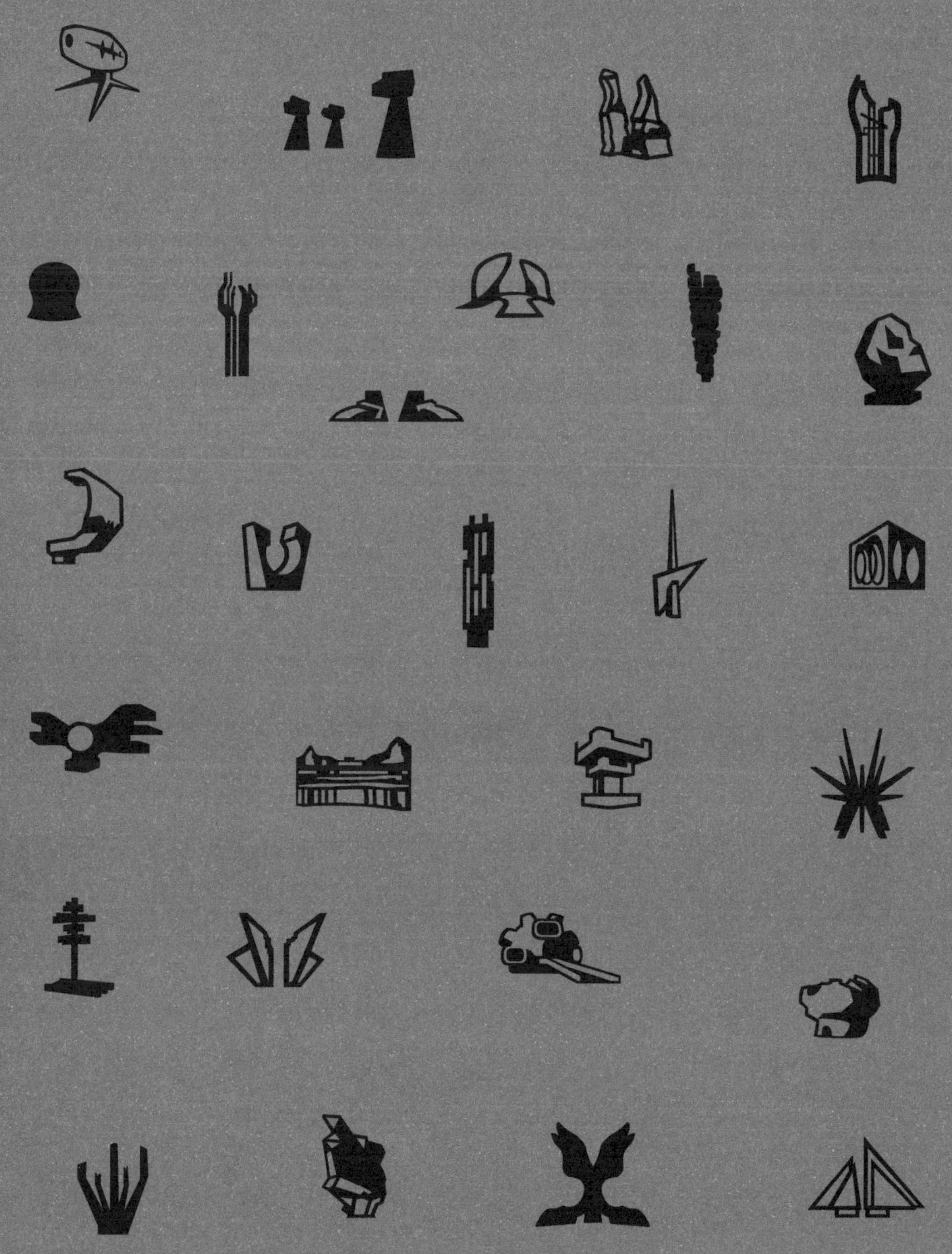